TO THE STUDENT: A Study Guide for the textbook is available through your college bookstore under the title STUDY GUIDE TO ACCOMPANY PRINCIPLES OF BUSINESS COMMUNICATION: THEORY, APPLICATION, AND TECHNOLOGY by Alfred B. Williams. The Study Guide can help you with course material by acting as a tutorial, review and study aid. If the Study Guide is not in stock, ask the bookstore manager to order a copy for you.

Business Communication Basics

APPLICATION AND TECHNOLOGY

Wiley Series in Business Communications

The manuscript for this book was developed under the guidance of C. Glenn Pearce, Consulting Editor for Business and Organizational Communication. Dr. Pearce is a professor at Virginia Commonwealth University.

Business Communication Basics

APPLICATION AND TECHNOLOGY

Ross Figgins California State Polytechnic University

Steven P. Golen Louisiana State University

C. Glenn Pearce Virginia Commonwealth University

John Wiley & Sons

New York Chichester Brisbane Toronto Singapore

This book is dedicated to

My daughter, Caryn Weiss, a.k.a., Ladybug
— Ross

My wife, Dorothy
— Steven

My sister, Earlene, and brother, Billy
— Glenn

Book designed by Sheila Granda.
Cover by Renée Kilbrite.
Book production coordinated by Deborah Pokos.
Copy editing supervised by Deborah Herbert.
Illustrated by John Balbalis, with assistance from the Wiley Illustration Department.
Photos edited by Elyse Rieder.

Copyright © 1984, by John Wiley & Sons, Inc.

All rights reserved. Published simultaneously in Canada.

Reproduction or translation of any part of
this work beyond that permitted by Sections
107 and 108 of the 1976 United States Copyright
Act without the permission of the copyright
owner is unlawful. Requests for permission
or further information should be addressed to
the Permissions Department, John Wiley & Sons.

658.45
F471

Library of Congress Cataloging in Publication Data:

Figgins, Ross.
    Business communication basics.

    Includes index.
    1. Communication in management.   I. Golen, Steven.
II. Pearce, C. Glenn.   III. Title.

HF5718.F53 1984   658.4′5   83-16792
ISBN 0-471-86538-9

Printed in the United States of America

10 9 8 7 6 5 4 3 2 1

Preface

"Dear Mr. President" was how the letter began. Its author, the director of the United States Patent Office, was urging President McKinley to close that bureau because, in his estimation, "everything that can be invented has been invented." The recommendation was offered in all seriousness but was respectfully disregarded.

The point of the anecdote is not to show the shortsightedness of a long-forgotten bureaucrat, but rather to point out that throughout our history the assumption has been made that human inventiveness and inspiration are finite. Today, there are those who view communication from this same myopic perspective. For them, nothing has changed in the world since they learned communication principles, and books of this sort on business writing should be chock full of form letters and fill-in report forms similar to the "letters for all occasions" that were so popular at the turn of the century.

If such were the case, most of our personal libraries would be much smaller than they are. We would have to buy only one book on each subject, once. The G. C. Merriam Company, for example, would have published "the" *Webster's Dictionary* many years ago, and each of us would own one. But, have you ever looked at the printing history of this work? Take it down sometime and check the dates; you can find them on the second page, immediately following the title page. Why do you think that that dictionary has gone through so many editions? Because the language has changed? Exactly! And so, too, have the techniques and styles we employ in using language well.

With the advent of computers and their adjuncts, word processors and electronic mail, we have limitless access to information. As a result, some are predicting the demise of courses in communication. But as Mark Twain said after reading his own obituary in the *New York Times,* "the reports of my death have been greatly exaggerated." The role of the communicator, in every field, is increasing, not diminishing. Our technology has made us more dependent, not less, on well-honed communication skills. The more people have access to communication and, hence, the more they come to rely on it, the more important messages become. If futurists such as Eric Toffler and John Naisbitt are correct, we are indeed entering the information age, where the ability to bridge the chasm between human minds is becoming the most important single asset of a successful professional.

The primary goal of this book is to explore the various kinds of written messages that are common to business and organizational situations. If we accept the idea that communication is a human process shared in differing contexts, then the circumstances of communication take on a significance equal to that of its content. The relative effectiveness of each communique thus depends on the relationship between *data,* the information being transmitted, and *form,* the nature of the message itself— more simply put, the *what* and *how* of writing. For this reason all communication should be considered in terms of its appropriateness to the reader and to the environment in which communication takes place.

ORGANIZATION AND CONTENT

The material in this book has been arranged to complement its goals. The sixteen chapters are divided into six specific working units, moving from the general question of what makes business writing effective to the specific question of how to write effectively. In addition, the last unit deals with effective speaking and listening skills.

The first area of study, in Unit 1, is written communication itself, in which fundamental techniques of style and tone are explored. The material focuses on how messages are planned and includes demonstrations and examples of good analysis and execution.

The title of Unit 2 is "Written Communication: Correspondence." Business correspondence includes letters and memorandums, and both are covered extensively. This unit is organized to emphasize practical applications, those situations encountered most often on a day-to-day basis. Beginning with an explanation of basic correspondence techniques, the coverage moves into the most valuable areas of application: how to prepare favorable, unfavorable, and persuasive messages. For easy understanding, this section is organized in a developmental manner: An ineffective example is presented; it is then critiqued and rewritten in a professional manner. This type of development parallels the genesis of effective messages through their various composing and editing stages. Put another way, this is the natural way to write!

Unit 3 is devoted to business reports. Once again, a process approach is used, beginning with planning a report project. Following the planning stage, the subject is presented developmentally: collecting data, both primary and secondary, then sorting and organizing, summarizing, evaluating, and outlining it. Also included in this unit is a discussion of the preparation and presentation of data in visual forms, including computer graphics. Following the discussion on visual aids is a presentation of how to write and prepare the format for a formal report. The final chapter is devoted to short, informal reports.

Unit 4 is a special section devoted entirely to word/information processing systems that are becoming so much a part of daily business life. The discussion begins with an orientation to the available technology and proceeds to a major discussion on how word/information processing equipment aids users in preparing, processing, and distributing business messages. How to prepare to dictate and how to dictate are discussed as well as how to prepare short, long, and form documents using word/information processing systems.

The most practical test of your skills in analyzing messages and responding to them is found in Unit 5: how to find the right job and achieve your career goals. The unit is divided into two sections, one on the employer's perspective and the other on the applicant's. The dynamics of the employment process are evaluated in terms of how to prepare the right message at the right time, how to deal with potential barriers, and how to increase your potential for success in various situations.

Unit 6 is devoted to those communication skills that are directly related to our ability to write well—speaking and listening. No professional person, especially one in a position of responsibility, can ignore the importance of being able to present ideas directly to others in face-to-face situations. At the same time, the ability to listen actively and respond intelligently is a hallmark of an effective communicator.

The reference section at the end of the book includes six related appendices. Appendix A reviews elements of grammar and includes helpful examples of each element. Appendix B covers business reference sources, including the latest information on computer assisted information services. Appendix C explains and illustrates how to prepare standard bibliographies, with sample citations of each form presented. Correspondence layout is presented in Appendix D. Letter and memorandum parts, punctuation styles, salutations and complimentary closes, margin requirements, and addressing procedures are found here. Appendix E is a presentation of reading techniques useful in reading business communications. The SQ3R procedure is presented as a tool for reading large segments of written information effectively. Appendix F is a reference guide to standard proofreading marks.

No communication can be effective unless there is common agreement about what words mean. For this reason, we have included a Glossary of the major terminology of business communication as it is commonly applied today and as it is used in this work. You are encouraged to refer often to the Glossary, especially when you wish to know the specific usage of a particular term in question.

Ross Figgins, *Pomona, California*
Steven P. Golen, *Baton Rouge, Louisiana*
C. Glenn Pearce, *Richmond, Virginia*

Acknowledgments

The essence of communication is intention. If this is true, and we believe that it is, our intention has been to prepare a book that is academically sound and useful. But no project with such broad goals could possibly be the product of one person or small group of authors. We were guided and assisted by a number of well-qualified people during the years that this book was being prepared for your use. We would like to acknowledge some of them by name.

First, we are grateful to the reviewers of the original proposal for the text. With their help, we formed the basic organization and content for the book. They are as follows: Hilda Allred, Kingston, Rhode Island; Russell A. Duke, George Mason University; Doris Engerrand, Georgia College; Patti Ernst, Fort Smith, Arkansas; Ed Goodin, University of Nevada, Las Vegas; Laura B. Greer, John Tyler Community College; Christine Horn, Grand Prairie Regional College; Hilda M. Jones, Oregon State University; C. Jeanne Lewis, Fayetteville State University; Martha H. Rader, Arizona State University; Bobbi Rothstein, University of Rhode Island; Gretchen N. Vik, San Diego State University; Jean W. Vining, Houston Community College; Alfred B. Williams, University of Southwestern Louisiana.

We are grateful for the assistance of several people who gave their time and good counsel in reviewing the manuscript as we wrote it. They kept us on the correct course by reacting candidly to what we were saying and how we were saying it. These people are as follows: Lois Bachman, Community College of Philadelphia; Ray Beswick, Harwick Word Processing Consultants; Doris Engerrand, Georgia College; Laura B. Greer, John Tyler Community College; Gretchen N. Vik, San Diego State University; Jean W. Vining, Houston Community College; Alfred B. Williams, University of Southwestern Louisiana; Mary Ellen Adams, Indiana State University; Vanessa Dean Arnold, University of Mississippi; Annelle Bonner, University of Southern Mississippi; Belford E. Carver, Southeastern Louisiana University; David P. Dauwalder, Central Michigan University; Pernell H. Hewing, University of Wisconsin-Whitewater; G. Pepper Holland, Mississippi State University; William Neal, Utah State University; Bill G. Rainey, East Central (Oklahoma) University; Natalie R. Siegle, Providence College; and Joann Spitler, Virginia Commonwealth University.

Several sections of the book were written by professionals with particular expertise in the subject matter of those sections. Marietta Spring and Gaye C. Dawson, both professors at Virginia Commonwealth University, wrote Chapter 13, "Word/Information Processing: The Communicator's New Tool." R. Jon Ackley, also a professor at Virginia Commonwealth University, wrote Appendix A, "Elements of Grammar." Merryll S. Penson, a librarian at Virginia Commonwealth University, wrote Appendix B, "Business Reference Sources," and Halsey Taylor, a professor at California State Polytechnic University, wrote Appendix E, "Reading Skills in Business Communication."

In addition to co-authoring a chapter, Gaye C. Dawson edited the original manuscript for style and tone before it was sent to the publisher, and we appreciate the outstanding job she did in this effort. Jean Vining, a professor and departmental chairperson at Houston Community College, prepared the Instructor's Manual. Her work is exemplary, and has resulted in a useful guide to using the book effectively. Dr. Vining also prepared the oral presentation rating sheet used in the chapter on oral presentations. Further, we acknowledge Raymond V. Lesikar of North Texas State University and Philip C. Kolin of the University of Southern Mississippi. Dr. Lesikar, a pioneer in the art of business communication instruction, was first to outline clear distinctions between short and long reports. The distinctions we have made between such reports on pages 270 and 271 are based on those made in his book, *Report Writing for Business*, 6th Edition, Homewood, IL: Irwin, 1981, pp. 109–111. Likewise, the system introduced on page 218 to show how to present visual aids effectively is based on the one suggested by Dr. Kolin in his book, *Successful Writing at Work*, Lexington, MA: Heath, 1982, pp. 298–300.

The continuing assistance over the course of many months by the staff at John Wiley & Sons should also be mentioned. We are particularly grateful to Leonard B. Kruk, Wiley's Business Education Editor, who encouraged us when we needed it, advised us on content and procedure, and carefully guided us through every step of the process. Dr. Kruk's assistants, first Cindy Zigmund and then Pat Fitzgerald, were always willing to help when we needed it, and we appreciate the valuable help they gave us. We also thank Claire Thompson, Managing and Development Editor, for her patience and skill in coordinating the manuscript development. We appreciate too the fine work of the copy editor, Sally Bailey, and of the designer, Sheila Granda, in making this an attractive book inside and out. The editorial production manager, Deborah Herbert, and the production supervisor, Deborah Pokos, deserve praise for keeping everything on schedule while being quite kind and encouraging about it.

We also thank Marketing Manager Joe Morse for the good faith he showed by traveling from New York to New Orleans to advise us and seek our advice about advertising the book long before there was a book to advertise. His work is ongoing still, and we acknowledge him and his staff members, particularly Carolyn Opper, for doing an outstanding job. Then, we are grateful to Alan B. Lesure, Executive Editor, for traveling from New York to Phoenix to consult with us on the project and to show his support even before we began to write the manuscript.

These acknowledgments would be incomplete unless we thanked the thousands of students we have taught during our careers as business communication instructors and consultants. While they must remain nameless here, we acknowledge them fully for the wonderful feedback they have given us. More than anyone else has, these students have told us how to teach business communication effectively. During the past few years, many have tested and reacted to much of the material in the book, and it is a better book because they have participated in these ways.

To all who use this book, both instructors and students, we thank you. We will appreciate your feedback about both content and organization at any time. Meanwhile, our wish is that you will take pleasure in using the book as we have taken pleasure in preparing it.

R. F.
S. P. G.
C. G. P

Contents

UNIT 2
WRITTEN COMMUNICATION: CORRESPONDENCE

Chapter Three
Fundamental Correspondence Techniques

Chapter Four
Favorable Correspondence

Chapter Five
Unfavorable Correspondence

Contents

Chapter Six
Persuasive Correspondence   121

UNIT 3
WRITTEN COMMUNICATION: REPORTS   149

Chapter Seven
Planning the Report Process   151

Chapter Eight
Collecting Research Data   167

Chapter Nine
Giving Meaning and Structure to
Research Data   193

Chapter Ten
Preparing Visual Aids   217

Chapter Eleven
Presenting the Research Results   243

UNIT 6
ORAL COMMUNICATION   375

APPENDICES   403

Contents

Business Communication Basics

APPLICATION AND TECHNOLOGY

UNIT 1

Written Communication Fundamentals

CHAPTER ONE

Fundamental Writing Techniques

The goals in studying the text and completing the activities in this chapter are to know

1. The process for planning and achieving writing objectives
2. Factors to consider in analyzing the reader before writing
3. How to achieve coherence in writing
4. How to gain credibility in writing
5. Emphasis techniques used in writing
6. How to assure that messages are readable
7. The process for proofreading messages
8. The factors involved in preparing attractive copy

Begin this chapter by taking a few minutes to look at the advantages of writing messages. On a sheet of paper, jot down the numbers of each of the following statements that describe a value of written messages:

1. Good way to present complex or detailed information
2. Good way to keep a permanent record
3. Useful way to review business transactions
4. Best way to allow receiver to choose the right time and place to receive a message
5. Good way to allow a receiver to control feedback

If you wrote down all five numbers, you are right, all are values of business writing. Writing is a good way in which to send complex or detailed information that requires careful study; a reader has time to reflect on written messages. Writing provides a useful permanent record, good for reviewing business transactions and for legal purposes. Readers can choose the best time and place in which to read written messages, and they also can decide what other messages to send and how to send them.

As you work, you probably find yourself often in situations where you should send messages in writing. How effective they are depends on how well the objectives are planned.

PLANNING AND ACHIEVING WRITING OBJECTIVES

Because you write business messages to reach certain goals or objectives, planning is necessary. Planning helps you to set clear objectives and at the same time gives you a system to follow when monitoring progress toward the objective. Through planning, the purpose for writing becomes clear, as does what to say and how to say it.

Planning gives order to the writing process. Here is a five-step method for organizing a writing plan:

Step 1   *Identify the purpose for writing.*

The purpose is the primary reason to write: the objective or desired result. For example, the purpose for a memorandum may be to schedule a meeting on plant safety rules on the company's assembly line.

Step 2   *Determine the message content.*

The points you make in the content fulfill the purpose. That is, they explain the reason by giving details about it. For example, a memorandum written to schedule a meeting on plant safety rules may include the following content:

a. Time and date of meeting
b. Place of meeting
c. Agenda for meeting
d. Type and amount of preparation needed
e. Materials to bring to meeting
f. Names of those attending meeting
g. Names of those conducting meeting

Step 3 *Organize the content by priority.*

Develop a step-by-step plan for including all content in the message by deciding which information to state first, which second, and so on. Base priorities on such factors as order of importance, psychological needs of the reader, and time and budget constraints. These points are discussed more fully in the chapters on correspondence and reports.

Step 4 *Set a time schedule.*

A short, simple written message such as a routine letter of inquiry about the availability of a product can be completed within a few minutes on a single day. A long report, however, may require many hours during a period of days or weeks. Set a reasonable time schedule and then adhere to it.

Step 5 *Devise a system for monitoring progress.*

Only long or complex writing projects that require several hours to several days or weeks to complete require a monitoring system. Because of the brief time involved, short-term projects require no system. For long projects, monitor the time schedule, quality, and the procedure used to complete the work.

Use steps 1 through 3 for every message you write. Also use steps 4 and 5 when writing longer projects, long reports, for example. The following is a checklist to help you use the plan faster:

1. *What is the purpose for writing?* Jot down the primary reason for writing.
2. *What content should be included?* Jot down each point to be made.
3. *Which presentational order should be followed?* Jot down the order in which to present the points to be made.

4. *Which time schedule is best?*   Jot down a time schedule that you can meet.

5. *Which monitoring system is best?*   Jot down times and procedures for checking your time schedule, work quality, and the procedure used to complete the work.

Remember, too, when writing a message that it will be read and interpreted by the reader and that readers differ one from another. Therefore, an additional step in the planning process is to analyze the reader so that messages can be written to the particular person being addressed.

ANALYZING THE READER

Since readers differ, each message should be adapted to a particular receiver. A problem here is that writers often know little about one another. True, you can write more effectively to people you know; and the more you know about them, the better your messages can be. However, the following nine points will help you to improve your writing, regardless of how well you know the reader:

1. *What is your relationship with the reader?*   Is the reader a customer or client? a colleague or peer? a superior? a subordinate? Answering this question will help you to write in a proper tone.

2. *What position does the reader hold?*   Is the reader an engineer, a sales manager, a production supervisor? Is that position managerial or nonmanagerial? What basic interests and objectives might a person have who holds that position?

3. *What is the reader's reading level?*   You can only guess the answer to this question, but a good guess can be made by noting the position that the reader holds within the company. Some jobs require a high school education, others a college degree; education is a good indicator of a person's reading level. When your writing falls within a three- to four-grade range of the receiver's actual reading level, that will be close enough for it to go unnoticed.

4. *What are the reader's interests?*   Knowing a reader's job-related or social interests can help you to personalize a message. As you are able to choose appropriate things to say, the tone of your messages will improve accordingly.

5. *What knowledge of the subject matter does the reader have?*   Are you free to write without explaining technical terms and concepts, for example? How much detail should you include to make the message clear?

6. *What is the reader's background?*   Is the reader in sales, finance, production, or homemaking, for instance? Does she or he live on the East Coast or West Coast? in France or Japan? You can answer these questions about almost any reader. As correspondence with people continues, you will learn more about their backgrounds.

7. *What biases and prejudices does the reader have?*   Avoid provoking a reader by using biased or prejudiced language. While you may not know a reader's particular biases or prejudices, you can always avoid generally irritating labels such as *communist, redneck, left wing,* and *right wing.* Referring to controversial life-styles and political and religious issues is risky.

8. *What are the reader's unspoken needs?*   Has the reader indicated unspoken but concrete needs for information that you are free to provide? This involves "reading between the lines," but you can open lines of communication by providing helpful information that you have no reason to withhold.

9. *Does the reader need information quickly?*   Be cooperative when information is needed quickly. A quick reply is always welcomed and sometimes needed.

After analyzing the reader to plan a general approach, the actual writing can begin. One of the most meaningful qualities of good writing is coherence, the unity of ideas.

ACHIEVING COHERENCE

Messages need unity to be coherent. Ideas in a coherent message are understandable and connect logically. Coherence is easily destroyed, though; one improperly chosen word can prevent a reader from understanding an entire sentence. For example, if "We must seek a *compromise*" becomes "We must seek a *concession,*" the meaning is distorted. Such a mistake can distort the meaning of an entire paragraph or, indeed, an entire message.

Message coherence is built on word choice, sentence and paragraph construction, and parallelism.

Using Appropriate Words

Appropriateness is one of the most important elements in business writing, and it begins with word choice. To choose appropriate words, choose those having the right denotative and connotative meanings, and use action verbs and descriptive adjectives and adverbs.

Denotative and Connotative Meanings

All words have denotative (literal) meanings, but many have connotative meanings as well. Most of us can agree on the meaning of such words as *automobile, day, week, window, pencil,* and *door* because only their denotative meanings are used commonly. Whenever these words are used in business messages, the reader's interpretation of them is certain.

The connotative meaning of a word is that feeling or impression conveyed along with the denotative meaning. For example, a *hallway* may be called a *breezeway.* While both words have the same denotation, *breezeway* also has a connotation. Also, while *duty, obligation, responsibility,* and *moral imperative* have the same denotation, their connotations differ. The following word groups show how denotation and connotation differ:

celebration - merrymaking	smile - smirk - grin
stamp out - extinguish	messenger - envoy
overweight - fat	child - brat
accept - acquiesce	limit - obstruct
purse - moneybag	decline - rebuff
mute - dumb	spokesperson - mouthpiece

Because readers interpret messages, you cannot be certain what connotation a reader will place on a particular expression. However, you can choose words that have acceptable connotations as far as you know.

Active Verbs

The verb is the nucleus of any complete thought. To construct a meaningful expression, first choose a proper verb. Verbs convey the degree of precision in the action being expressed. Thus, use an action verb to convey a precise meaning. For example, assume that you wish to say how a woman proceeded on foot down a street. You might say merely that she *walked* down the street, using an imprecise verb. To be more precise, though, use an active verb such as *sped, raced, dawdled, strolled,* or *hobbled.* Then you will say *how* she walked down the street.

Descriptive Adjectives and Adverbs

Descriptive adverbs and adjectives support active verbs, and like verbs, these descriptors may be precise or imprecise. Imprecise descriptors include words such as *good-better-best, real-really, fine, very, most-mostly,* and *fair-fairly.* If you say, for example, that you will be busy for *most* of the day tomorrow, the meaning is imprecise. But if you say that you will be busy between 10 A.M. and 3:30 P.M. tomorrow, the meaning is precise. Imprecise descriptors are useful in some contexts in business writing, however. For instance, you may begin a paragraph by calling a product the *best* on the market and then follow with an explanation of what makes it best. That way, the paragraph as a whole conveys a precise meaning.

Strong, emphatic descriptors may convey imprecise meanings also. Words such as *fantastic, fabulous,* and *amazing* are strong and emphatic, but they often overstate reality. For example, to say that you had a *fantastic* time last evening is stronger than saying that you had a *good* time. But if you had a *good* time and say that you had a *fantastic* time, the meaning is imprecise. This type of overstatement also erodes the credibility in messages.

Constructing Effective Sentences

The basic parts that make up a complete thought, a sentence, are words and related word groups (phrases and clauses). The way in which you construct sentences from these related word groups determines how effective messages will be. Sentences must be coherent and should be interesting, too, since readers pay more attention to interesting writing. Four guides to writing coherent and interesting sentences are the following:

1. *Vary sentence types.*   Use a variety of sentence types to add interest to a message or to change emphasis or tone. Any written message as long as a full page probably should contain simple, compound, and complex sentences. Because compound-complex sentences are often long and complex, use them sparingly. When you do use compound-complex sentences, read them a second time to make sure that they are clear. More information on sentence types is in Appendix A.

2. *Vary sentence length.*   Sentences should average 15 to 20 words. Too many short sentences leave messages choppy and without unity. On the other hand, too many long sentences leave messages unclear and hard to read. When sentences are all the same length, though, reading them is a monotonous chore. So for best results, vary the sentence length.

3. *Use connectives.*   Use connectives to smooth the thought flow. They show the progression of ideas and how they relate to one another. Here is an example: "We will finish revising the Lindauer contract this week, *and* all other work is on schedule." The connective *and*

binds the thoughts together giving them unity. The following is a list of useful connectives:

Time Connectives

after, afterward
first, second, etc.
for example
further
meanwhile
next
still
until
when, whenever
while

Comparison/Contrast Connectives

after all
although
briefly
but
generally
however
if, then
instead, rather
nevertheless
nor, or

not only, but also
since
so
specifically
therefore
though
thus
where, wherever
yet

Likeness Connectives

also
and
as, as if
just as
likewise
similarly

Cause and Effect or Association Connectives

because
consequently
for

4. *Vary sentence formats.* Vary sentence formats in either of two ways:

   a. Present some ideas as questions rather than as statements.

Rather than this:	This procedure has been ineffective. We should consider discontinuing its use.
Try this more tactful way:	This procedure has been ineffective. Why should we continue using it?

   or

   Must we continue using it?

   b. Begin some sentences with a clause or phrase.

Rather than this:	We must discontinue using this procedure because it is ineffective.
Try this more forceful way:	Because this procedure is ineffective, we must discontinue using it.

Developing Organized Paragraphs

Just as well-constructed sentences help to form effective paragraphs, well-organized paragraphs can help to form effective messages. The factors involved are structure, length, and thought flow.

Paragraph Structure

Structure sentences within a paragraph tightly enough to form a central idea, which is the total message sent in a paragraph, the whole idea. A paragraph consists of a *main thought* (called a topic sentence) and *supporting details*. Business writers use *deductive* (direct) and *inductive* (indirect) organization most often. Both structures convey a central idea, and both employ the main thought–supporting details format. A deductively organized paragraph begins with the main thought and follows with supporting details. An inductively organized paragraph begins with supporting details and follows with the main thought, just the reverse of deductive organization. Here are examples of each method:

Deductive (main thought in italics)
Sick leave in the office set a record yesterday, so we will have to hire temporary help to complete the Aspen Project. Sarah took a day of sick leave to take her son to see a physician. Raoul was hospitalized after crashing his car into an embankment while driving to work. Mary Ann was sidelined with a broken ankle. Eduardo and Renee were bedridden with influenza, which is epidemic here in Chicago.

Inductive (main thought in italics)
Sarah took a day of sick leave yesterday to take her son to see a physician. Raoul was hospitalized after crashing his car into an embankment while driving to work. Mary Ann was sidelined with a broken ankle. Eduardo and Renee were bedridden with influenza, which is epidemic here in Chicago. *Therefore, since sick leave in the office set a record yesterday, we will have to hire temporary help to complete the Aspen Project.*

The best way in which to construct these paragraphs is to write down the main thought first and use that as a framework for writing the supporting details. Deductive organization is more direct and, therefore, more understandable on the first reading. On the other hand, inductive is more persuasive. So a good rule to follow is to structure paragraphs deductively except when you need to persuade the reader to agree with your ideas; then structure them inductively.

Paragraph Length and Thought Flow

An effective paragraph may contain a few or several hundred words. Usually, letter and memorandum paragraphs are shorter than are those in reports because reports usually contain more details. Regardless of the type of business writing, vary the paragraph length.

Good thought flow within, between, and among paragraphs also helps to give a message unity. Here are three guides to help smooth thought flow:

1. *Organize the supporting details within paragraphs.* The content of the message itself gives the best clues about how to organize details. Several possibilities are

   a. From least to most important, or the reverse
   b. Through comparison and contrast
   c. In a time or date sequence
   d. By defining the main thought
   e. Through classification

   To illustrate, try a time sequence. Assume that you are writing a paragraph about the events of a single day. To arrange details in chronological order, begin with the earliest event of the day and continue to the last thing you did.

2. *Use connectives.* Use connectives within paragraphs to smooth the thought flow from sentence to sentence. Also use them between and among paragraphs for the same reason. For example, using words such as *however* and *therefore* at the beginning of a paragraph signifies that the ideas in the paragraph relate to those in the preceding one. A list of connectives is given on page 10.

3. *Repeat key ideas.* Repeating an idea cues the reader to note its importance. You can use repetition to stress key points. When you do this, either use a synonym or just restate the word or phrase. But avoid redundancy, that is, immediate restatement of an idea.

Using Parallel Construction

Parallel form guides a reader through ideas you present in a message and shows the balance between and among ideas that are equal in thought. As a result, you should express parallel thoughts in parallel grammatical form. The relationship may be from word to word, phrase to phrase, clause to clause, or sentence to sentence. Grammar should be parallel when elements are connected by coordinating or correlative conjunctions. (Commonly used coordinating conjunctions are *but, or, and, so, for, yet,* and *nor. Both-and, either-or, neither-nor, not only-but also,* and *whether-or* are commonly used correlative conjunctions.) Several examples of correct and incorrect parallel construction are

Incorrect	Jane's stockbroker advised her to sell Abcar shares but against buying Inovar shares.
Correct	Jane's stockbroker advised her to sell Abcar shares but not to buy Inovar shares.
Incorrect	Not only must we balance the books, but also taking the inventory is necessary.
Correct	Not only must we balance the books, but also we must take the inventory.

Incorrect	(headings in a report)
	A. Production Needs
	B. Sales Needs
	C. Needs in Inventory
Correct	A. Production Needs
	B. Sales Needs
	C. Inventory Needs
Incorrect	(headings in a report)
	I. Diseases in Peach Trees
	II. Diseases in Apple Trees
	III. Diseases in Orange Trees
	IV. Diseases in Winesap Trees
	V. Diseases in Golden Delicious Trees
Correct	(*Note:* Winesap and Golden Delicious are apple varieties.)
	I. Diseases in Peach Trees
	II. Diseases in Apple Trees
	A. Winesap
	B. Golden Delicious
	III. Diseases in Orange Trees

Violating parallel form can mislead a reader about the meaning of a message. This happens most often when the subject matter is unfamiliar to the reader and when the ideas are complex.

While messages must be coherent in order to understand them, they should be credible, in this case objective and fair.

GAINING CREDIBILITY

Credible writing is believable; nevertheless, truthful writing may not be credible. Much depends on how you say what you say. This section contains pointers on how to write credibly.

Being Objective

When it comes to sounding credible, using subjective statements is risky. Readers have more faith in objective statements, and therefore a close tie exists between being objective and being persuasive. This practice is easy as long as you are presenting facts. Yet you can present opinions objectively just by calling them what they are—opinions. In fact, the opinions of authorities are highly persuasive. Here are three ways in which to be objective in business writing:

1. *Cite sources.* Give the readers sources of your information, especially when presenting key ideas. For example, did your information come from a survey, from talking with superiors or from company records? If so, cite the source. Here is an example:

   The results of tests run July 20 by Philip Goldman, chief engineer at DuBont's Sprackling Division in Philadelphia, show that . . .

2. *Quote sources.* Paraphrasing is more effective than quoting because it is usually clearer. However, quoting can be more objective, so quote information when that is especially important. Here is an example:

   Louis DuBois, president of French Lines, said in a speech before the National Association of Business that "International tax laws must be changed if we are to . . ."

3. *Use figures and graphic aids.* Citing figures can show a reader why you have made certain statements. Graphic aids also help by illustrating ideas or showing relations between and among complicated data.

Showing Fairness

Fairness gives balance to writing, and balance implies thought and planning. Also, fairness, as does objectivity, makes writing credible. Here are several techniques to use.

Show Different Viewpoints

Showing differing viewpoints can give writing a balanced approach. Here are two examples of how this is done:

   While the majority of employees favored extending insurance coverage to include dental expenses, 25 percent were unwilling to pay the higher rates required for the added coverage.

   Groton's citizens believe that Dynamics Company should receive the defense contract. They favored Dynamics over Aerospace Company by a

450-to-60 vote. Portsmouth's citizens believe that Aerospace should receive the contract, however, by a 232-to-72 vote.

When appropriate to do so, showing different viewpoints can have a powerful effect on credibility.

Give Complete Information

Giving complete information also shows fairness to everyone concerned. Doing this helps especially when dealing with emotional issues. For example, assume that the matter of who should receive the defense contract in the preceding example is an emotional issue. In such a case, you might report the vote this way:

> Groton's citizens believe that Dynamics Company should receive the defense contract. They favored Dynamics over Aerospace Company by a 450-to-60 vote. Portsmouth's citizens believe Aerospace should receive the contract, however, by a 232-to-72 vote. Although the vote was not considered representative because it was taken on a Sunday morning when many citizens were unavailable, Newport's citizens favored Dynamics by a 23-to-10 vote.

Avoid Libel and Copyright Violations

Libel is a written defamation of another person's good reputation without good reason. To sue for libel, the injurious information must be (1) false, (2) communicated in writing or pictures, and (3) read by a third person. To collect damages, a desire to inflict injury and damage to one's reputation must be proven. Examples of libelous information include any false statement that damages a person's reputation, such as a charge that a person committed a crime. If a statement injures a person in his or her profession, libel is assumed and need not be proven.

A *copyright* is issued by offices of the United States Register of Copyrights to protect the publication rights of those who own original written material. If granted before 1978, a copyright lasts 28 years and is renewable for 47 years. If granted during or after 1978, it lasts for the owner's life plus 50 years. However, anonymous works and those created under pseudonyms are protected for 75 years from publication or 100 years from creation, whichever is shorter. When two or more people hold a copyright, protection lasts for 50 years after the death of the last survivor.

You may make *fair use* of copyrighted material, which usually means that you may make one copy for noncommercial use. The factors involved are

1. Purpose and character of use, including whether it is commercial or for nonprofit education purposes

2. Nature of the work

3. Amount and substantiality of the portion used in relation to the whole work

4. Effect of use on potential market for or value of the work

The penalties for libel and copyright infringement can be great. So if you question the legality of what you write or copy, either ask a lawyer about it or seek an alternative.

Avoid Unrelated Matters

Always try to leave the reader free to be persuaded by appropriate information. To do this, avoid mentioning unrelated matters; they can get in your way if they apply undue pressure. For example, reminding a reader that you are friends might be a form of undue pressure, as might be a hint that you are friends with her or his boss. These tactics imply that a reader should consider these relationships in making a decision about your message.

While no one can write persuasively without sounding credible, good writing includes other factors such as knowing how to emphasize important ideas.

USING EMPHASIS TECHNIQUES

Use emphasis techniques to stress key ideas you want a reader to pay special attention to. Remember, though, that "special" attention cannot be paid to every idea, so avoid emphasizing too much. The following are nine ways in which to emphasize ideas:

1. *Primacy and recency effect.*   Readers pay close attention to the first and last parts of a message. Therefore, we should open and close messages with key ideas. The special emphasis on the opening part of a message is called *primacy effect;* that on the closing part is called *recency effect.*

2. *Short paragraphs.*   Ideas presented in short paragraphs have special emphasis. For best results, limit these paragraphs to one sentence or perhaps two short sentences.

3. *White space.*   Surrounding parts of a message with additional white space (more blank lines or larger margins) emphasizes those parts.

4. *Listings.*   Along with being a good organizing device, listing is a good emphasizing technique that is quite useful when presenting points in

a particular order. Examples are points that proceed from most to least useful or in a time sequence. Here are four ways in which to arrange the ideas:

   a. Line spacing
   b. Enumeration (1, 2, 3 or I, II, III)
   c. Alphabetizing (a, b, c or A, B, C)
   d. Bullets (· · ·)

5. *Headings.* Headings are used most often in reports, but they are just as effective in long memorandums and letters.

6. *Capitalization and underlining.* You can emphasize a word, phrase, clause, sentence, or paragraph with capitalization or underlining. Limit this to six or fewer consecutive lines, however.

7. *Color.* Using one or more colors other than the color of the paper attracts a reader's eye. Use colors that contrast to the color of the paper. Also, use tasteful combinations and shades of colors.

8. *Figures and graphic aids.* In addition to clarifying ideas and making them more credible, figures and graphic aids also emphasize them.

9. *Repetition.* Repeating an idea later in a paragraph or in a later paragraph emphasizes it.

A final check in message construction is to make sure that your messages are easy to read. Easy-to-read messages are more likely to be read than are those that are hard to follow.

ASSURING READABLE MESSAGES

Readability, the ease with which a message can be read, can determine whether it will be read at all. Because we must be sure that our writing is read, readability is a crucial factor. The following is a method for determining the readability level of messages.

Fog Index Explained

Many formulas exist to compute readability. Of these, Robert Gunning's Fog Index is most often used in business and industry. Follow these four steps to compute the reading level of a message using the Fog Index[1]:

[1]Adapted from Robert Gunning, *The Technique of Clear Writing,* rev. ed. (New York, New York: McGraw-Hill, 1968, pp. 38–39. Used by permission.

Step 1   *Find the average sentence length.*

Choose a passage of continuous sentences containing at least 100 words; the passage may be a complete message or part of one. Count the number of words in the passage and then the number of sentences. (Count independent clauses as separate sentences. For example, "We read. We learned. We improved." This would be counted as three sentences, even if semicolons or dashes are used instead of periods.) Divide the number of words in the passage by the number of sentences to get the average number of words in a sentence.

Step 2   *Find the percentage of "difficult" words.*

"Difficult" words are those containing three or more syllables *except*

a. Words that are capitalized
b. Words formed by combining short words (*nonetheless* and *hereafter*, for example)
c. Verbs made into three syllables by adding *ed* or *es* (*confounded* or *disposes*, for example)

Now count the number of difficult words, counting each one each time it appears in the passage. Divide the number of difficult words by the total number of words in the passage and multiply the result by 100. The answer is the percentage of difficult words.

Step 3   *Add the answers in steps 1 and 2.*

Add the average sentence length to the percentage of difficult words.

Step 4   *Multiply by 0.4.*

Multiply the answer in step 3 by 0.4 to obtain the reading grade level (Fog Index) of the passage.

If you prefer to use a mathematical approach for computing a reading grade level, apply this formula:

$$\text{Fog Index} = \left(\frac{B}{C} + \left(\frac{A}{B} \times 100 \right) \right) \times 0.4$$

where A = number of "difficult" words in the passage
B = number of words in the passage
C = number of sentences in the passage

Note: In dates, count each word separately; for example, *January 10, 1984,* is three words. In numbers and symbols, count each word separately when spelled out or when spaces are left between: for example, *$250* is one word but *two hundred fifty dollars* is four words; *six and two thirds* is four words but *6 2/3* is two words.

Fog Index Applied

The "difficult" words in the following paragraph from a sales letter are underlined, and the Fog Index computation follows:

> The booklet has been received warmly. For example, the Information Service Institute has adopted it as a text for use in a statewide teacher training program for city organizations; these groups have included fire, police, and parks departments. This institute trains members of the departments to serve as teachers. Then the teachers conduct workshops within their own organizations. Many of these departments have purchased multiple copies of the booklet. Also, the booklet has been ordered by hundreds of private companies across the nation. In some cases, a copy was ordered for each person who conducted a workshop. In other cases, a single copy was bought for use as a reference manual for the company's training division.

Step 1	Number of words	116	
	Number of sentences	9	
	Average sentence length (116 ÷ 9)		13
Step 2	Number of "difficult" words	13	
	Percentage of "difficult" words (13 ÷ 116 × 100)		11
Step 3	Steps 1 and 2 answers added		24
Step 4	Reading grade level of passage (24 × .4)		9

The 9 reading grade level means that a person who reads in the ninth-grade range can read the passage easily. Business messages usually are written between grade levels 8 and 12. If you consistently write messages within this range, most readers will find them easy to read. Remember, though, that easily read messages may not be easy to understand. Also, Gunning's formula takes time to apply. When you cannot take time to apply the formula to a passage of your writing, remember that long sentences and words of more than two syllables increase the reading grade level.

Many good writers could be better if they would take time to reflect on the quality of their writing. Proofreading copy provides an opportunity for reflection.

PROOFREADING MESSAGES

Proofreading provides the only regular opportunity you have to reflect on the quality of your writing. Writing skills grow when nurtured, and proofreading nurtures that growth. Make it a practice to proofread your own work. When perfect copy is especially important, ask someone else to proofread it as well.

Types and Methods of Proofreading

The three types of proofreading are

1. *Context.*   Did you say what you meant to say in the way you meant to say it?

2. *Accuracy.*   Are there any language errors—spelling, punctuation, capitalization, grammar?

3. *Form and appearance.*   Is the layout correct—are all parts in place and the spacing correct? Does it look good?

Proofreading for everything at once is hard to do and usually results in overlooking some mistakes. A better practice is to proofread *separately* for context, accuracy, and appearance and form.

The four methods of proofreading are

1. Read forward.

2. Read backward.

3. Ask another person who writes well to read it.

4. Read it with another person who writes well.

Reading your own work forward is good for finding errors in context and accuracy. Reading backward is the best way to read for typographical errors. Asking someone else to proofread your work is excellent for finding context errors and good for finding accuracy errors; sometimes, we overlook our own mistakes. Proofreading with another person is excellent for finding context and accuracy errors. When doing this, each person should read from a separate copy. Because proofreading with another person takes additional time and effort, this method is best for especially important works.

The Three P's System

Proofreading long works such as reports is complex, and therefore overlooking errors is easy to do even when two or more people read the material. Using a *system* when proofreading can solve the problem. The *Three P's System* that follows is a practical and flexible system for finding errors in long documents. Either you or another person can use it independently, or you can use it when proofreading with another person. The three P's stand for *preconditions, procedure,* and *postconditions.* Here is how it works:

P1: Preconditions

1. *Allow at least 3 hours to lapse before proofreading a message.*   For even better results, allow about 24 hours to lapse, but do not wait

more than three days. Proofreading too soon allows too little time to reflect on the message, but waiting too long tests the memory.

2. *Proofread a rough draft when feasible.*   The rough draft allows more flexible use of the material.

3. *Learn to use standard proofreading symbols to mark changes.*   Using standard symbols makes it easy to interpret changes. A list of standard proofreading marks is printed in Appendix F.

P2: Procedure

First, *proofread for overall effect.* Reflect on the message as the reader will do. Does it say what you wish to say, only what you wish to say, and in the way you wish to say it? Then, proofread for the *Seven C's* of writing:

1. *Is it clear?*   Are all points clearly stated using familiar, direct language? Are complex points simplified? Are points stated in proper relationship with one another?

2. *Is it complete?*   Are all important points included? Has everything been said that should be said?

3. *Is it concise?*   Are only relevant points included? Is the message succinct? Is it worded precisely?

4. *Is it concrete?*   Are facts and figures used wherever needed? Is the language objective and specific?

5. *Is it considerate?*   Does the message focus on the reader's interests and needs? Does the language express the reader's viewpoint and include the reader in the action?

6. *Is it correct?*   Is the language level correct for the reader? Are grammar, spelling, punctuation, and capitalization correct?

7. *Is it courteous?*   Does the message sound sincere? Is the language positive?

P3: Postconditions

1. *Ask another person to proofread the message if (a) it is not satisfactory at this point or (b) it has special importance.*

2. *Revise the message if it is not satisfactory at this point.*   After revising the message, proceed again through P1 (preconditions) and P2 (procedure).

3. *Rewrite the message entirely if it is still not satisfactory at this point.*   While rewriting, refer to the revised message now being discarded only for facts. Avoid using an unsatisfactory revision for guidance on organization or expression. When you must rewrite a message, remember that you are starting over.

The Three P's System works well when followed closely. More time is needed to use it the first few times than when you learn to use it well. Here is a paragraph from a long report which was proofread using the system. A corrected copy follows. Consult Appendix F for standard proofreading marks.

The sixteen women and six men who shopped regularly at the Fan Market have incomes ranging from $15,000 to $55,000. Income level and sex showed no correlation. ③ women and one man had incomes between $15,000 and $25,000 and six women and men two had incomes between $25,000 and $35,000. ④ women and two men had incomes between $53,001 and $45,000, and three women and one man had incomes between $45,001 and $$55,000.

The sixteen women and six men who shop regularly at the Fan Market have incomes ranging from $15,000 to $55,000. Income level and sex show no correlation. Three women and one man have incomes between $15,000 and $25,000. Six women and two men have incomes between $25,001 and $35,000. Four women and two men have incomes between $35,001 and $45,000, and three women and one man have incomes between $45,001 and $55,000.

"Good looks" is very important in a written message. To ensure that the messages you sign look good, learn how to prepare attractive copy yourself.

PREPARING ATTRACTIVE COPY

The physical appearance of a message makes the *first impression* on a reader. To test this notion, notice what happens the next time you read a letter or take a first look at the title page of a report. If the message looks attractive, your initial impression will be positive. But if the message looks unattractive, your impression will be negative. The first impression should be positive, but good-looking messages require careful copy preparation.

How Copy Is Prepared

Written messages either are typewritten or printed whenever they are important enough to be recorded. While most messages written by managers today are prepared for mailing or routing by nonmanagerial employees, this procedure is changing. Already, many managers prepare messages on word/information processing equipment. Why not learn to use this equipment yourself? When you do, you will be able to produce better quality writing as a result of being able to do your own work. When you do not do your own work, check the work of those who prepare your messages before you sign or otherwise approve them. (See Chapter Thirteen for more details on using word/information processing equipment.)

Checkpoints for Preparing Copy

Here are four points to check before approving a message for mailing or routing:

1. *Do the pages look clean?*   Remove any visible erasures, corrections, or smudges. This may mean typing things again.
2. *Does the copy look sharp?*   Copy should be dark, contrasting sharply with the paper. Quality paper and a new typing ribbon help greatly.
3. *Is the message balanced on the pages?*   Frame the message with blank spaces on all sides of each page. Center the message slightly high on the page—called the "picture frame" effect.
4. *Are standard layouts and formats used?*   Readers expect to see standard layouts and formats. Nonstandard layouts and formats draw attention away from the message.

Other graphic factors also affect the reader's impression of the message. These include

1. Letterhead, memorandum forms, and envelope design and printing quality
2. Paper type and color
3. Type style and ink color

Most firms standardize selections of these items, requiring their use throughout the firm. Because a change may affect everyone in the firm, changing a standardized item normally requires approval from superiors.

SUMMARY

Because we write business messages to achieve objectives, it is important to plan first. The five steps in planning to achieve objectives are as follows: identify the purpose, determine the content, organize the content, set a time schedule, and devise a system for monitoring progress.

The next step is to analyze the reader. Having done this, you are ready to write the message.

To achieve coherence in writing, choose appropriate words, construct effective sentences and paragraphs, and use parallel grammatical form. Active verbs and descriptive adjectives and adverbs are appropriate, and simple, compound, complex, and compound-complex sentences may be used. Vary sentence types, lengths, and formats and use connectives to improve coherence and interest. Organize your paragraphs either inductively or deductively. Then use connectives, repeat key ideas, and organize supporting details internally to achieve good thought flow in paragraphs.

Your business writing should be credible as well. To achieve this, first be objective by citing and quoting sources and using figures and graphic aids where needed. Then, ensure fairness by showing different viewpoints, giving complete information, and avoiding unrelated matters.

Emphasis techniques are useful in business writing, and it is important to assure that messages can be read easily. A readability formula is useful to determine the reading grade level of a written message. The Gunning Fog Index is one that can be applied easily.

Proofread your messages before sending them, and send copy that looks attractive. Use the Three P's System to proofread. The three P's stand for preconditions, procedure and post-conditions. When preparing copy or monitoring copy preparation, check pages for cleanness and sharpness of copy. Also, balance the message on the page and use a standard layout and format.

Additional Readings

Bonner, William H., and Jean Voyles. *Communication in Business: Key to Success.* Houston, Tex.: Dame Publications, 1980, pp. 36-40.

Brown, Harry M., and Karen K. Reid. *Business Writing and Communication: Strategies and Applications.* New York: D. Van Nostrand, 1979, pp. 79-99.

Gunning, Robert D. *The Technique of Clear Writing,* rev. ed. New York: McGraw-Hill, 1968.

Haggblade, Berle. *Business Communication.* St. Paul, Minn.: West, 1982, pp. 67-91.

Huseman, Richard C., James M. Lahiff, and John D.

Hatfield. *Business Communication: Strategies and Skills.* Hinsdale, Ill.: Dryden Press, 1981, pp. 39-54.

Lesikar, Raymond V. *Basic Business Communication,* rev. ed. Homewood, Ill.: Richard D. Irwin, 1982, pp. 26-46.

Quible, Zane K., Margaret H. Johnson, and Dennis L. Mott. *Introduction to Business Communication.* Englewood Cliffs, N.J.: Prentice-Hall, 1981, pp. 38-56.

Treece, Malra. *Successful Business Writing.* Boston: Allyn & Bacon, 1980, pp. 120-121, 124-132.

Review Questions

1. What advantages do written business messages have compared with those sent by telephone or in person?

2. Name the steps in planning and achieving writing objectives.

3. Why should we analyze the reader before sending a written message?

4. What factors make written messages more coherent? Give an example of each.

5. Explain the ways in which you can be objective and fair in business writing to appear more credible.

6. Name five emphasis techniques that are

effective in writing business messages. Explain how to use each of them.

7. What does readability mean? Is a readable message always easy to understand? Explain.

8. Why should you proofread what you write?

Explain how the three major steps function in the Three P's System for proofreading.

9. Why is it important to send attractive-looking written messages to readers? Name three questions you should ask yourself about the physical appearance of a written message before mailing or routing it.

Exercises

1. List three verbs that show more action than the underlined word in each of these sentences:
   a. Agnes <u>went</u> to her noon appointment with Ted.
   b. Lars <u>talked</u> with Diane about the Stears project.
   c. Marvin Jenks <u>came</u> to the four o'clock meeting.
   d. Vennie <u>looked</u> at her work schedule.
   e. Connie <u>smiled</u> when she heard the news.

2. Examine the simple sentences following in each part of this exercise. Then rewrite the sentences to form compound, complex, or compound-complex sentences as indicated. You may add connectives when needed.
   a. The Jorgensens charged the purchase to their credit account. Marilyn then posted the charge on the record. (change to a *compound* sentence)
   b. The accounting staff needs another auditor. Sara Scranton applied for the job. (change to a *compound* sentence)
   c. A $55 balance was due. Olga paid it. She then bought a new radial tire for her car. (change to a *complex* sentence)
   d. Hilda Turner gives the orders here. She is the manager. (change to a *complex* sentence)
   e. The holiday season begins tomorrow. We will prepare for it. Afterward, we will cel-

   ebrate. (change to a *compound-complex* sentence)
   f. Helena Schmidt works in France. Josep Aulbert works in Austria. They exchange visits once a year. (change to a *compound-complex* sentence)

3. The following paragraph contains only simple sentences. Rewrite it so that it contains at least one each of the four sentence types: simple, compound, complex, and compound-complex. Use connectives wherever appropriate.

   Roberto and Joan spent two weeks campaigning for Alderman Pemberton's re-election. Both are busy with their jobs. They asked their neighbors to vote for the alderman. They passed out leaflets in South Philadelphia. They spoke to voters during rush hours. They posted handbills on telephone poles in the district. First, they got a permit to do this. Joan appeared on a local television program to promote the cause. Roberto promoted it among union members. Both Roberto and Joan believe the alderman is doing a good job.

4. Write *deductively* and *inductively* arranged paragraphs using the information presented. First, write a main idea (topic sentence) from the suggested idea. Next, write a deductively arranged paragraph using your topic sentence and the suggested ideas for details.

Then, rearrange the paragraph inductively. You may add words to smooth the thought flow.

Suggested Idea for Main Idea
K-C Company's new Zippy paper towel is the best on the market.

Suggested Ideas for Paragraph Details
The towel will absorb 20 percent more than other towels on the market. The towel is more tear resistant than any of the five leading brands. It will not get "soggy" when wet. The towel is more durable than those of any competitor. It comes in five new designs. Each towel is 15 percent larger than any major brand.

5. Find the parallelism problems in the parts of this exercise that follow and then rewrite them in a parallel form.
   a. Not only will we debit the account, but also making the disbursement is necessary.
   b. Shelley will choose the gift, arrange the retirement party, and the guests must be invited by her.
   c. Where we go and the things we do are often unplanned.
   d. (headings in a report)
      A. Finance Charges Increased
      B. Decrease in Profits
      C. Inventories Remained Steady
      D. Costs Fell Slightly
   e. (headings in a report)
      A. Selling for High Prices
         1. Planning the Presentation.
         2. Making the Delivery
         3. Buying for Lower Costs
      B. Salvaging for Resale
      C. Should Manufacture for Best Design
         1. Use Buying Plan
         2. Sell Old Stock

6. Apply the procedure for finding the Gunning Fog Index to the two paragraphs that follow.

Find one reading grade level for the combined paragraphs.

Millions of travelers enter the continental United States each year. Along with the usual souvenirs, they often bring many varieties of prohibited agricultural products. Currently, a number of these contraband products carried by travelers get through without detection.

Many of these agricultural products may carry pests not found in this country. Because these pests may not have natural enemies in the United States, they can flourish. The Mediterranean fruit fly is a prime example. This enemy of fruit growers has appeared in the country several times during this century. Thus far, we have been able to eradicate them each time using scientific methods. But can we always do this?

7. Make a photocopy of the first of the two paragraphs that follow or type it on a sheet of paper. Then proofread the paragraph so that when the corrections you suggest are made, the copy will read like the second paragraph.

Enter the new United Bank serve yourself sweepstakes is easy. Firstly conduct a transattion at any Serve Yourself Banking Center in area your between August 1st and September 30th. each transaction is actually an entry in the sweepstakes. Whether you check your balance or make a deposit, payment transfer or withdrawal of cash, you are entered automatically. Winners willbe notified before October 1st by mail.

Entering the new United Bank Serve Yourself Sweepstakes is easy. Simply conduct a transaction at any Serve Yourself Banking Center in your area between August 1 and September 30. Each transaction is actually an entry in the sweepstakes. You are entered automatically whether you check your balance or make a deposit, payment, transfer, or cash withdrawal. Winners will be notified by mail before October 1.

CHAPTER TWO

Style and Tone in Language

The goals in studying the text and completing the activities in this chapter are to know

1. The effects of style and tone in language
2. The three levels of language usage
3. How to use unbiased language
4. The factors involved in clarity in language
5. The factors involved in conciseness in language
6. The factors involved in accuracy in language
7. How to sound sincere in language
8. How to sound positive with language
9. The factors involved in vividness in language

Style! Things have it—furniture, clothes, jewelry. You can see an automobile's style in the way it looks. People are even said to have it—an athlete or actress has style! Writing has it, too. Look at the style in two opening passages from business letters:

> Pursuant to your request of the fourth instance for merchandise parcels, we beg to say that your gracious order was kindly received.

> Your order No. 311 was shipped this morning by railway express.

The style of the first passage was common in business writing of the nineteenth century. Although this wordy, indirect, stilted language isn't "stylish" today, remnants of it linger here and there. The second passage is more informative and direct. We prefer this style today.

Writing has tone, too. You can see it in these two passages, also from business letters:

> You should pay attention to our directions. Order merchandise from the warehouse nearest you, Little Rock in your case.

> For quicker delivery and better all-around service, you can place your next order with our warehouse there in Little Rock.

The demanding, preachy tone of the first passage really puts the reader off. On the other hand, the courteous, reader-centered tone of the second passage can make you want to place an order when you again need merchandise. This passage shows modern business writing tone.

Business writing has a unique style and tone. Although discrete qualities, they appear together to form the overall impression you have of what you read.

POINTS ABOUT STYLE

Writing style is the characteristic manner in which we express ourselves in writing. Although your writing style is unique in that no one else writes exactly as you do, you can change your style to suit the occasion. For instance, you may use one style when writing a business letter, another when writing a poem. Your business writing style, however, should draw as little attention to itself as possible. In fact, the less noticeable that style is to readers, the better the effect. Why? A writing style that draws attention to itself can direct the reader's attention from the content of the message and perhaps distort understanding. A writing style that draws little or no attention to itself leaves the reader free to concentrate on content.

POINTS ABOUT TONE

Tone in writing refers to the manner in which you express a certain attitude. What you choose to say and how you say it determine tone. The most effective business writing tone is friendly, conversational, businesslike, objective, and personalized. Tone is weak, however, when it is friendly enough to sound familiar, conversational enough to sound chatty, businesslike enough to sound too formal, objective enough to sound indifferent, or personalized enough to sound snoopy. The positive qualities of tone are reversed easily when used excessively. Consequently, practice restraint in business writing.

The major topics discussed in this chapter are language level, bias, clarity, conciseness, accuracy, positiveness, and vividness.

GENERAL LANGUAGE LEVELS

Three levels of language usage are *formal, informal,* and *nonstandard.* Each level reflects the degree of formality of the occasion for which it is appropriate. In business writing, however, use only the formal and informal language levels. Using nonstandard language in business calls attention to itself. An example is "The orders was placed last week, wasn't they?" In this example, the subject-verb disagreement diverts your attention from the message. A different example is "After reading your complaint, I don't know where you're coming from." Here, the slang expression, "where you're coming from," diverts the attention and may be misunderstood.

Informal language is almost always best for business writing. The exception is that formal language is best when a high degree of formality is needed, in legal contracts and treaties between nations, for example. The correct usage of language levels is shown in Figure 1.

Language level is determined by vocabulary, phrasing, sentence and paragraph length, and punctuation. Formal language calls for longer, more complex words and more complex phrasing. This level restricts pronoun use to the third person, uses no contractions, and contains strictly constructed, fully developed paragraphs. Sentences may average 25 to 40 words and paragraphs 200 to 300 words. As a result, punctuation is likely to be more complex. Use formal language in business writing only where formality is expected since it is more complex and more difficult to read than informal language.

Informal language is conversational and employs shorter, simpler words and simpler phrasing. Sentences and paragraphs are shorter, with

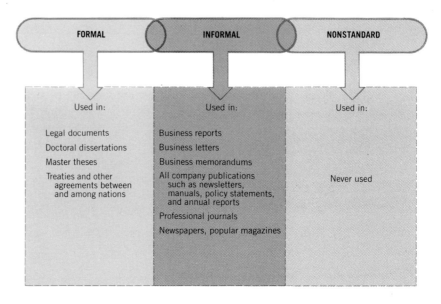

sentences averaging 15 to 20 words and paragraphs 100 to 150 words. (See Chapter One for more information on paragraph length.) In addition, punctuation is less complex and therefore easier to follow. *The language of business is informal.* The difference between formal and informal language is shown in these contrasting word groups and in the sentences that follow them:

Formal	Informal	Formal	Informal
anticipate	expect	pursuance	carrying out
appertaining	belonging	regulation	rule
ascertain	learn	statute	law
henceforth	after this	prior to	before
heretofore	up to now	undersigned	signer (or use name)
party	person or group of people	utilization	use
		vigilant	watchful
prophesy, prophecy,	predict, prediction	wherewithal	means, necessary means

Formal

The undersigned should ascertain prior to the deadline how the statute applies.

Informal

Miss Razo should find out how the law applies before the deadline.

| Henceforth, each regulation appertaining to Group 5 was underutilized. | After this, each rule belonging to Group 5 was underused. |

Modern writers use formal language less often than in the past, and the trend is toward using it even less. Insurance policies are sometimes written in informal language today, as are other legal documents. *Write as you talk* reflects the natural style and tone of informal language.

Another trend in business writing today is to use unbiased language.

UNBIASED LANGUAGE

A campaign is being waged in business today for equal treatment of minority groups in language use along with the quest for equal employment opportunities. For example, the use of masculine gender when a singular pronoun is needed to refer to both sexes is being questioned. What should the writer do then? Should the feminine gender now be preferred? The answer is no; reverse discrimination is not an answer. Rather, give equal treatment to both women and men in all business writing. The following discussion on using unbiased language is adapted from Judy E. Pickens, ed., *Without Bias: A Guidebook for Nondiscriminatory Communication*, 2nd ed. (New York: John Wiley, 1982).

Bias Against the Sexes

Perhaps the most obvious form of bias in business language today is sexually biased language. While women's groups have fought hardest to eliminate this practice, the language is often biased against men as well. Follow these six guides to erase sexual bias from the business messages you write.

Guide 1 *Include all people in general references by using asexual words and phrases instead of masculine and feminine words.*

Rather Than This	Try This
man-made	synthetic, artificial, constructed, manufactured
man-sized	husky, sizable, large, requiring exceptional ability
man-hours	hours, total hours, staff hours, working hours

mankind	people, humanity, human beings, human race
for the lady of the house	for the homemaker, for the consumer

Note: To avoid using *he* when a generic singular pronoun is needed, use one of these techniques: (1) reword the sentence to remove unneeded gender pronouns; (2) change the case from singular to plural; or (3) replace the masculine pronouns with *one, you, he* or *she,* or *her* or *his.* Avoid using the same technique repeatedly in a passage, however, because that will result in a monotonous repetition in the message.

Rather Than This

Each employee completes his timesheet at the end of his shift.

Try This

Each employee completes a timesheet at the end of the shift.

OR

All employees complete their timesheets at the end of their shifts.

OR

Each employee completes his or her timesheet at the end of the shift.

Guide 2   *Refer to women and men equally and make references consistent.*

Use the full name the first time you refer to a person in a message, but then use either the first or last name in later references.

Rather Than This

Sam Purdy and Miss Brown

Try This

Sam Purdy and Julia Brown

OR

Mr. Purdy and Miss Brown

Sam Purdy and Julia Brown were recently promoted. Purdy has been with the firm since 1970 and Julia since 1968.

Sam Purdy and Julia Brown were recently promoted. Purdy has been with the firm since 1970 and Brown since 1968.

OR

Mr. Purdy has been with the firm since 1970 and Ms. Brown (or

Miss or Mrs. if she prefers) since 1968.

OR

Sam has been with the firm since 1970 and Julia since 1968.

Guide 3   *Avoid unnecessary labels and stereotypes.*

Rather Than This	*Try This*
lady executive/banker	executive/banker
male cook/housekeeper	cook/housekeeper
just like a man/woman	avoid
ladylike	well mannered

Guide 4   *Avoid using "man" or "woman" as a suffix or prefix in job titles.*

Rather Than This	*Try This*
businessman/businesswoman	business executive, manager, entrepreneur
chairman/chairwoman	presiding officer, the chair, head, leader, moderator, coordinator, chairperson
foreman	supervisor, manager
salesman	salesperson, sales clerk, sales representative

Guide 5   *Use parallel language when referring to people by sex.*

Rather Than This	*Try This*
the ladies and the men	the women and the men; the ladies and the gentlemen; the girls and the boys
man and wife	husband and wife

Guide 6   *Use generic titles or descriptions for both women and men.*

General expressions refer to both sexes. Use them both in titles and descriptions of men and women.

Rather Than This	*Try This*
woman manager	manager
male secretary	secretary
authoress	author
aviatrix	aviator

Bias Against Racial and Ethnic Groups

Clichés and stereotypes about races and ethnic groups abound in the United States and abroad today. We hear of the fiery Spaniard, the hearty German, and the frugal Scot. Modern folklore is filled with these biased images, some of them so powerful that knowledge to the contrary does not change them. Avoid using them in business writing. Following are two guidelines to use in avoiding racial and ethnic bias in business writing:

Guide 1 *Avoid using qualifiers that reinforce racial or ethnic stereotypes.*

Do not add information that suggests that a person is an exception to a racial or ethnic norm.

Does This Sentence . . .	*. . . Contain This Hidden Stereotype?*
John Jones, a well-groomed black student, works as a part-time clerk.	Blacks are poorly groomed.
No retiring, quiet job for her, Betty Wong chose a dynamic career as . . .	Asians are shy, docile.
José Rodriguez, a steady and even-tempered worker . . .	Mexican Americans (or other people of Spanish heritage) are volatile, unpredictable.

Guide 2 *Avoid citing racial identification or ethnic origin except when pertinent to the message.*

If This Identification Is Inappropriate . . .	*. . . Is This Phrasing any Different?*
Judy, an outgoing white woman	Mary, an outgoing black woman

When proofreading messages, be alert for subtle bias implied in the context.

CLARITY

Misunderstandings in business result more often from unclear messages than they do from bad feelings or lack of goodwill. Unclear messages can be ambiguous, causing the reader to either have to guess the intended meaning or ask for a clarification from the writer. At other times, messages may be altogether unclear—the reader does not know what meaning the writer intends. When this happens, the reader either must disregard the message or call for clarification. In all these events, the chances of sending a successful message decreases.

Concrete and Abstract Expressions

Concrete expressions refer to actual objects whose natures people agree on. *Building, door, train,* and *briefcase* are examples. Abstract expressions on the other hand refer to qualities whose meanings are somewhat different for every person. Examples are *beauty, motivation, progress,* and *the American spirit.* Because clarity is essential in business messages, use concrete expressions where possible. Follow these three guidelines:

1. Add a word or phrase to an abstract term to define it more fully. For example, change *progress* to *organizational progress* or *economic progress.*
2. Replace the abstract term by explaining the meaning in sentences. Changing *progress* to *organizational progress* may yet leave the message unclear by leaving it incomplete. You may need also to explain the type of organizational progress meant. Does it mean that a new organizational structure is being adopted for the company, that the present system is being reviewed, or what?
3. Use the most specific concrete term possible when it is important to the meaning of the message. For example, if a *building* referred to has special importance to the message, go on to call it a *house,* a *store,* or whatever type building it is.

Specific and General Expressions

You probably would not be thoughtless enough to ask an old friend to meet you at a certain restaurant at *midafternoon,* but would you ask her or him to meet you there at *about noon?* While "about noon" is more specific than "midafternoon," it is not as specific as the situation will allow most of the time. If you intend to meet the friend at noon, for example, set that as the specific time to meet. Then if one of you is unavoidably late, the other likely will understand. Such practice is good training in using the specific language needed to conduct daily business affairs. Here is a list of general expressions commonly used in business messages that are too general to use. Rather than use them, be specific about what is meant.

above named	as in the above
as soon as possible	at an early date
at your convenience	in due course
in due time	of the above date
order has gone forward	give this matter your attention
under separate cover	without further delay

These expressions are used so often in business messages today that they are now stereotyped as well as too general.

Short, Simple Expressions

We may impress readers with our knowledge of language by using long, complex words. However, this may come at the high price of lifeless expressions or even misunderstanding. Short, simple terms convey meaning more directly and therefore more clearly than do long, complex ones. For example, use *people* rather than *personnel*, *home* or *address* rather than *residence,* and *send* rather than *furnish.* Here is a comprehensive list of such terms along with recommended alternatives.

Rather Than This	*Try This*
advise	write, tell
anticipate	expect
ascertain	find out, learn
comply	follow
constitute	are, be, is
deceased	dead
deem	think
desire	want, wish
disclose	show
effect (verb)	cause
endeavor	try
ensue	follow
execute	do
facilitate	make easy
forward	mail
indemnify	protect
indicate	say, show
initial	first
insufficient	not enough

Rather Than This	Try This
kindly	please
locate	find
prohibit	forbid
require	need
reveal	show
review	check
state	say
submit	give, send
subsequent	later
substantial	big, large
sufficient	enough
supply	send
sustain	suffer
terminate	end, stop
transpire	happen
vehicle	bus, car, truck

Many of the words in the preceding list also are stereotyped, another reason to avoid using them.

Unfamiliar Words, Foreign Expressions, and Jargon

While the English language does contain more than 700,000 words, only a few thousand of them are used commonly. In fact, most people use only 1000 to 1500 words in conversation and writing on a typical business day. Most words in the language are unfamiliar to most of us. For example, if you heard or read the word *piscatorial* (of fisherpeople or fishing, fishlike), would you have to guess at the meaning or look it up in the dictionary? How about *circumambient, terpsichorean,* and *tesselate?* Rather than use such unfamiliar words and risk misunderstanding, use more commonly known synonyms.

Avoid confusing unfamiliar words with technical terms. The technical terms of a profession may be used without an explanation when writing to a member of the same profession. For example, accountants speak of accruals and reversing entries among themselves. These terms may be used with an explanation when writing to a person who is not in the profession.

Using foreign expressions in business writing is also undesirable. While these expressions may sound "knowledgeable" or "stylish" to some, the risk of miscommunicating is great. Use the English equivalent instead. For example, rather than calling it a *tete-à-tete,* call it a *private conversation;* rather than saying *per se,* say *by itself* or *in itself.* The following is a list of commonly used foreign expressions to avoid.

Rather Than This	*Try This*
ad nauseam	to the point of disgust
a propos	to the point or purpose
au revoir	goodbye until we meet again
bona fide	in good faith
caveat emptor	let the buyer beware
coup de grace	a finishing stroke
de facto	in fact, actual
de jure	by right, by law
esprit de corps	group pride or honor in common interest or activity
in perpetuum	forever
in toto	as a whole, entirely
ipso facto	by the fact itself, by that very fact
magnum opus	a great work
modus operandi	procedure
non sequitur	it does not follow
par avion	by airplane, by airmail
per annum	by the year
per diem	by the day
quid pro quo	one thing in return for another
savoir faire	ready knowledge of how or when to do the correct thing; tact
sine qua non	a necessary thing
status quo	current situation
terra firma	solid ground
viz.	namely

Foreign expressions may be used as technical terms. For example, *per diem* and *de facto* may be used meaningfully in a legal or financial sense among professionals in the same field and in legal documents.

Jargon is the "slang" language of business. An example is the expression *initial outlay* as used in, *The initial outlay for the project will be. . . .* While jargon may sound "knowledgeable" to some people, it communicates little and thus should be avoided. A better practice is to say what you mean in simple, direct terms. Some terms are jargonized when used in one sense but not when used in another. For example, referring to an employee as an *activator* is jargon, but referring to a nuclear reactor's *activator* core is simply using a technical term.

Here is a list of commonly used terms that are jargonized in business. Avoid using them and other similar expressions. Notice that these terms also are stereotyped and clichéd.

characterization	knowledgeable (reliable,
commonality	informed) source
company man, company woman	logistical
computerize	maximize, minimize
conceptualize	prioritize
configuration	programmable
constraints	reorientation
contingency plans	space age tactics
expedite	subsystem
impact on	synchronized
implementation	systematized
incremental	technological advance
infusable	the foregoing
integral	the undersigned
interfacing	time phase
interrelationships	verifiable facts

Every profession has its jargon; when it is used strictly within the profession, meaning is clear. Common business jargon, however, is not professional; it tends to obscure meaning.

CONCISENESS

To be concise is to express a message completely in as few words as possible. Being concise results in increased effectiveness and decreased costs. Wordy expressions and redundancies are the problems to overcome to communicate concisely.

Wordiness

Wordiness plagues business writing today. Too many words are used to say too little. Wordy expressions are those that can be said in fewer words without losing meaning. For example, *about* or *near* says it more concisely than does *in the neighborhood of* or *in the vicinity of.* In the same way, *as you requested* is more concise than is *in compliance (or accordance) with your request,* and *many* beats *a large number of.* Thousands of wordy expressions are in regular use in modern business. Following is a list of wordy terms to avoid along with more concise alternatives.

Wordy	*Concise*
abovementioned, aforementioned	mentioned earlier, stated before
according to our records	we find
afford an opportunity	allow, enable
after the conclusion of	after
along the lines of	as with
are desirous of	want to
are of the opinion that	believe, think
as a general rule	generally
as per, as per your letter	acknowledge
as per your suggestion	as you suggested
as yet	still
at a later date	later
at all times	always
at the present time	now, at present
at such time, at which time	when
attached find, attached herewith is, attached hereto	attached, attached is, here is
attention is called	notice, please note
by means of	by
came into contact with	met
comes into conflict	conflicts
consider favorably	approve
costs the sum of	costs
despite the fact that	though
due in large measure to	because, since
during the time, during which time	while
during the year of	during
during this period of time	meanwhile
each of these	each
effects an improvement	improves
enclosed herewith, enclosed please find	here is, we are enclosing
equally as good	equally good
every effort will be made	we can, we will try
experience has indicated that	we have learned that
feel free to	please
first of all	first
for a total of	for
for the month of, for the period of	for
for the purpose of	for

Wordy	*Concise*
for the reason that	because, since
fullest possible extent	most
fully cognizant of	aware
give consideration (encouragement, instructions) to	consider (encourage, instruct)
have need for	need
held a meeting	met
hold in abeyance	postpone
I have your letter (or memo) of recent date	I have received, thank you for
if doubt is entertained	if doubtful
if you so desire	if you wish
in a careful manner	carefully
in a manner similar to	as with
in a position to	able to
in a satisfactory manner	satisfactorily
in a situation in which	when
in accordance with	by
in accordance with your request	as you requested
in addition to the above	also
in all probability	probably
in connection with	by, for, in
in large measure	largely
in order that	so that
in order to	to
in process of preparation	being prepared
in receipt of	received
in regard to	about, regarding
in spite of the fact that	even though
in the amount of	for
in the case of, in the event that	if
in the city (or any geographical location) of	in
in the nature of	as
in the near future	soon
in the normal course of	normally
in very few cases	seldom
in view of the fact that	because, since
in view of the foregoing	because, therefore
inasmuch as	since
inquired as to	asked

Wordy	*Concise*
is responsible for selecting	selects
it is in recognition of this fact that	therefore
it is recommended that consideration be given to	we recommend that
it would be advisable to	we suggest that, perhaps you should
kindly advise	please call, please write
let us hear from you	call us, write us
make a decision	decide
make an adjustment in	adjust
make inquiry regarding	inquire
make provisions for	does
may rest assured	may be sure
message to the effect that	message that
more or less	about, nearly
not in a position	cannot, unable
of a confidential nature	confidential
of the opinion that	believe, think
of the order of magnitude of	about
on the basis of	by, from
on the grounds that	because
on the occasion of	on, when
other things being equal	normally, usually
pending receipt of	until
pertaining to	about, of
please forward	mail
previous to, prior to	before
pursuant to our agreement	as we agreed
reason is due to	because
remember the fact that	remember
should take appropriate action to determine	should determine
take action	act
take pleasure	glad, happy, pleased
takes appropriate measure	acts, does
this will acknowledge receipt of	thank you for sending
thought occurred to us	we thought
through the use of	by, with
under consideration	considering
under date of	on
until such time as	until
we are awaiting your reply	may we have your answer

Wordy	*Concise*
we would like benefit of	we need, we want, we wish
will you be kind enough to	please
with a view to	to
with due regards to	for, regarding
with reference to, with regards to, with respect to	about
with the exception of	except

Some wordy expressions can be omitted altogether without any loss of meaning in the message. Compare these sentences:

Wordy   This is to inform you that your shipment was sent today.
Concise   Your shipment was sent today.

This is to inform you that is unnecessary to the meaning of the sentence. Avoid cluttering your writing with these "deadwood" expressions. The following is a list of the most frequently used "deadwood" expressions.

acknowledge your
allow me to express
along this line

answering your
as a matter of fact
at a loss to explain
at hand
do not hesitate
duly
has come to hand
have before me
hereto
hope to hear, hope to receive
I remain, we remain
in re
in reference to your request

in reply to, replying to
in reply wish to state, in reply would state
in response to, in response to same, in response to your favor, in response to your recent inquiry
in this connection
it goes without saying
kind favor
permit me to say
please be advised that, we wish to advise that
pursuant to your request
referring to your letter (or any message)
said (as in said response, said application)
take the liberty to
take this opportunity
thanking you in advance

Most of the wordy expressions listed in this section also are stereotyped, another reason to avoid using them.

Redundancies

To repeat an idea stated earlier in a passage can underscore its importance in the message. Therefore, this type of redundancy is effective. However, using other words that mean the same thing immediately after expressing an idea merely duplicates the meaning but adds nothing to it. An example is 7 P.M. *in the afternoon; in the afternoon* repeats P.M. unnecessarily. *A popular woman who is well liked, prejudge in advance,* and *joined together* are other examples. Here is a list of commonly used redundancies to avoid.

adequate enough	few in number	past history
advance warning	filled to capacity	perfectly clear
always and ever	filled to the top	personal opinion
and moreover	final completion	positively certain
assemble together	final outcome	proposed plan
awkward	first and foremost	real reason
predicament	first priority	refer back
basic fundamentals	fresh start	repeat again
begin first	full and complete	reverse back
big in size	gather together	serious danger
blue in color	grateful thanks	shuttle back and
burning flame	has got, have got	forth
close proximity	(used for *possess*)	sincere and earnest
collected together	important essentials	successful
combined together	instructional training	achievements
complete monopoly	last and final	surrounded on all
completely	local resident	sides
eliminated	mutual cooperation	thought and
consensus of opinion	my boss, she (or he)	consideration
depreciated in value	necessary requisite	throughout the whole
each and every	new beginning	of
end result	ordered sequence	true facts
entirely complete	original source	usual customs
exactly identical	pair of two	
fellow colleague	passing fad	

Business writing is concise only when both clear and complete.

ACCURACY

Because we communicate in business to achieve results, accuracy in expression is especially important. Just as a misplaced period can cause $50.00 to read $5000., so can an ill-chosen expression alter the meaning of a message. Using euphemisms, unwarranted superlatives, figurative cliches, and colloquialisms are four prime causes of inaccuracy in business messages. Rather than use these expressions, you should choose more accurate terms.

Euphemisms and Superlatives

Euphemisms are terms substituted for others we avoid because they are distasteful or offensive. However, they are always less accurate expressions, so use them *only* to avoid using a clearly distasteful or offensive term. Such euphemisms as *decline* used for *recession, had another setback* used for *failed again,* and *as events worked out* used for *unfortunately* can get across ideas less offensively. But euphemisms such as *terminated* used for *fired, laid to rest* for *buried,* and *golden years* for *older age* may appear pretentious or insincere. Euphemisms can be very inaccurate. For example, notice how ambiguous the term *sanitary engineer* is when used as a job title. A sanitary engineer might work as a garbage collection worker or supervisor, a janitor, a custodian, a garbage disposal worker or supervisor, or an engineer specializing in sanitation techniques and procedures.

The most extreme comparison of adjectives and adverbs is the *superlative* degree. For example, the superlative degree of *lovely* is *loveliest* or *most lovely;* that of *high* is *highest.* Using superlatives is good practice as long as the chosen word accurately describes the situation.

We use superlatives to stress points too often, however, and in doing so we often overstate points. For example, to use a strong adjective such as *amazing* often overstates the point; to use the superlative *most amazing* almost always does so. Disregarding accuracy, some business writers reach beyond conventional superlatives to coin expressions such as most *"fantabulous"* and *"amazeriffic."* Writing this way is inaccurate and causes the reader to question the writer's credibility. Therefore, use superlatives discreetly.

Figurative Clichés

Clichés are hackneyed or stereotyped expressions that are worn out through overuse in business messages. Figurative clichés can cause misunderstandings because a reader may assign literal meanings to them or figurative meanings different from those intended by the writer. Examples are *get on the ball* and *straight from the shoulder.*

Figurative clichés are culture bound as well; that is, only members of a society—Americans, for example—are likely to know their meanings. A Japanese with whom you are doing business probably will not know what you mean by *can't make heads or tails of it.* Therefore, avoid using these terms altogether.

The following is a list of figurative clichés used often by Americans in business messages.

a rude awakening

as pleased as Punch

bed of roses

beg the question

below the belt

blood is thicker than water

bone to pick with

bring to a head

bury the hatchet

by fits and starts

by leaps and bounds

can't tell whether I'm coming or going

cash in on

close call

counting chickens before they hatch

crossing bridges before coming to them

don't give a hoot

exception that proved the rule

fill the bill

flesh and blood

force of circumstance

grin and bear it

happy as a lark

high as the sky

horn of plenty

in due course

in the course of events

in the nick of time

it goes without saying

jolly as an elf

keep the wolf from the door

leave no stone unturned

let the cat out of the bag

looking through rose-colored glasses

make a bundle

mind your P's and Q's

never spoke a truer word

nip and tuck

oil on troubled waters

play the game

playing second fiddle

pride and joy

pull yourself together

pull up stakes

putting the cart before the horse

right on

say the word

shake a leg

shoot it straight

shoulder to the wheel

sleep like a log

snug as a bug in a rug

spearhead the drive

spic and span

stand your ground

stick to your guns

sticks and stones

strike while the iron is hot

take the bull by the horns

take to task

to the victor belongs the spoils

turn over a new leaf

up to no good

ups and downs

walk the straight and narrow

wise as an owl

with a grain of salt

with flying colors

without rhyme or reason

Colloquialisms

Colloquialisms are very informal expressions used instead of standard English terms. An example is

> **Colloquial** Miss Davis stood *in back of* Jenny Lomans.
> **Standard** Miss Davis stood *behind* Jenny Lomans.

Some colloquialisms are both inaccurate and draw attention to themselves because they come so close to nonstandard usage; an example is *owing to* for *because*. (See "General Language Levels" in this chapter.) Others may be as accurate as their standard English equivalents; compare *fizzle* with *fail*, for example. Here is a list of colloquialisms to avoid using in business messages.

Rather Than This	*Try This*
all done	completed, finished
all the farther	as far as
anywheres	any place
around this time	about this time
as to (when used for *about*)	about
be most happy	be glad, be happy
better than (when used for *more than*)	more than
but what (when used for *but that*)	but that
cannot help but	cannot but, cannot help
doubt but what	doubt what, doubt whether
get through	complete, finish
kind of, sort of (when used for *rather*)	rather
know how	knowledge, knowledge and experience
no good	worthless
no show	did not appear, did not arrive
nowhere near	not nearly
nowheres	no place
of no account	worthless
so (when used for *very*)	very
somewheres	someplace
sound out	explore, seek an opinion

Using accurate expressions represents a step toward credible writing.

SINCERITY

Appearing to be sincere is one of the most difficult tasks in business writing, yet one of the most necessary. Having honest intentions is not enough, the message itself must sound as though you have them. To help you appear sincere, you must show confidence, safeguard confidentiality, and avoid unnecessary humility and excessive flattery.

Showing Confidence

Sending messages that lack confidence is a certain way to cause readers to question your motives. Appearing confident, on the other hand, can assure that you will reach your objective. Follow these guidelines to improve confidence in business messages.

1. *Appear certain of the result.* Showing confidence about achieving the desired result can help you to achieve it. Notice the difference between the confidence level of these statements:

Lacks Confidence	*Sounds Confident*
Would you like to see our new fall catalog?	Call us today at 359-4678 for a copy of our new fall catalog.
When you can spare the time, please stop in to see our new spring suits.	Join us Thursday for the open house celebration of the arrival of our new spring suits by Halsey.

   Clauses such as *would you like to* and *when you can spare the time* are both hesitant and doubtful expressions. Others are *if you would like to* and *you should consider.* These statements destroy the success-oriented tone of good business writing.

2. *Avoid overconfidence.* An attempt to sound confident may sound overconfident because the writer takes too much for granted. Readers question the sincerity of presumptuous statements. Look at these examples:

Overconfident	*Confident*
We know that you will want to take advantage of this special offer today.	To take advantage of this special offer, just sign and mail the enclosed card today.

   Other overconfident statements begin with such clauses as *I am sure that, you will certainly find that,* and *of course, this is.* In addition to sounding insincere, these statements may annoy readers.

3. *Avoid appearing to harass or demand.*   Some attempts at sincerity not only sound insincere but also appear to harass the reader or to demand that the reader take some action. Here are examples:

Harassing and Demanding	*Avoids Harassing or Demanding*
You absolutely must pay your bill by June 21 to avoid a late payment charge.	Please pay your bill by June 21 to avoid a late payment charge.

Statements beginning with clauses such as *we cannot understand why, we are at a loss to understand,* and *your problem is unique, but* appear to harass readers or to sound demanding. Also, these statements provoke anger.

Safeguarding Confidentiality

Many company records, reports, and correspondence must be kept confidential for business, personal, or legal reasons. For example, information about new products that a company plans to market must be kept secret from the competition. Similarly, information on employment records needs safeguarding both to preserve the rights of employees and to avoid lawsuits. Even when we are discreet with information, the language we use can imply indiscretion. For instance, statements beginning with *I heard that* can cause a reader to suspect you of being indiscreet. In the same way, *we saw you at . . .* and *your secretary told me that . . .* can suggest that you are prying. Avoid using these expressions and others like them.

Excessive Humility and Flattery

Although it is important to show respect for your reader when writing, that can be taken so far as to sound insincere. In the extreme, one can appear unduly humble and flattering to the point of embarrassment. Here is an example of excessive humility:

May I kindly beg a favor of you?

This is better:

Will you please take a few minutes to . . .

Expressions such as *will you kindly be good enough to, I shall be eternally grateful if,* and *I am just a mere clerk (or any occupation), but* humble the writer unnecessarily. Avoid using such language; rather, ask directly for what you want and then go on to justify the request.

Here is an example of excessive flattery:

I know a person of your importance is busy, but will you take a few minutes of your valuable time to

This is better:

We need your opinion as an authority in the field. Will you please take a few minutes to

Other examples of such overstatement may begin with *You are surely one of the world's leading authorities in* or *You are held in such great esteem.* Sincere flattery works well when the situation justifies it. Excessive flattery sounds insincere, however. Sincerity helps to build a bond of trust between a writer and a reader.

POSITIVENESS

Look about you on that next shopping trip, walk, or drive; look about on the job as well. Written messages are everywhere, and far too many of them are expressed negatively:

No loitering. No parking. No talking. Do not enter. No fishing from bridge. No swimming. No vacancy. No trespassing. No refunds. No checks cashed. No breaking in line. No standing.

We live in a world colored by negative expressions, it seems. They appear wherever we go and in whatever we read. We grow accustomed to them and forget that they affect our attitudes and actions. Negative, selfish expressions give writing a negative tone, which in turn affects our attitudes about both writer and subject. To write positively, write from the reader's viewpoint and limit the use of negative expressions.

Writing from Reader's Viewpoint

The best business messages focus attention on the reader, observing the situation as the reader sees it. Reader's respond well to their own interests, so this technique works very well. As an example of this in action, suppose that you want a customer to buy more merchandise than usual this month. Your interest is that you want to win a company sales contest. To reach your objective—to get more orders—write about the benefits the reader will receive by buying the goods now. Talking about your winning the contest just isn't much of an appeal. So you might talk about discounts on volume orders, increased profit potential, and no risk because the goods can be returned later if not sold.

Along with highlighting the reader's interest, focus on the reader by using pronouns such as *you* and *your* rather than *I* and *me*. Here is an example:

Rather Than This I shipped the six dozen sweaters this morning by air express.
Try This Your order for six dozen sweaters was shipped this morning by air express.

We and *our* are also effective when referring to reader *and* writer because they emphasize the two as a unit.

Personalizing a message by calling the reader's name in the text also emphasizes the reader's interests. Use this technique in correspondence to emphasize the reader's viewpoint. Here is an example:

(In a letter to Mr. Lopez)   Therefore, your $30 refund should arrive next week, Mr. Lopez. Thank you for . . .

Use this technique sparingly; personalizing sounds insincere when over-used. Once or twice in a letter or memorandum is enough.

Avoiding Negative Terms

Perhaps few of us would be as blunt as Ben Franklin was in a letter to a former friend:

You and I were long friends; you are now my enemy, and I am
                                                        Yours,

Although Dr. Franklin must have felt that the situation justified the anger, he would have had a difficult time persuading this former friend to take positive action in the future. Angry statements in business writing generate enmity and then remain in the record long after the anger is gone. Even veiled anger can block success. Because anger is one of the moods that is hard to disguise, let it pass before writing a business letter or memorandum.

We also should avoid using the word *not* and contractions in a message wherever possible. Often it is just as easy to express an idea positively as it is to say it negatively—*remember* rather than *don't forget*, for example. Language should sound natural, however, so use contractions and *not* rather than awkward phrases.

Avoid using inherently negative expressions as well; these either accuse the reader unnecessarily or express doubt or sorrow. *Hope* (the verb), *claim* (the verb), *neglected, failed, hardly, scarcely, regret, unfortunately, sorry, apologize,* and *policy* (in letters) are among these inherently negative terms.

Here is an example:

You failed to enclose a check to pay for the supplies.

The verb *failed* accuses the reader of neglect and perhaps will provoke anger. Instead, just ask for a check to pay for the supplies. Here is another example:

I hope we will have the Mazula contract ready by next Thursday.

The verb *hope* suggests doubt that the contract will be ready at the suggested time, even though the writer may intend to appear confident.

Avoiding negative terms is covered in more detail in the chapter on unfavorable messages.

VIVIDNESS

Vivid language evokes clear mental images as it is being read. This makes the subject matter interesting. A reader will pay close attention to interesting writing and will enjoy reading it as well. As you apply the principles of style and tone discussed thus far in this chapter, your writing will become more vivid. Three points of grammatical construction can help further, however: effective use of voice, mood, and word selection.

Voice and Mood

Active voice is more vivid than passive because statements made in active voice are more direct. Examples are

Active voice   Miss Valences paid the insurance premium.
Passive voice   The insurance premium was paid by Miss Valences.

Use active voice whenever a message is positive to the reader. However, use the less direct passive voice whenever it is negative.

Mood is the verb form that shows the manner in which the action expressed in or the situation described in a thought is received. Thus, mood cues the reader about the manner in which to interpret information. Mood is *indicative, imperative,* or *subjunctive.* When you make statements or ask questions, you use indicative mood. When you give commands or directions or make requests, you use imperative mood. Examples are

Indicative mood   The invoice is cleared for payment.
                      Is the invoice cleared for payment?

Imperative mood   Clear the invoice for payment.
Will you please clear the invoice for payment.

Use indicative and imperative moods whenever they will deliver the message correctly because both are vivid and informal. However, you must use subjunctive mood in "that" clauses of command or demand, motion or resolution, or recommendations or orders. Examples are

Subjunctive mood   I move that the minutes *be* approved.
I insist that the passenger *go* aboard.

Converting subjunctive to indicative or imperative mood is easy. For instance, the subjunctive mood used in *If need be, I will go* converts easily to *I will go if needed* (or *If needed, I will go*).

Word Selection

Using specific nouns, action verbs, and descriptive adjectives and adverbs also makes writing vivid. Compare these examples:

Bland   A building was destroyed by fire.
Vivid   A raging fire burned the two-story brick home on the corner of Main and James Streets this morning.

Refer to Chapter Three for more information on word selection and to the grammar appendix for more on voice and mood.

SUMMARY

Writing style is the characteristic manner in which you express yourself. Writing tone is the manner in which you express a certain attitude. Formal, informal, and nonstandard are the three levels of general language usage. Use informal language for all but the most formal business messages—contracts, for example. In addition, business writing should be unbiased against sexes, races, and ethnic groups.

Two more elements of good business writing are clarity and conciseness. To be clear, choose concrete rather than abstract terms when possible and specific rather than general terms. Also, short, simple terms are clearer than are long, complex ones in most cases. Use them whenever they will express all the meaning that you intend to convey. In addition, control your use of unfamiliar words, foreign expressions, and jargon to make messages clearer. Wordy and redundant expressions are not concise. Some wordy expressions can be revised by substituting other terms, while others can be omitted altogether. Using a redundant term that repeats an idea immediately after using it is ineffective.

Business writing also should be accurate

and sincere. To be accurate, control your use of euphemisms and avoid superlatives that overstate the situation. Accuracy requires avoiding figurative clichés and some colloquialisms. To be sincere when writing, show confidence by appearing certain of the result, but avoid being overconfident or appearing to harass the reader or make demands. Sincerity also involves keeping confidential any private or sensitive information and avoiding excessive humility and flattery.

Writing from the reader's viewpoint is one way to be positive in business messages. To do this, focus on the reader's interests. Use *you*, *your*, *we*, and *our* often and *I*, *me*, *my*, and *mine* seldom. Also, personalize messages by using the reader's name in the text. In addition, positive messages contain no angry statements and limit the use of *not* and contractions; positive language does not accuse the reader of negligence or other faults, nor does it express doubt or sorrow.

Practicing the principles given in this chapter will help you to write vividly. In addition, use the active voice, as long as the message is positive to the reader; the indicative or imperative mood; and specific nouns, action verbs, and descriptive adjectives and adverbs.

Additional Readings

Bowman, Joel P., and Bernadine P. Branchaw. *Successful Communication in Business.* San Francisco, Calif.: Harper & Row, 1980, pp. 37–68.

Buchanan-Brown, John. *Le Mot Juste.* New York: Vintage Books, 1981.

Ewing, David W. *Writing for Results.* New York: John Wiley, 1979, pp. 171–209, 335–367.

Feinberg, Lilian O. *Applied Business Communication.* Sherman Oaks, Calif.: Alfred, 1982, pp. 64–78, 100–121.

Haggblade, Berle. *Business Communication.* St. Paul, Minn.: West, 1982, pp. 67–92.

Himstreet, William C., and Wayne Murlin Baty. *Business Communications.* Boston: Kent, 1981, pp. 50–81.

Lanham, Richard A. *Revising Business Prose.* New York: Scribners, 1981.

Lesikar, Raymond V. *Basic Business Communication.* Homewood, Ill.: Richard D. Irwin, 1982, pp. 48–69.

Miller, Casey, and Kate Swift. *The Handbook of Nonsexist Writing.* New York: Barnes & Noble, 1980.

Murphy, Herta A., and Charles E. Peck. *Effective Business Communications,* 3rd ed. New York: McGraw-Hill, 1980, pp. 30–94.

Persing, Bobbye Sorrels. *Business Communication Dynamics.* Columbus, Ohio: Charles E. Merrill, 1981, pp. 191–223.

Pickens, Judy E., ed. *Without Bias: A Guidebook for Nondiscriminatory Communication,* 2nd ed. New York: John Wiley, 1982.

Quible, Zane K., Margaret H. Johnson, and Dennis L. Mott. *Introduction to Business Communication.* Englewood Cliffs, N.J.: Prentice-Hall, 1981, pp. 17–56.

Sigband, Norman B. *Communication for Management and Business,* 3rd ed. Glenview, Ill.: Scott, Foresman, 1982, pp. 89–119.

Treece, Malra. *Successful Business Writing.* Boston: Allyn & Bacon, 1980, pp. 80–120.

Wells, Walter. *Communications in Business,* 3rd ed. Belmont, Calif.: Wadsworth, 1981, pp. 39–91.

Review Questions

1. Explain why style and tone are the two most important qualities of business messages.

2. Which of the three general language levels is most appropriate for business writing? Explain.

3. In what ways can business writing appear to be biased? Give an example of each.

4. Name four ways in which to make business writing clearer. Give an example of each.

5. Explain how wordiness and redundancy can affect conciseness in business writing. Give two examples of each.

6. Explain how euphemisms, superlatives, figurative clichés, and colloquialisms can affect accuracy in business messages. Give two examples of each.

7. Name the three major ways in which to sound sincere in business writing. Give an example of each.

8. How can writing from the reader's viewpoint make business messages more positive? Give an example.

9. Explain how to avoid negative expressions in business writing. Give two examples of each.

10. What value does vivid language have in business writing? Which is more vivid, active or passive voice? Explain.

Exercises

1. Name the types of bias shown in each of the following sentences and then rewrite it as an unbiased statement.
   a. Each employee's union dues are deducted from his paycheck.
   b. Julia Garner and Edgar received awards.
   c. Jerry Herrington is a male cook.
   d. Cynthia Tricou and Larry Miloni are our new salesmen.
   e. Gretchen is both a girl Friday and her husband's better half.
   f. Hanna LaFada, an even-tempered Italian, will negotiate the contract for management.
   g. Susan Amani, a hard-working black woman, heads the payroll department

2. Locate the wordy expressions in each of the following sentences and then rewrite the sentences using more concise expressions.
   a. As a general rule, a grievance is filed first.
   b. The plan at the present time is to file the grievance at a later date.
   c. Attached herewith is a form to write the grievance on.
   d. Each of these clerks came into contact with Mr. Largess in the hallway.
   e. Feel free to withhold the check first of all if you so desire.
   f. We are now in a position to give consideration to your plan.
   g. Our lawyer sent a message to the effect that the information is of a confidential nature.

3. Locate the undesirable colloquialisms in each of the following sentences and then rewrite the sentences to eliminate them.

a. Crowded conditions force us to store goods anywheres that space is found.

b. Ric will be most happy to take your order.

c. Lelia will get through with the inventory tomorrow.

d. We do not know but what she will arrive late.

e. Such mistakes happen in this day and age.

f. All these old records are no good.

g. When you are all done with the interviews, please sound out the records before hiring anyone.

4. Rewrite each of the following sentences to give them a more positive tone.

a. You neglected to enclose the invoice.

b. We are unable to find the merchandise you claim you sent.

c. Don't forget to meet the guests in the foyer.

d. I hope you will file the papers on schedule.

e. You are not the Schlesinger representative, are you not?

5. Rewrite the following sentences in active voice.

a. Susan was told about the award by Gaye and Phil.

b. A decision was made by the board of directors.

c. The truck is driven only by Miranda.

d. Business ethics should be practiced by everyone in the chamber.

6. Rewrite the following sentences in passive voice.

a. Lemuel drove the car to the garage.

b. Gayle threw the crumpled invoice into the wastebasket.

c. Therefore, we deny your request.

d. For these reasons, we chose another option.

UNIT 2

Written Communication
CORRESPONDENCE

CHAPTER THREE

Fundamental Correspondence Techniques

The goals in studying the text and completing the activities in this chapter are to know

1. Functions and objectives of correspondence
2. Three basic psychological formats for organizing correspondence
3. How to organize the three basic types of correspondence
4. How to write opening and closing statements for correspondence

Picture yourself as a sales representative for a computer software manufacturer and distributor. You like the work and you want to do the job well. Much of your work is handled through correspondence—letters and memorandums. Could the following story told at a sales representative's meeting have happened to you?

Two years ago while working as a sales representative for a small computer software manufacturing company in Iowa, I called on the purchasing supervisor of a large retailer of ladies' sportswear. The company has retail outlets in the Midwest and would have been a big account for us if we could have gotten the business. The firm uses computers to handle daily business transactions and to keep inventory records. They were using software supplied by the computer manufacturer, and we believed we could provide more reliable service at a lower price. We also believed our products were equal in quality to those of the present supplier.

The purchasing supervisor gave me an hour to sell her on using our computer software. As the meeting ended, the supervisor told me that she was interested in our products and asked me to summarize my message in a letter and mail it to her within ten days. She would then consider the information along with that of two competitors who also wanted the contract.

I wrote the letter and mailed it on the fifth day after our meeting, feeling confident that we would get the contract. Three weeks passed before a letter arrived telling me that another firm had won the contract. After thinking about it, I concluded that my follow-up letter was ineffective. I asked a fellow sales representative who was known to write effective correspondence to review the letter. He confirmed that the letter was poorly written. The writing followed no clear plan and the objective was unclear. Also, the opening was negative ("I regret the delay in writing"), and the closing lacked confidence ("I surely hope that I haven't goofed and let someone else make a better proposal").

That incident took place two years ago. Since then, I have completed two writing skills workshops and my correspondence has improved markedly as a result. Therefore, I recommend to each of you that you learn to write well if you are not now a good writer. Good writing ability is important to a successful business career.

Could you write effective letters and memorandums if you held such a position today? Many people feel that they could not. Your letters and memorandums can be more effective even if you are already a good correspondent, if you first take time to examine the functions and objectives of your correspondence before writing it.

CORRESPONDENCE
FUNCTIONS AND OBJECTIVES

By following the five-step plan presented in Chapter One, reaching correspondence objectives is more certain. As does all types of business writing, correspondence serves certain functions and can help you meet both general and specific objectives.

Correspondence Functions

In the broadest sense, correspondence *informs* others about company business, *directs* (or suggests) actions others should take, and *establishes* and *maintains* goodwill. Letters serve as the medium for corresponding outside the firm. By writing letters, you can seek business opportunities, maintain business relationships, or establish and monitor situations involving supplies, inventories, and services. Also, letters help to form the impression that customers and employees of other firms have of your company.

Memorandums serve as the medium for corresponding within the firm. Therefore, you can conduct internal business transactions with memorandums. Regardless of the physical distance involved, use the memorandum whenever the writer and receiver work for the same company. Even when written messages are sent within departments or from one department, division, or branch to another within the company, they take memorandum form.

Correspondence Objectives

General correspondence objectives serve as a framework for your writing and give a sense of direction when forming an overall plan for writing. Seven general objectives for corresponding are to

1. Get action
2. Direct a course of action
3. Instruct
4. Encourage
5. Send or seek ideas
6. Send or seek facts
7. Promote goodwill

Before writing a letter or memorandum, first identify the general objective you wish to achieve.

Once you identify the general objective, you must identify the specific objective to be met. Specific objectives serve as direct guides to use in choosing ideas to put in a letter or memorandum. Choosing a specific objective helps to focus the message on the prime reason for writing. Twenty-one specific objectives for corresponding are to

1. Make routine business requests
2. Respond to routine business requests
3. Make special business requests
4. Respond to special business requests
5. Order goods or services
6. Respond to orders for goods or services
7. Make a claim
8. Respond to a claim
9. Make a credit request
10. Respond to a credit request
11. Create goodwill
12. Maintain goodwill
13. Collect money or services due
14. Sell goods or services
15. Promote ideas or plans
16. Appeal for donations or contributions
17. Give orders or directions
18. Give information to improve the conduct of business activities
19. Congratulate
20. Say thank you
21. Give condolences or otherwise express sympathy

To improve the chances for success, attempt only one specific objective as a primary purpose for a single letter or memorandum. Much correspondence, however, does have secondary objectives. For example, building goodwill is always a secondary objective.

Once you identify the general and specific objectives, the best way to achieve these objectives is to first reflect on how the reader will probably interpret the message.

BASIC CORRESPONDENCE PSYCHOLOGY

How the reader interprets the message will be influenced by the reader's needs and interests. Because the reader (not the writer) interprets the message, direct control of the communication's success or failure depends on the reader's reaction to it. Therefore, writing from the reader's viewpoint increases the chances of success.

Messages can be made more successful by first anticipating how a reader is likely to interpret different types of messages. Such predictions can be made by looking at the psychological value of messages. For example, readers are glad to receive certain types of messages but not so glad to receive others. In fact, three basic ways of classifying the primary message of correspondence received are (1) favorable, (2) unfavorable, and (3) persuasive. That is, the prime message sent to readers in correspondence may be viewed in one of these ways.

Favorable Message Psychology

Favorable messages are those that the reader views as positive. The message either pleases the reader or has neutral value (such as simple information). Here are two examples:

Congratulations! You are now promoted to production supervisor.

The vacation period begins as usual on August 1.

Some messages please readers more than others do, but a message is favorable whenever the primary news is positive to the reader.

Unfavorable Message Psychology

Correspondence containing *unfavorable messages* involves a range of values from mildly to strongly negative. In any case, readers view the primary message as being unfavorable or disappointing, at least to some extent. Therefore, if the reader receives the primary message as unfavorable to any degree, the message is psychologically negative. Examples of unfavorable messages are

We have located another supplier. Please cancel our order.

We cannot pay for your entire trip to Hawaii, but we will pay for your hotel room rental.

The Schwim Model 360 bicycles you ordered are temporarily out of stock. You should receive them within two weeks.

The royal blue sweaters you ordered are out of production, but we have navy blue. Will those be acceptable?

Our company audits financial records exclusively. Goodtimes Tax Service, located at 2021 Arizona Avenue, will gladly prepare your tax return.

The LIFO inventory control method you prefer is too expensive for your company. You will save $20,000 yearly by switching to the FIFO method.

Persuasive Message Psychology

Persuasive messages, as are favorable messages, are positive to the reader. Their nature is more complex, however, and the positive value may not be evident. Although the reader is likely to receive the news with an open mind, the writer must be persuasive if the message is to be effective. The writer requests that the reader take some action but must justify the action to motivate the reader to take it. Examples of persuasive messages are the following:

The warranty on my electric blanket expires April 1 rather than February 1 as you suggested. The expiration date is from the date of purchase rather than from the date of manufacture.

You will be able to enjoy meeting with fellow real estate dealers and will have the opportunity to hear new ideas about selling real estate when you speak to the St. Louis Real Estate Dealers Association.

This new public address system is guaranteed to last ten years without repairs, five years longer than any comparable system on the market today.

You can help resolve your problems with purchasing procedures just by taking a few minutes to fill in the enclosed questionnaire.

Once you classify the primary message as favorable, unfavorable, or persuasive, then devise a plan for presenting ideas within the message to the reader. That plan can serve as a guide to help meet the objective for writing.

CORRESPONDENCE ORGANIZATIONAL PLANS

Even when the subject of a letter or memorandum contains an unfavorable message for the reader, you can present the message in a positive way. To do this, present the message parts in a sequence that will give the entire message a positive overall tone. Following are three plans to use in maintaining this positive psychology, one each for writing favorable, unfavorable, and persuasive messages.

Favorable Correspondence Plan

Use this plan when the primary message favors the reader—the reader will be glad to hear the news. Three steps to follow when using this direct (deductive) approach are

1. *Deliver the news.* Begin on the subject but keep it positive.

2. *Include necessary details.* Be concise but include all details needed to make the message clear.

3. *Close positively.* The nature of the message will determine what is said here.

Here is a sample letter using this three-step design:

Dear Mr. Ouida:

Please send descriptions and prices on the Crakow Series 2100 office furniture you advertised in Sunday's *Des Moines Register.*

We are presently refurnishing our executive suite and plan to buy natural wood-tone furniture. Your series 2100 line is the type furniture we wish to purchase.

As we plan to order all furnishings for the suite in mid-November, may wo havo tho information by Novombor 1?

Sincerely yours,

All favorable news letters and memorandums can follow this plan. Specific types of this correspondence are covered in detail in Chapter Four.

Unfavorable Correspondence Plan

Use the unfavorable correspondence plan whenever the subject is unfavorable to any degree for the reader. Five steps to follow in using this indirect (inductive) approach are

1. *Open with a buffer statement.* The best buffer statements open on some positive aspect of the subject.

2. *Begin giving reasons for refusing.* Include the strongest reason here (strongest from the reader's viewpoint). If you have just one reason, use it here. If you have two reasons, use the stronger one here and the second one in the fourth step. If you have several reasons for refusing, use one or two here and others in the fourth step.

3. *Refuse.* Either imply or state the refusal directly. Be sure to state the refusal clearly.

4. *Resume giving reasons for refusing.* When refusing without recourse for the reader, give at least one reason at this point. When offering a

substitute, making a referral, or offering a compromise or alternative method or procedure, make the suggestion at this point.

5. *Close positively.* If you offered the reader a recourse as mentioned in the fourth step, close the correspondence with an action request. For example, you may request that the reader accept your compromise offer. In other cases, close with a positive statement that is consistent with the content of the correspondence.

Here is a sample memorandum using this five-step design:

To: Wanda Brewer, Credit Department
From: Lindsay Morgan, Personnel Department
Subject: Request for Classified Information

The members of your personnel department were glad to learn that your annual review of credit files is nearing completion. Our review of the personnel files is nearing completion as well. Therefore, we should now have current information for use in making credit and personnel decisions.

Our information supervisor, Mabel Moses, has reviewed your request to see Joseph Lehrer's personal data file. She noted that the file contains classified information. Therefore, this information can be released only for review by a personnel review committee. Three company officers appointed by the president become members of such a committee. Committee members are appointed only after such a review is requested.

We shall be glad to ask the president to form a personnel review committee to hear your request. If all necessary information is available, a decision on the release can be made at the hearing.

Please complete the enclosed request for classified information and send it directly to me. Mabel and I will process your request the same day that we receive it.

Use this plan to organize all correspondence that delivers unfavorable messages to readers. Complete details for writing specific types of unfavorable messages are given in Chapter Five.

Persuasive Correspondence Plan

Use this plan whenever you must persuade the reader to take some action to reach your objective for writing. The ideas in this plan are arranged in a persuasive sequence, which like unfavorable messages is a type of indirect (inductive) approach. Use these four steps when writing persuasive letters and memorandums:

1. *Open with an attention-getting statement.* Be positive. The statement should stimulate the reader to continue reading. To do this, appeal directly to the reader's interests or needs.

2. *Get the reader interested in the topic.* Think of a central appeal, a main point of reader interest. This appeal should be the strongest you can think of that might move the reader to take the desired action. Then introduce any supporting appeals you wish to mention. These add to the overall appeal.

3. *Build a desire to take action on the topic.* Continue presenting reasons for taking the desired action. Point out the benefits derived by taking action and downplay obstacles that may stand in the way.

4. *Close with an action request.* Make a specific, direct request that the reader take the desired action. Keep the tone positive and courteous. For best results, make it easy to take the action you request.

An easy way to recall the steps in this plan is to think of the letters A-I-D-A (Attention-Interest-Desire-Action). Here is a sample letter using the four-step persuasive design:

Dear Mr. and Mrs. Bartz:

Do you remember going to summer camp as a child?
Remember how the lights of a campfire glisten on the water and light the dark night sky? Girls and boys sit around the campfire. They sing, play, laugh, and learn to grow into adulthood by sharing good times with their companions.

This year, summer camp at Ocher Retreat will fulfill the dreams of more than two thousand girls and boys aged 9 to 14 from Kansas City. Activities at Ocher Retreat will teach these youths to be productive members of the community. They will learn responsibility by maintaining a full schedule of daily activities. Daytime events include fishing, swimming, and boating at nearby Lake Rhonda, all supervised by trained counselors. Campers will hike in Vereen Woods, where they can study plant and animal life in a natural setting.

Evening activities will include games played around the campfire, storytelling, and conversation and friendship shared with fellow campers. Three evenings a week, these youths will learn good study habits, how to maintain their rooms at home, and how to care for their personal belongings. They will also learn to solve problems using microcomputers.

Responsibility. Sharing. Good times. New friends. They will enjoy all these and more at summer camp at Ocher Retreat. More than forty educational and recreational programs await the arrival of these Kansas City youngsters.

Please consider sending your son, Michael, and daughter, Heidi Marie, to Ocher Retreat this summer. They will surely have a great time and will learn many new things as well. The cost is only $800 a person for a four-week stay held June 1 to 28. Pay cash if you wish or pay in convenient installments of $73.09 monthly for twelve months.

You need send no money now! Cash payment or the first installment can be made any time before June 1. To save spaces for Michael and Heidi Marie, just sign and mail the enclosed return reply card by March 1.

Sincerely yours,

Complete details for writing specific types of persuasive correspondence are given in Chapter Six.

Regardless of the type letter—favorable, unfavorable, or persuasive—the opening and closing statements are the most troublesome parts to write. These statements should be especially effective, however, because they give the first and last impressions the reader gets of the message.

CORRESPONDENCE OPENING AND CLOSING STATEMENTS

Because opening and closing remarks receive the most emphasis because of their positions in messages, keep the tone positive in all cases.

Opening Statements for Correspondence

Here is a checklist to follow when writing opening statements for correspondence:

1. *Be positive.* The opening statement is in an emphatic position. Emphasize the positive effect.
2. *Sound cooperative.* Open in a cooperative context.
3. *Keep it short.* Short messages are more emphatic.
4. *Write from the reader's viewpoint.* Center the message on the reader's interests and needs.

Following are sample opening statements for the three basic organizational plans—favorable, unfavorable, and persuasive.

Favorable Message Opening Statements

Because the subject of favorable correspondence is positive for the reader, open on the subject itself. This approach emphasizes the subject. Examples are

> May I have a copy of the free brochure on home heating costs you advertised in *Newsweek* magazine's October 10 issue? (routine request for information)

> Here is your free copy of "Fifty Ways to Save on Home Heating Costs." (response to routine request for information)

> Please send the following items advertised in your new fall catalog. (order for goods)

Your new Zippy Model 250 electric blanket was shipped by parcel post today. (filling an order for goods)

Please send me a new Best Buy electric toaster, Model SZL, to replace the defective one I bought under a 90-day unconditional warranty last Saturday. (simple claim)

A new Best Buy electric toaster, Model SZL, was mailed to you today by express delivery service. (granting a simple claim)

May we have credit information on Suzy B. Delegal? (credit information request)

Suzy B. Delegal has an excellent credit record at Mercer's Department Store. (sending credit information)

We appreciate your doing business with us at Internal Auditing Associates this year. (expressing gratitude, which builds goodwill)

Congratulations, Genevieve, on your promotion to assistant vice president. (congratulations, which builds goodwill)

Please accept our sympathy in this time of bereavement. (expressing condolence)

Delivering the primary message in the opening paragraph emphasizes both the subject and the positive psychology of the message.

Unfavorable Message Opening Statements

Because these messages are negative at least to some degree, do not begin the correspondence with the disagreement. Instead, open with some positive aspect of the situation. Whenever this is impossible, open with a positive general statement—a note of thanks, for example. Examples are

Yes, the language of insurance policies should be clear. (refused request, opening with a point of agreement)

Thank you for ordering one of our Big Wow remote control units. (refused order or response to incomplete order, opening with thanks)

The preparation of your tax return is guaranteed for correctness and accuracy in computation. (refused claim, opening with a point of agreement)

Your application for an open credit account with Parisian Coterie has been examined by our credit manager. We appreciate your inquiry. (refused credit, opening with thanks)

These indirect opening statements begin correspondence with a positive tone, which can be continued in the remainder of the letter or memorandum. Being positive is possible even when the basic message is unfavorable.

Persuasive Message Opening Statements

Persuasive messages require attention getting opening statements. They should be positive and should create a desire to continue reading the message. Examples are

> Your reliable, quick service is the major reason that I used your agency for the past five years. (complex claim, opening with a statement of strong reader interest)

> Do you ever wish you had a more comfortable office chair to sit in while working? (selling a product, setting up an area of interest for a prospective customer)

> Do you need to buy but need to save as well? A dilemma, you say? Well, that is where we can help. You can *buy* and *save* at the same time. (selling a product or service, opening with a general statement)

> Helping others. That's a good feeling, and you can have it, too! (appeal for donation or contribution, setting up an area of interest)

> Your recent article in *The Atlanta Journal* has stimulated a lot of discussion here at Modem Corporation. (persuasive request for information, opening with an indirect — but clear — compliment)

Use these or similar ideas when writing the opening for a persuasive letter or memorandum.

Closing Statements for Correspondence

Here is a checklist to follow when writing closing statements for letters and memorandums:

1. *Be positive.* The closing statement is in an emphatic position. Emphasize the positive effect.

2. *Strike a "closing" tone.* The closing statement should sound as though you are closing the message.

3. *Sound successful.* An attitude of success is needed. To achieve this attitude, use confident expressions.

4. *Write from the reader's viewpoint.* Center the message on the reader's interests and needs.

5. *Be specific in action request closings.* When appropriate, ask for the specific action you want the reader to take. Is the reader to sign and return a form, for example? If needed, give a deadline date for taking the action.

Closing statements may be *general* or *action request* closings, depending on the objective. A general closing is a simple final remark designed to end your message. An action request closing asks that the reader take some specific action. Following are examples of both general and action closing statements.

General Closing Statements

In favorable and unfavorable correspondence, you may use a general closing. (Persuasive messages always require an action request closing.) Examples of general closing statements are

> Your interest in our shuttle bus service is appreciated. We look forward to discussing it with you next Thursday at the Commonwealth Club.

> If you need more information, we will be glad to help. Write us or call at 383-1729.

> When you are again in Boston, stop in for a visit. We will be glad to see you.

> Are you free next week to meet to discuss the O'Shea account? I will telephone Monday to see if we can arrange a suitable time.

> When we may serve you again, please write us or call at 699-2371. (for favorable messages only)

Action Request Closing Statements

Use an action request closing as needed in favorable, unfavorable, or persuasive correspondence. These closings are needed whenever the reader should respond directly to the writer's request for action. Examples of these closings follow.

For Favorable Messages   Use statements such as the following to close favorable correspondence:

> We need to have both tow trucks operating for the start of the tourist season on April 1. If the extensions are available, please ship them by March 15. (routine request for goods).

> An announcement is included about our October 12 sale for preferred customers only. Free coffee and cookies will be served all day. Be sure to stop in our Westover Hills office (43 Lackawanna Drive) that day to look at these exciting new fall coats. (filling order for goods; contains sales promotional material)

> I plan to go deep sea fishing with members of my fishing club on June 20. Will you please send the repaired fishing rod or a replacement by June 15. (simple claim; may use also for complex claim, a persuasive message)

For Unfavorable Messages   Use statements like the following to close unfavorable correspondence:

> If the triple-knit sweaters are acceptable, telephone us collect at 901-843-2462. We will ship the merchandise within two days after you call in your acceptance. (offer of substitute for original order)

> We will gladly repair your automobile headlights for the price of parts alone, $10.50. Call us today at 821-7333 so that we can begin the work. (refused request with compromise offer)

> Call me at Extension 7142 if this alternative procedure is acceptable. I will complete the work by Friday if you notify me by Tuesday to go ahead. (refused request with alternative proposal)

For Persuasive Messages   Use statements such as the following to close persuasive news correspondence:

> Just list the model number you prefer on the enclosed form and mail the order in the enclosed postage-paid, return-reply envelope. Do it today. (selling the product)

> Just check the proper box on the enclosed postage-paid, return-reply card and drop it in the mail today. Your delivery service will begin within three days after we receive your request. (selling a service)

> May we have with your acceptance a small photograph and a list of your recent professional activities by November 1? We will use these to begin publicizing the conference. (invitation to speak free of charge)

Both opening and closing remarks in correspondence require thoughtful preparation. Follow these examples when handling your business problems through correspondence. Also, please note that designs for correspondence format and layout are shown and discussed in Appendix D.

SUMMARY

Business correspondence is written to inform others about company business, to direct actions that others should take, and to elicit or convey goodwill. Letters are written outside the firm and memorandums within it. Identifying both a general and specific objective before beginning to write will improve the chances of corresponding successfully.

To reach a correspondence goal, first reflect on how the reader probably will interpret the message. Based on this idea, you can classify the primary message of letters and memorandums as favorable, unfavorable, or persuasive. Favorable messages are those that readers view as positive. A three-step design for writing these messages calls for delivering the news, including necessary details, and closing positively. Unfavorable messages are those viewed by readers as negative. A five-step plan for writing these messages calls for opening with a buffer statement, giving reasons for declining, declining, continuing with reasons for declining, and closing positively. Persuasive messages are those that require the writer to persuade the reader to take action. A four-step design for writing these messages calls for opening with an attention-getting statement, developing an interest in the subject, creating a desire to take an action, and requesting the action.

Because opening and closing remarks make the first and last impressions in correspondence, they should be especially effective. These parts may be the most difficult to develop, so a special section on writing them is included in the chapter.

Additional Readings

Bowman, Joel P., Bernadine P. Branchaw. *Successful Business Communication.* San Francisco: Harper & Row, 1980, pp. 69–79.

Feinberg, Lilian O. *Applied Business Communication.* Sherman Oaks, Calif.: Alfred, 1982, pp. 82–94.

Himstreet, William C., and Wayne Murlin Baty. *Business Communications.* Boston: Kent, 1981, pp. 84–89.

Murphy, Herta A., and Charles E. Peck. *Effective Business Communications.* New York: McGraw-Hill, 1980, 95–119.

Treece, Malra. *Communication for Business and the Professions.* Boston: Allyn & Bacon, 1978, pp. 163–174.

Wilkinson, C. W., Peter B. Clarke, and Dorothy C. M. Wilkinson. *Communicating Through Letters and Reports,* 7th ed. Homewood, Ill.: Richard D. Irwin, 1980, pp. 77–82.

Wolf, Morris Philip, Dale F. Keyser, and Robert R. Aurner. *Effective Communication in Business,* 7th ed. Cincinnati: South-Western, 1979, pp. 16–35, 58–83.

Review Questions

1. Explain the broad functions of correspondence.

2. Name three general correspondence objectives and give an example of each.

3. Name five specific correspondence objectives and give an example of each.

4. Describe a situation in which favorable message psychology should be used in correspondence.

5. Describe a situation in which unfavorable message psychology should be used in correspondence.

6. Describe a situation in which persuasive message psychology should be used in correspondence.

7. List and explain the three steps in the favorable correspondence plan.

8. List and explain the five steps in the unfavorable correspondence plan.

9. List and explain the four steps in the persuasive correspondence plan.

10. What is the difference between a general and an action request closing statement?

Exercises

1. Read the following statements and then identify a general objective and a specific objective that each message will meet:
   a. You receive a memorandum from a payroll clerk telling you that your union dues
   will be deducted from your paycheck as
   you requested.
   b. You receive a letter from the union shop
   steward telling you about the advantages
   of joining the union. She requests that you
   apply for membership.
   c. You write a letter to the union shop steward who requested that you apply to join
   the union telling her that you are unable
   to join at this time. You will apply next
   year, however.

2. Identify the correspondence plan that should
be used to write each of the following messages (favorable, unfavorable, or persuasive):
   a. You receive a memorandum from the
   head of your company's payroll department telling you that the payroll deduction for your major medical insurance policy is being increased by 20 percent.
   b. You receive a letter from the president of
   Cranberry Mint asking you to subscribe to
   a monthly issue of coins commemorating
   the birthdates of American presidents.
   The letter contains information about the
   coins themselves and their investment
   value. You will be able to pay in monthly
   installments if you wish.

   c. You receive a letter from a sales representative of a local savings and loan association telling you about the advantages
   of investing in All Savers Certificates.
   You are asked to call or write for an
   appointment to discuss the advantages of
   these certificates.

3. Write an opening and closing statement for
each of the following situations:
   a. You write a letter to the sales representative of the savings and loan association
   mentioned in problem 2(c). You are not
   interested in the All Savers Certificates.
   However, you are interested in investing
   in an Individual Retirement Account.
   b. You write a letter to your investment
   counselor saying that you wish to add
   $5000 to your investment portfolio. She
   should choose and buy stocks with the
   money.
   c. You write a memorandum to the members of your department at work asking
   each of them to donate blood to the blood
   bank. You point out the good work done
   by the blood bank and make an urgent
   request for Type O blood.
   d. You write a memorandum to members of
   your department at work telling them
   that a car pool will begin operating on the
   first day of next month. Members of the
   department have been requesting that
   such a pool be formed for some months
   now.

CHAPTER FOUR

Favorable Correspondence

The goals in studying the text and completing the activities in this chapter are to know

1. The types of favorable letters commonly written in business
2. How to write, critique, and revise favorable letters
3. The types of favorable memorandums commonly written in business
4. Special style and tone considerations in writing memorandums
5. How to write, critique, and revise favorable memorandums

The task of writing from the reader's perspective becomes easier whenever the primary message is helpful to the reader. When people receive favorable correspondence, they are either glad to get the news or need to know the information. Once you determine that the primary message of a letter or memorandum is favorable, you need only follow the steps in the following checklist:

1. *Deliver the news.* Be direct by beginning with the primary message that you are sending.

2. *Include necessary details.* Explain the primary message if needed. State any conditions or details needed to get across the complete message.

3. *Close positively.* Close with an action request if appropriate. If not, close with a general positive statement.

Following this broad outline will ensure that the message is delivered in the best sequence. Regardless of the type of news, you can use this broad outline effectively when writing favorable memorandums and letters.

FAVORABLE LETTERS

You write favorable letters when making routine requests, responding to routine requests, and expressing goodwill. The specific types of favorable letters are

1. Routine requests and responses
2. Orders for goods or services and responses
3. Simple claims and granting adjustments
4. Credit information requests and responses
5. Credit requests and responses
6. Goodwill messages

Routine Requests and Responses

Routine requests and responses to them are written more often than any other type of letter. Many managers conduct 50 percent or more of their daily business activities with this type letter. While the subject of the inquiry or response may vary widely, the routine nature of such letters results in receivers viewing their messages favorably. Thus, you should follow a direct approach when writing such messages. An example of a routine request letter written in this direct approach follows.

First Draft   Dear Mr. Abrams:

I read about your new wallboard. The advertisement I read was in the *Construction News*. It interested me.

We use 60,000 pounds of nails a year in putting up wallboard in commercial buildings. Will you send us information about your new wallboard? We need sizes, colors, and materials from which the product is made, and we need to know about delivery. Also, is the glue guaranteed for 100 years?

Sincerely yours,

Critique   These corrections should be made to the first draft of the letter:

1. Open with the request for specific information.
2. Combine sentences to remove the choppy effect caused by too many short sentences.
3. Rewrite the details explaining the request to improve the organization. Also present the details in parallel form.
4. Add a closing statement.

Now, study this revised draft of the letter:

Revised Draft   Dear Mr. Abrams:

Please send us information on the "New Era" wallboard you advertised in the April 15 issue of *Construction News*.

Because we use 60,000 pounds of nails yearly in constructing commercial buildings, this product could possibly lower our costs. Please include answers to these questions:

1. Of what materials is the wallboard constructed?
2. What sizes and colors do you offer?
3. What delivery methods are available?
4. Is the 100-year life of the glue guaranteed?

We will appreciate your sending this information.

Sincerely yours,

Here is an example of a response to the routine request just presented.

First Draft   Dear Miss Smitty:

We are writing in regard to your inquiry. We were glad to hear that we might be able to sell you our product.

Please find enclosed herewith a brochure with the information you requested. The wallboard is made from both white oak and yellow pine. The only size offered is 4' × 8'. Colors include the natural finish, tan, antique green, and white. Shipment is made at our expense by truck or rail. Yes, the 100-year life of the glue is guaranteed. Although you failed to ask, prices are included on the enclosed brochure. With kindest regards,

Yours truly,

Critique These corrections should be made to the first draft of the letter:

1. Open by sending the information requested.
2. Rewrite the opening paragraph from the reader's viewpoint. The first draft is centered on the writer's interests.
3. Omit the opening sentence (a statement of the obvious).
4. Rewrite the details of the explanation to improve the organization. List the details to make them more emphatic.
5. Omit the wordy expressions "in regards to," "please find enclosed herewith," and "with kindest regards." Also omit the negative expression "you failed."
6. Add a positive closing statement.

Here is a revised draft of the letter:

Revised Draft Dear Miss Smitty:

Here is the information you requested about the "New Era" wallboard you saw advertised in the April 15 issue of *Construction News:*

1. The wallboard comes in both white oak and yellow pine.
2. The size is a standard 4′ × 8′ panel.
3. Colors include natural white oak and yellow pine, tan, antique green, and white finishes.
4. Shipment is made at our expense by truck or rail.
5. The 100-year life of the glue is fully guaranteed.

Prices, materials, and colors are shown on the enclosed brochure. We appreciate your inquiry and look forward to serving you. Shipment will be made within two days after receiving your order.

Yours truly,

Orders for Goods or Services and Responses

Most companies place orders for goods and services on purchase order forms that are signed but are not accompanied by a letter. Letter responses to these orders are rarely sent. Whenever these orders are filled promptly and exactly as requested (a favorable response), companies include a packing list with the shipment of goods. An invoice is also sent, but no letter accompanies the shipment. Some companies still use letters, however—mostly small companies or those that seldom place orders.

If you write an order letter or respond favorably to one, list the goods or services. A list of items in the letter is easier to follow rather than writing the information in paragraph (narrative) format. Be sure to give *complete* information about the items—colors. sizes, order numbers, quantities, and so on. A sample order for goods follows.

First Draft

Dear Mr. Merserski:

We are beginning our annual "Spring Festival Jubilee" sale on April 1 and would like to include some of your books in the sale.

Please send us 8 copies of *How to Win Big in the Stock Market,* 25 copies of *Writing Winning Résumés,* and 6 copies of *Looking for a Pot of Gold.* A check for $155.68 is enclosed to pay for everything.

Sincerely yours,

Critique

These problems should be corrected in the first draft:

1. Open the letter with a direct request for the goods.
2. List the items being ordered. Include complete information about each item—author's name, edition, stock number, and the price for each book.
3. State the shipping method preferred unless you have no preference.
4. State the total cost of the books and the shipping cost.
5. Omit the general expression "at your earliest convenience." Instead, include a deadline if you need the books by a specific date.

Here is a revised draft with these problems corrected:

Revised Draft

Dear Mr. Merserski:

Please ship by parcel post the following books that are listed in your 1984 catalog:

8 copies of *How to Win Big in the Stock Market,* second edition, by John Winship, #24555, @ $2.75 each	$ 22.00
25 copies of *Writing Winning Résumés,* by Ophelia Ramm, #24557, @ $4.00 each	100.00
6 copies of *Looking for a Pot of Gold,* by Senegal Romumba, #24589, @ $2.60 each	15.60
Total	$137.60

A check for $155.68 is enclosed to pay for the books plus shipping costs of $18.08. We would appreciate receiving the books by April 1 so that we can offer them for sale during our annual "Spring Festival Jubilee" sale.

Sincerely yours,

Use the same format and techniques to write a favorable response for goods or services. Begin the letter with a statement that delivers the goods or services. Then state precisely which goods or services you are sending, and close with a positive statement. Be sure to list the items and state the delivery method.

Simple Claims and Granting Adjustments

When the writer and the reader readily agree that the writer is entitled to the claim, this is called a *simple* claim. In such cases, the writer merely needs to make the claim and give details needed to explain the claim and make it easy to grant.

Suppose, for example, that a shopper buys an electric toaster that is guaranteed for one year against defective parts. The guarantee offers a new toaster if any part becomes defective. After one month's use, a part breaks. Here is a sample letter placing the claim:

First Draft   Dear Ms. Ciccariaco:

Recently, I went down to Finest Goods' Laburnum Avenue store and bought a Sunrise electric toaster. I took it home and used it daily for a month. It worked fabulously, and I just thought it was about the most wonderfully amazing thing I had ever bought in my whole entire life.

Then the bottom fell out. One morning when I put in a couple of slices of my very own favorite Whoopsie-Poopsie Toastettes, the drop lever would not lower them into the toasting chamber. I discovered that the drop lever is broken. I want you to send me another toaster right away. I am put out by this problem, and I want it taken care of right away. I am having to make toast in the oven, and I find that extremely expensive and an enormously awful discomfort. I am sending the broken toaster to you today.

Sincerely yours,

Critique   The following problems should be corrected in the letter:

1. Open the letter with the claim, give details, and then close positively.

2. Improve the tone of the letter by
   a. Writing from the reader's viewpoint, including omission of many of the "I" references
   b. Substituting more correct words for excessive statements such as "fabulous," "most wonderfully amazing," "very own favorite," "extremely expensive," and "enormously awful"
   c. Expressing the claim in a less demanding way than "want it taken care of right away"

3. Enclose a copy of the guarantee.

Here is an improved version of the letter:

Revised Draft   Dear Ms. Ciccariaco:

Please replace the Model #64 Sunrise electric toaster I bought on October 2 at Finest Goods' Laburnum Avenue store.

The drop level broke on the toaster after one month's use. A copy of the one-year guarantee that defines the terms of our agreement is enclosed. Also, the broken toaster will reach you tomorrow by Speedy Delivery Service.

Your Sunrise brand toaster has been a joy to use because it browns evenly every time. Can you please deliver the replacement within two weeks because I am now having to make toast in the oven.

Sincerely yours,

A response that grants the adjustment to the simple claim letter follows:

First Draft

Dear Mr. Marable:

A new toaster is being shipped to you at the earliest opportunity. We are as pleased as Punch to send you a replacement.

It was a surprise to hear that the drop lever broke, but your guarantee is in effect and binding. You never spoke a truer word when you wrote that the toaster browns evenly every time. It does indeed beat all the competition. The drop lever in your new toaster is reinforced with a magnesium alloy plate that will withstand 20 pounds of pressure. This toaster also is guaranteed against defective parts for one year.

May we take this opportunity to thank you for your business.

Sincerely yours,

Critique

The following problems need correcting in the adjustment letter:

1. Improve the insincere tone in the first paragraph.

2. Improve the accusative tone suggesting surprise in the second paragraph. Also, improve the bragging tone of the reinforcement statement that the toaster does brown evenly every time.

3. Be specific about details of shipping the replacement toaster.

4. Omit these expressions in the rewriting:

   a. The figurative clichés "as pleased as Punch" and "never spoke a truer word"
   b. The redundant expression "in effect and binding"
   c. The general, stereotyped expression "at the earliest opportunity"
   d. The deadwood, stereotyped expression "may we take this opportunity"

The following is a rewritten version of the letter:

Revised Draft

Dear Mr. Marable:

A new Model #64 Sunrise electric toaster was shipped to you this morning by parcel post. You should receive it within five days.

Your new toaster has a drop lever that is reinforced with a magnesium alloy plate that will withstand 20 pounds of pressure. Only 1 pound of pressure is needed to lower two slices of bread into the toasting chamber.

We are delighted to hear that you enjoy using the Sunrise model. Tests performed by Consumer Laboratories showed that this model does indeed brown toast more evenly than any competing model on the market today. We appreciate your business and look forward to your next visit to Finest Goods.

Sincerely yours,

Credit Information Requests and Favorable Responses

Whenever a consumer or firm requests a credit arrangement for payment of goods or services, most companies check credit references before granting the request. These references come from other firms from which the applicant bought goods or services on credit in the past. Requesting and granting such credit information is routine business among companies today. Here is a sample letter requesting credit information from a credit supervisor:

First Draft   Dear Miss Bonevac:

I am writing this letter to request that you send me credit information on Alpine Sporting Goods Company. The company applied for credit with us and gave your firm as a reference.

Mr. Rodriguez of Alpine asked that the company be allowed to charge $1000 monthly on open account for goods they will purchase from us. Because we don't know whether we can trust them, we need credit information from you.

Will you please fill in the attached credit information form and return it to us as soon as possible. We are sorry to inconvenience you but need the information.

Sincerely yours,

Critique   The first draft of the letter follows the desirable practice of addressing the person charged with giving credit information. Address the company or credit department only when you are unable to obtain the name of the person charged with the duty. While the letter does follow the basic plan for organizing favorable requests, the tone is negative. This negative tone is established by the combined effect of the second sentence of the middle paragraph and the last sentence in the letter.

These corrections should be made:

1. Omit the obvious opening statement, "I am writing this letter."

2. Omit the negative statement, "Because we don't know whether we can trust them." The verb *trust* implies doubt, which is unwarranted at this time.

3. Omit the negative statement, "We are sorry to inconvenience you." This statement implies that the credit information request process is unusual. Because the process is routine, present the request as favorable news.

4. Omit the stereotyped statement, "as soon as possible." If you need the information quickly, state the date by which you need it and the reason why you need it by that date.

Here is a rewritten letter with these mistakes corrected:

Revised Draft   Dear Miss Bonevac:

Please send us credit information on Alpine Sporting Goods Company. The firm applied for credit with us and gave your company as a credit reference.

Mr. José F. Rodriguez of Alpine asked that the company be allowed to charge $1000 monthly on open account for goods purchased from us. Because this is their first such application with us, we shall appreciate as much information as you can give us.

Alpine requested that the first order be shipped by April 10. So that this request can be met, can you complete and return the attached credit information form to us by April 5?

Sincerely,

The following is a favorable response to the credit information request:

First Draft   Dear Mr. Bailey:

We understand from your letter that Alpine Sporting Goods has applied with you for the purchase of goods on credit terms. We are happy to supply you with this information.

On account of their timely repayment on the account with us, we are happy to give them our most fabulous recommendation to you for the purpose of credit purchases. Allow me to say that you will enjoy doing business with them.

You will find that we shoot straight from the shoulder in the attached credit information form being returned to you. We hope this is what you wanted.

Yours truly,

Critique   The first draft of the letter has a positive tone except in two places: (1) the statement about giving a "most fabulous" recommendation and (2) the closing statement *hoping* that "this is what you want." In addition, the basic plan for delivering favorable news is not followed and several changes should be made in language.

Here are the specific points to correct in the letter:

1. Reorganize the basic plan to return first the form delivering the favorable news about the status of Alpine's credit standing with the com-

pany. Follow this with details about the credit standing, but avoid repeating details provided on the credit information form itself. Then close on a positive note.

2. Substitute "because" for the undesirable colloquialism, "on account of."

3. Omit the presumptive, wordy expression, "you will find."

4. Omit the figurative cliché, "shoot straight from the shoulder," or substitute an accurate expression for it.

5. Substitute "best" or "highest recommendation" for "most fabulous recommendation."

6. Omit the deadwood expression, "allow me to say that."

7. Omit the doubtful expression, "we hope this is what you wanted." It is thought that the requested information is being sent and the letter should give that impression.

The following is a corrected version of the first draft of the letter:

Revised Draft   Dear Mr. Bailey:

As the enclosed credit information form shows, Alpine Sporting Goods Company has our highest recommendation for credit purchases from your firm.

Alpine always pays us on time. Also, they seem eager to maintain a sound business relationship with us. Therefore, we think you will enjoy doing business with them.

Just write or call us at 843-0098 when we can supply you with credit information again.

Yours truly,

Credit Requests and Favorable Responses

You may make a direct request for credit terms in cases where you are certain that your financial condition merits a favorable response. Both individuals and firms use the same procedure in making such requests. Many firms that offer credit terms ask applicants to fill in financial disclosure statements that they provide. Others request that you prepare a financial disclosure statement yourself. A good idea is first to inquire about the proper procedure before requesting credit terms; following this procedure can save time and effort.

Here is a sample credit request sent by an individual to the credit manager of a furniture retailing store:

First Draft   Dear Mr. Devereaux:

I was in your store the other day and saw a living room set that my wife and I think is out of this world, and I want you to know that I would just about break a leg to have it to make my wife and me happy by making our home look smarter than a castle.

The set contains nine pieces—a three-piece sectional sofa, two chairs, two end tables, and a two-piece coffee table—which you call the Jefferson Manor Group, and I am prepared to buy it if I can get it on credit terms for the $900 purchase.

Enclosed please find a financial disclosure statement which your clerk gave us to complete and which my wife and I have completed.

Sincerely yours,

Critique

The first draft of the letter needs these corrections:

1. Follow the basic format for a direct request. Begin with the request for credit terms. Then include details about the goods you wish to buy, including the cost. State that you are enclosing a completed financial disclosure statement and close positively.

2. Shorten the average sentence length. The three sentences in the first draft average 42 words, whereas a desirable average length is 15 to 20 words.

3. Correct the rambling style of the letter; the thoughts tend to run together.

4. Omit the figurative clichés, "out of this world" and "break a leg."

5. Omit the wordy and stereotyped expression, "enclosed please find."

6. Improve the tone by omitting some of the references to "I." The first draft is writer centered.

A corrected version of the letter might read this way:

Revised Draft

Dear Mr. Devereaux:

Will you please open a line of credit for my wife and me.

A completed copy of your standard financial disclosure statement is enclosed. Your standard one-year repayment plan at 18.5 percent simple interest is our choice of available plans.

We wish to buy your nine-piece Jefferson Manor Group living room set priced at $900. The group is just what we have been looking for, and we look forward to making the purchase.

Sincerely yours,

A favorable response to the credit request made to Mr. Devereaux follows:

First Draft

Dear Mr. Lovejoy:

We are happy to extend credit to you to cover the purchase of a furniture group from us. The reason is because your credit appears to be good.

We trust that our interrelationships will be positive in perpetuum. The modus operandi is that your monthly payment is due on the first day of each month.

The Jefferson Manor Group you wish to purchase can be delivered free of charge within two days after you call us to set a delivery date. This set will blend with almost any decor, perhaps the reason it has become our most popular living room group. Thank you for choosing Abacus Furniture Company for this purchase. We look forward to a continuing business relationship.

Cordially yours,

Critique   The first draft of the letter has a generally positive tone despite the doubt expressed in the second sentence of the first paragraph and the first sentence of the second paragraph. The third paragraph is more effective than either of the first two. Also, the basic format is followed effectively in this first draft.

These problems should be corrected:

1. Deliver the favorable news more directly in the first paragraph.
2. Omit the undesirable colloquialism, "the reason is because," from the first paragraph.
3. Omit the negative, doubtful expression, "trust," and the jargon, "interrelationships," from the second paragraph.
4. Omit or substitute other expressions for the expressions, "in perpetuum" and "modus operandi."

Here is a corrected version of the first draft of this favorable response:

Revised Draft   Dear Mr. Lovejoy:

A $1000 credit line is now open for you here at Abacus Furniture Company. After reviewing your credit application, we are glad to open the joint account for you and Mrs. Lovejoy.

A statement will be sent to you during the second week of each month, and a payment is due on the first day of each month. Interest accrues at 18.5 percent yearly, computed as simple interest.

Free delivery of the Jefferson Manor Group you are purchasing will be made within two days after you call to give us a delivery time. This furniture set will blend with almost any decor, just one reason it has become our most popular living room group.

Thank you for choosing Abacus for this purchase. We look forward to a continuing business relationship.

Cordially yours,

Goodwill Messages

You will need to write some messages just to create and maintain goodwill with those with whom you do business. Some concrete information may be sent in these messages, but the primary reason for writing goodwill letters is to generate good feelings toward you and your company. When you do write these messages, they are especially meaningful because most people neglect to write them. Taking time to write goodwill messages shows courtesy, thoughtfulness, and empathy. In addition, it can boost your own company's sales while creating a good atmosphere in which to do business.

Examples of goodwill messages are those expressing thanks, congratulations, and condolences. These three types all follow the three-step plan for presenting favorable messages.

Thank You Messages

A simple expression of thanks is a powerful goodwill builder. You may write a follow-up letter thanking a person for granting you a specific favor, for example. Another example is writing a customer or client expressing thanks for doing business with your company. Still another example is writing a supplier to express thanks for the timely and correct filling of your orders. Probably you can think of other examples.

Notice how important a sincere tone is to the effectiveness of this revised (mailable) draft of a thank you message:

Revised Draft   Dear Ms. O'Reilly:

Filling your orders for the past seven years has been a pleasure, and we are grateful for your business.

Your regular orders, placed promptly and correctly, have allowed us to supply you with the right merchandise in time to meet your needs. Further, you have paid for these goods by the due date every time. Customers like you make doing business enjoyable.

You have our best wishes for continuing success with your fine retail store. We look forward to another seven years—and more—of a rewarding business relationship with you.

Cordially yours,

Congratulatory Messages

Congratulating others is another goodwill builder in business situations. These messages are appropriate for special occasions such as promotions and successful completion of special projects or assignments. Business associates, clients, and customers can be congratulated on special occasions in their personal lives as well. An example would be on a marriage or birth of a child.

Here is the revised (mailable) draft of a congratulatory message sent on the occasion of a job promotion:

Revised Draft   Dear Mr. Linowitz:

Congratulations on your promotion to vice president for foreign investments at Universal Virginia Bank. We were glad to hear the news.

Your advice on financing our foreign operations during the past ten years has been outstanding. We are aware that much of our success with those operations resulted from your wise counsel. Now that you head that operation at Universal Virginia Bank, we are especially happy about the prospects of a continuing fruitful relationship.

You have our wishes for success in your new job, Mr. Linowitz. We look forward to working with you in your new role with your firm.

Sincerely yours,

This letter to Mr. Linowitz follows the basic plan for favorable messages: deliver the news, add details, and close positively. Note also that the letter is both complimentary and written from the reader's viewpoint.

Condolence Messages

Condolence is the expression of sympathy to those in grief. Because a direct approach works best, use the favorable news organizational plan when writing these messages. Sincerity is especially important, as are positive statements. Taking a positive approach requires that only general references be made to the cause of grief because of the negative nature of this situation. The message must be supportive as well.

Here is the revised (mailable) draft of a condolence message sent to a business associate whose husband died recently:

Revised Draft   Dear Mrs. Mendes:

You have our sympathy in this time of bereavement.

We think of you daily and wish that soon you will be feeling well again. Your most critical job duties have been assumed by John Tyler, who asked me to tell you that he is glad to be able to help in this way. John is making sure that your work load will be normal when you are able to return to work.

You are missed by all your associates here at the Meyer Group. Your return to work will be a happy event for us all.

Sincerely,

FAVORABLE MEMORANDUMS

As you write memorandums to fellow employees, you will be more successful with them if, first, you consider the general conditions involved. Memorandums do carry messages other than the primary news being sent. For example, they deliver secondary news about your knowledge of and attitude toward your job. Further, memorandums reflect the quality of interpersonal relationships among fellow employees. As a result, the way in which you write them can make your job duties easier or more difficult.

Information travels upward, downward, or laterally within a company, and therefore the tone may vary somewhat as a result of differences in rank in an organization. No one should write in a condescending tone, yet the status of the interpersonal relationship between sender and receiver should be reflected in the tone. A more personal tone is effective where a close working relationship exists; but the same tone is inappropriate when writing to those you scarcely know or do not know at all.

Style may vary in memorandums as well. As noted in Chapter Two, informal style is correct for memorandums. The degree of informality used depends upon the writer's preference, regard for authority lines, and the interpersonal relationship between the sender and the receiver.

Favorable memorandums help to conduct internal routine business affairs. Through memorandums, you may request routine information or other assistance or give such information or assistance. Also, some managers prefer the favorable news plan to give written orders through memorandums. While managers give orders only to subordinates, information and other assistance may be given to superiors, peers, or subordinates.

The specific types of favorable memorandums are

1. Routine requests for information and responses
2. Routine requests for assistance and responses
3. Giving orders

Routine Requests for Information and Favorable Responses

Routine requests for information and favorable responses to them are often made through memorandums. These include information sent or received about credit, financial, and personnel records; policies and procedures; status of projects and research development; physical plant and maintenance; and inventories. You should write both the request and the response as favorable news whenever the sender and receiver normally handle such information as part of their daily (routine) job duties.

Here is a revised (mailable) draft of a routine request for information about the status of a product inventory:

Revised Draft   To: Leila Schwartz, Inventory Supervisor
From: Cary Branham, Information Processing Center Supervisor
Subject: Inventory of Film Ribbons

Do we have three dozen Number 877 correctable film ribbons in stock to fit our Omyden 2000 memory typewriters (stock number 4455)?
We are trading these typewriters for word processors on September

15 but need three dozen ribbons in stock to last until that time. Mabel Moseley, Omyden's sales representative, told me that she will accept return of any unused ribbons toward the purchase of a supply to fit the new models. Since replacement machines will be selected this week, I will tell you the type and quantity of ribbons to order for them by Friday.

We appreciate your helping us make this change, Leila.

This memorandum follows the favorable plan—deliver the news, include necessary details, close positively. The tone is friendly, yet businesslike. Specific details are given where needed, and the status of the transaction is reported accurately. Notice how the writer personalized the closing statement by using the receiver's name.

Here is a revised (mailable) draft of a typical favorable response to a routine request. This memorandum answers the inquiry made above in the routine request for information.

Revised Draft

To: Cary Branham, Information Processing Center Supervisor
From: Leila Schwartz, Inventory Supervisor
Subject: Supply of Film Ribbons

Yes, we have 50 Number 877 correctable film ribbons in stock to fit your Omyden 2000 memory typewriters.

We expect to have 14 ribbons to return to Omyden in exchange for ribbons to fit your new models. We will then be able to stock the correct ribbons by September 15 to fit your new word processors.

We are pleased to be able to help you make this change, Cary.

This response to the routine request made earlier follows the same favorable news plan. Notice that each major point made in the inquiry is answered in the response. Such complete responses are needed to make these exchanges of information work well.

Routine Requests for Assistance and Favorable Responses

Routine requests for assistance are quite similar to routine requests for information, as are favorable responses to them. The assistance requested varies as widely as do job duties in the company. Your decision to write the request in the favorable news plan should depend upon whether the request is routine. If the assistance requested and to be given is part of the sender's and receiver's regular job duties, use the favorable news plan.

Here is the revised (mailable) draft of a routine request for assistance:

Revised Draft To: J. Stuart Laws, Corporate Legal Counselor
From: Amanda R. Loos, Personnel Assistant
Subject: Preparation of EEO Report

Will you please help me prepare the state requirements section of our annual equal employment opportunity report?

As a result of changes in the state legal code this year, we must meet additional requirements. Therefore, I need your legal assistance in preparing Section 6 of the report.

This will take only about 15 minutes of your time. I can meet you any day this week or next, whatever suits you best. The report must be mailed to the Equal Employment Opportunity Commission within three weeks.

Because legal assistance is part of Mr. Laws's regular job duties in the company, the request is made as favorable news. Notice that Ms. Loos told him what advice is needed, how much time is required, and when the report is due. These details will help him to respond properly to the request and to prepare properly for the meeting.

Here is the revised (mailable) draft of the favorable response to the request for assistance:

Revised Draft To: Amanda R. Loos, Personnel Assistant
From: J. Stuart Laws, Corporate Legal Counselor
Subject: Meeting for EEO Report Preparation

Let's meet in my office (Suite 245) this Friday at 10:30 A.M. to complete Section 6 of your annual equal employment opportunity report.

You must now provide two items of information that were not required last year:

1. What procedure was followed in advertising available jobs to members of minority races?
2. What procedure was followed to assure that an applicant's place of residency was disregarded in hiring practices?

Please bring this information with you to the meeting in addition to information you normally include in this section of the report.

I look forward to meeting with you on Friday, Amanda.

This brief, yet detailed, response will set the stage for a successful meeting. Listing the new items of information needed emphasizes those important ideas. Also, the tone of the memorandum is courteous and friendly, yet businesslike.

Giving Orders Using Direct Approach

Managers usually speak to employees rather than write them. However, when dealing with routine matters, orders may be sent in writing. Also, when a manager needs to document that orders were given, they may be put in writing, even if also given orally. In addition, they may be put in writing when they contain quite a few details or facts that might be easily forgotten. Managers who prefer a direct approach when giving orders use a favorable news plan when writing them, starting each memorandum with the order itself.

Here is the revised (mailable) draft of an order given in this direct approach:

Revised Draft

To: D. Wayne Humen, Administrative Assistant
From: Michelle M. Corletto, Vice President of Sales
Subject: Arrangements for Sales Supervisors' Meeting

Please reserve and prepare Banquet Room M for a luncheon meeting of our sales supervisors for 12:30 P.M. to 2:00 P.M. on June 19. You and I will meet with all ten supervisors at that time.

Because we will set sales quotas and plan strategy for next year, please make these arrangements:

1. Arrange the seating so that everyone has a full view of everyone else.
2. Place a note pad and two sharpened pencils at each station.
3. Serve a buffet lunch without dessert or alcoholic beverages.
4. Play soft music in the background.
5. Ask Jake LaMonta in Room 2110 next door to the banquet room to keep both doors to his office closed while the meeting is in session. This should guarantee us a quiet working environment.
6. Tape record the entire business session.

Thanks for making these arrangements, Wayne. I will return from Milwaukee the morning of June 19 and will be in the office by 11 A.M. You and I can review our plans for conducting the session just before it begins.

In using this direct approach, the order is given first, details follow, and then a positive statement closes the memorandum. Please note that the arrangements are listed in an easy-to-follow plan.

SUMMARY

Follow a favorable news plan when writing correspondence in which the message favors the reader. Also, use this direct approach when giving information that the reader needs to know to carry out his or her own work. Three steps to follow in order are (1) deliver the news, (2) include necessary details, and (3) close positively.

Write these types of letters as favorable messages:

1. Routine requests and favorable responses to them
2. Orders for goods or services and favorable responses to them
3. Simple claims and replies granting adjustments as requested
4. Credit information requests and replies giving the information
5. Credit requests and replies granting the credit requested
6. Goodwill messages, including saying thank you and giving congratulations and condolence

The chapter contains sample letters in two drafts. The first draft includes typical mistakes made in writing these letters. A critique of each first draft explains the errors before the revised version is shown.

Write these types of memorandums as favorable messages:

1. Routine requests for information and favorable responses to them
2. Routine requests for assistance and favorable responses to them
3. Orders given in a direct approach

The chapter also presents sample final draft memorandums to use as guides when writing internal correspondence.

Additional Readings

Feinberg, Lilian O. *Applied Business Communication.* Sherman Oaks, Calif.: Alfred, 1982, pp. 158–194.

Himstreet, William C., and Wayne Murlin Baty. *Business Communications: Principles and Methods,* 6th ed. Boston: Kent, 1981, pp. 104–128.

Lesikar, Raymond V. *Business Communication: Theory and Application,* 4th ed. Homewood, Ill.: Richard D. Irwin, 1980, pp. 148–203.

Londo, Richard J. *Common Sense in Business Writing.* New York: Macmillan, 1982, pp. 161–186.

Murphy, Herta A., and Charles E. Peck. *Effective Business Communication.* New York: McGraw-Hill, 1980, pp. 161–260.

Treece, Malra. *Successful Business Writing.* Boston: Allyn & Bacon, 1980, pp. 169–198.

Wilkinson, C. W., Peter B. Clarke, and Dorothy C. M. Wilkinson. *Communicating Through Letters and Reports,* 7th ed. Homewood, Ill.: Richard D. Irwin, 1980, pp. 103–177.

Wolf, Morris Philip, Dale F. Keyser, and Robert F. Aurner. *Effective Communication in Business,* 7th ed. Cincinnati: South-Western, 1979, pp. 176–246.

Review Questions

1. List and explain the steps for writing favorable correspondence.
2. Give five specific types of favorable letters.
3. How often do managers write routine request letters and favorable responses to them.
4. Do managers often place orders by writing letters? Explain your answer.
5. Explain when you should write a simple claim letter.
6. Explain the difference between a credit information request and a credit request.

7. Explain how a writer can benefit from writing a goodwill message.

8. Explain how style and tone may vary in memorandums.

9. List and explain four topics you might discuss in a memorandum to request routine information.

10. Explain when a manager might give orders effectively in a memorandum.

Exercises

Letter Cases

1. As manager of an electronics dealership, you often receive requests from charitable organizations for donations of radios, television sets, and other electronic equipment. A local nonprofit retirement home asked you to donate a television set to place in its recreation room. You agree to do this but need to know whether they want a portable or console model. Write a letter to get this information. Address: James Oliver, President; Yarborough Senior Citizens Center; 8765 Franklin Street; Yarborough, Massachusetts 09311.

2. As personnel director of Oriental Express Insurance Company, you are in charge of new employee orientation. Each new employee receives an orientation booklet, but your company's booklet is now three years old and needs revision. Before you undertake revision, you want to look at orientation booklets from other companies. Write a form letter requesting a copy of an orientation booklet or other orientation materials that a company might have. Offer to send a copy of your booklet after you have revised it.

3. You have just moved from San Francisco, California, to Lynchburg, Virginia. Two weeks before moving, you bought a new 10-speed, 26-inch Model 96 Twixt bicycle for your son's birthday. Because you were about to move, you delayed unpacking the bicycle for assembly until you made the move to Lynchburg. When you unpacked the bicycle yesterday, you discovered that the rear brake assembly is missing. Twixt bicycles are not sold anyplace in Virginia, and your son's birthday is two weeks away. Write a letter to the San Francisco dealer asking that a rear brake assembly be express mailed to you. Enclose a copy of your sales receipt. Address: Twixt Bikes Unlimited; 422 Acadian Way; San Francisco, California 94555.

4. Assume that you are the bicycle dealer mentioned in Exercise 3. Write a letter to accompany the rear brake assembly that you are sending by express mail today. Also include a bracket wrench (Stock Number 39) and 12 $\frac{1}{2}$-inch Willy bolts (Stock Number 45-1) that are needed for the assembly. Include resale material (ideas that will reassure the customer of the quality of the product) in your letter to the customer. Address: Timothy L. Waxen; 3622 Lexington Avenue; Lynchburg, Virginia 24221.

5. You are the claims manager for Finest Products Company, a retail discount store. Two weeks ago, a customer bought an elec-

tric toaster that is guaranteed against defective parts for one year. The customer, who lives on a ranch some 60 miles away, returned the toaster today with a letter saying that the toaster will not heat. He requested that you either repair the toaster or send him a replacement. You check the toaster and see that the electric circuitry does not work and cannot be repaired. Write a letter to the customer saying that you are shipping a new toaster by parcel post tomorrow. Address: Walter Abbott; Route 1, Box 805; Depot City, Wyoming 66006.

6. You are the credit manager for X-Tra Department Stores. Today, you received a credit information request from the credit manager at Minton Department Stores. Harriet McKenzie has applied to open a credit account with Minton and gave your store as a reference. Write a letter to the credit manager at Minton telling him that Ms. McKenzie is a good credit risk. She has a $1500 credit line with your store and has owed you as much as $1200 at a time. She has always paid her monthly installment payment within 10 days of receiving a statement. Address: George J. Macklin, Credit Manager; Minton Department Stores; 682 Waverly Lane; St. Paul, Minnesota 53182.

7. You recently graduated from Southwestern University in Dallas, Texas, and took a job as a management trainee with Optimal Oil Company. You work in the research and development division in Optimal's home office in Dallas. You decide to apply for a BankNational Credit Card through your local bank, Major National Bank. So you pick up an application at the bank and fill in all the required information. Write a letter to accompany your application in which you request that an account be opened in your name. Address: Cynthia Trecou, Supervisor; BankNational Credit Card Department; Major National Bank; 33154 San Antonio Road; Dallas, Texas 77743.

8. You are the president of Richland Fabricating Company, a builder of metal tanks for storing liquids underground. You have just received a large order from Mason Fuel Company. This company has placed orders regularly for five years now and always has paid you on time. Write a goodwill letter to the president of Mason thanking her for doing business with your company. Address: Elaine Gruver, President; Mason Fuel Company; Post Office Box 946; Columbia, South Carolina 25610.

9. You own and manage a retail flower shop in Vancouver, Washington. One of your suppliers, an orchid grower, is also a good friend. You have just learned that his wife died last week in a tragic automobile accident. Write a letter of condolence expressing your sympathy. Address: Harry J. Soccer, President; Washington Orchid Growers, Incorporated; Beaverton, Oregon 95540.

10. You are sales manager for Spicy Chicken Restaurants, a fast-growing retail franchiser. Last month, your company awarded its one-hundredth franchise. Write a letter to the new owner of the franchise congratulating him on receiving the franchise. Address: Ralph C. Snodgrass; Spicy Chicken Restaurant; 1369 Ocean Drive; Bridge City, Louisiana 70010.

Memorandum Cases

11. Small and Inverness, an accounting firm, has decided to begin advertising for business for the first time. You were hired as

the new advertising director and are now designing an advertising program. You need a 15-minute appointment with each of the firm's 15 account supervisors to discuss their ideas about how best to advertise the firm. Write a form memorandum to be routed to each of the supervisors.

12. You are one of the account supervisors mentioned in Exercise 11. Write a memorandum to the new advertising director telling him that you will be glad to meet with him to discuss the new advertising program. Suggest that you meet next Wednesday morning or Thursday afternoon in your office. Address: Manuel Lopez, Advertising Director; Suite 495; Munter Building.

13. You are a chemist with Robertson Pharmaceuticals Company, a manufacturer of prescription drugs. You are now developing a new drug that will relieve asthma symptoms. The drug works best in time-released capsule form, and the granules of the active ingredient must be coated in zilfin. Zilfin is sticky when wet, and you do not know whether the production department can manufacture the drug in that state. Write a memorandum to the production manager asking her assistance in preparing sample capsules of the product in your laboratory. The objective is to determine whether your manufacturing design will work. Enclose a drawing of your design. Address: Lily Tao, Manager; Production Department; 18 Bridges Lane Building.

14. You are the production manager mentioned in Exercise 13. Write a memorandum to the chemist who wants your assistance in preparing sample capsules of the asthma symptom relieving drug. Agree to meet in his laboratory and suggest that the meeting be held either Monday or Tuesday of next week. Address: Dr. Abraham Minkovitz, Lantz Memorial Laboratory; Twin Crosses Building.

15. You are traffic control manager for Birdland Industries, an importer of retail merchandise. You provide free parking spaces in company owned lots for employees, who work in 8-hour shifts in a 24-hour operation. Each employee is given a parking sticker with instructions to display it on the left rear bumper of his or her car. Any violation of this rule carries a $25 penalty. Yesterday, you walked through two parking lots and counted 15 cars with bumper stickers displayed on the right rear bumper. Yet the members of your traffic control force have issued no tickets for such a violation for two months. Write a form memorandum to be routed to each of the 15 members of your traffic control force. Tell them to begin issuing tickets for this violation on Monday morning at 8 o'clock.

CHAPTER FIVE

Unfavorable Correspondence

The goals in studying the text and completing the activities in this chapter are to know

1. How to avoid being too direct and too indirect in writing unfavorable correspondence
2. Ways of reducing the negative effects of refusals
3. The types of unfavorable letters commonly written in business
4. How to write, critique, and revise unfavorable letters
5. Special tone factors to consider in writing in business
6. How to write, critique, and revise unfavorable memorandums

Just as a direct approach works best for writing favorable messages, an indirect approach works best for writing unfavorable ones. Readers receive bad news most positively when the negative message is justified before it is stated. This indirect or inductive approach gives the writer a chance to explain an action before saying what the action is or will be. Some business writers have strange ideas about how to be indirect, however.

Writing in *The Wall Street Journal,* Thomas Petzinger, Jr. observed that

> Even in the best of times, [corporate executives are] prone to murky prose. But when the economy turns lousy, the traditional letter to shareholders in annual reports can get more baffling than usual.
>
> The executive double talk springs from a special vocabulary. It [allows] troubled firms to depict themselves as victims of sinister forces beyond their control. Corporate wordsmiths indulge at these times in various forms of understatement, overstatement, and nonstatement.[1]

This strategy of using "gobbledygook" to send bad news is found in many types of business correspondence today. Rather than accept responsibility for the way things are, writers try to "double talk" their way around it. Some are crafty enough to go in two directions at once, saying that they are "cautiously optimistic." Yet readers can see the situation clearly and can also see that the writer is shirking responsibility for it. Then, being too indirect in delivering unfavorable news doesn't work. On the other hand, being too direct does not work either.

AVOIDING OVERLY DIRECT, NEGATIVE APPROACHES

Being too direct and negative includes accusations, bluntness, and blaming others for what has gone wrong. Examples are "You neglected to enclose a receipt with your request." "We cannot understand why you haven't fulfilled this obligation." "You claim you included a check with your letter." "Therefore, we will *not* (or certainly will not) accept these terms." Statements such as these anger readers. Telling the truth without being too direct or too indirect works best.

Bad news is received best when told clearly, in understandable language, while relying on sound reasons for your actions or refusal to act. This may sound difficult to do at first, but actually unfavorable news is as easily written this way as any other. The first step is to follow an

[1]Thomas Petzinger, Jr., "Double Talk Grips Business Reports as Firms Try to Sugarcoat Bad News," *The Wall Street Journal,* March 31, 1982, p. 31.

indirect overall writing plan, one that allows you to explain your actions before you say what the actions are. (Note that the language is not indirect, just the plan.)

The next step is to use appropriate language and explain your ideas fully. The result is that the reader hears your reasons for refusing first without having to deal emotionally with your refusal while hearing the reasons. Using this plan allows you to be heard with an open mind. In that way, you will have the chance you need to justify your actions fully. Good writers can build goodwill even while delivering unfavorable messages.

PLANNING UNFAVORABLE MESSAGES

A five-step plan to follow in delivering unfavorable messages in letters and memorandums follows:

1. *Open with a buffer statement.*   Buffer statements are used to establish a common ground between the reader and the writer. The best of them open on some positive aspect of the subject. This allows a smooth transition into the next step.

2. *Begin giving reasons for refusing.*   Include the strongest reason here (strongest from the reader's viewpoint). If you have just one reason, use it here. If you have two or more reasons, use at least one here and save at least one for step 4.

3. *Refuse.*   Either state the refusal directly or imply it. Be sure to say it clearly.

4. *Resume giving reasons for refusing; this option is called "refusing without recourse."*   Other options you can use at this stage are to make a referral or offer a substitute, compromise, or alternative method or procedure. Offering options is called refusing *with recourse.*

5. *Close positively.*   If you offered the reader a recourse in step 4, close the correspondence with an action request. For example, you may request that the reader accept your compromise offer. When you decline without recourse, close with a positive statement that is consistent with the other ideas in the correspondence. Resale of goods or services or sales promotional material may be included in the closing paragraph when appropriate.

Bad news may range all the way from slightly bothersome to disastrous, and the writer may not always know how bad the news is. For example, this can be seen in the delay of an order for goods: if the customer does not need the merchandise for a month, then a two-week delay may not be so bad. On the other hand, if production is held up until the goods arrive, then the delay may be disastrous. So, the degree to which information is negative depends on the reader's viewpoint, which is sometimes clear but sometimes not.

A writer does know, however, if messages are *likely* to be unfavorable. In all cases where the news is likely to be unfavorable from the reader's viewpoint, you should follow the unfavorable correspondence plan.

REDUCING NEGATIVE EFFECTS OF REFUSALS

When your interests are like those of your customers, clients, and business associates, everyone is happy because the situation favors everybody. When interests are different, however, the situation is always negative for someone and very often for everyone. Two ways of reducing the negative effect in unfavorable correspondence are to (1) imply the refusal whenever the situation allows and (2) offer the reader a recourse.

Implying the Refusal

Sometimes you can imply a refusal just as clearly as you can say it directly. Whenever you can do this, the negative effect is reduced. For instance, assume that you have been asked to release information that must be kept confidential as required by law. A reason for refusing followed by a direct refusal might go like this: "Because this information must be kept confidential as required by federal law, I am unable to release it to you." To *imply* the refusal might be more effective: "The information you requested must be kept confidential as required by federal law. To release it would be illegal."

An implied refusal is also more effective, for example, when a business associate asks you for an appointment on January 16 to discuss a contract. You are eager to talk but you will be attending your daughter's wedding on January 16. A reason for refusing followed by a direct refusal might read as follows: "I will be in Wilmington attending my daughter's wedding on January 16. Therefore, I will be unable to meet with you that day." A better way to put it might be to imply the refusal: "I will be attending my daughter's wedding in Wilmington on January 16 but can meet with you on January 17 or 18." In this case, you have implied the refusal and suggested an alternative in the same sentence.

Notice that the implied refusals given in the last two paragraphs are *clear*. An *unclear* implied refusal can anger your reader and force an extra exchange of messages just to clear the situation. Another problem is that some writers both imply the refusal *and* say it directly. An example is the following: "The information you requested must be kept confidential as required by federal law. To release it would be illegal. Therefore, I am unable to send it to you." This practice also adds to the negative effect of refusing.

Direct refusals can be effective. Be careful, though, that they are not expressed too directly. For example, "we are therefore unable to meet your request" may be quite effective. On the other hand, "we therefore will not do what you ask" is too direct. Stronger statements such as "we therefore certainly will not do what you ask" are insulting, regardless of how well you have handled the reasons for refusing.

Offering the Reader a Recourse

Very often, you can help a reader even though you are unable to do what was requested. For instance, after refusing a request, you might make a referral. To show how this works, assume that you operate a wholesale shoe business. You sell shoes to retailers who then sell them directly to consumers. One day, you receive a mail order from a consumer for a pair of shoes. You then write to say that you sell only to retailers. After declining to fill the order, you might include the name, address, and telephone number of a local retailer who sells the shoes.

In the same way that the referral is made, you might offer substitutes or compromises or suggest alternative methods or procedures when appropriate. Doing this increases goodwill and can actually increase your business profits.

Unfavorable letters are most effective when written according to the indirect plan. By carefully developing these messages, you may be able to turn around negative situations and move them in positive directions.

UNFAVORABLE LETTERS

Situations requiring unfavorable letters include those refusing requests for information or assistance, handling various problems with orders, refusing to grant claims on goods or services, and refusing to extend credit.

Refused Request for Information or Assistance

One-half or more of the unfavorable business letters you will write will be refused requests for information or assistance. This happens because your needs and interests often differ from those of your customers, clients, and business associates. Often the problems are small enough that you work them out to everyone's satisfaction. An attitude of willingness to cooperate should show up in the tone of your letters even when you must refuse flatly a request.

Here is a first draft of a letter refusing a request to speak at an insurance club meeting followed by a critique and a revised draft:

First Draft Dear Mrs. Winokur:

I received your request directed to my secretary that I come speak to your insurance club on March 10, which was received with warmest regards.

I was in an insurance club such as yours when I was in college, so I want you to know that I think well of them. Insurance is the name of the game in business today, and I am thoroughly excited about seeing graduates such as you prepare for service in the field. People who get into this field will surely find that it is right for them and will find it much more rewarding than they had imagined beforehand.

I do hope that you will be able to find someone to speak at your meeting. I will be in Omaha, Nebraska, the entire week of March 10 and therefore cannot be with you at the same time. You'll find somebody, I know, because many insurance agents are interested in college insurance club members just as I am. Our district manager in Richmond, Mary Cox, may consent to do it, so why don't you call her?

By the way, we have the right insurance policy for you should you ever decide that you want outstanding coverage designed to meet your specific needs. Good luck with your projects.

Cordially yours.

Critique The writing style of this first draft is appropriate for a business letter, but tone problems are serious. Corrections that should be made follow:

1. The letter does not follow the unfavorable correspondence plan. The refusal, which is implied *and* stated, should follow the reason for refusing rather than precede it.

2. The opening statement, "I received your request," is an obvious statement. Also "which was received with warmest regards" is misplaced in the sentence.

3. Tone problems are as follows:

   a. Overuse of the word *I* focuses attention on the writer, so the tone is selfish.

   b. The third sentence in the second paragraph contains two presumptive statements: "will surely find" and "will find it much more rewarding than they had imagined." The second statement also suggests that people who have considered getting into insurance have imagined insurance practice to be unrewarding. Also, the third sentence in the third paragraph is presumptive: "You'll find somebody, I know".

c. The tone of the first sentence in the second paragraph is preachy: "I want you to know".

d. The first sentence in the third paragraph is doubtful: "I do hope".

e. The opening sentence contains the wordy, stereotyped, and old fashioned expression, "with warmest regards."

f. The second sentence in the second paragraph contains an excessive superlative: "thoroughly exciting."

g. The closing sentence, "Good luck with your projects," is stereotyped.

h. The first sentence in the last paragraph follows a poorly handled refusal and therefore will anger the reader. Sales promotional material is effective in refusal letters, though, when it follows an effective refusal.

Revised Draft   Dear Mrs. Winokur:

Beta Eta Xi is an outstanding insurance organization, and I appreciate your invitation to speak at your career day activities this year. The program you sent looks both appropriate and timely.

On March 10, the day your program is being held, I will be in Omaha, Nebraska, attending a seminar on changes in insurance laws. These changes affect our policy writing procedures here at the Williamsburg Agency, so we need to know about them to serve our clients' insurance needs properly.

Mary Cox, our district manager in Richmond, is an excellent speaker. I talked with her last Friday about your needs, and she told me that she will be happy to speak to your group. Ms. Cox lives in Richmond, so it will cost nothing for her to speak at your seminar. If you would like her to speak to the group, please call her before February 15. The telephone number is 358-1687.

Whenever you need further support with your programs, call or write us. We will be glad to do whatever we can to assist you.

Cordially yours,

Problems with Orders for Goods or Services

When you receive an order for goods or services that you cannot fill or cannot fill on time, then the buyer deserves to know what has happened. Problems with orders include cancellations, substitutions, and back orders or delays. If you can offer a substitute, that may be the best option. A substitute should be about equal in quality and price to the goods or services that were offered, though. If the quality is much poorer or the price much higher, consider delaying delivery until you can provide the proper goods or services. A delay should be reasonable, though—two weeks, perhaps three or four, depending on the buyer's needs. If you decide to offer a substitute or delay an order, give the buyer a chance to accept or reject your offer.

Canceling an order is sometimes necessary, but that is the least effective option. When you must do this, refer the customer to a source of the goods or services if possible; give the full name, address, and telephone number of the prospective supplier that you mention.

Here is a first draft of a letter refusing part of an order for merchandise followed by a critique of the first draft and a revised draft:

First Draft   Dear Mr. Royalton:

We wish to say that we appreciate your order Number 8181, which we are now attempting to fill.

We can't send the Jamaican ginger, however, because it is out of stock at the moment; but we do have everything else on the order. We're going ahead and shipping the remainder of the order this afternoon. Because Jamaican ginger is the best available and many customers will buy only that type, we feel it the better part of wisdom not to substitute another type.

We will have another supply of Jamaican ginger within 30 days, and we will ship it at that time unless we hear otherwise. We will gladly substitute Indian or American ginger or will send a 30-day supply to last until the Jamaican ginger arrives. If either option is preferred, call us toll free at 1-800-200-4176. We will be most happy to follow your instructions to the letter.

Yours truly,

Critique   This letter does not use the good news that the order is being filled and shipped. The message is written almost entirely from the writer's viewpoint as shown by the excessive use of "we." In several places, the writer could have conveniently said "you" but did not do so. Another major problem is that the refusal comes before the reason for refusing, so the unfavorable correspondence plan is not followed. Other problems to correct are as follows:

1. Nothing is said about how the order is being shipped or about how quickly a substitute order can be sent.

2. "We wish to say that" in the opening sentence and "going ahead and" in the second sentence in the second paragraph are wordy expressions.

3. "Which we are now attempting to fill" in the opening sentence expresses doubt about whether or how to fill the order. This leaves the impression that the writer has not decided what action to take even though action is being taken.

4. "At the moment" in the first sentence in the second paragraph is a stereotyped expression.

5. "Better part of wisdom" in the third sentence in the second paragraph and "to the letter" in the closing sentence are figurative clichés.

6. "Be most happy" in the closing sentence is an ineffective colloquial expression.

Revised Draft   Dear Mr. Royalton:

Your purchase order Number 8181 is now being filled and the goods will be shipped this afternoon by Poulus Freight Lines, as you requested.

Because of a rainy harvest season, our fall supply of Jamaican ground ginger has been delayed 30 days. Since our stock of this ginger is now depleted, your order will be delayed until the new shipment arrives. Because many of our clients' customers will buy only Jamaican ginger, we are reluctant to ship another type.

Your Jamaican ginger will be shipped by April 30. If you prefer, however, you can have Indian or American ginger shipped now. You may order a 30-day supply of either or you may substitute the order entirely. If one of these options is better for you than waiting until April 30, please call us toll free at 1-800-200-4176. We will ship the order prepaid by air express within 24 hours after receiving your instructions.

Yours truly,

Refused Claims on Goods or Services

Follow the unfavorable correspondence plan whenever you write a refusal to grant an adjustment on goods sold or services rendered. Whether you refuse to grant all or part of a claim, the news is at least somewhat unfavorable for the reader. Claims adjusters in various types of businesses often write this type of letter; but most people in business write them occasionally, regardless of the type work they do. For instance, real estate dealers and supervisors in utility companies sometimes must refuse to return nonrefundable deposits or fees.

Here is a first draft of a refusal to grant a claim on an insurance policy, followed by a critique of the first draft and a revised draft of the letter:

First Draft   Dear Mr. Chan:

We were informed by you this morning that you are requesting an additional $500 as reimbursement compensation for repairs to your sports car, which is insured with this business concern.

All Ways Insurance is always willing to ascertain information from clients to help the company make just and fair decisions on claims. Your case is no exception. Upon inspection of your Fiat sports car last month after the accident but prior to the repairs, our appraiser estimated that the damage could be repaired for the amount of $1500. She recommended three shops that would fix your car for that amount but told you that you could have it repaired wherever you like as long as the cost did not exceed our estimate, and I received notification from Jiffy Automobile Repairs who stated that they had given you a $1500 estimate. Therefore, pursuant to the regulations of our policies in handling claims, you became the party responsible for paying the override when you had the car repaired at Old Faithful Repair Studios. All Ways Insurance Company denies your request.

Your business heretofore has been appreciated. Call on us whenever we can be of assistance again.

Sincerely yours,

Critique   The style of this first draft is too formal, so the message is stiff and detached. These problems should be corrected:

1. The words "informed" and "business concern" in the opening sentence are too formal.

2. "Ascertain" in the first sentence of the second paragraph and "prior to" in the third are too formal. "Received notification" in the fourth sentence of the second paragraph and "pursuant to," "regulations," and "party" in the fifth are also too formal. In addition, "heretofore" in the closing sentence is too formal.

3. Personification of the company also is too formal an approach. An example is in the first sentence, second paragraph: "All Ways Insurance is always willing".

The overall tone of the letter is unresponsive, blunt, and selfish, and it blames the receiver for the problem in a negative way—it's the owner's problem, so he should handle it. These problems should be corrected:

1. The first and second sentences in the second paragraph are selfish, implying that the company *always* does the right thing.

2. The effect of the refusal in the last two sentences in the second paragraph is too direct—"you became the party responsible" and "denies your request." Actually, the refusal is repeated unnecessarily.

3. The closing sentence evokes anger mostly because the reasons for refusing and the refusal are poorly written.

4. Specific language problems are

   a. "Reimbursement compensation" in the opening sentence and "just and fair" in the first sentence in the second paragraph are redundant.

   b. Avoid referring to "policies" in a letter as is done in the fifth sentence in the second paragraph. Policies are internal guidelines that companies follow, so they should not be mentioned to customers.

c. "Your case is no exception," the second sentence in the second paragraph, is stereotyped.

d. "For the amount of" in the third sentence in the second paragraph is wordy.

e. "Override" in the fifth sentence in the second paragraph is jargon.

Other problems are as follows:

1. The opening sentence is a statement of the obvious.

2. The refusal is too close to the end of the letter to allow enough space to re-establish a good tone before closing.

3. The third and fourth sentences in the second paragraph are too long; also, the fourth sentence rambles.

Revised Draft   Dear Mr. Chan:

We were glad to learn that your car has been repaired and that you are again able to drive it to work.

When our appraiser, Judy Nix, inspected the damage to your car on August 1, she estimated that it could be repaired for $1500. She then gave you a check for that amount and recommended three shops that would fix the car. The manager of one of them, Jiffy Automobile Repairs, sent us a copy of a $1500 estimate that he gave you on August 2. Had you been unable to get your Fiat repaired for $1500, we would have appraised the damage a second time.

You will still continue receiving the $50 yearly "safe driver" deduction given drivers who do not cause an accident. Then, next year, you will be eligible for a $100 deduction if this safe driving record continues.

The enclosed pamphlet, just published by the American Driving Association, gives tips for long distance traveling by car. Because you do travel regularly in your work, I thought you would enjoy reading it.

Sincerely yours,

Refusing Credit

Lending institutions, such as banks and businesses that sell goods and services, finance loans and credit purchases. When a consumer or business applies for credit, the financing agency will investigate the applicant's credit record. If the applicant is judged to be a poor credit risk, the message is usually delivered by letter. The law requires a complete explanation of why credit is refused. Here is the first draft of a letter *refusing credit* to a young married couple who have applied for an account with a furniture company. A critique of the first draft is then given, followed by a revised draft of the letter.

First Draft

Dear Mr. and Mrs. Mertz:

I do trust that you are enjoying your new Chesapeake living room suite that you bought from us last month. Let us know if it doesn't meet your expectations.

When I learned that you plan to furnish your apartment as soon as you can save the money, I suggested that you apply for credit with us so that you could furnish the entire apartment now. Your decision to do so seemed wise then.

Your credit application has been reviewed according to our modus operandi. Your credit rating and credit references are favorable, although combined together you have bought little on credit in the past. However, your present debt-to-income ratio is too high to allow us to give you $5000 installment credit as you requested.

You are eligible for $2000 credit, though, according to the above-mentioned plan. Is that suitable? If it is, come in after the conclusion of any workday and buy whatever you wish as long as it doesn't exceed $2000. At your convenience choose that new bedroom suite, or whatever, pursuant to this agreement.

Sincerely yours,

Critique

While this letter appears to follow the unfavorable correspondence plan, careful study reveals that it does not. As discussed in point 3, following the refusal is hinted clearly before the major reason for refusing is given. The overall tone of the letter is negative, so negative, in fact, that the readers are likely to refuse to do further business with this company. The problems that contribute to this negative tone are these:

1. The verb "trust" in the opening sentence implies doubt about whether the readers are enjoying the furniture they bought already.

2. "Let us know if it doesn't meet your expectations," the second sentence in the opening paragraph, compounds the problem in the first sentence. It confirms the doubt by suggesting the possibility that the reader will not be pleased with the merchandise.

3. The second sentence in the second paragraph, "Your decision to do so seemed wise then," implies that the credit application will be refused. This clear hint that the credit is being refused destroys the psychology of the unfavorable plan. Although restated later, the refusal does come before the reason for refusing.

4. A clause in the second sentence in the third paragraph is a negative reminder—"although combined together you have bought little on credit in the past." Because the credit rating and references are favorable, the negative issues considered in making those decisions need not be mentioned.

5. "Debt-to-income ratio" in the third sentence in the third paragraph is financial jargon. The readers may know "about" what is meant by the phrase, but they deserve to know the details about it.

6. "Is that suitable?" the second sentence in the fourth paragraph, is a negative suggestion.

7. "As long as it doesn't exceed $2000" in the third sentence in the last paragraph is a negative reminder. "Pursuant to this agreement" in the closing sentence is the same thing. These statements reprimand the readers without cause.

8. Taken together, the last three sentences leave the impression that the writer doesn't really want the credit business. If so, then credit terms should have been refused altogether. If the writer does want the business, then these sentences should make in specific terms a strong appeal to buy.

Other specific language problems are as follows:

1. "Modus operandi" in the first sentence in the third paragraph is a foreign expression. Also, "combined together" in the second sentence in the third paragraph is redundant.

2. "Above-mentioned" in the first sentence in the last paragraph is wordy. Also, "after the conclusion of" in the third sentence in the last paragraph is wordy.

3. "At your convenience" in the closing sentence is general and stereotyped.

4. "Pursuant to this agreement" in the closing sentence is wordy and formal.

Revised Draft   Dear Mr. and Mrs. Mertz:

Your application for a $5000 installment loan to buy furniture from us has been reviewed by Joan Lanham, our credit supervisor. Thank you for making the application.

Ms. Lanham first checked each of your credit ratings and found them favorable. Next, she checked your credit references and found them favorable also. Then, she compared your monthly expenses with your monthly incomes. This comparison showed that your monthly expenses of $1200 leaves you $175 when deducted from your $1375 monthly income after deductions. A $5000 loan at 18 percent annual interest for 48 months would cost you $187 monthly, $12 more than you have left after paying the bills. Based on these figures, you would be unable to assume payment of a $5000 loan.

You are eligible, however, for a $2000 loan at 18 percent annual interest for 48 months. On this loan, your monthly payment will be only $75. We encourage you to accept this loan so that you can purchase many of the furnishings you want now. If you will accept this agreement, we will gladly review your application after 24 months to see if you are eligible for an additional loan then.

The Chesapeake bedroom suite you looked at last month is on sale now at a 20 percent discount, a $400 savings. This classic suite will match perfectly the living room suite you bought from us last month.

Please stop by the store this week after work to take advantage of this offer, which expires Saturday. We are open every weekday until 9 P.M. Sincerely yours,

Some internal business matters are unique as are some external matters. But business transactions that employees and employers conduct among themselves are often similar to those that they conduct with people outside the company. Because of this, the content of unfavorable memorandums is often about the same topics as those of unfavorable letters. An example is denying a request for information or assistance.

UNFAVORABLE MEMORANDUMS

As discussed in Chapter Four, a memorandum differs from a letter largely because of necessary differences in tone. Two factors are especially important:

1. Rank and status within a company should be observed in the style and tone of a memorandum. For example, you should observe the lines of authority in the tone. In some cases the style may be more formal when writing to superiors than when writing to peers or subordinates.

2. Closer personal relationships are more likely to exist among people who write memorandums to one another than among those who write letters. The positive aspects of working relationships that you have with fellow employees should be reflected in the tone of memorandums you write to them.

Three common situations in which you may write unfavorable memorandums are to refuse (1) requests for information or assistance, (2) requests for changes in policies or procedures, and (3) excessive claims against the company.

Refused Requests for Information or Assistance

Some common reasons to refuse information to a fellow employee are that it is confidential, that you lack the authority to release it, or that you do not have the information. Common reasons to refuse assistance are that you cannot take time from your own work to do it, that your superiors will not allow it, or that you lack knowledge, equipment, or facilities to do it.

The following is the first draft of a memorandum refusing a request to provide information about cosmetics to an internal auditor. The first draft is followed by a critique and then by a revised draft of the memorandum.

First Draft
To: Jackson Pallock, Internal Auditor
From: Mabelline Yurich, Sales Supervisor of Cosmetics
Subject: Response to Request for New-Life Cosmetics Sales Records

In reference to your request for last quarter's sales records for our line of New-Life Cosmetics, I am unable to give them to you by March 12 as you requested.

According to Section 6 of our policy manual (copy attached), "only the vice president for sales may release classified sales records internally or externally." Cosmetics sales records are classified. The vice president for sales, Jack Grayson, is vacationing and cannot be reached until he returns to work March 17. Jack's assistant, Ms. Mary Smith, told me that the records that you are desirous of can be sent immediately in toto if Jack approves their release when he returns next Thursday. She asked me to tell you that unfortunately we must hold your request in abeyance until he returns.

I am sorry this happened, Jackson. If you need information on man-hours spent on sales, I can fill the bill now. Otherwise, we will meet your request in due time if it is approved. You'll still have time to complete your audit by March 30, though.

Critique
The memorandum follows a direct rather than an indirect approach. As a result, the refusal becomes a rebuff. The sudden direct quote from the policy manual shows how being too objective can sound cold. The apology in the closing paragraph sounds false following such a cold refusal. Also, the closing sentence is presumptive and sounds flippant in the overall context of the memorandum.

Other specific problems to correct are the following:

1. "In reference to your request" in the opening sentence is wordy and stereotyped.

2. Since Jack Grayson was not referred to as "Mr." in the second sentence of the second paragraph, referring to Mary Smith as 'Ms." in the third sentence of the same paragraph appears to be sexually biased.

3. "Are desirous of" in the fourth sentence of the second paragraph is wordy and too formal.

4. Saying that the records can be sent "immediately" (fourth sentence, second paragraph) is vague; it does not say when they will be sent.

5. "In toto" in the fourth sentence of the second paragraph is a foreign expression.

6. "Unfortunately" in the fourth sentence of the second paragraph is a strongly negative connective.

7. "Hold your request in abeyance" in the last sentence of the second paragraph is wordy and too formal.

8. Saying "sorry" in the apology in the first sentence of the last paragraph is negative and might sound false. The writer apologizes for a matter she cannot control.

9. "Man-hours" in the second sentence of the last paragraph is sexually biased; "fill the bill" in the same sentence is a figurative cliché.

10. "In due time" in the third sentence of the last paragraph is general and therefore vague.

Revised Draft   To: Jackson Pallock, Internal Auditor
From: Mabelline Yurich, Sales Supervisor for Cosmetics
Subject: Response to Request for New-Life Cosmetics Sales Records

     I have reviewed your request to see last quarter's New-Life Cosmetics sales records by March 12 with Mary Smith, the assistant to the vice president of sales, Jack Grayson.

     Mary and I checked Section 6 of our policy manual and confirmed that Jack must give permission to release any classified records either internally or externally. All cosmetics sales records are classified. Jack is vacationing in Tibet and cannot be reached until he returns to work on March 17. Mary said that these records are complete and can be sent to you on March 17, if Jack approves.

     Should you need any unclassified cosmetics records to help you complete your audit by March 30, I can send them to you now. Records such as those of staff hours spent on selling cosmetics are unclassified. Call me at Extension 7165 to tell me what else you need, if anything.

Refused Requests for Changes in Policies or Procedures

Policies are the rules that companies follow to conduct their business, the overall guidelines. Procedures are the methods used to put policies into effect, so procedures should never conflict with policies. Changes in policies always require the consent of company officials, perhaps even the board of directors if the company is a corporation. Depending on the nature and importance of procedures, changes in them may require the consent of company officials as well. Here is a first draft of a refused request for a change in the vacation schedule. Meeting the request would have required a change in departmental procedure, but making the change would have required a change in company policy as well.

     The first draft is followed by a critique, which is then followed by a revised draft of the memorandum:

First Draft   To: Donna Crenshaw, Account Executive
From: Ernest Smithson, Account Supervisor
Subject: Response to Request for a Change in the Vacation Schedule

     Your trip to Paris sounds exciting. Many people are taking such trips. You want to switch your vacation to June 16 to 30 from May 1 to 15 so you can take the trip. But five people already chose that date. Only five people may vacation at one time.

I checked with everyone in the department. Nobody is willing to change.

I already checked with Mr. Jones to see if we can let you go anyway. He said no.

You may switch to another two-week period. Your parents might change their plans. However, keep your choice between May 16 and August 30. Also, do not choose August 1 to 15.

I must know about any change by March 1, the deadline for setting vacation dates.

Critique
This memorandum gives the impression that the writer does not really care about the reader's request despite two attempts to help. The main reason for this is that the ideas are not explained fully. Also, the tone is curt and may be taken as somewhat insulting in places.

Other than to explain the ideas fully, here are other specific problems to correct:

1. The memorandum contains too many short paragraphs and sentences. They contribute to the curt tone.

2. The second sentence, "Many people are taking such trips," is rude because it implies in this context that the reason for the request is trivial.

3. The second sentence in the fifth paragraph, "Your parents might change their plans," may be received as an insult.

Revised Draft
To: Donna Crenshaw, Account Executive
From: Ernest Smithson, Account Supervisor
Subject: Response to Request for a Change in the Vacation Schedule

Your choice to vacation in Paris this summer with your parents does sound exciting. They were thoughtful to invite you to join them.

As we discussed when you chose your vacation dates, only five people in the department may vacation during any two-week period. When I received your request to change your vacation from May 1 to 15 to June 16 to 30, I checked to see how many people are scheduled for vacations then. The roster showed that five people requested June 16 to 30.

Next, I asked each of these five people if any of them will make a change. Having planned their vacations completely, all of them declined. Then, I asked Mr. Jones if we might make an exception and let you go anyway. He declined, saying that we must meet the two-thirds staffing requirement all summer to serve our customers adequately.

You may reschedule your vacation for another two-week period if that will help. Perhaps your parents can reschedule their vacation so this plan can work. Any other two-week period between May 16 and August 30 is acceptable except August 1 to 15, when five people are scheduled already. If you do wish to make a change, please tell me before March 1, the deadline for setting vacation dates.

Refused Claims Against the Company

Employee claims against a company may range from requests for reimbursement of travel expenses to suits against the company for injuries or other personal losses. If federal or state laws are involved in a refusal, the company's lawyers will take charge of the company's interests. But when claims merely violate company policies or procedures, a financial officer normally refuses to grant all or part of the adjustment.

The following is a first draft of a refusal to grant a claim for travel expenses followed by a critique of the first draft and a revised draft of the memorandum:

First Draft

To: Mark Johnson, Salesperson
From: Maria Cillias, Controller
Subject: Reimbursement for Travel Expenses

As per your request, we are processing your request for reimbursement of travel expenses for your December 2 to 5 trip to Denver.

Your attention is called to two items for which you are seeking reimbursement: tolls and taxicab fares. You listed tolls totaling $10.50 and taxicab fares totaling $27.50 on the request form but neglected to enclose receipts for these expenses. Company rules require that receipts be attached to the form for all expenses for which you seek reimbursement except meals and tips.

To facilitate reimbursement of your travel expenses, will you kindly advise us whether you can furnish these receipts. When you comply with this constraint, we will reimburse you without further delay.

Critique

The style of this memorandum is too formal. The tone is too negative, and that problem is compounded by several violations of sound business writing principles.

Specific problems to correct are as follows:

1. "As per your request" in the opening sentence is wordy, stereotyped, and too formal.

2. "Your attention is called to" in the first sentence in the second paragraph is also wordy, stereotyped, and too formal.

3. The word "neglected" in the second sentence in the second paragraph is negative because it directly accuses the reader of causing the problem.

4. The words "facilitate" and "furnish" in the first sentence in the last paragraph are more complex than are needed. Also, they help make the style more formal. "Kindly advise" in the same sentence is wordy, stereotyped, and formal.

5. "Comply with this constraint" in the last sentence is wordy and formal. Also, "constraint" is jargon. "Without further delay" in the same

sentence is general and therefore vague; also it is a stereotyped expression.

Revised Draft   To: Mark Johnson, Salesperson
From: Maria Cillias, Controller
Subject: Reimbursement for Travel Expenses

Your request for reimbursement of travel expenses for your December 2 to 5 trip to Denver is now being processed.

In reviewing the form you submitted for reimbursement, we noted that you listed tolls and taxicab fares for which no receipts were attached. Company procedures require that receipts be submitted for all refunded expenses except meals and tips. Will you please send us the receipts for $10.50 in tolls and $27.50 in taxicab fares. Then, we can send you a check for $56.35, the full amount of your request.

We will issue your reimbursement check within two days after receiving the receipts.

You can use letters and memorandums shown in this chapter as guides for writing your own unfavorable correspondence regardless of the type of job you hold. Whenever you need to write the same message again and again, you may want to prepare a form letter or memorandum to use as a more specific guide each time you write the message. Form correspondence is discussed in Chapter Thirteen.

SUMMARY

Many business writers make the mistake of using language that is too indirect and obscure when writing unfavorable correspondence. On the other hand, some writers use language that is too direct and negative. Telling the truth without being either abrupt or vague works best. Use this five-step, indirect organizational plan for delivering the news: (1) open with a buffer statement, (2) begin giving reasons for refusing, (3) refuse, (4) resume giving reasons for refusing, and (5) close positively.

Two ways in which to reduce the negative effects of refusing reader requests are to imply the refusal whenever possible and to offer the reader a recourse. Implied refusals should be clear and any recourse offered should be realistic.

Unfavorable letters include refusing requests for information or assistance, handling problems with orders, refusing to grant claims, and refusing to extend credit. Problems with orders include cancellations, substitutions, and back orders or delays. Offering a substitute is normally the best option, followed by delaying orders; cancel orders only when you can do nothing else.

Claims adjusters often write letters refusing to grant claims made on goods or services; other people in business write them, too, for example, real estate brokers and supervisors in utility companies. Letters refusing credit may be written by people who work for lending institutions or businesses that finance the sale of their own goods and services.

Memorandums differ from letters in style and tone. Two primary factors involved are (1) rank and status within companies and (2) personal relationships among people within companies. Common types of unfavorable memorandums include denying (1) requests for information or assistance, (2) requests for changes in policies or procedures, and (3) claims against the company.

Common reasons why you may decline to give information to fellow employees are that it is confidential, you do not have the authority to release it, or you do not have the information. Common reasons for refusing to give assistance are that you cannot take time from your own work to do it, your supervisors will not allow it, or you lack the knowledge, equipment, or facilities to do it.

Policies are rules companies follow to conduct their business; procedures are the methods used to put policies into effect. When employees make claims against a company, the company's lawyers will take charge if federal or state laws govern any aspect of the claim. If the claim is governed only by company policies or procedures, a financial officer normally handles the situation.

Additional Readings

Bowman, Joel P., and Bernadine P. Branchaw. *Successful Communication in Business.* San Francisco: Harper & Row, 1980, pp. 151–172.

Feinberg, Lilian O. *Applied Business Communication.* Sherman Oaks, Calif.: Alfred, 1982, pp. 195–203.

Himstreet, William C., and Wayne Murlin Baty. *Business Communications: Principles and Methods,* 6th ed. Boston: Kent, 1981, pp. 129–154.

Lesikar, Raymond V. *Basic Business Communication,* rev. ed. Homewood, Ill.: Richard D. Irwin, 1982, pp. 140–162.

Londo, Richard J. *Common Sense in Business Writing.* New York: Macmillan, 1982, pp. 187–212.

Murphy, Herta A., and Charles E. Peck. *Effective Business Communications.* New York: McGraw-Hill, 1980, pp. 261–327.

Sigband, Norman B. *Communication for Management and Business,* 3rd ed. Glenview, Ill.: Scott, Foresman, 1982, pp. 439–454.

Swindle, Robert E. *The Business Communicator.* Englewood Cliffs, N.J.: Prentice-Hall, 1980, pp. 230–242.

Wells, Walter. *Communications in Business,* 3rd ed. Boston: Kent, 1981, pp. 264–287.

Wilkinson, C. W., Peter B. Clarke, and Dorothy C. M. Wilkinson. *Communicating Through Letters and Reports,* 7th ed. Homewood, Ill.: Richard D. Irwin, 1980, pp. 204–263.

Review Questions

1. Why does an indirect approach work best as an organizational plan for writing unfavorable correspondence?

2. Can a writer of unfavorable messages be too indirect? Explain your answer.

3. List and define the five steps in the unfavorable message organizational plan.

4. Give two ways of reducing the negative effects of refusals. Give an example of each.

5. Give an example of a business situation in which you would refuse in a letter to give information or assistance.

6. What are the types of problems that you might have with orders for goods or services that might cause you to write an unfavorable letter?

7. Give an example of a business situation in which you would refuse in a letter to grant a claim on goods or services.

8. Name two reasons why you might refuse a request to purchase goods or services on credit terms.

9. Name and discuss two factors that are especially important in setting the right tone in an unfavorable memorandum.

10. How do policies and procedures differ? Give an example of a situation in which a policy or procedural change might be refused in a memorandum.

Exercises

Letter Cases

1. Your company just received a request from the Neighborhood Beautification Committee of Wentswood. The committee is asking that all businesses in Wentswood erect fences around their buildings and repave their parking lots. You believe that the committee is doing a good job. However, you must decline this request. You did repave your parking lot last year, but erecting a fence is too expensive for you to do at this time. Write a letter refusing the request. Address: Neighborhood Beautification Committee of Wentswood; 1001 Dennison Parkway; Wentswood, Kentucky 44974.

2. You work for WRSF-AM radio station as an advertising account executive. John Williams, the president of Parkersburg Civic Club, wrote the station manager asking that someone speak to the club. The topic is radio advertising, and the presentation is to be made at the next monthly meeting. The station manager asked you to do it, but you will be in Charleston on business at the time of the meeting. No one else at the station can do it either. The club is one of the most prominent organizations in the city, and the station would have gained valuable public relations if you could have made the presentation. Write a letter explaining the situation. Address: John Williams; 1267 Lapsburg Highway; Parkersburg, West Virginia 20111.

3. You work as a marketing representative for Duxbury Computer Company. Recently, you sold a new computer system to Total Automobile Parts Company. As a part of the sales agreement, you agreed to train one of the firm's employees to use the equipment. Then today you received a letter from Total's president asking you to train three of that firm's employees. Besides not having agreed to do this, you have no available training spaces. Write a letter refusing the request. Address: Lydia Perkinson, President; Total Automobile Parts Company; 88 Lyons Parkway; Savannah, Georgia 31405.

4. You manage the mail-order department for a large retail merchandising firm. Each year, you publish an expensive catalog of your merchandise. Five years ago, you had to begin charging $2.00 for copies of the catalog to recover some of the expense of producing it. This year, the cost went to $7.00, and you wrote all your catalog customers telling them about the increase. Yesterday, you received a request for a new catalog from a customer accompanied by a $2.00 check. You must refuse the request and ask for an additional $5.00. If you prefer, return the $2.00 check and ask for a $7.00 check. Address: Mabel Kowalski; 188 Philadelphia Street; Pittsburgh, Pennsylvania 15762.

5. You buy merchandise and equipment for Tas-T Bakery in Lima, Ohio. This year, you asked for bids for 50 delivery trucks. The successful bidder was a firm in New York City, and you placed the order last month for delivery in four months. Now a new competitor has taken so much of your business that sales are off 25 percent. So you believe it wise to buy only 25 delivery trucks at this time. Perhaps you will be able to order the other 25 next year. Send a letter to New York to tell them the news. Address: Tom Brownlee Auto Mart; 413 East 121 Street; New York, New York 10039.

6. You own and manage the Bestways Tax Service, a firm that prepares both individual and business tax returns. Most of your business comes from individuals, and your busiest season is February through April. In January, you receive a letter from a local home for senior citizens (men and women ages 65 and older). The supervisor of the home requests that you give free tax counseling in February and March to 50 residents of the home. The commitment will require about 200 work hours for your seven tax counselors. Write a refusal letter. Address: Brenda Bushway, Supervisor; Bozeman Home for Senior Citizens; 888 Stafford Street; Bozeman, Montana 52390.

7. As sales manager for Lucky People Fashions, you offer a close-out sale of your slow-selling merchandise each year. Your inventory space at the factory is too small to allow you to store this merchandise. This year, you offered a 50 percent discount on men's jackets and pants with the agreement that no merchandise could be returned. Today, you received a letter requesting permission to return six dozen Number 5768 Trimline jackets that a customer was unable to sell. Write a refusal letter. Address: Johnny L. Davenport, Manager; Paris Best Fashions; 2424 Lawrence Avenue; Topeka, Kansas 61321.

8. You are sales manager for Computerville, a local dealer specializing in microcomputer sales. Last month, one of your representatives sold an Orange III microcomputer to a restaurant in the city. Two weeks ago, one of your technicians went to the restaurant to repair the microcomputer, which had broken down. Your sales agreement with the customer reads that a customer will not tamper with the machine when it breaks down but will call the company to send a technician to repair it. The technician saw that the casing on the machine had been pried open and that the seal was broken. She told the restaurant owner that this violated the sales agreement and left a bill for $200 for repairs. Today you received a letter from the customer saying that the guarantee is still effective and that he will not pay the bill. Write a letter refusing to cancel the debt and include a copy of the sales

agreement. Address: Hugh M. Willoughby, Owner; Round-O-Loin Steak Restaurant; 411 North Gates Avenue; Rochester, New York 11876.

9. You manage a local retail credit company. Two weeks ago, a young couple came into your office. They plan to add a room onto their home for a child they are expecting in six months. You saw that they really wanted the new room, so you asked them to complete a credit application. When you checked their credit references, you learned that they have made payments on some accounts as much as 120 days late. Write a letter refusing to lend them the $5000 they want. Address: Judy and Glen Pearson; 45244 Huntington Beach Boulevard; Long Beach, California 91098.

10. You own your own vehicle leasing company. Four years ago, a friend who lives in another state bought a new van from you on a lease/option agreement. While he did make the payments, he sometimes paid as much as 90 days late. The debt has now been paid, but it cost you in both interest and stress. Now, he has written you with plans to buy a camper. Write him a letter that will refuse the request but maintain your friendship. Address: Jerome Topping; 906 West Avenue; Lewiston, Maine 01211.

11. You own and manage a plumbing supplies company. Recently, you granted credit to a new customer, Wellsville Fixtures Company. Your decision was based on information supplied by Wellsville. Although your credit check did not uncover a problem, you learned by chance that this company's manager gave you false information about having bought merchandise on credit terms before. As yet, Wellsville has not pur-

chased anything on credit terms from a supplier. Write a letter retracting the offer to sell goods on credit terms. Ask that the firm buys from you for cash. Address: Walter Roush, Manager; Wellsville Fixtures Company; 105 North Lane; Wellsville, New York 14892.

Memorandum Cases

12. You work for a large paper manufacturer as personnel director. One morning, an employee came into your office and asked for information about another employee who wants to buy a sailboat from him. He wants to know if the other employee can afford to pay for the sailboat and asks about the man's income. You tell him that the information is confidential and refuse to disclose it. This week, you received a memorandum from the same employee making the same request. Write the man telling him once again that the information is confidential. Address: Percy Hamberg; Shift A; Littleton Building.

13. You are production manager in an office furniture factory. Yesterday, you received a memorandum from the marketing manager asking that you manufacture 475 Scepter desk chairs for next month's promotional sale. Your stock of the special aluminum alloy needed to make the chairs is depleted; a new supply will arrive in three months. Write a memorandum explaining the situation. Offer to make the chairs from steel alloy stock that you do have in inventory. Address: J. Terence Landry, Marketing Manager; Suite 45-A; Main Building.

14. As vice president for a large investment company, you just received a request from the supervisor of the word processing center. He tells you that the center's work load

is two weeks behind schedule. One answer is to allow employees to work on weekends, which they will do if paid double-time wages. Your company has always had a policy of never paying double-time wages. Also, you think it will set an example that employees in other departments might expect to follow if you grant this permission. You are willing to hire additional temporary employees if the supervisor can document the problem. Write a refusal memorandum. Address: J. Baxter Lanager, Supervisor; Word Processing Center.

15. As president of an automobile parts manufacturer, you received a memorandum today from an assembly-line employee. Last month, she tore her work uniform on a piece of equipment on the assembly line. She asked her supervisor to pay for a replacement. The supervisor refused, saying that the equipment is safe and that the tear must have been caused by carelessness. Write a memorandum to the employee telling her that the authority to make such a decision has been delegated to her supervisor. However, you will ask one of the vice presidents to discuss the incident with her supervisor. Address: Laura P. Zeigler; Bearings Assembly Room.

CHAPTER SIX

Persuasive Correspondence

The goals in studying the text and completing the activities in this chapter are to know

1. How to choose and write persuasive appeals in correspondence
2. The types of persuasive letters commonly written in business
3. How to write, critique, and revise persuasive letters
4. How to overcome special objections to taking favorable action on a persuasive request
5. Special tone factors to consider in writing persuasive memorandums
6. The types of persuasive memorandums commonly written in business
7. How to write, critique, and revise persuasive memorandums

For 20 years, Ellis Gladwin wrote a monthly newsletter called "Letter Logic" for employees of the Connecticut Mutual Life Insurance Company. In the final issue of the newsletter, written just before his retirement, Gladwin left his readers with this advice about persuasion, taken from Feodor Dostoevski's novel, *The Brothers Karamazov*:

> If people around you are spiteful and callous, and will not hear you, fall down before them and beg their forgiveness, for in truth you are to blame for their not wanting to hear you.

While the reaction suggested here does not fit any business situation, the nature of the advice is appropriate for writing persuasive correspondence. Once you become willing to assume the blame for any lack of success in messages you write, you will assume the responsibility for writing effectively. The result of taking charge of situations is that your efforts become more successful.

Persuasion in business correspondence is the *active* attempt to alter someone's attitudes or beliefs to get that person to take a desired action. For example, you may seek special assistance from or seek to sell a product or service to a reader. The persuasive process itself involves learning to

1. Reinforce presently held beliefs that support your proposition.
2. Weaken presently held beliefs that oppose your proposition.
3. Encourage the undecided reader to share your position.

To reach your goal (getting the reader to take the desired action), you will need a plan of attack. This plan will provide a framework to use in developing the discussion as you present ideas.

PLANNING PERSUASIVE CORRESPONDENCE

The A-I-D-A approach is an effective overall plan to use as a guide in writing persuasive letters and memorandums: Attention, Interest, Desire, and Action. This plan is organized inductively (indirectly) in that the writer justifies an action before requesting that the reader take the action.

Here is an outline and explanation of how the persuasive plan works:

1. *Open with an attention-getting statement.* The purpose of the opening statement is to interest the reader in reading the rest of the letter

or memorandum. You can gain reader acceptance most effectively by appealing to the reader's interests or needs. In doing this, be positive and brief and talk about some aspect of the topic itself.

2. *Get the reader interested in the topic.*   Begin by discussing appeals to engage the reader's interest in the topic of your letter or memorandum. Appeals are arguments you will use to generate reader interest. Focus on the central appeal since that will interest the reader the most. By starting with the central appeal, its position in the message will be emphasized (primacy effect). Continue building the persuasive effect of your argument by using supporting appeals and additional selling points.

3. *Build a desire to take action on the topic.*   Continue presenting reasons why the action is desirable for the reader. For example, point out the benefits of taking the action. Also, use words to picture the reader enjoying the benefits. If needed, play down any obstacles that stand in the way—the price of buying a product, for example.

4. *Close with an action request.*   Request *directly* but courteously that the reader take the desired action. Be positive and write in a confident tone showing that you are certain that taking the action is desirable and that the reader will take it. Suggest a specific time for taking the action and make it easy to do.

This overall plan is easy to follow, but just following it will not guarantee results. Rather, each step must be carefully developed and woven into the whole message. For ideas on how to open and close persuasive correspondence, consult the section on "Correspondence Opening and Closing Statements" in Chapter Three, Fundamental Correspondence Techniques.

Choosing and Writing Persuasive Appeals

Any logical and tasteful reason that will motivate a reader to take the action you request can become an appeal in a letter or memorandum. Once you decide to make a persuasive request, list the possible reasons or appeals that might be attractive to the reader. Look at these *entirely* from the reader's viewpoint. What will encourage the reader to act on your request? That is, what value is in it for the reader? For example, when making a persuasive claim on a faulty product, you might appeal to the reader's sense of fair play and desire to maintain good customer relations. On the other hand, if your appeal is that you deserve an adjustment, you are appealing to your own interests, not those of the reader.

If an appeal will benefit both you and the reader, add it to your list.

Remember, though, that readers are motivated by self-interests. For example, a request for a charitable donation may benefit the writer's cause, but an appeal to the reader's prestige or sense of satisfaction is more likely to motivate an action. In such a case, focus on the reader's rewards when writing the letter. A list of qualities that can make effective appeals in persuasive correspondence is shown in Figure 1.

Selecting Central and Supporting Appeals

When your list of appeals is completed, the next step is to choose the *central appeal* from the list. That appeal should be the one that you think will be *most* persuasive. To show how this works, suppose that you own a small investment counseling firm and that you both counsel clients about investments and make investments for them. Now you want to expand your services to include tax return preparation.

When you list your appeals before writing letters to your clients, they might include

1. Guaranteed correctness of the returns
2. Reliability of your service in the past
3. Knowledge of your clients' financial backgrounds
4. Efficiency of doing more financial business in one place
5. Lower prices than the competition
6. Quicker service than the competition
7. Expertise in preparing returns

The central appeal might be any one of the seven or even one not listed here. In fact, your choice may differ from client to client because their

---

POSSIBLE APPEALS FOR PERSUASIVE CORRESPONDENCE

1. Gaining sense of satisfaction
2. Giving comfort or convenience
3. Saving time, money, effort, or merchandise
4. Creating and maintaining goodwill
5. Increasing health benefits
6. Adding prestige, exclusiveness, or distinction
7. Gaining attractiveness (beauty and style of product, physical appearance)
8. Adding taste or wholesomeness
9. Gaining safety or security
10. Getting durability

FIGURE 1 Qualities for use in writing persuasive appeals.

needs and interests may differ. On the other hand, a single appeal may be the right central appeal for all of them.

Among the seven appeals listed, the first and seventh may be necessary to offer to get the business under any circumstances. However, neither of them may make the best central appeal because your competitors can make the same offers. The second appeal is an advantage for you that at least some of your competitors cannot offer; but perhaps some of them can—the bank, for instance. The fifth and sixth appeals are always attractive in a situation such as this, but they might be important only when combined with other appeals. The third and fourth appeals are strong incentives that you perhaps can offer exclusively. The third appeal seems especially strong because you already counsel these clients about investments and make investments for them. Then, you might choose "knowledge of your clients' financial backgrounds" as the central appeal.

Using a deductive procedure as in the one just described will help you to find the best central appeal for every persuasive letter or memorandum you write. When making considerations, look at the clients' specific interests and needs and then at how you can serve those interests and needs best. You will know for certain that you have chosen an effective appeal only when you get the readers' reaction to it. The procedure does work, however. Problems occur only when you do not have enough information about your reader to select appropriate appeals.

All appeals not chosen as the central one can become *supporting appeals*. As was true when choosing the central appeal, all six remaining ones may qualify. However, each of them should be examined to see if it is appropriate. In each case, an approach may persuade one client but not another. When this happens, different letters should be written to different clients. To show how to proceed in examining potential supporting appeals, here is a sample analysis of the remaining six.

Because the first and seventh appeals probably are needed to get the business under any circumstances, they should be included. Include the second and fourth appeals because they give you an advantage over at least some competitors. If your prices are low and your service quick (the fifth and sixth appeals), you might include these appeals. Include them if they are better than what the competition can offer. However, if they are not advantages, disregard them. Remember not to apologize for or try to reason away negative items (such as a high-priced service) because this merely will emphasize the negative aspects. Instead, ignore them; say nothing about them at all rather than emphasize them.

Assuming that the fifth and sixth appeals are not advantages, then the first, second, fourth, and seventh remain as supporting appeals to include in your letter. Along with the central appeal (the third item), these items form the basis for persuading clients to give you their tax return preparation business—steps 2 and 3 in the persuasive process. In all, you will have five appeals to write about in the letter.

Writing the Appeals

Here is a sample persuasive appeal for the letter to clients asking for their tax return preparation business that was discussed in the last section. The first paragraph develops the central appeal, and the second and third paragraphs develop the supporting appeals.

> Our clients have been asking us to prepare their state and federal tax returns ever since we opened for business in 1980. Many of them tell us that we know more about their financial needs than anyone else and therefore they want us to prepare their tax returns. This makes sense because we do counsel you and our other clients about your financial investments and make investments for you. Your investment portfolio is reviewed weekly in this office, and we can use this up-to-date knowledge of your financial background to determine exactly what tax deductions are available to you.
>
> To make certain that you get the best possible service, Janice Moriarity has joined our staff to work full time in offering this new tax service. Janice has fifteen years' experience in preparing tax returns. She is also a Certified Public Accountant and has a university degree in tax accounting. The correctness of your returns will be guaranteed.
>
> You will get the same reliable service that you have received from us in the past. We will review your tax records each time your investment portfolio is reviewed and will keep all these records in the same file. In addition, you can enjoy the convenience of doing more of your financial business in one place—no more running around the city at tax time to find someone to prepare your returns.

Notice that the central appeal appears first in the letter and that more is said about it than about any supporting appeal. These practices emphasize the central appeal, the major selling point. By following the central appeal with supporting appeals, they reinforce it. Also, they continue to persuade the reader to take the action that will be requested. If the appeals work well, the reader should be ready to take the action by the time you actually request it.

Putting Together the Complete Message

Once the appeals have been written, you only need to add opening and closing statements. The opening statement should grab the reader's attention so that he or she will read the appeals. The closing statement should request the action courteously and confidently; that request should be as specific as possible, and you should make the action easy to take.

Here is a complete version of the letter appealing for the tax return preparation business:

Dear Ms. Brown:

Serving your financial needs since (name the year) has been a pleasure. Now, there is a way to serve these needs more fully.

Our clients have been asking us to prepare their state and federal tax returns ever since we opened for business in 1980. Many of them tell us that we know more about their financial needs than anyone else and therefore they want us to prepare their tax returns. This makes sense because we do counsel you and our other clients about your financial investments and make investments for you. Your investment portfolio is reviewed weekly in this office, and we can use this up-to-date knowledge of your financial background to determine exactly what tax deductions are available to you.

To make certain that you get the best possible service, Janice Moriarity has joined our staff to work full time in offering this new tax service. Janice has fifteen years' experience in preparing tax returns. She is also a Certified Public Accountant and has a university degree in tax accounting. The correctness of your returns will be guaranteed.

You will get the same reliable service that you have received from us in the past. We will review your tax records each time your investment portfolio is reviewed and will keep all these records in the same file. In addition, you can enjoy the convenience of doing more of your financial business in one place—no more running around the city at tax time to find someone to prepare your returns.

Ms. Moriarity is ready now to begin reviewing your investment portfolio, but she needs your permission to go ahead. So that she will have plenty of time to get acquainted with the information in your file and begin studying your needs thoroughly, will you please give us your consent to go ahead by January 1. All you need do is sign the enclosed form and mail it in the enclosed postage-paid, return-reply envelope.

Sincerely yours,

The completed message follows the A-I-D-A approach to persuasion. All your letters and memorandums can follow this general outline successfully regardless of the specific type.

WRITING SPECIFIC TYPES OF PERSUASIVE LETTERS

The five types of persuasive letters that managers write frequently are (1) special requests for information or assistance, (2) requests to grant complex claims, (3) appeals for donations or contributions, (4) appeals to buy goods or services, and (5) appeals to pay debts. (Persuasive job application letters are discussed in the chapter on finding a job.)

Requests for Information or Assistance

A special request and a routine request for information or assistance differ. The routine request is made whenever the action you request is a part of the reader's normal job duties. Because of this, you should follow the favorable correspondence plan discussed in Chapter Four when making routine requests directly. When the action being requested is not regarded as a part of the reader's normal job duties, you should write a special request following the persuasive correspondence plan.

A special request must be reasonable to be effective. Such appeals work best when they involve the reader's self-interests. For example, if you want a customer to fill out a questionnaire telling you what type of insurance coverage she or he prefers, then appeal to the reader's needs to get what you want.

Here is the first draft of a letter in which this is done. The first draft is followed by a critique and then by a revised draft. (The questionnaire that accompanies this letter is shown in Figure 6 in Chapter Eight.)

First Draft | Dear Ms. Magnuson:

We are conducting a survey among men and women across the country pertaining to life insurance needs. The objective of the research is not only to find out what your needs are but providing them as well.

Your name was selected in a computer-derived random sample from a list of our customers who now have automobile insurance with Trumpeters. We value your business and now seek utilization of your opinions about other insurance that customers like you might need.

Your initial outlay will be to take a few minutes to complete the enclosed questionnaire. You have our assurances that your answers will be held in strictest confidence and will be used only for bona fide research purposes. No salesman will call on you as a result of your sharing your opinions with us.

Please complete and return the questionnaire as soon as possible. A postage-paid envelope is enclosed for your convenience.

Sincerely yours,

Critique | This letter is ineffective and is therefore likely to be ignored. The opening statement begins to develop an interest in the topic without first getting the reader's attention. No appeals are developed; the reader merely is asked for a favor without being given any incentive to grant the request. The most effective parts of the letter are the attempts to overcome reader resistance: (1) assuring that the information will be kept confidential and (2) promising that no salesperson will call. However, these assurances are undermined by the lack of certainty about how the information will be used.

The style is too formal for a business letter, and tone problems abound. Specific errors to correct are as follows:

1. The letter should open with an attention-getting statement followed by a clear statement of the purpose, which includes how the information will be used. Follow this with the appeals to take the action and then attempt to reduce the reader's resistance to granting the request. Then close with a specific action request.

2. The following expressions are too formal: (a) "pertaining to" in the opening sentence, (b) "utilization of" in the second sentence of the second paragraph, and (c) "you have our assurances" in the second sentence of the third paragraph.

3. The second sentence in the first paragraph is not grammatically parallel—"not only to . . . but providing".

4. The objective stated in the second sentence of the first paragraph implies a hidden motive. The reader might wonder why the writer wants to provide for her needs if no sale is being made. This implication is repeated in the second sentence of the second paragraph: "that customers like you might need." Then, the implication is repeated again in the first sentence of the third paragraph: "Your initial outlay" implies that something more is to follow. As a result of these implications, the assurances given in the third paragraph sound suspicious.

5. "Computer-derived" in the first sentence of the second paragraph and "initial outlay" in the first sentence of the third paragraph are jargon.

6. "Strictist confidence" in the second sentence of the third paragraph is redundant, and "bona fide" in the same sentence is a foreign expression.

7. "Salesman" in the third sentence of the third paragraph is sexually biased.

8. "As soon as possible" (first sentence, last paragraph) and "for your convenience" (last sentence in the letter) are general expressions and are stereotyped as well.

Revised Draft   Dear Ms. Magnuson:

Would you exchange one favor for another if it were very easy to do?

We need your help and would like to offer you our help in return. We are willing to deduct $2.00 from your July automobile insurance premium payment if you will take about five minutes to give us your opinions. And it won't cost you a penny.

For several years now, many of our customers have been asking us to offer them a life insurance plan. They want more complete insurance coverage from the company that insures their automobiles. At first, we were reluctant to do this, believing that we should continue to specialize in automobile insurance. But now we wonder if perhaps we can better serve our customers by offering broader coverage. Therefore, we are considering offering a life insurance plan.

You can help by telling us whether we should offer this extended coverage and, if so, what type coverage you think should be offered. A questionnaire is enclosed to make it easy for you to share your opinions. No salesperson will call on you as a result of your answering this questionnaire. Also, your answers will be kept confidential and will be used only for research purposes.

All you need to do is to complete the questionnaire and mail it in the enclosed postage-paid envelope by June 15. Then, $2.00 will be deducted from your premium before a statement is sent to you in July.

Sincerely yours,

Requests to Grant Complex Claims

The two types of claims on goods or services are *simple* and *complex*. A simple claim is one that clearly is justifiable to both the writer and the reader. The writer needs only to make the claim directly to have it granted and therefore will follow the favorable correspondence plan in placing it.

In a more complex claim, the reader might question or resist taking action for one reason or another, but the writer feels fully justified in making the claim. For example, assume that you have had your tax return prepared by a tax service that made certain guarantees about the quality of the service. Later, you find that one or more of the guarantees were not met, and thus you feel justified in seeking an adjustment. Such a claim letter should be written using the persuasive plan.

Here is the first draft of a letter in which this was the case. The first draft is followed by a critique and then by a revised draft of the letter.

First Draft   Dear Mr. Grantham:

Your "know all the latest changes in the tax codes" advertisement was the first and foremost reason for my selecting Quick-n-Easy Tax Consultants to prepare my federal tax return this year.

On February 3, I had my return prepared by one of your tax consultants, Jack Custou. Mr. Custou reassured me that you guarantee correct computations of all entries on returns, but nevertheless he would accompany me to the tax office if my returns were audited.

Wouldn't you know what would happen? On November 20, my

return was audited, and Mr. Custou went with me to the tax office as promised as mouthpiece for your company. While all entries on the return were computed correctly, the auditor told me that I could have deducted an additional $400 for an office that I maintained in my home and $300 depreciation on a personal computer that I purchased last year. I quite distinctly remember asking Mr. Custou about both these deductions when he prepared my returns, and he said that federal regulations did not allow for such deductions.

Because Mr. Custou did not "know all the latest changes in the tax codes," I feel that the fee in the amount of $75 that I paid your company to prepare the return should be reimbursed posthaste. Enclosed herewith is a copy of your advertisement guaranteeing your services. I'll expect payment soon.

Sincerely yours,

Critique   This letter does follow the persuasive correspondence plan, yet it is ineffective. While the style is informal, tone problems are serious enough to defeat the writer's objective, which is to recover the $75 fee. The abrupt opening and demanding tone throughout the letter will irritate the reader. The closing paragraph is unorganized. Also, the action request is not specific even though the request itself is repeated—"posthaste" and "soon."

Specific problems to correct are as follows:

1. Two sentences are too long for easy reading—the third sentence in the third paragraph (42 words) and the first sentence in the last paragraph (37 words).

2. Quoting the advertisement in the opening statement gets attention in a negative way by making clear that a complaint is looming. Closing the letter by repeating the quotation compounds the problem. These quotations are too direct and therefore are irritating.

3. "First and foremost" in the opening sentence is redundant as is "but nevertheless" in the second sentence in the second paragraph.

4. The first sentence in the third paragraph, "Wouldn't you know what happened?" can be omitted without losing any meaning. Also, the statement is flippant and presumptive.

5. The connotative meaning of "mouthpiece" in the second sentence of the third paragraph is demeaning.

6. "Quite distinctly" in the fourth sentence in the third paragraph is didactic (preachy). The connective "and" in the same sentence is incorrect; "but" is correct in this case.

7. "In the amount of" in the first sentence in the last paragraph is wordy. "Posthaste" in the same sentence is demanding, old fashioned, and indefinite.

8. "Enclosed herewith is" in the second sentence in the last paragraph is wordy and stereotyped. "I'll expect payment soon" in the last sentence in the letter is demanding and indefinite.

9. The second sentence in the last paragraph is misplaced and therefore changes the thought flow abruptly.

Revised Draft　　Dear Mr. Grantham:

Your advertisement that your tax consultants keep up with the latest changes in the tax codes led me to select your company to prepare my federal tax return this year.

Jack Custou, one of your consultants, prepared my return on February 3. At that time, he reassured me that you guarantee that the return is computed correctly. He also said that he would accompany me to the tax office if the return were questioned.

On November 20, the return was audited, and I was called to the tax office to explain several deductions. Mr. Custou went with me as promised and explained how the deductions were computed. While the auditor agreed that they were computed correctly, she also said that the tax code would have allowed me to deduct an additional $700. I could have deducted $400 for an office that I maintained in my home and $300 depreciation on a personal computer. When I asked Mr. Custou about these deductions when he was preparing the return, he said they were not allowed.

Because the consultant did not know about these changes in the tax code, the $75 fee I paid for preparing the return should be reimbursed. Therefore, will you please send this payment by December 31, the close of the tax year.

Sincerely yours,

Appeals for Donations or Contributions

Appeals for donations or contributions should always be written as persuasive requests. These appeals range from requests for money to requests for clothing, food, or some other goods. Write these appeals as letters when appealing to people who do not work for your own employer and as memorandums when writing to fellow employees.

The following is a first draft of an appeal for children's clothing, followed by a critique of the letter and then a revised draft:

First Draft　　Dear Mrs. Xavier:

Children are a source of joy in the lives of their families. When a two-year-old smiles or calls your name, you feel special.

Feeling special to someone else is something all of us can appreciate, especially when that someone is a child. Wouldn't it be nice if all children could be taken care of and provided for?

How many times have you disposed of your children's clothes thinking it a waste that they outgrow them before they wear them out? Here at the Weygandt Home for Children, our children's needs are basically provided for. But they are in need of winter clothes to warm them on these cold winter nights in Lubbock. You can help these children in a special way if you will donate the hand-me-downs from your family. The coat that your Susie or Jack outgrew last winter would provide warmth for our Susie or Jack this winter. The children at Weygandt get very excited when our cars come back from picking up donations. They are like children; they love to get something new, new to them at least.

Have your donations (sizes 3 to 12) picked up by calling 732-6570 between now and November 5. If you prefer, you are welcome to bring the clothes to the Weygandt Home yourself and meet the little orphans while you're here.

Donations to the home are tax deductible and receipts will be provided. But these donations provide more than tax deductions. They provide a real opportunity to do something for a child and to feel the warmth that comes from being important in a child's world.

Yours truly,

Critique   The style of this letter is appropriate, and the language flow is effective. The major problem is that the tone, which is warm in the beginning, builds relentlessly into a blatant appeal to pity. The central appeal is to sorrow for the children, a strongly negative way to persuade. For example, statements such as "new to them at least" and "meet the little orphans" are unabashed appeals to pity.

Other problems to correct in the letter are as follows:

1. The attention-getting opening sentence is not emphatic enough and perhaps is not interesting.
2. "Taken care of and provided for" in the second sentence in the second paragraph is redundant.
3. "In need of" in the third sentence in the third paragraph is wordy.
4. "Hand-me-downs" in the fourth sentence in the third paragraph is a figurative cliché.
5. "They are like children" in the seventh sentence of the third paragraph is incorrect factually. They *are* children.
6. The last two paragraphs should be interchanged. The mention of the tax deduction for donations in the fifth paragraph is a minor appeal and should precede the action request, which is now located in the fourth paragraph.
7. "Real opportunity" in the last sentence in the letter is redundant.

Revised Draft   Dear Mrs. Xavier:

Helping children grow up happily can be a joyful experience. When a young child smiles at you or calls your name, it makes you feel special.

Feeling special to someone else is something that all of us can appreciate, especially when that someone is a child.

How many times have you thrown away your children's clothing thinking it a waste that they outgrew them before they wore them out? Here at the Weygandt Home, our children's needs basically are provided for through generous donations by the citizens of Lubbock. But right now, some of them do need warm clothes for the winter.

You can help in a special way by donating some of the used clothing (sizes 3 to 12) that your children have outgrown. We especially need overcoats, gloves and mittens, and pants and skirts. The clothes that your children outgrew last year would serve our children well this year.

Donations to the home are tax deductible and receipts will be provided. But these donations will provide more than tax deductions. They provide an opportunity to feel the warmth that comes from being special in a child's world.

We will gladly pick up your donations any weekday between 9 A.M. and 5 P.M. If you prefer, you are welcome to bring them to the home at 18 Cross Lane and meet the children while you're here. Please call us at 732-6570 before November 5, the closing date of the appeal.

Yours sincerely,

Appeals to Buy Goods or Services

Called *direct-mail advertising,* selling goods or services in writing is practiced widely. You may write persuasive requests to mass audiences of hundreds or millions, to small groups such as the members of a club, or to individuals. In deciding whether you can afford to advertise by direct mail, consider the nature and size of the audience, the type and cost of the product, and the cost of preparing and mailing the letter and any enclosures. These considerations will lead you to a decision about whether you can sell an audience by mail and whether you can make enough profit to make doing so worthwhile.

Choosing Appeals and Screening Audiences

When writing a sales letter to an individual, you will have no need to vary the central or supporting appeals. Likewise, you may be able to send the same version of a letter to the members of a small group because of their similar interests.

When writing to mass audiences, however, you may need to vary both the central and supporting appeals to suit the special interests of subgroups within an audience. This need is especially evident with the central appeal. For example, assume that you want to sell solar-powered water heaters to homeowners. A high-income subgroup of your audience may be most interested in the tax deduction they can get if they buy the product; if so, then the tax deduction will make the best central appeal for this group. On the other hand, members of low-income subgroups may be most interested in the money they will save on their utility bills if they buy the heater; if so, this will make the best central appeal for this group. Such appeals are chosen according to certain demographic or psychographic factors, such as income (a demographic factor) in this example.

You also may decide about *whether* to mail a letter to a certain group of people based on demographic or psychographic factors. Called *screening the audience*, this is done to ensure that the people to whom you appeal are potential customers and therefore could be persuaded to buy. For example, assume that you want to sell portable radios by mail. You might first screen your audience to make sure that everyone you write is an adult who can be obligated legally to pay for the radio if he or she buys it. If owning the radios might appeal to people in a certain age group, say, people ages 18 to 30, you might further screen your audience by age. If you see that people who travel often might have a special interest in buying the product, then you might screen the audience further for a list of names of those who do travel frequently. This process can continue until you have a list of people who are the best candidates to buy the radios. Screening an audience in this way can increase your profits by decreasing your selling costs.

You can screen an audience yourself as just discussed or you can buy a mailing list that has been screened already for the demographic or psychographic factors that interest you. Some companies are in business solely to sell mailing lists, and companies that offer credit cards sell them too. For a fee, these companies will provide you with a list of names and addresses of people who fit the description you provide.

Overcoming Special Objections

The central and supporting appeals in your letter will overcome many and perhaps all of the objections your audience will have to buying the goods or services you offer for sale. Sometimes, however, audiences need special help in overcoming some types of strong resistance. Most special objections are about *low quality* or *high price*, and often there is a trade-off between these two factors. If the quality is high, the price may be high also. If the price is low, the quality may be low as well.

The best way to handle special objections to low quality is to offer guarantees; the better the guarantee you can afford to offer, the more you will be able to overcome the resistance. Ways to overcome special objections to a high price include low or no down payments, discounts, deferred buying plans, and pointing out that purchases are tax deductible when they are.

To show how this can work, first reread the letter on page 127 that is selling a new tax return preparation service. Then assume that the price of the service may be a special objection because some competitors have a lower-priced service than yours. To handle this, you could add this paragraph offering deferred payments just before the closing paragraph:

> If you prefer, we will gladly add the cost of preparing your returns to your monthly deferred payment for maintaining your investment portfolio. We estimate that most of our clients' monthly payments will increase by only about $5.00, depending on the amount of time required to prepare the return.

Here is the first draft of a letter selling a group of college students on the idea of coming in to look at the newest model of a car. That draft is followed by a critique and then by a revised draft.

First Draft

Dear (Student's Name):

Tired of heretofore missing the bus to classes? Tired of walking to the college day after day?

The time has come to terminate that experience by buying a BAMBI! Space Cadet Motors has the newest model of BAMBI. The car is a sleek, slant-backed model, ready to take you around Springfield or up to Chicago. BAMBI's 4-cylinder, 125-cubic-inch engine powers the most advanced ideas in sporty and economical cars. This configuration makes BAMBI look good.

Smirk at your friends. Acquiesce to their compliments. Avoid long gas lines. You can choose between a three-speed automatic transmission that gets 50 miles to a gallon of gasoline and a five-speed manual transmission that gets 60 miles to a gallon.

Features of the car include two fold-down, bucket-shaped, contoured front seats; a rear seat; a trunk; and pretty upholstery.

For students at Northside College who have approved credit, we have a special offer—no money down and low monthly payments. Those first 25 Northside students who come in to see the car will receive a free sweater. Stop by or call in to place your order. You'll get off on riding in your new BAMBI!

Sincerely yours,

Critique

The letter does not follow the persuasive correspondence plan. For example, the request to buy the car in the first sentence of the second paragraph is premature. (Cars are too expensive to sell outright in a letter, so the writer should focus on the idea of coming in to see and test drive the car.) Also, several of the appeals are given about the same amount of discussion with no one of them treated as a central appeal. Although less effective than they could be, the best ideas in the appeals are the attempts to have the reader visualize the experience of owning the car. These attempts are made in the third sentence of the second paragraph and the first two sentences of the third paragraph.

Specific problems to correct in the letter are as follows:

1. The ideas in the first paragraph are negative and lack emphasis. Also, "heretofore" in the first sentence is too formal.

2. "Terminate" in the first sentence of the second paragraph is a more complex word than is needed. "Configuration" in the last sentence of the same paragraph is jargon.

3. "Smirk" in the first and "acquiesce to" in the second sentence of the third paragraph have negative connotations. The fourth sentence of this paragraph says that the transmission gets the gas mileage rather than that the car gets it.

4. The fourth paragraph offers a list of the car's features without actually selling them.

5. A second attempt to sell the car by mail is made in the last paragraph. The action request should be to visit the showroom to see the car and perhaps to test drive it. To be specific, a date for the visit should be suggested. "Get off on" in the last sentence of the letter is a figurative cliché.

Revised Draft   Dear (Student's Name):

Want to get off your feet and into the driver's seat?
Want to put away that moped or those walking shoes?
Space Cadet Motors has a twofold answer for you: a smart new car and a plan to help you buy it *now*. Sound interesting?

The car is a new minicompact called BAMBI, and you can afford to drive it. The five-speed manual transmission model gets an outstanding 60 miles to a gallon of gasoline. No other car on the road today can match that performance. At the present price of unleaded gasoline, you can cruise around Springfield or up to Chicago for just 2 cents a mile! But if you prefer not to shift gears, you can choose the three-speed automatic transmission model, which gets 50 miles to a gallon. That performance too is unmatched in its class.

A lot of performance is under the hood too! The BAMBI has a powerful 125-cubic-inch, clean-burning, 4-cylinder engine that will accelerate to 50 miles an hour in just 7.6 seconds. You'll be charmed by the interior as well. The car has two bucket-shaped, fold-down seats that are contoured for comfortable driving for hours at a time. The 4-cubic-foot rear seat is ideal for carrying groceries, luggage, or a large dog. Then there's a roomy trunk, attractive triple-weave upholstery, and more.

How does the car look? The new BAMBI is a sporty-looking, slant-backed model that closely resembles an expensive European sports car. Just look at its sleek styling shown in the enclosed brochure. Compare those good looks to the ordinary box-shaped cars that so many people drive today.

You can own a BAMBI much more easily than you might think. As a Northside College student with approved credit, you can drive away in your new BAMBI with *no down payment*. Monthly payments are as low as *$77.50,* and you can take up to five years to pay.

Starting Monday, the first 25 Northside students who come in to see the new BAMBI will receive a free gold and black sweater with the Northside Rams logo on the back. Stop by our showroom at 9 Chamberlayne Avenue to see this smart new car. Test drive it while you're here. You *can* get off your feet and into the driver's seat, now!

Sincerely yours,

Appeals to Pay Debts

The most effective way to collect debts is to approach collections as a process. Three stages in the process are *reminder, inquiry,* and *persuasive.*

Reminder Stage

The first step in the reminder stage is to send only a statement of the amount due. If the customer pays within the proper time period, that is all there is to collecting a debt. But when the due date passes without payment, you may wish to send another copy of the statement as a reminder. This second reminder may be stamped "Second Notice," or you may include a brief favorable plan letter reminding the customer that payment is due.

Assume throughout the reminder stage that the customer intends to pay the account on time. Therefore, you are merely prompting payment. If you decide that you cannot afford the time it takes to send a second reminder, then send only the first reminder and proceed to the inquiry stage.

Inquiry Stage

Once you decide that something may be keeping the customer from paying the account on time, you should then write an inquiry letter. Perhaps the customer did not receive the statement or has not paid for some other simple reason. You should assume at this stage that the customer intends to pay you. So write to ask for payment or an explanation by a certain date. Follow the favorable correspondence plan when writing this letter.

Persuasive Stage

Once you decide that a customer must be prodded to pay a debt, you should then write persuasive appeals following the A-I-D-A approach presented in this chapter. You could choose from among the following appeals.

1. *Appeal to integrity.* An appeal to integrity is an appeal to the customer's sense of fair play or honesty. The idea is that "you owe the debt and therefore should pay it."

2. *Appeal to economic self-interests.* An appeal to economic self-interests is based on the fear of the consequences of nonpayment. These interests include possible loss of credit with your firm, loss of a good credit rating, and the cost of paying for having the account collected through legal recourse.

3. *Appeal to pride.* An appeal to pride can be both positive and powerful. The idea is that "paying the debt is a way to keep your self-esteem."

The persuasive appeal includes three steps if you wish to follow through completely with this stage of the process. The first step is a *mild appeal* in which you point to the benefits of paying the account and ask for payment by a certain date. The second step, called an *urgent appeal*, is a strong appeal to pay by a certain date. This appeal should be based on a vivid picture of the consequences of nonpayment. The third step, called an *ultimatum*, is a last attempt to collect the debt before taking an appropriate action to collect it. Appropriate action includes turning the account over to your lawyers or a collection agency for collection. This action may include suing the customer to collect the debt if necessary.

The letters in the first two steps of the persuasive stage may be written by the credit manager. But to lend authority to the last letter, a company officer usually writes it, perhaps the treasurer or a vice president.

Here is a revised (mailable) draft of a first step (mild appeal) persuasive stage letter written to collect a debt that is overdue:

Revised Draft Dear Mr. Jones:

Credit terms keep business activity alive. The buyer gets merchandise when he or she needs it, and the seller makes a sale.

We have appreciated the chance to sell merchandise to you on credit terms for the past two years. The arrangement has been good for you and good for us as well. Now, though, payment of your account is 60 days overdue. Although we have received no response to our inquiry about the problem, we still believe that you intend to pay the debt.

This oversight is causing a serious problem, however. The matter can result in the loss of your privilege to buy goods from us on credit terms. Also, perhaps you know that we are a member of the Detroit Credit Bureau Association. A requirement of that membership is that we report to the bureau all delinquent accounts that are 90 days overdue. Such an action could affect your good credit standing.

To avoid serious consequences that result from late payment, please send us a check for $1500 by October 1. That will place your account in good standing again and will allow you to continue buying merchandise from us on credit terms.

Sincerely yours,

WRITING SPECIFIC TYPES OF PERSUASIVE MEMORANDUMS

When writing persuasive memorandums, follow the same A-I-D-A approach that you follow when writing persuasive letters. While memorandums do differ in format from letters, they may also differ in tone. Remember that a natural tone is best. To write naturally, you should consider the rank of people to whom you write memorandums and your personal and working relationships with them. For example, your tone may differ when writing to superiors from when writing to peers or subordinates. Also, you may write in a different tone to a close friend in the company than to someone you do not know.

The topics of your persuasive memorandums will vary according to the nature of the work you do and the type of business in which the company is engaged. Two common reasons that employees write memorandums are to make special requests for information or assistance and to sell a service or idea.

Special Requests for Information or Assistance

Persuasive requests for information or assistance cover a wide range of topics. While routine requests are written as favorable news as discussed in Chapter Four, special requests should be written as persuasive news. Remember that special requests are those that the reader will not regard as a part of his or her normal job duties.

Here is a special request for an appointment to discuss adopting a flexible work schedule in a word processing center. A first draft of the memorandum is presented, then a critique of the first draft, and then a revised draft.

First Draft

To: Janet Schich, Director, Employee Services
From: Carroll Jauber, Director, Word Processing Center
Subject: Advantages of Flexible Work Schedule

I need your help with a big problem that I have in the word processing center.

About 80 percent of the center's employees are homemakers who find it difficult to work the 9 A.M. to 5 P.M. work schedule we keep. As a result, we have often had to lower our job requirements just to get enough employees to fill the jobs we have had available.

Now our competitors in the area, CopyRight Company and CompuText Industries, have adopted a flexible work schedule in their word processing centers. Their employees can report for work as early as 6 A.M. or can stay as late as 7 P.M. Also, they can work as little as 30 hours a week if they choose. Consequently, our competitors are stealing our employees who are homemakers.

Were we to adopt a work schedule like theirs so that we could compete with them effectively, we would need to hire five more employees. We could do this without increasing the total number of hours worked a week. So, without increasing our labor costs, we could offer our employees greater freedom in choosing the hours they will work. Therefore, those homemakers who now work for the center will be encouraged to stay on with us and other qualified homemakers will be encouraged to apply for a job with us.

Adopting these changes will cut our turnover rate. Your department will then enjoy a lower cost of hiring and training new employees.

I look forward to hearing your feelings about this proposal.

Critique   The most effective parts of this memorandum are the developments of the second and third steps (developing interest in the topic and creating a desire to take action). The appeal could be strengthened in two ways, however:

1. The idea that competitors are stealing employees who are homemakers (third paragraph) could be made more credible by offering facts in addition to the opinion.

2. The plan presented in the fourth paragraph could be more effective if the benefits were presented before the needed action is mentioned. That is, say that the proposed change will cost nothing before saying that additional employees are needed.

The writing style and language flow are effective. The least effective parts of the memorandum are the opening and closing statements. Even though a forthright request can be effective, the opening statement is self-centered and negative. The closing statement does not suggest any particular action and therefore just leaves the problem hanging.

Revised Draft   To: Janet Schich, Director, Employee Services
From: Carroll Jauber, Director, Word Processing Center
Subject: Advantages of Flexible Work Schedule

Could I interest you in a plan that will reduce your hiring and training costs and will reduce the employee turnover rate in the word processing center at the same time?

About 80 percent of the center's employees are homemakers who find it difficult to work the 9 A.M. to 5 P.M. work schedule we now keep. As a result, we often have had to lower our job requirements just to get enough employees to fill the jobs we have had available.

Now our competitors in the area, CopyRight Company and CompuText Industries, have adopted a flexible work schedule in their word processing centers. Their employees can report for work as early as 6 A.M. or can stay as late as 7 P.M. Also, they can work as little as 30 hours a week if they choose. Consequently, our competitors are stealing our employees who are now homemakers—8 within the last month alone.

We could adopt a flexible work schedule to allow us to compete with them without increasing our labor costs. Just by hiring five more people, we could allow our employees to work fewer hours if they choose. Yet the total number of hours worked in the center will remain the same. Homemakers who now work for the center will then be encouraged to stay on with us. Also, other qualified homemakers will be encouraged to apply for jobs.

Hiring these new employees and changing to a flexible work schedule will result in your department's enjoying a lower total cost of hiring and training new employees. At the same time, the center's turnover rate will be reduced.

May I have an appointment with you next week to discuss these proposed changes? I will be in Santa Barbara on business all day Wednesday but will gladly meet with you on any of the other four workdays.

Selling a Service or an Idea

You may sometimes need to sell a fellow employee on buying or adopting a service or on adopting or allowing you to adopt an idea. While the topics of these memorandums will vary, you should follow the A-I-D-A approach of the persuasive correspondence plan when writing them. Here is a revised (mailable) draft of a memorandum selling a new employee on the idea of joining the company's credit union.

Revised Draft

To: Jason Kupzik, Financial Analyst
From: C. O'Dell Aprisner, Credit Union Supervisor
Subject: Financial Services of Company's Credit Union

Congratulations on assuming the duties of your new job as a financial analyst with the company.

As a part of the company's orientation program for new employees, we want to introduce you to the company credit union. The credit union exists solely to serve employees. Once you become a member, you can borrow at the lowest interest rates available anywhere today—13 percent annually. Members can borrow as much as $5000 at a time and can take as many as five years to pay. Just imagine driving that new car you've been wanting or getting that new furniture for your home or apartment. Perhaps you've already tried to save enough cash to make such a major purchase but just needed the right plan to make your savings program work. The credit union offers a plan that works every time.

By investing as little as $50 monthly, you can become a credit union member. Your money is safe when invested in the program because every penny you invest is guaranteed by a federally insured protection plan. You won't need to rush around town on your lunch hour to make financial transactions; the credit union office is right here in the building. In addition, a full 10 percent annual interest rate, compounded daily, is paid on all your deposits.

A brochure containing details about how the credit union investment program works for you is enclosed. This month, we are making a special offer to employees who wish to apply for membership. By depositing as little as $50, you will receive *12 percent* interest on all deposits made during the next 12 months. Please stop by the credit union office in Room 114 before April 30 to talk with us about the program. We look forward to meeting you then.

The persuasive correspondence plan works regardless of the topic of the letter or memorandum you need to write. Therefore, any time that persuasion is needed to get the action you want, use the A-I-D-A approach. Then, if the style, tone, and content are appropriate, your persuasive correspondence will be effective.

SUMMARY

Persuasive letters and memorandums are written when you want a reader to take some action but must justify your request. An indirect method, called the A-I-D-A approach, is an effective overall plan to follow when writing these messages. These letters stand for Attention, *Interest*, *Desire*, and Action, which represent these steps:

1. Open the correspondence with an attention-getting statement.

2. Interest the reader in the topic.

3. Build a desire to take the desired action.

4. Close the correspondence with an action request.

In the second and third steps, you should persuade the reader to take action on your request by using central and supporting appeals. A central appeal is that reason for tak-ing action that will motivate the reader the most. Supporting appeals support the central appeal by continuing the persuasive process. The best procedure to follow is to first identify and write the appeals and then to add an opening and closing statement. The opening statement should grab the reader's attention, and the closing statement should include a specific request to take action.

Five common types of persuasive letters are (1) special requests for information or assistance, (2) requests to grant complex claims, (3) appeals for donations or contributions, (4) appeals to buy goods or services, and (5) appeals to pay debts. A special request for information or assistance asks for an action that is not a regular job duty for the reader. A complex claim differs from a simple claim in that a reader is likely to question a complex claim unless it is fully justified.

An appeal for donations or contributions

ranges from requests for money to requests for clothing, food, or some other goods. A request to buy goods or services is called direct-mail advertising. When selling by direct mail, you may need to vary the appeals to fit the interests of various subgroups of your audience. Also, you may need to screen your audience before writing to decide which ones are prospective customers. In addition, any special objections to taking action, such as quality and price considerations, should be overcome in the message so that readers will respond favorably.

Three stages in the debt collection process are reminder, inquiry, and persuasive. The first two stages call for writing in the favorable news plan, but the third stage calls for writing in the persuasive news plan presented in this chapter.

Persuasive memorandums should follow the same A-I-D-A approach that you use to write persuasive letters. The format of memorandums differs from that of letters, however. The tone of memorandums will differ from case to case depending on the rank of persons to whom you write and your personal and working relationships with them. Two common types of memorandums that employees write are those making special requests for information or assistance and those selling services or ideas. For both types, the subjects you write about will vary according to the nature of your job and the type business in which your employer is engaged.

Additional Readings

Bonner, William H., and Jean Voyles. *Communicating in Business: Key to Success.* Houston: Dame Publications, 1980, pp. 93–123.

Bowman, Joel P., and Bernadine P. Branchaw. *Successful Communication in Business.* San Francisco: Harper & Row, 1980, pp. 173–219.

Himstreet, William C., and Wayne Murlin Baty. *Business Communications: Principles and Methods,* 6th ed. Boston: Kent, 1981, pp. 155–199.

Huseman. Richard C., James M. Lahiff, and John D. Hatfield. *Business Communication: Strategies and Skills.* Hinsdale, Ill.: Dryden Press, 1981, pp. 164–186.

Lesikar, Raymond V. *Business Communication: Theory and Application,* 4th ed. Homewood, Ill.: Richard D. Irwin, 1980, pp. 239–307.

Murphy, Herta A., and Charles E. Peck. *Effective Business Communications.* New York: McGraw-Hill, 1980, pp. 328–393.

Sigband, Norman B. *Communication for Management and Business,* 3rd ed. Glenview, Ill.: Scott, Foresman, 1982, pp. 457–492.

Swindle, Robert E. *The Business Communicator.* Englewood Cliffs, N.J.: Prentice-Hall, 1980, pp. 243–256.

Treece, Malra. *Successful Business Writing.* Boston: Allyn & Bacon, 1980, pp. 228–285.

Wilkinson, C. W., Peter B. Clarke, and Dorothy C. M. Wilkinson. *Communicating Through Letters and Reports,* 7th ed. Homewood, Ill.: Richard D. Irwin, 1980, pp. 264–307, 379–430.

Review Questions

1. Define persuasion as it is used in business correspondence.

2. Explain how the A-I-D-A approach to persuasion works. Discuss each step in the process.

3. Define a central appeal and explain how

this appeal is chosen in persuasive correspondence.

4. Define a supporting appeal and explain how this appeal is chosen in persuasive correspondence.

5. Explain the difference between special and routine requests for information or assistance. Which correspondence plan should you follow to write each of them?

6. Explain the difference between simple and complex claims on goods or services. Which correspondence plan should you follow to write each type of these claims.

7. Explain how to screen an audience before writing an appeal to buy goods or services.

8. How can you overcome special objections that people may have to buying goods or services? What are the most common types of special objections?

9. What are the three stages in the debt collecting process? Define each stage.

10. Give two situations in which you might write a persuasive memorandum to a fellow employee to sell a service or idea.

Exercises

Letter Cases

1. Business at your furniture store has fallen off 40 percent. The cause of the problem is a nationwide recession. Unemployment is especially high in your area. Experts agree that economic conditions should improve in about four months. You have information to show that it will improve in your area along with nationwide improvement. Write your major furniture supplier to ask for a four-month delay in making payments on your account. You will gladly pay interest charges on the balance during that time. Address: J. P. Ownby, Credit Manager; White Hall Furniture Company; 749 Pine Lane; High Point, North Carolina 28714.

2. The apartment you rent needs repairs. The plumbing fixtures leak, the paint is peeling from the walls, and several windows are broken. The owner of the building in which you live is a local bank that is noted for spending little money to maintain its rental units. Write the bank's real estate manager to request repairs. Persuade her that the bank will benefit by making the repairs and then maintaining the apartment thereafter. Address: Elvira M. Jessup, Supervisor; Real Estate Division; Valley National Bank; Grand Rapids, Michigan 43256.

3. You work for Tomaz Research Associates as a research analyst. One of your clients, Willis Record Shop, asked you to study the effects of declining record sales in its market area. You prepared a questionnaire that will be mailed to the record shop's customers to get their opinions. Now write a form cover letter to accompany the questionnaire. Persuade the customers to take 10 minutes to complete the questionnaire and return it to you within two weeks.

4. While on a visit to Toronto, you found a chair in a store there that you liked so much that you bought it. The chair is an unusual design that you have never seen before. When it arrived by railway express one month later, you unpacked it eagerly.

Although the shipping carton was not damaged and the packing was done correctly, both arms have fallen off the chair. The product carried no guarantee, but you feel that the company should replace it or pay for repairs. Write a persuasive letter to the store manager. Address: Alec LeMeire, Manager; Toronto Furnishings Limited; 1121 Bloor Street; Toronto, Ontario E5N 3K5.

5. While visiting Albuquerque on business, you had a suit cleaned by a dry cleaners near your hotel. Because you didn't wear the suit as planned at that time, you inspected it only after arriving home. When you did look at it, you found a 4-inch burned spot on the left leg of the trousers. Then you found a similar burned spot on the lapel of the coat. You cannot wear the suit again, and it cannot be repaired. Write a letter to the cleaners asking for a check to pay for another suit. The suit cost $350 and is three weeks old. Ship the damaged suit to the dry cleaners for inspection. Address: Lamont Cleaners; 81 West Lomas Boulevard; Albuquerque, New Mexico 81742.

6. You serve as director of the Yarborough Senior Citizens Center, a home for people ages 65 or older. The residents of the center told you that they would enjoy having a color television set in their recreation room. The center is a nonprofit operation, and no funds are available to buy the television set. Write a letter requesting that a local business donate a television set to the center. Address: Sandra Albemarle, President; Yarborough Electronics; 159 Center Street; Yarborough, Massachusetts 09311.

7. You serve as a volunteer worker for Helping Hand, a local charitable organization. Your job is to administer the record-keeping system. Currently, records are kept manually, which is an inaccurate and time-consuming method. You wonder if a large company in your city might donate a used microcomputer for your use. Another solution is for the company to allow you to keep your records on its system; if this can be done, you would manage all the data and maintain the records yourself. Write the letter. Address: Pierre Meyer, President; Little Town Distributing Company; 9870 Pearl Road; Cleveland, Ohio 40033.

8. You own and manage a women's formal wear store, which just opened for business. As a part of your advertising campaign, you decide to write a letter to women whose engagements are announced each week in the local newspaper. You should describe your product line and service. Also, you might wish to offer a special discount or some other incentive to get them to visit the store. Write the form letter.

9. As sales supervisor for a large lighting fixtures company, you just received an order for 200 Model 98 antique brass porch lamps. The buyer is one of your best customers. While you will be glad to fill this order, these lamps have been selling slowly for other customers. Besides that, you recently imported a different line of antique brass porch lamps from Copenhagen, Denmark. These lamps are selling better than any such lamp you have ever stocked, but they cost $10 more per unit than the model the customer ordered. Because the customer has a small store, you know that an additional order is unwarranted. Therefore, you decide to write a letter to persuade the customer to buy the new model instead. Address: M. Mary Renquist, President; Pine Bluff Lighting Company; Pine Bluff, Arizona 77329.

10. You have just opened a house cleaning service with a staff of 25 employees. This service will appeal best to people who earn between $25,000 and $40,000 yearly. As a part of your advertising campaign, you bought a mailing list of names and addresses of individuals and couples who might buy the service. Now you are preparing to write a form letter to persuade them to become customers. Write the letter and include an introductory offer as a special incentive.

11. As sales representative for a music store, you specialize in selling keyboard musical instruments. Also, you are responsible for seeing that your customers pay their accounts. Six months ago, you sold a piano to a young couple whose son is taking music lessons. They paid one-half of the $3500 price and agreed to pay the remaining $1750 in three months. You sent them a statement three months ago and followed with an inquiry letter six weeks ago. You have heard nothing from them. An additional problem is that they live 300 miles away and have never answered their telephone when you have called. Write a first-step persuasive appeal letter to the couple. Persuade them to pay the debt. Address: Mario and Annie Lipitzer; 4321 East Van Buren Street; Colorado Springs, Colorado 82225.

12. Assume that you are the sales representative mentioned in Exercise 11. You received no response from the Lipitzers. You checked to see if they still live at the address they gave you, and they do. However, they still do not answer the telephone when you call. Write an ultimatum telling them to pay you or you will turn over the account to your company's lawyers for collection.

Memorandum Cases

13. You manage the personnel division for a large investment counseling service in your city. The company has three branch offices in addition to the main office in which you work. When you were closing the office yesterday, you noticed a stack of confidential contracts laying atop a work table. When you picked them up to put them away, you also noticed three employee information files on the table as well. The next day, you ask the supervisor who did it. She doesn't know. Then you call the supervisors at the three branch offices and learn that they have had the same problem you're having. You decide to write a form memorandum to all personnel employees. Remind them of the need to secure all confidential files before leaving work each day. Also, remind them of the procedure to follow in securing confidential files.

14. You work as a marketing representative for a data processing vendor in Birmingham, Alabama. You are about to try to make a large sale to a local company that you have visited several times already. You believe that if a systems engineer from the Chicago office would come to Birmingham and accompany you on the next visit to the firm, you could make the sale. This is an unusual practice, but this is a special situation. Write a memorandum to the sales manager in the Chicago office making the request. Address: Alexander Hallman, Sales Manager; Computer-X Company; 49999 Wacker Drive; Chicago, Illinois 66674.

15. You work as a senior internal auditor at Drexler Industries in Madison, Wisconsin. As a part of your job, you often write reports to upper-level managers. Most of these reports contain statistical data. To

help you prepare more effective tables and figures for these reports, you want to attend a computer graphics seminar that will be held in Houston, Texas. The seminar is entitled "Applying Computer Graphics to Accounting Problems." Write a memorandum to your supervisor asking her to give you the time off from work to attend the seminar and to grant permission for reimbursement of your expenses. Address: Amy D. Lowe, Vice President; 400 Statler Wing; Masters Building.

UNIT 3

Written Communication

REPORTS

CHAPTER SEVEN

Planning the Report Process

The goals in studying the text and completing the activities in this chapter are to know

1. The importance of reports in business
2. The role of reports in the communication process
3. The value of the audience in report writing
4. The logic of the problem-solving report process
5. How to define and limit a research problem clearly
6. How to determine the scope of a problem or to formulate hypotheses to solve a problem
7. The importance of a research plan in report writing
8. The various parts normally found in a research plan

In today's businesses, reports are becoming increasingly important. As you learn and practice effective reporting skills, you will become more valuable on the job. One reason for this is that your reporting skills will become systematic and thorough rather than overburdening. In addition, managers who read your reports will be able to observe your skills.

Good reporting skills require more than writing ability. Other communication skills—reading, listening, speaking, and observing—are just as important for writing effective reports. The completed report is the product of a series of communication tasks that are linked together as a related process.

REPORT DEFINITION

A report is the result of a process whose purpose is to transmit meaningful data to an individual(s) for either informational or decision-making purposes. A report may be presented in either written or oral form. Your manager may ask you for both a written and an oral report for the same project. In addition to presenting data in a report, you also should arrange and analyze the data so as to make it meaningful to your reader. A business report is intended to achieve one of two objectives: (1) to provide managers with information, such as the sales history of a certain territory, or (2) to aid them in decision making, such as your analysis of a new inventory system.

CLASSIFICATIONS OF REPORTS

Businesses require many different types of reports. These reports can be classified by *function, directional flow,* and *formality.*

Reports Classified by Function

The first type of functional report is *informational.* This report presents facts in a comprehensive and organized manner but does not analyze or interpret facts.

Some common types of informational reports are

Accident reports	Process descriptions
Annual reports	Employee manuals
Committee reports	Inspection reports
Credit reports	News releases

Periodic reports	Recruiting brochures
Personnel reports	Sales reports
Policy statements	Service manuals
Progress reports	Training manuals

The second type of functional report is *analytical.* This report presents facts, but also it analyzes and interprets those facts. Based on the purpose of this report, your analysis and interpretation will result in your drawing a conclusion and perhaps making a recommendation for a course of action.

Some common types of analytical reports are

Accounting reports	Physical research reports
Budget reports	Product analyses
Feasibility reports	Proposals
Market analyses	Sales analyses

Reports Classified by Directional Flow

Reports classified by directional flow are called vertical, horizontal, or external reports. This classification is based not on function but rather on movement within or outside the business where the report originates.

The *vertical* report moves either up or down within the organizational structure of the company. A periodic departmental activity report may move upward within the organization whereas a policy statement may move downward.

A *horizontal* report moves among individuals, departments, and divisions within the organization. For example, a personnel report may flow from the marketing department to the personnel department.

An *external* report flows outside the business. These types of reports include annual reports sent to stockholders and recruiting brochures sent to prospective employees.

Reports Classified by Formality

Based on their style, you may classify reports as either formal or informal. Generally, formal reports are traditional, long reports written in an impersonal writing style. Informal reports, however, are usually short and are written in a personal writing style in either a letter or memorandum format. For information about style, consult Chapter Two. For information on how to write and design the format of formal reports, consult Chapter Eleven; for the same information on informal reports, consult Chapter Twelve.

REPORTS AND THE COMMUNICATION PROCESS

The communication process is followed in researching and writing reports just as in other types of communication. Figure 1 shows a model of the communication flow for a marketing report from the beginning of the idea to the delivery of the report.

Assume that the marketing problem is to determine whether a new product should be added to the current product line. This problem has been identified either by the marketing manager or a subordinate. Once the problem has been identified, the marketing staff member conducts the research and presents the results in final report form to the marketing manager. Once the marketing manager receives the report, he or she reads it and interprets the findings. (Note in Figure 1 the broken line between the decoder or receiver and the destination. This broken line means that the marketing manager could have been the last person to receive the report.) This manager could then make a decision based on the report's findings. In this model, however, the vice president of marketing makes the decision and directs the action to be taken concerning whether to add the product line. Because the vice president of marketing used this report to make the decision, the purpose of the report has been fulfilled. The broken line at the bottom represents feedback that provides information about the report back to the information source.

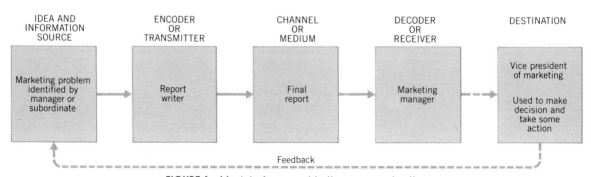

FIGURE 1   Model of a report in the communication process.

Barriers Affecting the Report Audience

To write reports, you need to be aware of those barriers that may affect the report's audience. A barrier is *any* element that inhibits the free flow of information between the sender and receiver. Four of these barriers are prevalent in a reporting situation:

1. *Use of technical language.*   Define any terms that your audience may not understand.
2. *Lack of knowledge in the area.*   Provide your audience with sufficient clarifying information.
3. *Poor organization of ideas.*   Organize your report so that your audience can follow your logic.
4. *Lack of interest in the subject matter.*   Create interest in your report project by convincing your audience of the possible benefits of your ideas by using good persuasive writing techniques.

Writing for the Report Audience

Regardless of the report writing situation, remember who will be the receiver of your message. A report writer can lose sight of the reader because of the writer's involvement in the project. For example, when you begin to write the report, you may assume that your reader has the same basic understanding of the topic as you do. As a result, you may omit needed information.

In addition to being aware of the barriers affecting the audience, the following are some questions you may ask yourself regarding your analysis of your audience:

1. What does your audience want to know?
2. For what purpose is the audience using your reports?
3. Will there be more than one reader?
4. If there are two or more readers, who are they?
5. What is your audience's educational level?
6. Does your audience have a positive attitude toward your subject?

Having information about the audience of your report will help you to determine what content and organizational flow to follow in writing it. If your audience is unfamiliar with the topic, then perhaps you may have to lengthen your report so as to include more preliminary information. Therefore, when you begin to write a business report and even when you prepare your final report, you need to remember not only your report's purpose but also your audience's needs.

Each report writing project has as its focal point a problem that needs to be solved. Fully understanding the problem is the key to your success in report writing.

PROBLEM ORIENTATION

You can follow five basic steps to solve a problem. These steps are common to all types of business research reports. The flow chart in Figure 2 shows the steps involved in the problem solving process. The first step shown in the model is to define the problem. Because it is the core that each succeeding step must have as its base, problem definition is the most crucial step in the entire process. Using this approach will allow you to progress to each step in the process properly oriented toward your ultimate goal.

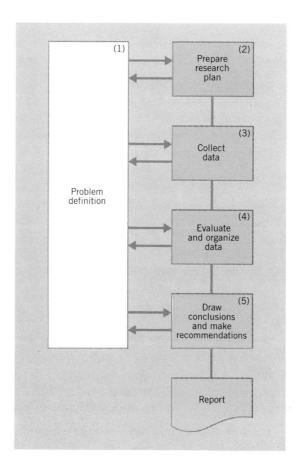

FIGURE 2 Model of the problem-solving report process.

In the remainder of this chapter, you will look at the first two steps of the problem solving process. The last three steps are covered in Chapters Eight and Nine.

Defining the Problem

As mentioned earlier, the problem you are defining is the key to successful report writing; this problem should be made clear at the beginning of the report process. However, defining the problem may not be an easy task. Therefore, criteria that will help you to define the problem clearly in your mind are (1) doing preliminary research, (2) limiting the problem, (3) determining the scope, (4) identifying the factors, and (5) formulating the hypotheses.

Doing Preliminary Research

When you are asked to write a report, one of two possible situations may exist. First, you may be so familiar with the problem subject area that you can clearly define what the problem may entail. An example is an accountant who may be asked to write a report on an accounting problem. Second, you may not have a clear idea of what the problem is; therefore, you may have to do some preliminary research into the background of the problem.

Whatever the situation, you should begin by making sure that you understand specifically what the authorizer (person granting permission to conduct the study) wants from your report. Does the authorizer just want information, or does he or she want a recommendation? Sometimes this person may not be completely familiar with the problem; therefore, you may need to read background material. Or you may have to talk to experts who may be familar with the problem area. As you read, talk, and collect preliminary background information, think constantly about this information as it may relate to your problem. The result of this thought process is a clear understanding of what the problem entails. Then depending upon the reader's knowledge of the subject, a section on background of the problem may be needed in the final version of the report.

Limiting the Problem

As you familiarize yourself with the problem, write it down in such precise terms that you know exactly the goal of your research. Often, the problem or purpose of your report will be so broad that you will have to limit it. One way in which to limit your problem is to ask yourself these five questions:

1. *What* is it that you want to do?
2. *Why* are you doing it?
3. *When* is the report due (time period)?
4. *Who* is going to be studied?
5. *Where* is the geographical area to be studied?

To apply these questions to a problem situation, assume that Beta Sporting Goods, located in Chicago, Illinois, is thinking about expanding to another location. The owner has asked you to look into this possibility. What do you do now? The first thing you should do is to ask yourself these five questions to help you to clarify your answers to the owner, the report authorizer in this case:

1. *What:* A study of three possible expansion sites
2. *Why:* To determine whether the expansion is feasible
3. *When:* Within the next two years
4. *Who:* Beta Sporting Goods
5. *Where:* Chicago, Illinois

After you have limited the problem to three expansion sites and to the possibility of expanding within the next two years within the Chicago, Illinois, area, you can now write a precise problem statement.

Here is a problem statement:

Problem: to analyze three possible expansion sites within the Chicago, Illinois, area for Beta Sporting Goods and to determine whether expansion is feasible within the next two years.

This problem statement was written in an infinitive phrase form. This form is perhaps the most commonly used today. However, you can also write the problem statement in question or declarative form. Here are examples:

What is the feasibility of Beta Sporting Goods expanding to one of three locations within the Chicago, Illinois, area within the next two years?

The problem of this study is to analyze three possible expansion sites within the Chicago, Illinois, area for Beta Sporting Goods and to determine whether expansion is feasible within the next two years.

Determining the Scope

When you analyze the problem situation, another criterion to keep in mind is the scope of the problem. In other words, what are the qualifying boundaries of the study? You will need to determine what problem areas are to be studied as well as what problems are not to be studied. This process allows you to identify how thorough your research needs to be to solve the problem.

For example, assume that the business you presently work for is considering buying a new copying machine for under $4000. Your supervisor has asked you to investigate this situation. After doing preliminary research and thinking about the problem, you write the problem statement. Now assume that you have written the problem statement and have limited your study to three copy machines. A possible scope statement may be as follows:

> This study will focus on three copying machines priced below $4000. A comparison of these machines will be based on an analysis of their costs, operating features, and special input-output qualities. This study will not include a comparison of their physical features such as their weight, dimensions, and color because all three copying machines have fairly similar physical features.

Note that this scope statement is tentative; that is, items may be added or deleted as you continue to research. However, this statement helps you to identify how much depth your research will require.

Identifying the Factors

After you determine the scope of the problem, the next step is to identify factors that are involved. Sometimes these factors are called elements, descriptors, criteria, or categories. Whatever term you prefer, try to identify those key factors that will help you to solve your problem. Your analysis of these items will form the basis of any conclusions you draw and any recommendations you make.

These factors will provide you with a framework with which to begin the collection phase of your report process. Also, you are beginning to develop a tentative outline for the writing phase. Note that these factors serve as a tentative outline; therefore, you may have to add or delete some of them as you get into your collection phase.

Look again at the Beta Sporting Goods problem. Remember that this problem basically deals with the feasibility of expanding the company's business operations to another location in Chicago, Illinois. What factors that you uncovered in the preliminary research could you list that may be considered in solving your problem? Please note that these factors will extend your scope.

Here are some factors that you may identify:

1. Cost
2. Site selection

3. Competition
4. Demand
5. Employee availability
6. Traffic flow

While you may think of other factors to include, the point is that you can see that the problem is starting to become more structured and orderly. In other words, you have the items that allow you to begin your research effort.

Formulating the Hypotheses

Sometimes you may have a problem situation that requires you to analyze alternative solutions. Therefore, you should formulate hypotheses statements rather than identify factors. When you formulate hypotheses statements, you are trying to determine some alternative solutions to a problem that you will test during your research. These statements will serve as a basis for your findings.

You can write a hypothesis statement in either the directed or null form. A directed hypothesis predicts the alternative solution that you expect to occur. An example is

> Using individualized instruction for in-service managerial training will result in higher achievement than will using the traditional large-group instruction.

A null hypothesis, however, states that there are no differences between the alternative solutions. Two ways of writing a null statement are

1. No significant difference in achievement will result when using individualized instruction for in-service managerial training than when using the traditional large-group instruction.
2. The type of instructional method used in in-service managerial training will have no effect on achievement.

The null hypothesis statement is used more often in research for two basic reasons. First, the null form makes the statement more objective. Second, it reduces any of the researcher's bias about the results.

Preparing a Research Plan

A research plan is merely a logical and organized pattern of material that gives the researcher guidance throughout the collecting, evaluating, and writing phases of a project. Put another way, the process of preparing the plan at the beginning of the research effort allows the researcher to decide what needs to be accomplished to solve a problem. Also, a well-developed research plan contains virtually all the items needed for the introductory section of the final report. (General suggestions about planning your writing are given in Chapter One.)

Sometimes researchers refer to a research plan as a proposal. Although many items included in a research plan also are contained in a proposal, they do differ. In business, proposals are written generally to get projects accepted either within or outside the company or to seek money by obtaining grants. Therefore, the approach used in writing a proposal is somewhat different from the research plan because it requires additional information. Proposal writing is presented in Chapter Twelve on special applications of report writing.

Research Plan Format

Formats for research plans may vary because of specific requirements identified by the report authorizer. However, the following items usually are included:

1. Statement of the problem
2. Background of the problem (if applicable)
3. Scope of the study
4. Statements of hypotheses (if applicable)
5. Sources and methods of data collection (may include a tentative bibliography)
6. Tentative general outline
7. Work progress schedule or timetable

Note that the first four items come directly from the problem definition phase of the report process. The tentative general outline actually will be an extension of the factors you have identified. The sources and methods of data collection section provides a step-by-step description of how the data will be collected. If the research is to be purely bibliographic (material collected from books and periodicals), you may wish to include a tentative bibliography. If you plan to collect data through conducting interviews or administering questionnaires, then these methods need to be identified. Also, if your data require statistical analysis, include a discussion of the statistical methods that you will be using. How to collect data is discussed in Chapter Eight.

The work progress schedule is an important aid in the planning stage of research because it forces you to think about the time needed to complete your report. In other words, you develop self-imposed intermediate goals for accomplishing each task of the report process.

RESEARCH PLAN FOR ABSENTEEISM PROBLEM
AT DELTA MANUFACTURING COMPANY
HOUSTON, TEXAS

Statement of the Problem

The problem of this study is to review the effect of the high absentee rate among operations personnel and to examine feasible remedies.

Scope of the Problem

This study will focus on absentee plans that are objective and concrete. It will not consider those plans involving personality evaluation or modification; for example, plans that require supervisors to become more authoritarian or that require a personnel manager to study carefully the personality traits of prospective employees will not be covered.

Sources and Methods of Data Collection

The data for this study will be collected from company files on absenteeism and from interviews with supervisors and operations personnel. Also, data will be collected on various absentee plans from journals and books about management and personnel supervision.

Tentative General Outline

I. Absenteeism situation
    A. Rate of absenteeism
    B. Cost of absenteeism
II. Types of absentee control plans available
    A. Desriptive control plan
    B. Disciplinary control plan
    C. Reinforcement control plan
    D. Other types of control plans
III. Comparison of alternative plans
IV. Conclusions and recommendation

Work Progress Schedule

January 14–January 20	Review absentee files in personnel office
January 21–February 5	Interview supervisors and operations personnel
February 6–February 20	Collect data on absentee plans from professional journals and books
February 21–March 2	Organize and evaluate the data
March 3–March 10	Write the report
March 11–March 15	Type and proofread the report
March 15	Submit final report to personnel manager

FIGURE 3 Illustration of a research plan.

When preparing a work progress schedule, allocate your time realistically. By setting realistic intermediate goals and by following your schedule closely, you can establish work priorities for the time you have available. Also, you can reduce anxiety about the completion date of the report. In business, sometimes you may be called upon for a report of your progress on a particular project. If you have followed your schedule closely, this task will be easy.

Research Plan Preparation

Assume that you work in the personnel office at Delta Manufacturing Company in Houston, Texas. The personnel manager has just had a conference with the plant manager about the high rate of absenteeism among operations personnel at the plant. This situation is critical, and the personnel manager has asked you to look into this problem. Figure 3 is an example of a research plan which you might prepare regarding this absenteeism problem.

SUMMARY

A report is the result of a process whose purpose is to transmit necessary data to people for either information or decision-making purposes. Reports may be classified by function, directional flow, or formality. Two types of functional reports are informational and analytical. Directional flow reports are called vertical, horizontal, or external reports. Based on formality, reports are either formal or informal.

The audience should be analyzed when planning the research. And, in doing so you should be aware of communication barriers.

The five basic steps in solving a research problem are (1) define problem, (2) prepare research plan, (3) collect data, (4) evaluate and organize data, and (5) draw conclusions and make recommendations. The first two steps are discussed in this chapter.

Defining the problem involves doing preliminary research, limiting the problem, determining the scope, identifying the factors, and formulating hypotheses. In doing preliminary research, consult with the report authorizer and read background material if needed. Ask *what, why, when, who,* and *where* to limit the problem. Setting the scope is qualifying the boundaries of the study. Factors are the key elements that will help you to solve the problem. An hypothesis predicts the problem solution that you expect to occur.

Preparing a research plan is done merely to design a logical, organized way in which to collect and evaluate data and write the report. The plan should have a clear and detailed format and should be completed before the research begins. A completed research plan is shown in Figure 3.

Additional Readings

Brown, Harry M. *Business Report Writing.* New York: D. Van Nostrand, 1980, pp. 191–196.

Brown, Leland. *Effective Business Report Writing,* 3rd ed. Englewood Cliffs, N.J.: Prentice-Hall, 1973, pp. 3–16, 67–74.

Himstreet, William C., and Wayne Murlin Baty. *Business Communications: Principles and Methods,* 6th ed. Boston: Kent, 1981, pp. 282–286.

Leedy, Paul D. *Practical Research: Planning and Design,* 2nd ed. New York: Macmillan, 1980, pp. 41–63.

Lesikar, Raymond V. *Report Writing for Business,* 6th ed. Homewood, Ill.: Richard D. Irwin, 1981, pp. 1–28.

Lewis, Phillip V., and William H. Baker. *Business Report Writing.* Columbus, Ohio: Grid, 1978, pp. 3–13, 23–40.

Murphy, Herta A., and Charles E. Peck. *Effective Business Communications,* 3rd ed. New York: McGraw-Hill, 1980, pp. 539–543, 630–632.

Sigband, Norman B. *Communication for Management and Business,* 3rd ed. Glenview, Ill.: Scott, Foresman, 1982, pp. 148–153, 186–187.

Smith, Charles B. *A Guide to Business Research: Developing, Conducting, and Writing Research Projects.* Chicago: Nelson-Hall, 1981, pp. 15–47.

Treece, Malra. *Effective Reports.* Boston: Allyn & Bacon, 1982, pp. 3–26, 111–129.

Wilkinson, C. W., Peter B. Clarke, and Dorothy C. M. Wilkinson. *Communicating Through Letters and Reports,* 7th ed. Homewood, Ill.: Richard D. Irwin, 1980, pp. 433–447.

Wolf, Morris Philip, Dale F. Keyser, and Robert R. Aurner. *Effective Communication in Business,* 7th ed. Cincinnati: South-Western, 1979, pp. 360–370, 383–389.

Review Questions

1. Why is it important to develop effective reporting skills?

2. What is a report? What purposes does a report serve? Give some specific examples of reports with different purposes.

3. Explain the difference between an informational report and an analytical report.

4. Why do report writers need to be aware of barriers to effective communication?

5. What effect does audience analysis have on effective reporting?

6. Discuss the importance of clearly defining the report problem?

7. Why is it so important to determine the scope of a problem?

8. What is the purpose of identifying factors? formulating hypotheses?

9. Why is a research plan a valuable aid to a report writer?

Exercises

1. Using the list of common types of informational reports in the text as a guide, locate an actual business informational report. Identify key items in it and explain why the report is informational.

2. Identify a report problem situation from one of the business areas (accounting, data processing, finance, etc.). Then, apply it to the model of the communication process in this chapter. Discuss your findings.

3. Using the following broad topics, write a problem statement for each topic that limits the topic precisely:
   a. Inflation accounting
   b. Consumer price index
   c. Capital budgeting
   d. Word processing
   e. Commercial lending

4. Using the problem statements you wrote in Exercise 3, what are some factors that apply to each problem? (Note: If you cannot identify any factors from your own knowledge, you might then do some preliminary investigation.)

5. Using the following problem situations, write a hypothesis statement for each in both the directional and null form:
   a. Effect of the N.O.W. account (negotiable order of withdrawal) on Third National Bank
   b. Change in inventory methods at Crane Plumbing Supplies, Incorporated, from FIFO (first-in, first-out) to LIFO (last-in, first-out)
   c. Results of use of MBO (management by objectives) techniques at Lee Motors
   d. Increasing the advertising budget for Shine-it Furniture Polish
   e. Effects of use of microcomputers at the Smith and Porter law firm

6. Select one of the problem situations from Exercise 5 and prepare a research plan.

CHAPTER EIGHT

Collecting Research Data

The goals in studying the text and completing the activities in this chapter are to know

1. The four typical applications of secondary research data
2. The various business reference sources in the library
3. The effect of technology on the research process
4. The three common primary research methods
5. The various sampling procedures
6. The importance of validity and reliability in primary research
7. The guidelines for effective questionnaire development
8. The advantages and disadvantages of common survey techniques

Collecting data is the next step in the research process after defining the problem. This involves accumulating data or facts that you will need to evaluate and interpret in the next phase of the process. Since this step can be both complex and time consuming, you should take time to develop an overall plan before you begin. Then take an organized approach to each stage as you proceed.

Research data come from either primary or secondary sources. Primary data come from an original source such as from observation or questionnaires. Secondary data come from an intermediate source such as material from books or microfilm. In other words, you get information directly from the source in primary research but indirectly from the source in secondary research. Some studies require collecting data from both primary and secondary sources.

COLLECTING SECONDARY RESEARCH DATA

Before you actually begin collecting secondary research data, stop to consider the uses you might make from it. Four typical uses of secondary data are to use them to

1. Determine whether similar research has been done already. If similar research has been done, you may be able to use that information to solve your problem, or you may be able to use it as a guide for conducting your own study.

2. Support an action that you take to solve a problem.

3. Identify any related areas that should be researched. Perhaps other problems need to be solved in addition to the one you are considering.

4. Justify the need for a proposed research study in cases where the need might be questioned.

In any research effort, you should be aware of all the sources that will help to solve the problem. The first step is to prepare a bibliography for your subject area.

Preparing a Bibliography

A bibliography used in this context means that you begin to identify and list all the sources that may contain some data that you believe are related to your subject. The purpose is to list all the sources that you will locate and review later in the library. Sources you might include are company publications, general reference books, books, periodicals and government documents. See Appendix B, Business Reference Sources, for a detailed compilation of sources that may be of value to your area of research.

Company Publications

Company publications are developed, produced, and written for a specific organization. These may include newsletters, bulletins, brochures, pamphlets, handbooks, manuals, and company records and reports.

General Reference Books

General reference books include sources such as almanacs and biographies. Two major guides to specific reference books in your area of interest are the *Guide to Reference Books,* 9th ed. (American Library Association, 1976; 1980 and 1982 supplements available), by Eugene Paul Sheehy and *Where to Find Business Information* (John Wiley, 1979) by David M. Brownstone and Gorton Carruth.

Books

Other sources that can be added to your bibliography are books related to your topic that are located in the library. The key to finding what you want in the library is the classification system. Books may be classified or cataloged either in the Dewey Decimal or the Library of Congress system.

In the Dewey Decimal System, the books are classified by numbers into 10 categories. In business and economic research, you probably would be interested in two categories: 300 – Social Sciences and 600 – Technology. In the Library of Congress system, the books are classified by letters into 20 categories. Of these 20 categories, one category would contain specific sources for business and economic subject matter: H – Social Sciences.

Understanding the Catalog System   The catalog system is an alphabetical index of books and perhaps periodicals and reference sources. The index may be on cards or on microform. (Microform is discussed in a later section of this chapter.) Each book in the catalog system is classified in at least three separate ways: according to author, title, and one or more subject areas. Figures 1, 2, and 3 are examples of these three classifications in the Library of Congress system.

In beginning your search through the catalog, you may not know of any specific books or authors in your research area. However, because you do know the subject area, you can consult the subject catalog for that area. If you cannot find any books under your subject heading or those closely related, consult the *Subject Headings Used in the Dictionary*

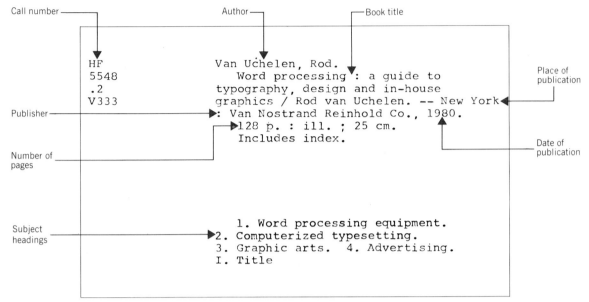

FIGURE 1 Author classification.

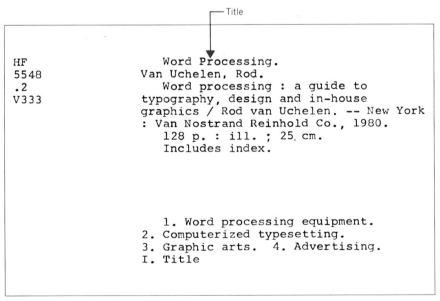

FIGURE 2 Title classification.

```
                                  ┌─ Subject
                                  │
                                  ▼
  HF                 Word processing equipment.
  5548               Van Uchelen, Rod.
  .2                   Word processing : a guide to
  V333               typography, design and in-house
                     graphics / Rod van Uchelen. -- New York
                     : Van Nostrand Reinhold Co., 1980.
                         128 p. : ill. ; 25 cm.
                         Includes index.




                       1. Word processing equipment.
                     2. Computerized typesetting.
                     3. Graphic arts.  4. Advertising.
                     I. Title
```

FIGURE 3   Subject classification. (*Note:* Three additional subject entries will be catalogued under "Computerized typesetting," "Graphic arts," and "Advertising.")

Catalog of the Library of Congress, which is usually located near the catalog files.

Using Other Sources to Find Books   Very likely, your local library will not have many books in your subject area. To find out what other books are available, you can consult three different sources: *Cumulative Book Index, Publishers' Weekly,* and *Subject Guide to Books in Print.* The *Cumulative Book Index* includes books published since 1928 by author, title, and subject area. *Publishers' Weekly* lists books, pamphlets, and paperbacks that are published each week. *Subject Guide to Books in Print* identifies books presently available in the United States.

If you do not find books that you need from one of these sources, you may be able to get them from another library near you. If not, your librarian may be able to borrow them from some other library through what is called an interlibrary loan service.

Periodicals

Periodicals are those magazines, journals, and newspapers published at regular intervals, such as weekly or monthly. These publications provide the most current data you will be able to find about your research topic. You can find the source of appropriate articles in magazines and journals by checking various indexes. Two of the most helpful indexes for business research are *Readers' Guide to Periodical Literature* and the *Business Periodicals Index*. For newspaper sources, consult your local newspaper index (if available), *The Wall Street Journal Index*, or *The New York Times Index*.

If you do not find enough material through the indexes that relates to your research topic, consult either the *Ayer Directory of Publications* or *Ulrich's International Periodicals Directory*. These directories contain the names of periodicals that relate to your subject area.

To find out what libraries hold the periodicals you want, consult the *Union List of Serials in Libraries of the United States and Canada*. This resource provides you with a comprehensive list of periodicals and the libraries that hold them. This list is updated by the *New Serial Titles*.

Once you have identified which library has the periodicals you need, you can ask your librarian if copies of the periodicals can be borrowed through the interlibrary loan service. You should note that some libraries will not lend the entire periodical, but they will make photocopies of articles contained in them.

Government Documents

Various federal, state, and local governmental agencies publish a vast amount of data of interest to researchers. For example, the state commerce department and the research divisions of state universities are two places where you can find data related to many areas of interest to a business researcher. In addition, you can find publications from your state, as well as other states, by consulting the *Monthly Checklist of State Publications*. When you are searching for U.S. government publications, the first place to look is in the *Monthly Catalog of United States Government Publications*. In this guide, current publications for all federal agencies are listed. Monthly and annual indexes also are prepared.

If you have sufficient time to collect governmental data, you can write the U.S. Government Printing Office in Washington, D.C., and ask for a list of its publications in your research area. Once you receive this list, you can determine what publications you may want to purchase from them. Another source to help you find the various periodicals available from the federal government is the *Index to United States Government Periodicals*.

Many other materials are published by the federal government, ranging from statistical data from the Bureau of the Census to the Small Business Bibliography series from the Small Business Administration (see Appendix B). Other sources that you may consider are those records and reports available to you through the Freedom of Information Act. This act allows any individual the right to review all records of federal agencies of the executive branch unless those records are exempted specifically by the act. The exemptions range from defense and foreign relations classified information to information involving an individual's personal privacy. This act does not apply to records of the U.S. Congress, federal courts, state and local governments, or private organizations. In making a Freedom of Information Act request, describe as accurately as possible the type of records you want. If these records need to be photocopied, you will have to pay the cost.

Other Sources of Secondary Research Data

Several other sources of data are available for researchers (see Appendix B). Two of these other sources that may interest you are

1. *Trade and professional associations.*   Various materials from trade and professional associations are available. You can consult the *Encyclopedia of Associations* for names, addresses, and publications offered through these associations.
2. *Subscription services.*   Libraries and some companies subscribe to certain financial services. These include services ranging from investment and income tax to general information about companies and the economy. This information is available through the mail and by computer terminal. Some of the better known firms offering these services are Dun & Bradstreet Corporation; Standard & Poor's Corporation; Commerce Clearing House, Inc.; and Prentice-Hall, Inc. To determine what services may interest you, you can consult the *Directory of Business and Financial Services.*

Technological Developments for Secondary Research Data

New technological advancements are providing researchers with the opportunity to find data quickly and accurately. Two developments that are being used in libraries are microforms and computerized literature search services.

Microforms

With the amount of data increasing each day, microforms have been developed to reduce the size of the data and make them easier to file through a photographic process. The two common microforms are microfilm and microfiche. Many libraries carry only microforms of periodicals.

Microfilm comes in 16mm (millimeter) or 35mm reels that contain data that are viewed sequentially on a reel-to-reel reader. Microfiche comes in 6″ × 4″ cards that contain a limited amount of data printed in a grid system. The viewing process allows you to gain access to the data randomly rather than sequentially as with microfilm. Both forms can be copied with the use of a photocopy attachment. Therefore, if you want copies of any data located on either form, the copies can be reproduced for you.

Computerized Literature Search Services

The use of the computer is easing the time-consuming process of locating secondary data manually. The computer can access various files or data bases for many subject areas. The result of this process is a computer-produced bibliography that often contains abstracts of the citations contained in the data base. After reviewing the abstracts, you can decide whether to locate and read the entire article.

Establishing a search strategy is extremely important before conducting the computer search. You need to determine key word descriptors for your topic because the computer will search through all the citations in the data base that contain the key word descriptors. You also have to decide what data bases you want to search and any publication date limitations. Obviously, having a broad topic and searching all available data bases with no date limitations can be a costly process. However, your librarian will work with you to determine the best strategy. Also, see sources in Appendix B.

Once you have located a particular source through your search effort, you need to record the specific data that will be helpful in solving your problem.

SUGGESTIONS FOR EFFECTIVE NOTE TAKING

The recording or note taking phase in research is often viewed as a rather routine or passive process. This phase, however, should be treated as an active and thought-producing process that contributes to your knowledge base. If you treat this phase with a questioning attitude, you will begin to identify and understand the relationship of the printed data to your overall problem.

Once you begin the actual collection process, use these questions as guidelines as you read, think about, observe, and review the data you find:

1. Are the data *directly* related to the problem or are they just nice things to know?

2. Will the data have a definite effect on solving the research problem?

3. Will the report audience need the data to make a decision about the results of the research study?

4. Are the data related to the current factors being studied and do they support or refute these factors?

5. Could these data be subfactors of the factors being studied or could they be new factors?

6. Do these data lead in any directions other than that of the problem itself?

7. Are these data current or are they too old to use?

8. Are the data from valid and reliable sources? For example, what reputation does the publisher or author have?

9. Are the data accurate? If opinions are presented, are they supported fully?

10. Do the data include all aspects of a particular issue?

The answers to these questions will help you to screen secondary information to come up with the most effective data to use to solve your problem.

Using these questions as a basis for your recording phase, you should follow a systematic and orderly plan to take notes. This plan includes the following steps:

Step 1   *Review pre-established factors.*

When you analyzed your research problem as discussed in Chapter Seven, you began to identify factors relating to your research problem. These factors should be reviewed and should serve as the starting point for finding related data.

Step 2   *Prepare a tentative list of pre-established factors.*

This tentative list will give you direction on how your factors relate to one another as well as provide you with a foundation for your written outline. As you find additional factors or related factors, you can write them on the list in the appropriate area.

Step 3   *Scan the source for major or related factors.*

If the source is a book, you might review the table of contents or index for factors. If the source is a periodical, you might concentrate on the major headings and their topic sentences. This process will give you a general overview, and it will help you in determining whether the data are worth pursuing.

Step 4   *Prepare a bibliography control card.*

Once you determine that a particular source contains data that you would like to record, prepare a 5″ × 3″ index card. Also, prepare a separate index card for every other source you use. These index cards will serve as a control measure that will be keyed to your note cards. The control cards serve two purposes. First, you only have to write the bibliographical reference once on the control card with a corresponding key symbol. Second, when the search is completed, all you have to do for typing your bibliography is to alphabetize the cards.

The key symbol system can be based on numbers, letters, or a combination of the two. Regardless of the system used, each source should be assigned its own key symbol. On each card, the entire bibliographical reference should be written. For example, periodical sources should include the author(s), article title, name of magazine or journal, volume and number of issue, date of publication, and page numbers. The proper format for writing bibliographical entries is discussed in Appendix C. Also, you should write the catalog classification number on the control card just in case you need to locate the source again at the library. An example of a bibliography control card for a book is shown in Figure 4.

Step 5 *Prepare one note card for each factor.*

Your next step is to use either a 6″ × 4″ or 7″ × 5″ index card for your actual note taking. In preparing your note card, write the key symbol for the source on either top corner of the card. Then, write the factor near the top of the index card. After you have written the factor, leave

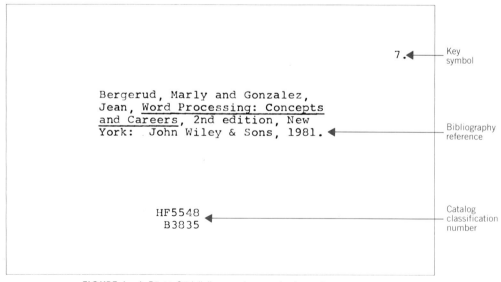

FIGURE 4   A 5″ × 3″ bibliography control card.

space and then write the page number and the corresponding note (see Figure 5). To aid you in organizing data, prepare a separate note card for each new factor or subfactor. Even when you find a discussion of the same factor in two different sources, prepare separate note cards. One comment or idea per card will provide maximum flexibility in the organizational process.

Step 6   *Determine the type of note.*

In the note that is illustrated in Figure 5, a direct quotation was copied. In addition to a direct quotation, there are three other types of notes: paraphrasing, outlining, and summarizing. In a direct quotation note, you should copy the note word by word without changing the punctuation or spelling. Paraphrasing is writing the major idea of the data in your own words. Although the data are in your own words, you still should footnote the source in your report. Footnote documentation is discussed in Appendix C. In an outline note, record the key word(s) from a particular paragraph, page, article, or chapter in an organized format. A summary note, which is similar to a paraphrased note, allows you to condense the major ideas from all or part of an article or book chapter. Reference the sources of both outline and summary notes.

If you wish, jot down some of your own ideas at the bottom of the note cards. This will help further when you evaluate and interpret the data later.

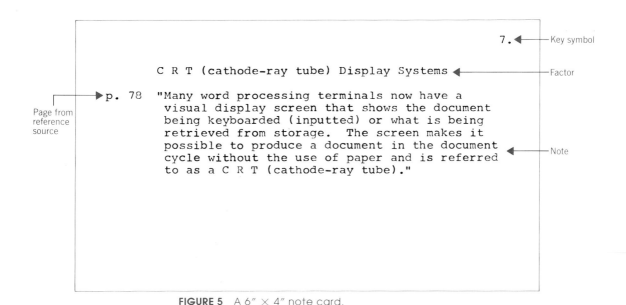

FIGURE 5   A 6″ × 4″ note card.

Step 7   *Arrange note cards in a logical order.*

This last step of note taking actually is the first step of your organizational phase. As you record a note for a factor or subfactor, include the note immediately with your other corresponding notes. From this arrangement, combined with a tentative list of all your factors and subfactors, you will now be able to prepare your writing outline. The organizational phase of report writing is presented in the next chapter.

When you begin to find the same data repeatedly in different sources, close your data search. By this time, you probably will have collected three, four, or five times the amount of data that you will need to solve your problem.

Very often, secondary data are not available to support a solution to a business problem. The nature of business problems often requires going directly to the source to get the information that is needed.

COLLECTING PRIMARY RESEARCH DATA

In collecting primary research data, you should consider two important aspects: time and expense. For example, conducting personal interviews and preparing and administering questionnaires can be time consuming and expensive. These factors are considered in selecting the research method you will use. Other research considerations are sampling procedures and the data collection procedures.

Primary Research Methods

Primary research data can be collected by one of three research methods: *experimental, observational,* and *survey* or by a combination of these methods.

Experimental Research Method
The experimental research method seeks to determine whether a change of one factor causes change in another. For example, assume that a bank wants to know whether opening on Saturday morning would increase the number of customers. To find out, an experiment can be conducted to measure the effect of the Saturday morning hours (factor A) on the number of customers (factor B).

A major consideration in conducting this experiment is to develop a research design that ensures that the change in the number of bank customers is due only to the change in hours. This means that you must consider such outside influences as similar promotions by competing banks or unusual changes in the weather. Many research designs exist, and you should become familiar with the techniques and the limitations of these designs before conducting experimental research.

Observational Research Method

The observational research method involves either a human or a mechanical viewing of the actions or results of some person or group of people. It may also involve other senses: hearing, touching, smelling, and even tasting. Perhaps you may have observed an individual on a street corner counting automobiles. That is an example of collecting data by observation. Another example is the filming of a process on an automobile assembly line to study the efficiency of procedures being used. Observational research can be used to examine external actions. Therefore, observers must be instructed about what to look for and how to record observations in a consistent and accurate manner.

Survey Research Method

In the survey research method, the researcher collects data from respondents by asking questions or posing statements to be responded to on questionnaires. The purpose is to determine opinions, attitudes, beliefs, or reactions about various work situations, issues, policies, procedures, or products, for example. The survey method is used most often in business because the type of information most often needed can be collected only by this method.

Combination of the Various Research Methods

Although it is very likely that you will choose one of the three primary research methods for collecting primary data, you should not eliminate the possibility of combining methods. For example, you may conduct an experimental study testing the effectiveness of large-group instruction and individualized instruction in your company's training program. In addition, you may want to survey the participants to get their attitudes about the training in which they were involved. This survey could be administered either by having the participants complete a questionnaire or by conducting personal interviews.

Sampling Procedures

In collecting primary research data, the ideal would be to use *every* member of a large group or *population*. The term "population" as used in this context refers to all the members of a large, representative group. For example, the population could be all business administration majors in a college of business or perhaps all the registered Democrats or Republicans in a state. If you were to question each member of the population, you would secure the information you need for each member of this large group. Attempting to question the entire group, however, can be costly and time consuming. Therefore, instead of trying to collect information from the entire group, you can use a *sample* of respondents from this large group.

Sampling requires selecting from a large group or population a subgroup or sample that is representative. The representative sample will have similar characteristics to those of the population. If the sample is representative of the population, you will be able to generalize or apply your findings to the entire population.

Once you have identified the population for the study, you must determine how the sample will be chosen. Various sampling methods are available, but they generally are classified into probability and nonprobability sampling methods.

Probability Sampling Methods

Three common types of probability sampling methods are simple, systematic, and stratified random sampling. For each of these techniques, you must have some list, directory, or roster that identifies all the members of the population. For example, one list may be all the real estate brokers in a particular state.

Simple random sampling involves the selection of a sample where every member of the population has an equal chance of being selected. For example, you could put all the names of the real estate brokers in a box or container and then pick out the number of names that would be representative of the entire population. Another procedure would be to use a table of random numbers. Consult a text or reference book on basic research methods and procedures for tables of random numbers and instructions on how to use them.

Systematic random sampling is similar to the simple random sample technique except that you would pick the sample based on some predetermined interval. In other words, every nth member of the population is chosen from the list for the sample.

Stratified random sampling consists of dividing the population into subgroups based on similar characteristics. Then a simple random selection is made within each subgroup to form the sample. In the case of the real estate brokers, you could stratify them according to sex, geographical location, educational level, or a combination of these subgroups.

In selecting the proper sample, you must be aware of the relative proportion of the subgroup to the total population. For example, assume that the list of brokers' names consists of 70 percent males and 30 percent females. Also assume that you want a sample size of 1000 brokers. Then you would select at random 700 names from the male subgroup list and 300 names from the female subgroup list. Therefore, the use of stratification offers you the opportunity of having more representation in the sample based on certain population characteristics.

Nonprobability Sampling Methods

In nonprobability sampling, the members of the sample group are not selected at random because

1. The entire population list is not available for the study.
2. Enough money or time is not available to use a probability sampling method.
3. You may not need to generalize the results of the research to the entire population.

The two common nonprobability methods are judgment and quota sampling.

Judgment sampling requires you to select a representative sample based on your informed opinion that the sample would have some characteristics of the entire population. For example, if you want to question corporate controllers about some accounting policy, you may sample several controllers who are members of a local accounting association. You cannot generalize the results to all corporation controllers, but the findings would offer some indication or direction of the accounting policy.

Quota sampling, however, involves the selection of a representative sample based on certain characteristics of the population that are proportionate to the sample. For example, assume that the population of the corporate controllers in a state is 30 percent employed in large-sized corporations, 50 percent in medium-sized corporations, and 20 percent in small-sized corporations. A quota sample of 1000 controllers would be to select 300 controllers from large-sized corporations, 500 from medium-sized, and 200 from small-sized. This technique is similar to the stratified random sampling technique, except that the quota sample is filled based on a nonrandom technique.

Data Collection Procedures

In survey research, once you have identified a population and selected a sample group of respondents, you are ready to determine what answers you need to solve the research problem. In other words, you will need to plan, design, and select a series of questions or statements for the respondents. Their answers will give you the data needed to solve the problem. The list containing your questions or statements is called a *questionnaire*. For data collected by questionnaires to be useful, they must be both valid and reliable.

Validity and Reliability

An objective of all research is to collect valid and reliable data to use to solve a problem. Simply put, research procedures are valid when they measure the concepts or issues that they are intended to measure. For example, when you design a study to measure employees' attitudes about a business policy, does your study actually measure their attitudes about the policy? Reliability refers to data that are measured consistently and accurately. In other words, would the same study produce the same results if repeated later. A researcher can increase the validity and reliability of the data through exercising care in sampling and questionnaire development.

Questionnaire Development

As with every other part of the research process, the questionnaire must serve the purpose of the study. Because questionnaire items must be geared to the population, audience analysis is extremely important at this stage.

As the researcher, you may be seeking factual data or attitudes or opinions, for example, how well a new product is selling or how a procedure works. An example of attitudes or opinions is how well a respondent likes a new product or how well he or she thinks a new procedure is working. The questionnaire items could be derived from factors such as a review of some related secondary data, from talking with people familiar with the problem, or from your experience. Regardless of the method you use to get ideas about how to design the questionnaire, the questions or statements you pose must be those that will give you the appropriate data. In other words, they must be valid and reliable.

One common way of proving the validity of a questionnaire is to use a panel of experts. These panel members may be professionals or practitioners who are familiar with the target population or the problem, or both. For instance, if you conduct a study on a company's personnel practices, you might include instructors of personnel management and personnel directors on the panel. These experts will review the content, clarity of the directions, vocabulary difficulty, item arrangement, ambiguities, and length of the questionnaire before using it. The reliability of the questionnaire can be determined statistically. Although the statistical analysis is beyond the scope of this book, you as a researcher should become familiar with various statistical methods that are available. Very often, these methods require that a pretest or pilot study be conducted. To do this, you would administer the questionnaire to a group of people who are similar to the population to see if the questionnaire gives reliable results. If it does not, then you can revise it before administering it to the sample group.

In addition to the points already discussed, follow these guidelines as you develop the questionnaire:

1. Word the items in a parallel manner so that respondents will interpret them the same way. Common problems in wording are the use of abstract words, jargon, ambiguous or general expressions, and negative terms. When you must include abstract words or technical jargon, define these terms when you use them in a question or statement. If you must use general expressions like *frequently,* then include specific reference points like *once a week* to clarify them. Here is an example:

How frequently are you required to make oral presentations of your written reports?

Very frequently (almost daily)	1. _____
Frequently (once a week)	2. _____
Occasionally (once or twice a month)	3. _____
Seldom (once or twice every 3 to 6 months)	4. _____
Rarely (once a year)	5. _____
Never	6. _____

Note: Notice that the response column is placed at the right of the responses. This fits more naturally with the way in which people fill out questionnaires than does placement at the left.

You should always phrase questionnaire items positively and let the respondent agree or disagree with them from that viewpoint. Here is an example:

Resistance to change is an important concern [instead of saying "*not* an important concern"] when deciding whether to install a new computer system:

    1. yes _____   2. no _____

2. Design items that require a response to only one aspect of an issue in each item. In other words, do not include compound questions or statements in a questionnaire item. For example, avoid a question such as the following:

Do you favor leasing or purchasing a computer system?

    1. yes _____   2. no_____

This structure would confuse the respondent because the question is actually asking about two aspects of the issue. Instead, pose separate questions.

3. Write items that do not suggest or influence a particular response. For instance, a question such as "Do you believe Gamma Corporation would provide the best after-sales computer service?" suggests a particular response. Instead, ask, "What company do you believe would provide the best after-sales computer service?" Then, include the possible responses.

4. Include *only* items that are needed to solve the research problem. As a courtesy, do not waste the respondent's time by asking "nice to know" items. If a respondent detects that you are doing this, then the responses to necessary items could be affected.

5. Write items that are phrased in a way to avoid damaging the respondent's pride or bringing up his or her biases. In other words, do not ask sensitive questions directly. Generally, be careful when asking questions about age, income level, education, church affiliation, political party membership, or any other personal characteristic. Age and income level are especially sensitive items. A way to get more accurate responses when you need this information is to give a range interval to choose from. For example, give intervals such as "21 to 30" and "31 to 40" for age and "$5000 to $9999" and $10,000 to $14,999" for income. These intervals should be mutually exclusive; that is, there is no overlap between intervals.

6. Design items that request current and easily remembered data. When respondents must rely too much on their memories, they may either guess or not respond at all. In either case, their answers will not give you valid or reliable data.

7. Arrange the sequence of the items in a way that starts in an easy and otherwise nonthreatening way. If a respondent sees that the first few questions are complex or otherwise threatening, he or she may choose not to complete the questionnaire. Also, group the sequence of items in a logical and coherent order. If possible, group together all items about a particular topic or subject. Such grouping will help the respondent think more logically about the issues involved and will show that you care enough about these issues to plan the questionnaire thoughtfully.

8. Design the overall format of the items in a way that will help you tabulate, organize, and evaluate the data easily. Generally, the easier a questionnaire is to complete, the easier it will be to deal with the data once you have it. Other than to write items clearly and group

them logically, you could devise a coding system. Coding is especially important when data will be analyzed with a computer program.

To show how coding works, assume that you are surveying commercial bankers to determine the type of bank in which respondents are employed. Here is the question:

In what type of bank are you employed?

> National   1. _____
>
> State   2. _____

Notice that each response is coded with a number: 1 and 2 in this case. This coding procedure will make either the manual or computer tabulation and analysis easy to perform. All responses in the examples given thus far in the discussion have been coded. A further discussion of coding is presented in the next chapter.

Questionnaire items can be written in two types of formats: unstructured or open-ended responses and structured or closed-ended responses.

Unstructured or Open-Ended Response Items In the unstructured or open-ended response questionnaire items, the respondents are free to express any response to the item in their own words. Very often this type of item would lend itself to gathering general data or, more important, to identifying other issues or problems the researcher may not have considered.

The following example illustrates this type of item:

> Please indicate the one major problem area in your office.
>
> _____

In this item, the respondents might indicate problem areas, such as low productivity, low morale, or outdated equipment.

Additional examples of unstructured or open-ended response items are the following questions that might be asked of a bank officer's perceptions in evaluating and declining a loan:

1. If your first impression is that a loan request is weak, how will you proceed to investigate the loan request?_____

   _____

2. When you decline a loan, how much consideration if any do you give to its effect on a family or community?_____

   _____

3. What alternatives and/or suggestions to the loan applicant do you give when you decline his or her loan?_____

_____

Structured or Closed-Ended Response Items   The structured or closed-ended response questionnaire items provide the respondents with a set or list of possible responses to use in choosing appropriate responses. Three common types of structured or closed-ended response items are dichotomous items, multiple-choice items, and rating scales.

Dichotomous items are those that allow only two alternatives, such as "yes-no" or "male-female." The following is an example:

Do you own a personal computer?
　　　1. yes _____   2. no _____

Sometimes these items include a third response, which is neutral. This third item is used when it is possible that the respondent may not have an opinion ("no opinion") or may not know the answer ("don't know").

Multiple-choice items provide three or more alternatives that identify all the responses that are possible for each item. Also, an "other" category should be included in case the researcher has not identified a possible alternative. The item that follows is an example:

Please check your present position in your public accounting firm.

Partner	1. _____
Manager	2. _____
Senior Staff	3. _____
Junior Staff	4. _____
Other (please	5. _____
specify _____)	

A *rating scale* is a type of multiple-choice item where the alternatives are based on some continuous scale. For example, the following is a rating scale based on a frequency of writing business reports:

How frequently do you write business reports?

Very frequently (almost daily)	1. _____
Frequently (once a week)	2. _____
Occasionally (once or twice a month)	3. _____
Seldom (once or twice every 3 to 6 months)	4. _____
Rarely (once a year)	5. _____
Never	6. _____

When you wish to determine the respondents' attitudes toward a particular object, issue, or statement, for example, you might use one of two commonly used attitude scales, namely, the *Likert scale* or the *semantic differential scale*. When using the Likert scale, respondents identify the degree of agreement or disagreement with a statement by selecting a response from a list of alternatives. The following example illustrates the Likert scale:

Computer programming is one of the most important courses in the business curriculum.

1. Strongly agree ____   2. Agree ____   3. Neither agree ____   4. Disagree ____   5. Strongly disagree ____
nor disagree
(neutral response)

Using the semantic differential scale, respondents give their attitudes on a series of seven-point scales with bipolar adjectives at each end (large-small, for example).[1] A degree of feeling about a statement can be indicated precisely. The following is an example of the semantic differential scale:

Please indicate your attitude toward Theta Corporation's management development program by selecting one alternative for each of the following scales:

good	: ____	: ____	: ____	: ____	: ____	: ____	: ____ : bad
useful	: ____	: ____	: ____	: ____	: ____	: ____	: ____ : useless
successful	: ____	: ____	: ____	: ____	: ____	: ____	: ____ : unsuccessful
adequate	: ____	: ____	: ____	: ____	: ____	: ____	: ____ : inadequate
important	: ____	: ____	: ____	: ____	: ____	: ____	: ____ : unimportant

Figure 6 shows a complete questionnaire about insurance needs that uses a Likert scale in Part I. The questionnaire is designed to be mailed to respondents, and a cover letter requesting that respondents fill out and return the questionnaire is shown in Chapter Six.

Common Survey Techniques

After you have developed a questionnaire, there are three commonly used ways of gathering the data. These three techniques are mail questionnaires, personal interviews, and telephone interviews.

[1]Charles E. Osgood, George J. Suci, and Percy H. Tannenbaum, *The Measurement of Meaning* (Champaign: University of Illinois Press, 1957).

INSURANCE PLAN QUESTIONNAIRE

Directions: Please check the appropriate answer for each statement in both Part I and Part II of this questionnaire about family insurance needs.

Part I

	Necessary	Important	No Opinion	Not Important	Undesirable
1. Anyone between the ages of 18 and 55 can enroll in the plan.	a. _____	b. _____	c. _____	d. _____	e. _____
2. My spouse can enroll in the plan for an additional 50 percent premium.	a. _____	b. _____	c. _____	d. _____	e. _____
3. My child or children can enroll in the plan for an additional 25 percent premium for each child.	a. _____	b. _____	c. _____	d. _____	e. _____
4. Cash benefits up to $200,000 will be paid if I die from any illness or accident before reaching age 55.	a. _____	b. _____	c. _____	d. _____	e. _____
5. Cash benefits up to $200,000 will be paid if I die from any accident after age 55.	a. _____	b. _____	c. _____	d. _____	e. _____
6. Cash benefits up to $100,000 will be paid if I die from any illness after age 55.	a. _____	b. _____	c. _____	d. _____	e. _____
7. Questions will be asked about my health before I can enroll.	a. _____	b. _____	c. _____	d. _____	e. _____
8. I may cancel the policy within 60 days after I enroll.	a. _____	b. _____	c. _____	d. _____	e. _____

Part II

1. I am: a. Married _____   b. Single _____   c. Divorced or separated _____
            d. Widowed _____

2. I am: a. Under age 18 _____   b. Age 18 to 35 _____   c. Age 36 to 55 _____
            d. Over age 55 _____

3. I have: a. No children _____   b. One child _____   c. Two children _____
            d. More than two children _____

FIGURE 6   A sample questionnaire.

Mail Questionnaires   This technique requires the researcher to prepare, print, and distribute questionnaires by mail to a group of people. Through the use of this technique, you can survey a large number of people and in a wide geographic area.

The cost of administering a mail questionnaire is relatively inexpensive compared with using personal or telephone interviews. In addition, respondents do not have to be in their offices or at home to be contacted and thus can complete the questionnaire when they have time. On the other hand, the response rate is usually low when using mail questionnaires. Also, respondents do not have the opportunity to seek clarification about the questions or statements. In addition, you cannot be sure that the person who completes the questionnaire is the one to whom you mailed it. Finally, it takes more time to mail the questionnaires and wait for responses than it does to conduct interviews.

Personal Interviews   The purpose of personal interviews is to acquire data through questions and answers in a face-to-face situation. This face-to-face technique encourages the respondents to give in-depth responses. Also, when respondents do not understand a question or statement item, they have the opportunity to ask the interviewer to explain. Conversely, if the interviewer does not understand the response, he or she could ask for an explanation. A limitation in conducting personal interviews is that it takes time to establish contact and then to interview the members of the sample group. Also, the training of interviewers and travel expenses may be costly. Another factor to consider is that in the interview itself, each item should be asked the same way and in the same order to eliminate any bias. In dealing with this technique, as well as telephone interviewing, you should review the material on interviewing in Chapter Fourteen and listening skills in Chapter Sixteen.

Telephone Interviews   With this technique, the interviewer can contact the respondents quickly and at a lower cost than in personal interviews. Although you are not able to see the person to whom you are talking, you can ask for and give explanations. The telephone interview should be structured in a way that will not take a great deal of time to administer. People resent talking on the telephone for a long time. Other limitations of telephone interviewing are that some people do not have telephones or have unlisted telephone numbers.

SUMMARY

The collection of data to solve a research problem can come from either secondary or primary sources. Secondary research data come from an intermediate source, for example, from books or microform. Primary data come from an original source, for example, from observation or questionnaires.

The first step in collecting secondary data is to prepare a bibliography. Sources to consider are company publications, general reference books, books, periodicals, and government documents. In addition, the resources of trade and professional associations and subscription services may be helpful. Microforms and computerized literature search services are also available in many libraries.

Effective note taking is essential to good secondary research. First, review pre-established factors and then prepare a tentative list of these factors. Then scan the source for major related factors and prepare a bibliography control card. Prepare one note card for each factor you have identified and determine the type of note that you are dealing with. After recording your notes, arrange the note cards in a logical order.

The three primary research methods are experimenting, observing, and surveying. Sometimes, you may combine two or all three of these methods in a single research study. The experimental research method seeks to determine whether a change of one factor causes change in another. The observational method involves either a human or mechanical viewing of actions or results of some person or group of people.

In the survey research method, the researcher collects data from respondents by asking questions or posing statements to be responded to on questionnaires. Usually, the respondents are a sample group of people chosen from a larger population. Three probability sampling methods are simple, systematic, and stratified random sampling. Nonprobability methods are judgment and quota sampling.

Survey data are collected with a questionnaire. The data must be both valid and reliable. Valid data measure the concepts or issues that they are intended to measure, and reliable data are measured consistently and accurately. Questionnaires should be geared to the sample group and should be easy to complete. They may contain unstructured or structured response items. Unstructured items leave the respondent free to express any response in her or his own words. Structured items call for specific responses. The data may be collected by mailing the questionnaires or by personal or telephone interviews.

Additional Readings

Babbie, Earl R. *Survey Research Methods.* Belmont, Calif.: Wadsworth, 1973.

Berdie, Douglas R., and John F. Anderson. *Questionnaires: Design and Use.* Metuchen, N.J.: Scarecrow Press, 1974.

Brown, Harry M. *Business Report Writing.* New York: D. Van Nostrand, 1980, pp. 199–217.

Brown, Leland. *Effective Business Report Writing,* 3rd ed. Englewood Cliffs, N.J.: Prentice-Hall, 1973, pp. 181–222.

Clover, Vernon T., and Howard L. Balsley. *Business Research Methods,* 2nd ed. Columbus, Ohio: Grid, 1979, pp. 42–167.

Dillman, Don A. *Mail and Telephone Surveys.* New York: John Wiley, 1978.

Emory, C. William. *Business Research Methods,* rev. ed. Homewood, Ill.: Richard D. Irwin, 1980, pp. 117–353.

Lesikar, Raymond V. *Report Writing for Business,* 6th ed. Homewood, Ill.: Richard D. Irwin, 1981, pp. 30–65.

Lewis, Phillip V., and William H. Baker. *Business Report Writing.* Columbus, Ohio: Grid, 1978, pp. 41–50, 61–79.

Smith, Charles B. *A Guide to Business Research: Developing, Conducting, and Writing Research Projects.* Chicago: Nelson-Hall, 1981, pp. 49–79.

Treece, Malra. *Effective Reports.* Boston: Allyn & Bacon, 1982, pp. 132–172.

Tull, Donald S., and Gerald S. Albaum. *Survey Research: A Decisional Approach.* New York: Intext, 1973.

Review Questions

1. What is the difference between primary and secondary sources of data?

2. What are four ways in which secondary research data can be used? Give a specific example for each one.

3. Discuss the effect of the Freedom of Information Act on business research.

4. Explain the role that technology has played in secondary research?

5. Why is it important to develop a computer search strategy?

6. Explain the difference in experimental, observational, and survey research methods.

7. How does a population differ from a sample?

8. Why are validity and reliability important when conducting primary research?

9. What are some of the major concerns in questionnaire design?

10. What are the advantages and disadvantages of mail questionnaires, personal interviews, and telephone interviews?

Exercises

1. Compile a bibliography of sources consisting of both books and periodicals on one of the following areas:

   a. Office of the future
   b. Worker productivity
   c. Price-level accounting
   d. Computer graphics
   e. Executive development programs

2. Choose one book from the list you compiled for a specific area and determine how many subject classifications there are for it. What value do these other subjects have in your research effort?

3. Choose a specific date, such as your birth-date. Then, locate a newspaper on microfilm for that date. Locate the major business, world, fashion, entertainment, and sporting events printed in the newspaper on that date. What changes have taken place since that date?

4. From the following research situations, explain which type of research method (experimental, observational, or survey) would be best to use and say why.

   a. Number of customers visiting a store
   b. Consumer preference for a particular product
   c. Supervisors' attitudes toward a new bonus plan
   d. Learning differences based on classroom instruction and on-the-job training
   e. Customer satisfaction of after sales service

5. From the following improper questionnaire items, give the reason why each one is improper and then correct the item:

   a. Having a competitive attitude is not important for a beginning salesperson.
      1. yes _____ 2. no _____
   b. Are quantitative and verbal skills necessary for a computer programmer?

c. Do you read *Management World* often?
d. What is your salary?
e. When did you buy your first bicycle?

6. Prepare three to five statements or questions for a questionnaire for the following types of structured or closed-ended response items:

a. Dichotomous
b. Multiple choice
c. Rating scale
d. Likert scale
e. Semantic differential scale

CHAPTER NINE

Giving Meaning and Structure to Research Data

The goals in studying the text and completing the activities in this chapter are to know

1. The techniques of classifying, editing, and coding primary research data
2. The applications of summarizing primary data
3. The various types of summary statistics
4. The effect of logical reasoning when evaluating and interpreting data
5. How to prepare an outline that follows effective basic techniques of organization

In the collection phase of the problem-solving report process, you have gathered secondary data, primary data, or a combination of both. The key to effective research, however, is not the accumulation of data. Rather, it is the ability to analyze, evaluate, and interpret the data to arrive at valid conclusions and recommendations that aid in solving problems. The product of the process is the presentation of credible data that provide useful information for the report audience.

The discussion in this chapter deals with three aspects that give meaning and structure to research data: (1) sorting and summarizing, (2) evaluating and interpreting, and (3) outlining. Although these three aspects suggest an independent and continuous process, this is not entirely the case. Rather, it is likely that parts of these aspects will begin just as soon as you begin to define the research problem.

SORTING AND SUMMARIZING RESEARCH DATA

Research data should be collected within the framework of the problem definition. When you identify the factors or write a hypothesis statement when you define the problem, it will give you direction about the type of data that will be collected and the type of analysis that will be needed. In addition, the sorting and summarizing of research data are completed with the problem in mind. Actually, you start this process when you begin to identify the factors that lead to the problem definition. These factors provide you with a framework to begin the collection phase.

In the sorting and summarizing phase, you actually are organizing the data for a comprehensive evaluation and interpretation. When you began to take notes from secondary sources, you sorted and perhaps summarized these notes in a logical arrangement. This arrangement, combined with the tentative list of your factors and subfactors, brought organization to your collection phase. Therefore, if you clearly have stated your research problem and your research plan and have taken effective notes, your secondary research data are ready for further evaluation and interpretation.

The collection phase is easily combined with the sorting and summarizing phase because secondary research data are primarily qualitative. On the other hand, with primary research data, you are dealing with original data that are primarily quantitative. For this reason, the sorting and summarizing of primary research data follow the collection phase. Basically, the sorting phase deals with three procedures: classifying, editing, and coding. The summarizing phase deals with tabulating and computing summary statistics.

Classifying the Data

The classification procedure involves identifying mutually exclusive intervals or groups of data that can be divided into manageable levels of related data. In other words, data should be grouped systematically. To show how this works, here is an example of how closed-ended and open-ended questionnaire responses can be classified.

The preparation of structured or closed-ended responses lends itself to a natural classification system. Any further classification would not be necessary because the data would already be grouped when the responses were made. For example, the items with two alternatives would be classified as "yes-no," "male-female," or whatever the alternatives are. The multiple-choice items would be classified into three or more alternatives. Also, rating scale items would be classified into a list of alternatives.

If some of the questionnaire items contained unstructured or open-ended responses, you cannot know in advance what the responses will be. Because the respondents are free to express any response to the item in their own words, the responses may vary. Therefore, a classification system would have to be formed after the responses were received. For example, consider the following questionnaire item and response:

Item: Please indicate the one major problem in your office. _____
Response: "It seems as if every time I start typing a report, the typewriter starts acting up."

One way in which to classify this response would be as "equipment problems" that stem from using outdated typewriters. Therefore, regardless of the type of responses you receive, you will want to classify them into meaningful groups.

Editing the Data

Once you have classified the data, your next step is to edit them. Editing requires you to check carefully for problems with the data. Typical problems are data that are missing (no response to an item) or data that are inaccurate (respondent checks one particular response repetitively to most or all items). If data are missing, you must decide how to handle the response. For example, you may include it as a "no answer" response, eliminate the item from the analysis, or contact the respondent for a response. If you find a repetitive response to a series of items, it is possible that these data are inaccurate. If this is the case, you may decide to eliminate all the items from the analysis.

Coding the Data

The coding procedure involves assigning a number to each response classification. This coding system is necessary especially if the data are to be keypunched and analyzed by a computer program. You could combine the classifying and coding procedures with the preparation of closed-ended response questionnaire items. For example, when you decide on the alternatives for a particular response item, assign a number to each alternative at that time.

The following questionnaire item has been classified and coded:

Please check your age category.

21–30	1. _____
31–40	2. _____
41–50	3. _____
51–60	4. _____
Over 60	5. _____

Tabulating the Data

Tabulating the data involves counting the number of responses in each response classification for each statement or question. This counting procedure could be completed either manually or by computer. If you are dealing with a large sample, you might consider computer tabulation because of the time and effort it would save you.

Whether the tabulation is completed manually or by computer, this procedure places the data in a frequency distribution. A frequency distribution shows how many responses were tabulated or tallied for each alternative for a particular item. As a researcher, you could tabulate responses to one item at a time or two or more at the same time. Tabulating two or more items at a time is sometimes referred to as a cross-tabulation. Figure 1 contains an example of a tabulation for one item based on the respondents' age (multiple choice). Figure 2 illustrates a cross-tabulation that combines age with a rating scale questionnaire item. Notice that cross-tabulation shows the relationship between or among two or more items.

Tabulating responses involving weighted alternatives is done differently. Figure 3 presents a tabulation of semantic differential responses with a weighted scale. As you can see from the tabulation and assignment of the weighted scale, the 14 managers' attitudes toward the management development program were favorable.

If you have few data or the relationships among your data are simple, you could evaluate the data immediately after the tabulation. On the

Age	Number of Respondents
21–30	11
31–40	32
41–50	44
51–60	10
Over 60	3
Total	100

FIGURE 1 A tabulation for one questionnaire item.

Item: How frequently do you write business reports?

Alternatives	21–30	31–40	41–50	51–60	Over 60	Total
	\<span\>Age\</span\>					
Very frequently (almost daily)	2	15	10	3	—	30
Frequently (once a week)	3	12	23	3	2	43
Occasionally (once or twice a month)	5	3	8	4	1	21
Seldom (once or twice every 3 to 6 months)	1	—	3	—	—	4
Rarely (once a year)	—	2	—	—	—	2
Never	—	—	—	—	—	0
Total	11	32	44	10	3	100

FIGURE 2 Cross-tabulation for two questionnaire items.

other hand, if relationships are complex or you have many data, you can carry the summarizing phase one step farther and compute summary statistics.

Computing Summary Statistics

As in the tabulation procedure, the purpose of computing summary statistics is to reduce the data to a more manageable and meaningful level. Basically, the summary statistics consist of three areas: percentages, measures of central tendency, and measures of dispersion.

Item: Please indicate your attitude toward Theta Corporation's management development program by selecting one alternative for each of the following scales:

FIGURE 3 A semantic differential tabulation with a weighted scale.

Percentages

Percentages are ratios that show a relationship between one or more data response classes to a base of 100. For example, 250 insurance agents were interviewed. The review showed that 185 agents worked as insurance agents for major insurance companies. The percentage that would be computed in this example for major insurance company agents would be 74 (185 ÷ 250), which is a ratio of 3 out of 4. Very often, percentages are computed immediately after the tabulation procedure is completed; and they are shown with the number of responses. Figure 4 illustrates this point.

Measures of Central Tendency

Measures of central tendency involve summary statistics that measure or represent the center value of a distribution of data. These measures include the mean, median, and mode.

The Mean   The mean or arithmetic mean is computed by taking the sum of all the responses and dividing that sum by the number of responses. For example, a study revealed the following number of word processors purchased by six different companies: company A purchased 24; company B, 14; company C, 18; company D, 25; company E, 18; and company F, 21. To compute the mean, sum all the word processors (120) and divide this sum by the number of companies (6). The result would be a mean of 20.

The usefulness of the mean can be distorted when there are some unusually high or low figures in the distribution. An example of this distortion would occur if a seventh company in the survey reported purchasing 118 word processors. The sum of all the word processors in the distribution would be 238, and the number of companies would be 7. Therefore, the mean would be 34. Because one company is so far out of line with the others, the mean is skewed and is therefore not an effective measure of central tendency.

Item: What type of insurance company do you work for?

Company	Number of Respondents	% of Total
Major insurance	185	74%
Independent insurance	65	26
Total	250	100%

FIGURE 4 Results of a tabulation and their corresponding percentages.

The Median   The median is the midpoint in a distribution of responses. To find the median, arrange the responses either from the highest to the lowest figure or from the lowest to the highest; then select the midpoint of that distribution. For example, if you were to arrange each of the seven companies' number of word processors from lowest to highest, they would be arranged as follows: company B, 14; company C, 18; company E, 18; company F, 21; company A, 24; company D, 25; and company G, 118. Thus, the median for this distribution would be 21. In this case, the median is meaningful and it is not distorted by the unusually high number of word processors in company G.

In finding the median for an even number of responses, you only need to find the two middle responses, add them together, and divide the answer by 2. For instance, if you use the original six companies, the median would be computed as follows: the lower middle response (18) plus the higher middle response (21) divided by 2 would produce a median of 19.5.

The Mode   The mode is found by identifying the most frequently occurring response in a distribution of responses. If you were to use the original six companies as an example, you might recall the initial distribution as follows: company A, 24; company B, 14; company C, 18; company D, 25; company E, 18; and company F, 21. The most frequently occurring response, and thus its mode, is 18.

Measures of Dispersion

Where the measures of central tendency deal with the center value of a distribution of data, measures of dispersion deal with the variation or spreading out of the data in a distribution. The three most common types of measures of dispersion are range, semi-interquartile range, and standard deviation.

Range   The range is the difference between the value of the highest response and the value of the lowest response in a distribution. For example, the stock market quotations include the high and low prices of stock sold on a particular day. This range for each stock is a measure of dispersion. To find the range in a distribution, subtract the value of the lowest item from the value of the highest item. In the example of the word processors in the six companies, the range would be the difference between company D's number of word processors and company B's number (25 − 14). The range would be 11. However, if the seventh company were to be used (company G = 118), the range would be 104

(118 − 14). Therefore, you can see the effect of unusual or extreme values in a distribution.

Semi-interquartile Range   If there are unusually high or low values in a distribution, then you could find the semi-interquartile range. This range can be found by taking one-half of the difference between the highest and lowest values of the middle 50 percent of all the values. For ease of computation, use eight companies rather than seven, with the eighth company (H) having three word processors. Thus, the values in the distribution, arranged from highest to lowest, would be as follows: company H, 3; company B, 14; company C, 18; company E, 18; company F, 21; company A, 24; company D, 25; and company G, 118. The middle 50 percent of the values in this distribution is companies C, E, F, and A. Thus, the semi-interquartile range would be 3 (24 − 18 ÷ 2).

Standard Deviation   Computing the standard deviation involves six steps. To show how these six steps work, consider the example of the six companies with word processors. The distribution of the number of word processors purchased by each company is company A, 24; company B, 14; company C, 18; company D, 25; company E, 18; and company F, 21. The first step in calculating the standard deviation of a distribution is to compute the mean. In this example, the mean is 20. The second step requires you to subtract the mean from each value in your distribution; this step is as follows:

Company	No. of Word Processors	−	Mean	=	Difference
A	24	−	20	=	4
B	14	−	20	=	−6
C	18	−	20	=	−2
D	25	−	20	=	5
E	18	−	20	=	−2
F	21	−	20	=	1

To complete the third step, you square each difference obtained in step 2. This means that you multiply the difference by itself in each case. These squared differences follow:

Company	Squared Difference
A	$4 \times 4 = 16$
B	$-6 \times -6 = 36$
C	$-2 \times -2 = 4$
D	$5 \times 5 = 25$
E	$-2 \times -2 = 4$
F	$1 \times 1 = 1$

The fourth step is to sum or add all the squared differences. This total is 86 (16 + 36 + 4 + 25 + 4 + 1). The fifth step involves dividing the total from step 4 by the number of values in the distribution (86 ÷ 6 = 14.33). In the sixth step, you take the square root of the result of step 5 to find the standard deviation. The square root of 14.33 is 3.79 (rounded to hundredths), which is the standard deviation. Actually, you could determine the square root without mathematical computations by consulting square root tables found in the appendix of most basic statistics books. You can also use a pocket calculator with a square root key or a word processor or microcomputer with appropriate software packages to find it.

You should compute and report as many types of summary statistics as necessary to give your report audience a clear understanding of the characteristics of the distribution. Word processors or microcomputers with software packages and computers can be used to compute these statistics easily. Remember, though, that just reporting summary statistics is not helpful unless you use these statistics along with tabulation to evaluate and interpret the data.

EVALUATING AND INTERPRETING RESEARCH DATA

Although evaluation and interpretation of the data are concluded at this stage of the research process, this process actually begins the moment you begin defining your problem. Deriving meaning from the data, at any stage of the research process, requires that you think logically to make sound judgments. Insight is needed, as is intuition. Throughout the entire process, the common denominator is the problem definition. This section includes the specific aspects of evaluating and interpreting either primary or secondary data that would flow naturally after you have sorted and summarized them. The major segments of these aspects are statistical and nonstatistical.

Statistical Evaluation and Interpretation of Data

Some summary statistics can be used to make inferences from the data about the problem being studied, especially in primary research. Basically, this means that you test the accuracy and significance of the data and identify relationships among them to help you draw valid and reliable conclusions about the problem. Thus, any inferences (sometimes called generalizations) that you make about the population should be based on the accuracy, significance, and possible relationships of your sample data. If you need more sophisticated statistical procedures than those discussed in this chapter, consult any basic statistics textbook or reference book.

Because of the nature of many business research studies, you might not need to calculate any statistics. Often, you will need only a few characteristics of the sample. For example, you might want to know what percentage and/or what proportion of insurance agents work for major insurance companies in a particular area. Or you might want to know the average number of word processors owned by certain types of companies. Regardless of what is needed, you could evaluate and interpret these statistics by simply describing why they were used to analyze your data and perhaps what some of the implications of these data are. Another way of evaluating and interpreting these statistics might be to compare them with published regional or national norms. Or you might compare these statistics with those from related studies.

You might report a combination of the mean and standard deviation to show a good representation of the overall distribution. These statistics also could be used for making comparisons with similar distributions. For instance, you might compare the representativeness of two sample means. Assume that the means for word processors purchased by companies in two separate samples were 20 and 21, respectively, and that their standard deviations were 3.79 and 10.15, respectively. By reporting these statistics, you could derive more meaning from the data than you could by reporting only the data.

In evaluating and interpreting data with statistics, you have to exercise not only knowledge of your subject and understanding of the statistical procedures, but also you have to apply patterns of logical thought and reasoning.

Nonstatistical Evaluation and Interpretation of Data

Nonstatistical evaluation and interpretation of data deal primarily with secondary research, but many aspects can apply to primary research as well. When you defined your problem and identified your factors, you started this phase by showing a relationship of the factors to the problem. Next, when you began your collection phase, you continued the process. At this point, you might want to review the section on collecting secondary research data in Chapter Eight.

As you took notes about your data, perhaps you wrote down your own ideas, suggestions, comments, and reactions. Again, this process guided your thoughts about the relationships that were forming and the direction the information was taking. Then, this is the point at which to take this evaluation and interpretation one step farther to arrive at conclusions and make recommendations. Appropriate conclusions and recommendations result only when logical reasoning is applied to the results of the data analysis.

Using Logical Reasoning

Logical reasoning is necessary in the research process just as in any other communication process. The two types of logical reasoning are *deductive* and *inductive.*

Deductive Reasoning   In deductive reasoning, your thought processes move from a general premise or proposition to a specific or particular conclusion. If the premises are true, then the conclusion drawn from the premises will be true also. Conversely, if the premises are false, then the conclusion drawn will be false as well. A syllogism will show how deductive reasoning works. A major premise, minor premise, and a conclusion are the parts of a syllogism. The following is an example:

Major Premise	Word/information processing systems are increasing paperwork efficiency in the office.
Minor Premise	Porter Company has just purchased a word/information processing system for its office.
Conclusion	Porter Company probably will increase its paperwork efficiency in the office.

The important aspect of applying this type of reasoning in research is that the reader is likely to accept your reasoning as truth. Each statement you make deductively should be accurate, and you should give reasons that support each statement.

Inductive Reasoning   Inductive reasoning involves moving from a specific premise or proposition to a general conclusion. This approach allows you to identify specific research data that will form patterns that will lead to a general conclusion. When you conduct business research, this reasoning process begins when you define your problem and identify your factors or form your hypotheses. These factors or hypotheses will be supported by factual data, which lead to a conclusion.

To show an example of inductive reasoning, assume that you are evaluating various types of pension plans that your company might consider adopting. The specific premises would be the various aspects of each type of plan. An evaluation of each plan then would lead to a generalized conclusion about which plan is best. Or another example might be that your company has selected a particular pension plan subject to employee approval. Your job is to evaluate employee reactions to the plan. After you evaluate each employee's reaction, you would then generalize that they favor or do not favor the plan.

Drawing Conclusions

If your research purpose is purely informational for the report audience, you probably will not have to draw any conclusions. If, however, your research purpose is analytical or evaluative, you will have to draw some conclusions and perhaps make some recommendations. All conclusions that are drawn must be based on the evaluation and interpretation of the data. Under no circumstances should new data be presented when drawing your conclusions. If new evidence is presented in the conclusion, then your overall problem analysis does not flow logically. Drawing conclusions implies bringing your data together logically to form a conclusion that will solve your research problem. Each conclusion must be supported by your data, and it should not merely restate the data. The problem of stating findings from the data as conclusions occurs most often when research studies include hypotheses.

To show how this might happen, look at this hypothesis taken from Chapter Seven.

> Using individualized instruction for in-service managerial training will result in higher achievement than will using the traditional large-group instruction.

If you found a significant difference between the two methods that favored the individualized method, then reporting this significance is not a conclusion but a finding. However, an objective conclusion can be drawn from this finding, such as

> The findings of this study support the hypothesis that individualized instruction is likely to produce more favorable results than is large-group instruction in the in-service managerial training program.

If you know about other studies that have arrived at conclusions similar to yours, you might cite them as support for your conclusions. This will make your conclusions more credible.

Making Recommendations

The conclusions that were drawn from your findings in an analytical report are the basis for making your recommendations. The recommendations you make indicate some type of action of how the report audience can use the results of your research study. For example, a recommendation based on the conclusion given in the previous section might be

> The individualized instruction method should be used in the in-service managerial training program rather than the large-group instruction method. In addition to producing more favorable achievement, the individualized instruction method would allow the in-service managers to work at their own pace. Also, they could work at a time more convenient to both the manager trainee and his or her supervisor.

The first sentence in this example contains the recommendation itself. In addition, some implications for using the individualized instruction method are cited. You have more flexibility in making recommendations than in any other part of the research process. For example, given the same conclusion, you may make recommendations different from those that another researcher would make. However, any recommendations you make should be drawn logically from the conclusion.

Evaluating and interpreting your data should follow processes of logical reasoning and judgment. This logical reasoning should be based on verifiable and supportive evidence. As a researcher, you should become familiar with common fallacies of reasoning because they can affect your data evaluation and interpretation. Many fallacies do exist; however, the following five fallacies are common in research reports: argumentum ad hominem, begging the question, false analogy, false dilemma, and post hoc, ergo propter hoc.

Argumentum ad Hominem   Argumentum ad hominem is a Latin term that basically means "argument to the person." In other words, the reasoning is associated with the personality or character of individuals rather than with the arguments presented. The following is an example of this fallacy:

> Our policy of promoting managers from within the company doesn't work because gloomy old Mr. Johnson was promoted to vice president last week.

Begging the Question   Begging the question implies making a statement that is not supported by some sort of proof. An example of this fallacy is

> It seems to me that the only method of dealing with these absenteeism problems is to fire those people who are involved.

False Analogy   False analogy occurs when two different statements or ideas are considered to be similar when they are not. For instance, consider the following example:

> Learning how to program a computer is like learning how to ride a bicycle. Once you learn, you never forget.

False Dilemma Known commonly as the "either-or" fallacy, false dilemma implies that there are only two sides to an issue when there can be others. The following example illustrates this fallacy:

> The solution to this morale problem is either to give the employees more money or to shorten their working hours.

Post Hoc, Ergo Propter Hoc Post hoc, ergo propter hoc is a Latin term that basically means "after this, therefore because of this." In other words, this fallacy suggests a logical error in the cause and effect relationship. An example of this fallacy is

> Because we hired the graduates from Gamma University to work in the main office, our sales have increased.

Applying the principles of reasoning gives you the entire picture of your solution to your problem. Completing the evaluation and interpretation of your data then leads you to the next phase of your problem-solving report process. This phase is the organizing of your data for writing or simply outlining.

OUTLINING RESEARCH DATA

An outline involves placing the various factors that you have identified into a logical and systematic pattern of data presentation. This pattern will show the relationship of your factors to the solution of your problem. By reviewing the outline, you can determine if it follows a logical and related pattern, thereby revealing any gaps in your reasoning. An outline can help to show if there is any overlapping among the factors and if each factor is getting enough coverage.

An effective outline will help you in organizing your report and will serve as your guide throughout the writing phase. The outline will aid you in labeling various section and paragraph headings in your report as well as in preparing your table of contents and report summary.

Deciding on an Organizational Plan

The outline reflects your decision on how to present the final sequence of your report. This decision depends upon the purpose of the report, the nature of the data, the type of report, and the requirements of the report audience. Although this decision will not affect your findings or conclusions, it does determine the physical presentation of your data when you begin to write. Generally, there are four common organizational plans: inductive, deductive, chronological, and geographical and/ or functional.

Inductive Organizational Plan

The inductive organizational plan is indirectly arranged and is probably the most common plan for organizing business research reports. In this plan, the physical presentation moves from the specific to the general or from the known to the unknown. In other words, you start with your introductory statement, proceed to your findings, and then end with a summary, conclusions, and recommendations. This plan is normally used when you have to write formal reports. A more important reason for using inductive organization is that it is the best arrangement for presenting your findings in a way to convince your report audience of the merits of your conclusions. In fact, this plan is sometimes called the persuasive plan. An example of the inductive plan is

Introduction

Federal Reserve Effect on Interest Rates

Development and Growth of Money Funds

Advantages of Investing in Money Funds

Disadvantages of Investing in Money Funds

Expected Returns of Money Funds

Conclusions About Money Funds Investments

Recommendations for Investing in Money Funds

Deductive Organizational Plan

The deductive organizational plan is a direct plan that presents the results of the report from the general to the specific or from the unknown to the known. Put another way, you start with your recommendations and conclusions, follow with your findings that supported your recommendations and conclusions, and end with a general summary. The deductive plan has become a popular pattern with managers who need to know what the major solutions are for a particular problem quickly. If necessary, they could then review and follow the logic of the researcher's findings to confirm the recommendations and conclusions. The following is an example of a deductive plan:

Recommendation for Purchasing a Computer

Conclusion About Purchasing a Computer Supported by Findings

Effects of Purchasing a Computer

Results of Leasing a Computer

Effects of Using Services of a Computer Firm

Summary of Three Computerization Alternatives

Chronological Organizational Plan

In the chronological organizational plan, the findings of a study are presented as they occurred over time. This plan is very commonly used in informational reports, where the data are presented as they occurred but no analysis is required. However, this plan could be used in combination with the inductive or deductive plans. For instance, in combining the inductive with the chronological, you might administer an attitudinal survey about a new health insurance plan when you first offer it. Then, after each quarter for the next year, you would administer the survey again. When you prepare your report, you would present your findings based on each quarter and then draw some conclusions about any changes in attitudes each time. An example of a chronological plan for an informational report is

Introduction

First Quarter Production Results (January 1 to March 30)

Second Quarter Production Results (April 1 to June 30)

Third Quarter Production Results (July 1 to September 30)

Fourth Quarter Production Results (October 1 to December 31)

Summary of Annual Production Results

Geographical and Functional Organizational Plan

The geographical plan presents the results of a study based on relationships in space rather than in time. As in the case of the chronological plan, the geographical plan is commonly used in informational reports. For example, a sales manager for a particular region might receive a report on the sales produced for each territory within that particular region. Or the vice president of marketing might receive a report on the sales activities for each region. The following is an example of a geographical plan:

Introduction

Northern Regional Sales Activities

Eastern Regional Sales Activities

Southern Regional Sales Activities

Western Regional Sales Activities

Summary of National Sales Activities

Closely related to the geographical plan is the functional plan where reports may be presented based on company divisions, departments, or other sections. As an example, the vice president of finance might receive a report that describes the activities of the auditing, tax, and general accounting services departments.

Selecting a Type of Outline Heading

The wording of an outline should be grammatically parallel; that is, you have applied some consistent pattern to the wording of your topics and subtopics. Generally, there are three common heading or caption types: topic, phrase, and sentence. Remember that when you select one of these types, you should use it consistently throughout your entire outline.

Topic Heading

The topic heading consists of using one, two, or three key words that show the specific factors you will be discussing in your report. As an example, consider the following topical heading outline for a report on managerial functions:

> Introduction
>
> Planning Function
>
> Organizing Function
>
> Controlling Function
>
> Directing Function
>
> Management Functions Summary

Phrase Heading

The phrase heading is an extension of the topic heading that more fully describes the factors. The phrase heading could take any of the following forms: infinitive, noun, participial, or decapitated sentence phrases. Examples of these are

> *Infinitive Phrase*
>
> To Develop Long-Term Plans
>
> To Determine Cash Requirements
>
> To Establish Capital Budgets
>
> *Noun Phrase*
>
> Development of Long-Term Plans
>
> Determination of Cash Requirements
>
> Establishment of Capital Budgets

Participial Phrase

Developing Long-Term Plans

Determining Cash Requirements

Establishing Capital Budgets

Decapitated Sentence

Long-Term Plans Developed

Cash Requirements Determined

Capital Budgets Established

If you decide to use the phrase outline heading, this does not mean that you have to select only one of the four forms. For variety or clarity, you can use a couple of these forms throughout the entire outline. However, if you do use more than one form, remember to use parallel construction. In other words, if you decide to use a participial form for your first major factor, then use it for other major factors. The major factors are equal to one another; therefore, their construction should be parallel.

The subfactors of a major factor may take another form, but they should be grammatically parallel to one another. For example, the following outline shows how a variety of headings can be used while maintaining parallel construction.

Presentation of Operating Budgets (noun phrase)
    Developing a Sales Budget ⎫
    Determining a Production Budget ⎭ (participial phrases)

Illustration of Cash Budget (noun phrase)
    Cash Inflow or Generation Estimated ⎫
    Cash Outflow Measured ⎭ (decapitated sentences)

Sentence Heading

The sentence heading states each factor in a simple and complete sentence that generally should not run longer than seven words. The point of using a sentence heading is to provide one complete thought but to do it concisely. Sentence headings are more descriptive than other types. An example of a sentence outline is

Copiers Differ in Input-Output Qualities
    Beta II Holds Slight Edge in Input Qualities
    Alpha I Allows for Diversity in Output

Copier Costs Vary Substantially
  Alpha I Bears Highest Initial Cost
  Gamma III Offers Lowest Price for Maintenance Agreement
  Beta II Provides Lowest Price per Copy

Using a Pattern of Outline Symbols

One way of bringing a more systematic structure to your outline is to use a pattern of outline symbols that correspond to each main factor or subfactor in it. In other words, each division is identified by a symbol that signifies its rank in the entire outline. The two most common patterns of outline symbols are Roman numeral-letter-number and decimal. The use of either of these patterns is a matter of the report writer's preference. The decimal pattern is used more often, however, in technical and scientific report writing. The following illustrations are examples of these two patterns of outline symbols:

Roman Numeral-Letter-Number
  I. First main division, topic, or heading
    A. First subdivision of first main division
    B. Second subdivision of first main division
      1. First subdivision of B
      2. Second subdivision of B
        a. First subdivision of 2
        b. Second subdivision of 2
 II. Second main division, topic, or heading
    A. First subdivision of second main division
      1. First subdivision of A
      2. Second subdivision of A
        a. First subdivision of 2
        b. Second subdivision of 2
    B. Second subdivision of second main division
III. Third main division, topic, or heading

Decimal
 1. First main division, topic, or heading
    1.1 First subdivision of first main division
    1.2 Second subdivision of first main division
      1.21 First subdivision of 1.2
      1.22 Second subdivision of 1.2
        1.221 First subdivision of 1.22
        1.222 Second subdivision of 1.22

    2. Second main division, topic, or heading
       2.1 First subdivision of second main division
          2.11 First subdivision of 2.1
          2.12 Second subdivision of 2.1
             2.121 First subdivision of 2.12
             2.122 Second subdivision of 2.12
       2.2 Second subdivision of second main division
    3. Third main division, topic, or heading

Notice that both these patterns divide the information in a similar way. Therefore, only the symbols used are different. The following outline illustrates the use of the Roman numeral-letter-number pattern. This is an outline from which you can write your report. The decimal pattern could be used in this outline instead of the Roman numeral-letter-number pattern if you prefer.

     I. Introducing the Problem
    II. Determining the Accounting Function in Banking
       A. Record Bank Assets and Liabilities
       B. Report Accounting Information
          1. Reporting to Bank Management
          2. Reporting to Customers and Potential Investors
          3. Reporting to Regulatory Agencies
       C. Maintain Internal Control
    III. Evaluating Effects of Computers on Recording Function
       A. Storing Accounting Information
       B. Inputting Accounting Information
       C. Outputting Accounting Information
    IV. Examining Effect of Computers on Reporting Function
       A. Provide Speed and Accuracy to Report Generation
       B. Allow Flexibility in Special Report Preparation
     V. Analyzing Effects of Computers on Internal Control Function
       A. Verification of Input and Output Information
       B. Maintenance of Bank Information Security
    VI. Summarizing and Concluding Remarks

In reviewing the patterns of outline symbols, notice that there are no single divisions or subdivisions at a level. This implies that you must have at least two or more divisions. If you were to end up with only one division at a level, then you have two choices to correct this. You could incorporate the single division item into a larger division. Or you could add a second division item at the same level. An example illustrating both situations follows:

Original
   II. Financing the Business
      A. Commercial Bank Loan

Possible Alternatives

II. Financing with a Commercial Bank Loan

or

II. Financing the Business
   A. Commercial Bank Loan
   B. Private Investors

SUMMARY

The ability to derive meaning from your data is the key to the effective solution of your problem. Once you have collected your data, you must organize them for evaluation and interpretation. This phase of the research process involves sorting and summarizing your data in a way that will aid in the evaluation and interpretation phase. Generally, much of your sorting and summarizing of secondary research data is done as you collect the data. This is possible as long as you follow a systematic approach in searching for secondary sources and use an effective system of note taking.

In sorting and summarizing your primary research data, however, you need to get the data ready for evaluation and interpretation by classifying, editing, coding, and tabulating them. Also, you might compute summary statistics, such as percentages, measures of central tendency, and measures of dispersion if needed.

Once you have your data sorted and summarized, you can begin a more detailed evaluation and interpretation of them. In this phase, you would evaluate or interpret the data using either statistical or nonstatistical methods. The statistical methods involve the use of summary statistics. When you evaluate and interpret data using nonstatistical methods, apply the basic principles of logical reasoning. You need to be familiar with common fallacies of reasoning that could affect your logical thought processes.

After you have your data evaluated and interpreted, you need to organize them into an outline to aid in writing the research report. Four organizational plans for writing reports are inductive, deductive, chronological, and geographical and/or functional. After deciding on a particular organizational plan, add outline headings and symbols.

Additional Readings

Brown, Harry M. *Business Report Writing.* New York: D. Van Nostrand, 1980, pp. 131-160, 196-198, 217-220.

Brown, Leland. *Effective Business Report Writing.* 3rd ed. Englewood Cliffs, N.J.: Prentice-Hall, 1973, pp. 231-253.

Clover, Vernon T., and Howard L. Balsley. *Business Research Methods.* 2nd ed. Columbus, Ohio: Grid, 1979, pp. 169-218.

Dawe, Jessamon. *Writing Business and Economic Papers.* Totowa, N.J.: Littlefield, Adams, 1975, pp. 75-86, 96-103.

Emory, C. William. *Business Research Methods,* rev. ed. Homewood, Ill.: Richard D. Irwin, 1980, pp. 369-402.

Himstreet, William C., and Wayne Murlin Baty. *Business Communications: Principles and Methods,* 6th ed. Boston: Kent, 1981, pp. 89-97, 315-331.

Lesikar, Raymond V. *Report Writing for Business,* 6th ed. Homewood, Ill.: Richard D. Irwin, 1981, pp. 69–95.

Lewis, Phillip V., and William H. Baker. *Business Report Writing.* Columbus, Ohio: Grid, 1978, pp. 81–85, 101–103.

Sigband, Norman B. *Communication for Management and Business,* 3rd ed. Glenview, Ill.: Scott, Foresman, 1982, pp. 77–86.

Smith, Charles B. *A Guide to Business Research:* *Developing, Conducting, and Writing Research Projects.* Chicago: Nelson-Hall, 1981, pp. 81–97, 125–129.

Treece, Malra. *Effective Reports.* Boston: Allyn & Bacon, 1982, pp. 174–188.

Wolf, Morris Philip, Dale F. Keyser, and Robert R. Aurner. *Effective Communication in Business,* 7th ed. Cincinnati: South-Western, 1979, pp. 29–33, 62–68.

Review Questions

1. Explain what is meant by "the sorting and summarizing of research data are completed with the problem in mind." Does it matter whether the research is primary or secondary?

2. Discuss the importance of classifying, editing, and coding primary research data.

3. What are the benefits of tabulating primary research data?

4. Define mean, median, and mode. What do these measures of central tendency offer to you as a researcher?

5. What are three common measures of dispersion? How can each measure contribute to your research effort?

6. Deductive and inductive are two types of logical reasoning. What is the difference between the two? Is one more effective than the other?

7. What five fallacies are common to research reports? Why should you be aware of these fallacies?

8. What are the advantages of preparing a writing outline?

9. Discuss the use of the four common organizational plans. Why would one be used over another?

10. Why should you maintain parallel construction when selecting an outline heading?

Exercises

1. Based on responses to unstructured or open-ended questionnaire items, how would you classify each of the following statements:

   a. "My boss doesn't listen to me."
   b. "I was just thrown into the new position created by the supervisor."
   c. "I can't seem to learn this new technique for preparing vouchers."
   d. "The inventory process always takes too long."
   e. "Our labor leaders don't seem to represent us well enough."

2. Determine whether the following semantic differential data are favorable or unfavorable regarding a new computer system. Then, write a short paragraph discussing your findings.

untimely:	///	////	___	///	////	///	///	timely
passive:	////	///	////	___	//	ЖТ	//	active
weak:	/	ЖТ	___	___	ЖТ	ЖТ /	///	strong
foolish:	///	///	___	//	ЖТ	///	////	wise

3. The number of unit sales of microcomputers for the past five weeks were:

Week:	1	2	3	4	5
Microcomputers sold:	20	15	14	16	14

Calculate the mean, median, mode, range, and standard deviation.

4. The following accounting test scores came from the training department of Maxwell Industries, Inc.:

92	86	91	79
81	88	85	92
89	74	90	96
94	90	72	84
79	96	84	82

Calculate the mean, range, and standard deviation.

5. From the following statements, discuss the type of reasoning fallacy each statement violates and why:
   a. "Our personnel problems have decreased since we started to promote only employees with 10 or more years of service."
   b. "This product will never sell because the marketing effort will be headed up by Bill Thomas."
   c. "The only problem we have is employee apathy."
   d. "We either should hire more operations employees or just close down the manufacturing process."
   e. "This whole hiring process reminds me of a lottery. You're hired if you're lucky enough to get your name picked."

6. The three partial outlines that follow violate some basic rules for wording outline headings. Tell why each outline is improper and then correct it.
   a. Accounting Methods Used in the Petroleum Industry
      New Accounting Method Proposed by the SEC
      Analyzing the Effects of the Change in Accounting Methods
   b. Monetary Considerations of Fringe Benefits
      Types of Fringe Benefits Offered
      Fringe Benefits and Productivity: Is There a Relationship?
   c. The Question of Actual Cost
      Analyzing Overall Performance and Riding Comfort
      Considering Operating Expenses

CHAPTER TEN

Preparing Visual Aids

The goals in studying the text and completing the activities in this chapter are to know

1. **The role of visual aids in report writing**
2. **The common requirements for presenting visual aids effectively**
3. **The techniques for preparing tables from both quantitative and qualitative data**
4. **How to apply the basic techniques of graphic design when constructing figures**
5. **Effect of technology on graphic preparation**

Today, because of the increased demand for quantitative and qualitative data for decision making, businesses are using visual aids more than ever. Visual aids make data more meaningful and more interesting when included in reports. They can substitute for narrative descriptions, or they can be used in conjunction with them.

To illustrate the effect of a visual aid in helping the report audience to understand the narrative explanation better, look at this material adapted from an article in *The Wall Street Journal.*[1] Assume that this explanation was included in a report on trade relations between the United States and China:

> In January 1981, the United States exports to China amounted to $423.6 million. One year later, the amount of exports to China was only $288.3 million. This change represented a 32 percent decrease in exports. However, during the same time period, China exports to the United States increased from $119 million to $248.6 million. This change constituted a 52 percent increase in exports. The net result was that the United States trade surplus decreased from $304.6 million in January 1981 to $39.7 million in January 1982.[8]

Note: The superscript at the end of the excerpt shows that the material was taken from a secondary source.

Notice that the financial data as presented could be confusing if they were not read carefully. Therefore, a visual aid can help reinforce the explanation. Here is a slightly revised version of the data followed by a visual aid to complement the explanation (see Figure 1).

The data in Figure 1 were summarized in narrative form, and then the major effects of the change in exports for the year were illustrated. In this manner, the reader is given both a verbal and a visual picture, which complement each other.

While effective visual aids can clarify ideas, ineffective aids can confuse report audiences.

PRESENTING VISUAL AIDS EFFECTIVELY

Visual aids must be presented to the report audience clearly to be fully effective. Five requirements must be met each time a visual aid is included in a business report. The key words for these requirements are *identify, document, introduce, interpret,* and *place.*

---

[1]*The Wall Street Journal,* March 22, 1982, p. 26.

The overall change in exports between the United States and China in January 1981 and January 1982 is shown in Figure 1. In January 1981, the United States exports to China amounted to $423.6 million. One year later, the amount of exports to China was only $288.3 million. This change represented a 32 percent decrease in exports. However, during the same period, China exports to the United States increased from $119 million to $248.6 million. This change constituted a 52 percent increase in exports. The net result was that the United States trade surplus decreased from $304.6 million in January 1981 to $39.7 million in January 1982.[8]

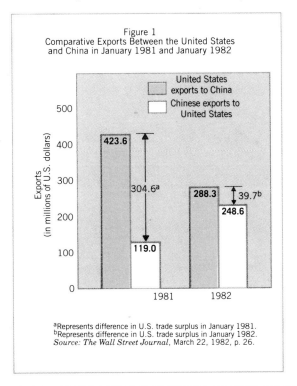

Figure 1
Comparative Exports Between the United States and China in January 1981 and January 1982

[a]Represents difference in U.S. trade surplus in January 1981.
[b]Represents difference in U.S. trade surplus in January 1982.
Source: The Wall Street Journal, March 22, 1982, p. 26.

FIGURE 1 A narrative explanation with a visual aid.

Identifying Visual Aids

With the exception of an informal table, you should label, number, and title all visual aids used in reports. (Informal tables are discussed in the table preparation section of this chapter.) You may label visual aids as a table, graph, chart, figure, map, or exhibit. A common way to handle the labeling procedure is to call them either "Table" or "Figure."

You would use the "Table" label for visuals presented in tabular form consisting of columns and rows of data. The "Figure" label would be used for all other visual aids except tables. An exception to this procedure would be the specific request of the report audience for another labeling procedure. For example, in this textbook the publishers request that all formal visual aids be labeled as "Figure" even though some of them are tables.

Generally, when the visual is labeled either as a "Table" or "Figure," further identification continues by assigning arabic numbers to each group of visuals. The numbering should be presented in sequence for each group of tables and figures, such as "Table 1," "Table 2," and so forth, and "Figure 1," "Figure 2"; "Figure 1" is assigned to the first illustration in this chapter.

Titling is the descriptive name you give each visual aid in a report. This descriptive name should reflect the order in which the information is presented in the visual aid. Notice the descriptive title used in the example for "Figure 1," which is shown in Figure 1 for the chapter:

Comparative Exports Between the United States
and China in January 1981 and January 1982

Once the complete identification is made, the label, number, and title are placed either above or below the visual.

Documenting Visual Aids

Documentation involves acknowledging the source of the visual aid. Basically, documenting has three applications: (1) primary source, (2) secondary source visual constructed from narrative, and (3) secondary source visual presented verbatim. When you construct a visual aid from your data (primary source), you can document it in one of two ways: (1) place the words "Source: Primary" directly below the visual or (2) omit the source note, which implies that the visual aid was constructed from your own primary data.

When you prepare a visual from secondary sources consisting of narrative data, include the specific citation of the secondary reference in the documentation. For example, notice how the documentation in Figure 1 reads as follows: "*Source: The Wall Street Journal,* March 22, 1982, p. 26."

When a visual that already appears in a secondary source is used verbatim, then you must acknowledge the entire reference along with the table or figure number. An example of this procedure follows:

Source: Jeffrey E. Long, "WP Survey: Who's Using What," *Management World,* Vol. 2, No. 4, April 1982, p. 15, Table 3.

If the final report is intended for publication, the researcher must get permission from the copyrightholder to reproduce the visual.

Footnotes are used to explain or discuss some item contained in visual aids. In such a case, use a superscript of a letter or an asterisk ([a], [b], *) rather than a number. An example of this is shown in Figure 1.

Introducing Visual Aids

A reference to the visual aid must be made within the narrative or text of the report before presenting the visual aid if the information is to be clear. One reference should refer both to the content of the visual and to its label and number.

Here is an introductory sentence that leads into the model "Figure 1," which is shown in Figure 1 for this chapter.

The overall change in exports between the United States and China in January 1981 and January 1982 is shown in Figure 1.

Notice that in the example, the emphasis in the lead-in sentence is placed on the content of the visual rather than on the visual's label and number. An alternative is to put the label and number in parentheses right after the lead-in sentence:

. . . in January 1981 and January 1982 (see Figure 1).

Now notice how the emphasis shifts to the label and number when they are presented first:

As shown in Figure 1, there was an overall change in exports between the United States and China in January 1981 and January 1982.

Although all these examples are used in reports, the first example is used most often. Use the same procedure to refer to a visual aid in an appendix as you do to refer to one included with the narrative.

Interpreting Visual Aids

Interpretation that accompanies visual aids can explain and emphasize ideas. Interpretation should not just repeat all the data that appear in the visual. Instead, you should explain the significance of the data to your overall discussion of the topic.

An example of how to interpret a visual aid is shown in the narrative in Figure 1. This explanation includes a discussion of the significance of the data. For example, consider the reference to the change in exports between the two countries represented by percentages. Although the percentages were not included in "Figure 1," the writer identified their significance by including the percentages. This interpretation of the data contained in "Figure 1" provides the reader with a more meaningful understanding of the dramatic change in exports between the United States and China.

Placing Visual Aids

A visual should be placed as close as possible to its introduction and interpretation in the text or narrative of the report. Generally, the size of all visuals should be at least one-quarter of an $8\frac{1}{2}'' \times 11''$ page. Anything smaller than a quarter of a page could be difficult to read. If the size of the visual aid is less than a half page, place it right after its introduction and interpretation. When typing the report, leave about three line spaces above and below the visual to separate clearly the visual aid from the text. Sometimes writers prefer to place at least some visual aids in a report between the introduction and the interpretation.

If the size of the visual aid is a half page or more, place it on the first full page that comes after the introduction. A full-page visual aid can be placed either vertically or horizontally on the page. Use vertical placement if the visual aid will fit within the normal margins of the report text.

The label, number, and title for a horizontally placed visual should appear centered and at the left-hand margin of the page. The label, number, and title for a vertically placed visual should appear centered on the top of the page.

Once you understand the five requirements for preparing visual aids, you can apply them to the appropriate type of visual aid for the report audience.

USING THE APPROPRIATE VISUAL AID

Several types of visual aids are available that you could use to convert quantitative and qualitative data into a meaningful summary. These are *tables, graphs,* and *miscellaneous visual aids.*

Tables

You can use tables to present quantitative data in a systematic order of columns and rows. The data used in tables usually come from primary research. While tables usually contain quantitative data, you can show qualitative data, such as lists of words or phrases, in tables.

Tables may be either informal or formal. Informal tables (sometimes referred to as spot or minor tables or listings) can be used to emphasize or highlight several items by indenting these items after a simple lead-in sentence. The informal table becomes a part of the regular narrative. Although an informal table might have column or row headings, it does not have a label, number, or title.

For example, consider the following sentence that contains some numbers referring to Beta Corporation's operating expenses for the four quarters of 1982 that might appear in a report.

> Beta Corportation's 1982 quarterly operating expenses were $32,000 for the first quarter, $28,000 for the second quarter, $35,000 for the third quarter, and $37,000 for the fourth quarter.

Now here is how that same data can be shown using an informal table:

Beta Corporation's 1982 quarterly operating expenses were

First quarter	$32,000
Second quarter	28,000
Third quarter	35,000
Fourth quarter	37,000

Because a formal table summarizes greater amounts of quantitative and qualitative data, you should separate them from the narrative of the report. The two types of formal tables are general and special purpose.

A general purpose table contains complex or general reference data, such as a computer printout of data or a list of questions used in an interview. These tables usually are placed in the appendix of the report.

The special purpose table contains specific data that are related to a particular discussion in the text. You should place these as close as you can to the discussion. Headings are used to indicate the row items and column categories. The row items, sometimes called stubs, are placed at the left-hand side of the table and are followed by the columns of data. A common table format, along with the identification of the major parts of the table, is shown in Figure 2.

This table has horizontal lines drawn between major divisions—a ruled format. You could, however, set up your table in two other formats: open and boxed.

Here is an abbreviated example of an open format:

		Cumulative
Position	Number	Number
Partner	39	39
Manager	57	96
Senior staff	80	176
Junior staff	74	250
Total	250	---

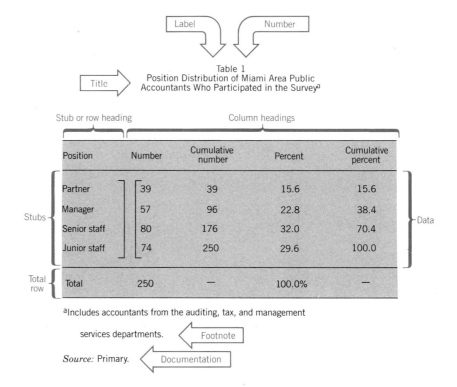

FIGURE 2 A common table format with major parts identified.

Generally, you would use the boxed format when you have several columns to place close together. An abbreviated example of this format is shown as follows:

Position	Number	Cumulative Number
Partner	39	39
Manager	57	96
Senior staff	80	176
Junior staff	74	250
Total	250	---

Generally, qualitative data, such as instructions, guidelines, or rankings are placed in a listing format. The same rules apply to a qualitative table as do to a quantitative table. A ruled table presenting qualitative data in a listing format is shown in Figure 3.

TABLE 1
The Ten Most Serious Communication Barriers
in the Accountant-Accountant Relationship

Rank	Communication Barrier
1	Tendency not to listen
2	Lack of credibility
3	Lack of trust
4	Hostile attitude
5	Personality conflicts
6	Poor organization of ideas
7	Know-it-all attitude
8	Either-or thinking
9	Defensiveness
10	Resistance to change

Source: Steven Golen, "An Analysis of Communication Barriers in Public Accounting Firms," *The Journal of Business Communication,* Vol. 17, No. 5, Fall 1980, p. 43.

FIGURE 3 A ruled table in a listing format.

Graphs

Graphs or charts are visual presentations of quantitative data. You can use them to show relationships between or among two or more data items. Graphs help report audiences to picture data by associating them with the various graphic forms. Three general types of graphs are *bar, line,* and *pie* or *circle.*

Bar Graphs

Bar graphs use rectangular bars or boxes that have similar widths to illustrate the relationship between data. Choosing the appropriate bar graph depends on the nature of the data and the overall effect you wish to convey. Three commonly used types to choose from are *simple, grouped,* and *segmented.*

Simple Bar Graph   The simple bar graph shows a comparison of two or more values. This bar graph, which could be drawn either vertically or horizontally, shows the values by the height or length of the bars. The bar graph has both a vertical and horizontal axis, where the beginning point for each axis is zero.

Each bar shown in the graph must have the same width, and each scale must have equal intervals. Any variation from these two aspects would distort the true meaning of the data and lead to interpretation errors. Vertical and horizontal simple bar graphs, along with the identification of the major parts are shown in Figure 4.

Notice that the exact quantities were placed at the ends of all the bars. These quantities could have been placed inside the bars instead. If it is not necessary to identify the exact quantities for the report audience, the exact figures could be left out. For additional emphasis you could use colors, shadings, or cross-hatchings for the bars.

Because the quantities of data being represented by the bars are sometimes at the high end, you may not need part of the scale. In such cases, break the scale between zero and the first interval that is needed. Note that distortion could occur when you use a very high number for the first interval. Two common types are Z scale breaks and straight-line breaks. They are illustrated for simple bar graphs in Figure 5. This technique can be used for other types of graphs as well.

Grouped Bar Graph   A grouped bar graph is used to compare two or more different values over a period of time or for a particular point in

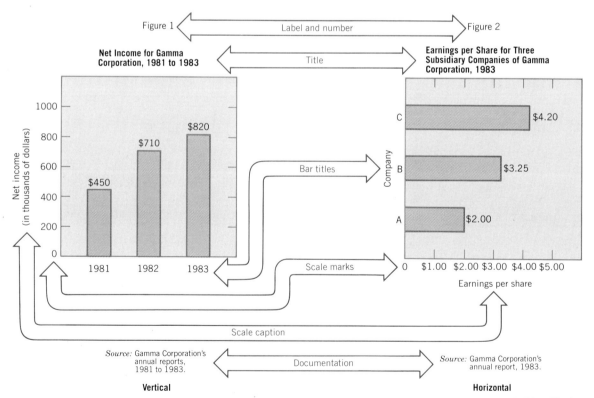

FIGURE 4   Vertical and horizontal simple bar graphs with major parts identified.

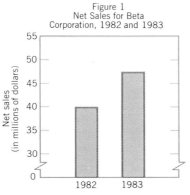

Figure 1
Net Sales for Beta
Corporation, 1982 and 1983

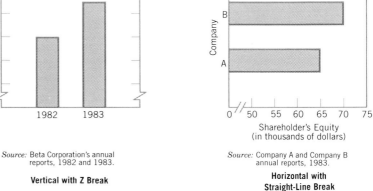

Figure 2
Shareholder's Equity for
Company A and Company B, 1983

FIGURE 5 Vertical and
horizontal simple bar
graphs with a Z break and
straight-line break,
respectively.

Source: Beta Corporation's annual
reports, 1982 and 1983.

Vertical with Z Break

Source: Company A and Company B
annual reports, 1983.

**Horizontal with
Straight-Line Break**

time. Each group should be limited to three or fewer items to avoid confusion.

You should use colors, shadings, or cross-hatchings to identify the different items being compared. Also include a legend or key placed on the graph to explain these designations. A grouped bar graph, along with a legend, is shown in Figure 6.

Notice in this example that different shadings were used to designate the three divisions. When using shadings, you should always place the darkest item at the left and then progress to lighter shades.

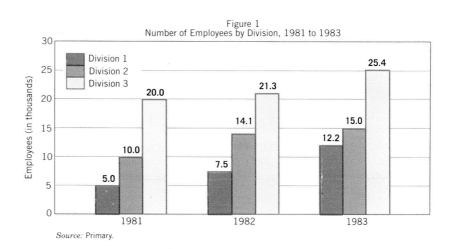

Figure 1
Number of Employees by Division, 1981 to 1983

FIGURE 6 A grouped bar
graph.

Source: Primary.

Segmented Bar Graph   The segmented bar graph shows the different parts of value that comprise the whole amount. You could use this graph to illustrate the parts of one value to compare the parts of several values. Generally, the total amounts being represented are absolute, such as dollars or some other type unit.

Each bar is divided into parts or segments that correspond to the amounts they represent. You should color, shade, or cross-hatch the segments and explain them in a legend. A segmented bar graph comparing three items is illustrated in Figure 7. Notice that both shadings and cross-hatches are used in this example.

Line Graphs

You can use line graphs to show trends—changes in data over a period of time. These graphs illustrate a continuous movement of data for the particular time period. Three commonly used types of line graphs are *single*, *multiple*, and *cumulative*.

Single Line Graph   A single line graph shows one series of value. This graph has both a vertical and horizontal axis. The vertical axis begins with zero and shows the amount that will be measured. The horizontal axis reflects a time period (or some method of classification when dealing with frequency distribution). Also, as in the bar graph, the vertical and horizontal scales should be marked in equal intervals.

Each amount, along with its time period, is plotted by placing a dot on the graph. Once you plot each amount, then connect the dots to show the continuous movement of the value. Also, when the amounts are all at the high end of the scale, then the scale could be broken using either a Z or straight-line break. A single-series line graph is shown in Figure 8.

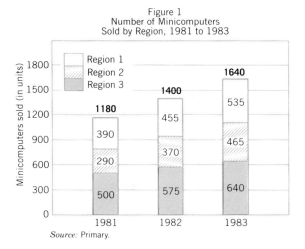

FIGURE 7 A segmented bar graph.

Figure 1
Number of Minicomputers
Sold by Region, 1981 to 1983

Source: Primary.

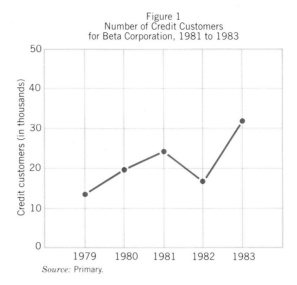

FIGURE 8 A single line graph.

Multiple Line Graph   Use multiple line graphs to compare two or more values over a time period or for a particular point in time. Usually, you should graph no more than four values to keep the graph simple and therefore easy to follow.

Because you have more than one line, some type of indicator should be used to distinguish each line, particularly if the lines cross over each other. Some common line indicators are the single colored solid line, different-colored solid lines, dots, dashes, and combinations of dots and dashes. A key that identifies each line should be placed in a legend. A multiple line graph is illustrated in Figure 9.

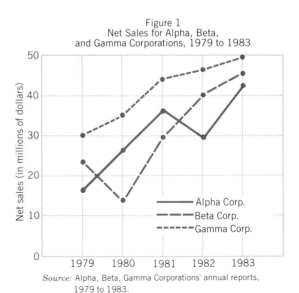

FIGURE 9 A multiple line graph.

Cumulative Line Graph   The cumulative line graph shows the parts of a particular series of a value that comprise a whole amount. Only one series can be plotted in this type graph, and the parts are in absolute terms, such as dollars or units.

For emphasis, each part could be distinguished with color, shade, or cross-hatching. Then, either a legend or proper labeling should be used to designate each part. A cumulative line graph is shown in Figure 10. Notice that a right vertical line was drawn to give the line graph a complete cumulative effect.

Pie or Circle Graph

You can use pie or circle graphs to compare the parts of one value for a particular point in time. Each part represents a portion of the total amount of the value. A pie graph must contain at least two parts but should not contain more than eight parts to avoid cluttering and confusion. Label each part of the graph, and if you wish, use color, shading, or cross-hatching for emphasis. In preparing the graph, compute percentages of the total for each part and then multiply each percentage by 360 degrees.

Next use a compass or some other object to draw a circle with at least a 2- or 3-inch diameter. Then, with a protractor, mark the degrees for each part starting with the largest part at the 12 o'clock position. You should then move clockwise by marking the degrees in a descending order. The only exception to this rule is the other or miscellaneous category. This part should be the last item marked even though the number of degrees it contains might be more than the other parts of the pie.

A completed pie or circle graph is shown in Figure 11. Notice that

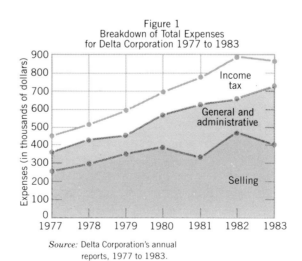

Figure 1
Breakdown of Total Expenses
for Delta Corporation 1977 to 1983

Source: Delta Corporation's annual
reports, 1977 to 1983.

FIGURE 10   A cumulative line graph.

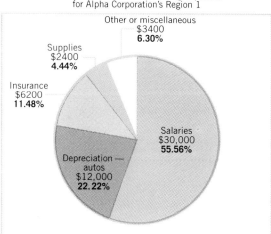

Figure 1
Breakdown of 1983 Total Selling Expenses
for Alpha Corporation's Region 1

Other or miscellaneous
$3400
6.30%

Supplies
$2400
4.44%

Insurance
$6200
11.48%

Salaries
$30,000
55.56%

Depreciation —
autos
$12,000
22.22%

Source: Primary.

FIGURE 11   A pie or circle graph.

when a segment is small, an arrow could be drawn from the label to the part.

Miscellaneous Visual Aids

Several other types of visual aids are used commonly in business reports. These include (1) *flow charts*, (2) *organizational charts*, (3) *time charts*, (4) *maps*, (5) *pictograms*, and (6) *photographs, drawings* and *diagrams.*

Flow Charts
Flow charts are used generally to present some type of process or procedure, such as the steps involved in operating a computer or preparing a tax return. In preparing a flow chart, you could use the same basic symbols used by computer programmers, or you could use your own system of symbols.

A flow chart using programming symbols is shown in Figure 12. Notice that no directional flow arrows are needed when the flow is downward, which is usually the case. Also notice that the diamond shape is a decision symbol, which allows the process or procedure to branch to an alternative.

Organizational Charts
Use organizational charts to identify the overall structure and directional line of authority for an organization. The parts are represented by rec-

Figure 1
Purchasing and Testing a Personal Computer

```
                        ┌──────────┐
                        │  START   │
                        └──────────┘
                             │
                        ┌──────────┐
                        │ Evaluate │
                        │ various  │
                        │ personal │
                        │computers │
                        └──────────┘
                             │
                        ┌──────────┐
                        │ Purchase │
                        │ personal │
                        │ computer │
                        └──────────┘
                             │
                        ┌──────────┐
                        │Run sample│
                        │ computer │
                        │ program  │
                        └──────────┘
                             │
                          ╱────╲              ┌────────────┐
                         ╱ Does ╲    No       │    Get     │
                         ╲program ╱──────────▶│professional│
                          ╲work? ╱            │   help     │
                           ╲────╱             └────────────┘
                             │                      │
                           Yes                      │
                        ┌──────────┐                │
                        │ Complete │                │
                        │ personal │◀───────────────┘
                        │ project  │
                        └──────────┘
                             │
                        ┌──────────┐
                        │   END    │
                        └──────────┘
```

FIGURE 12 A flow chart.

tangular boxes, and the chart should follow one of three basic patterns: (1) functions (finance, production), (2) departments (accounting, contracts), or (3) specific position titles (president, vice president of marketing). In the organizational chart, direct or line relationships between the boxes are shown with solid lines, whereas indirect or staff relationships are shown with broken lines. Specific position titles for a corporate accounting area are presented in Figure 13.

Time Charts

Use a time chart to show a schedule of activities or events that are to be completed over a period of time. Generally, a time chart serves as a visual work progress schedule for a particular project, and it is used often in proposals and progress reports.

Either bars or lines could be used to designate the times. A time

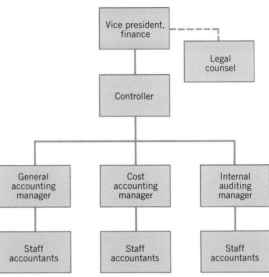

Figure 1
Zeta Corporation's Accounting
Area Organizational Structure

FIGURE 13 An
organizational chart

chart is illustrated in Figure 14. Notice that this time chart was prepared from the work progress schedule data included in the research plan shown in Chapter Seven.

Figure 1
Work Progress Schedule for Absenteeism
Project at Delta Manufacturing Company, January 14 through March 16

Activities	Time periods—week beginning								
	Jan. 14	Jan. 21	Jan. 28	Feb. 4	Feb. 11	Feb. 18	Feb. 25	Mar. 4	Mar. 11
Review absentee files in personnel office	▬								
Interview supervisors and operations personnel		▬▬							
Collect data on absentee plans from professional journals and books				▬▬					
Organize and evaluate the data						▬			
Write the report							▬		
Type and proofread the report									▬
Submit final report to personnel manager									▏

FIGURE 14 A time chart.   *Source:* Work progress schedule in Figure 7.3.

Maps

Use maps in business to show a geographical representation of either qualitative or quantitative data. For example, a real estate developer may include in a report to potential investors a map of the area that he or she will be developing. Or a corporation may include a map in a report to its stockholders showing the number and location of its franchises.

For emphasis, parts of the map could be colored, shaded, or cross-hatched. Also, a legend should be used if the colors, shades, or cross-hatches, as well as other symbols, represent data related to a specific geographical area. A map is shown in Figure 15.

Pictograms

Pictograms are visuals that use pictorial symbols to represent data. The best use of this visual aid is to present quantitative data to a nontechnical or general public audience.

A common pictorial symbol is stacking coins to represent sales or expenditures. Or you could use cars to represent the number of cars sold, or airplanes to represent the number of air miles flown. To avoid misrepresentation, each symbol should be drawn in the same proportion and

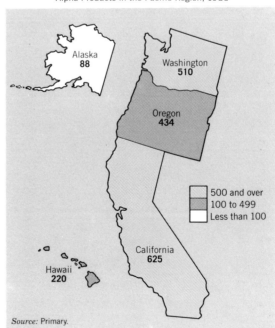

Figure 1
Number of Distributors of
Alpha Products in the Pacific Region, 1983

FIGURE 15   A map.

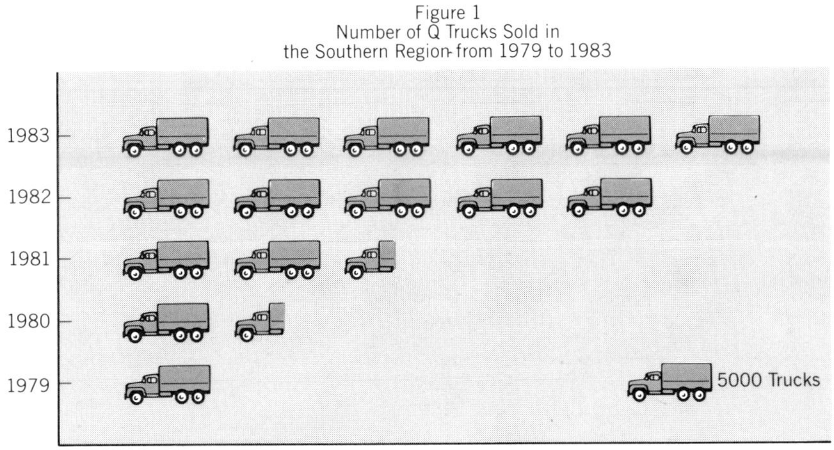
Figure 1
Number of Q Trucks Sold in
the Southern Region from 1979 to 1983
1983
1982
1981
1980
1979
5000 Trucks

Source: Primary.

FIGURE 16 A pictogram.

size. If needed, include a legend to show what each symbol represents in terms of a particular quantity. A pictogram is shown in Figure 16.

Photographs, Drawings, and Diagrams

You can use photographs effectively to show how an object or scene actually looks. In other words, photographs show surface detail. For example, when discussing a certain problem in a production line, you might include a photograph of the problem area. The photograph should show clearly the problem area without too many distractions.

Drawings and diagrams are used essentially the same way as photographs are, but drawings and diagrams do not include as much detail. A drawing is used to present the physical characteristics of an item or an area. For example, a drawing might be made of a building or a piece of equipment. A diagram, however, might present a brief sketch of an item or show how a particular process works. For example, a cutaway diagram could illustrate the inner parts of a piece of equipment. Or a schematic diagram could show the overall structure of a computer or electrical circuit.

You can use colors, shades, or cross-hatches to emphasize certain parts of the drawing or diagram. Also use arrows and labels if needed. An example of a drawing is presented in Figure 17.

Providing effective visual aids can be both time consuming and difficult to do. Recent advances in technology have brought an answer to this problem, however. The result is that highly effective visual aids (called computer graphics) can be produced automatically on computers.

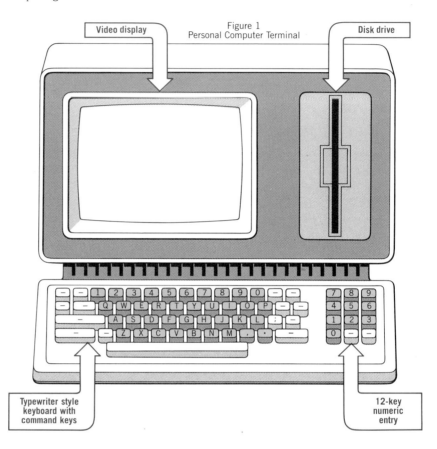

Figure 1
Personal Computer Terminal

Video display

Disk drive

Typewriter style
keyboard with
command keys

12-key
numeric
entry

FIGURE 17   A drawing.

REALIZING THE
EFFECT OF COMPUTER GRAPHICS

Computer graphics has provided the report writer with a new dimension for more effective and less time consuming reporting. Every visual aid that was presented in this chapter, with the exception of a photograph, could be produced by the computer.

Computer graphics can turn raw data into visual aids in both black and white and color. Using plain English instructions, managers can create graphics on their own display terminals right in their offices. These managers could even perform "what-if" functions on the terminals by manipulating the data to see what might be the outcome of particular decisions before a final decision is made.

Because of technological advancements during the past few years, the cost of a computer graphics system has declined greatly. Many computer graphics software systems ("software" is used to program computers to perform various functions) are available that could be used with a company's existing computer. In addition to software, the company would need related graphics equipment ("hardware"), such as a graphics display terminal and a printer. Computer graphics examples appear in Figures 18 and 19. With proper equipment, you can produce color prints, transparencies, and 35 millimeter slides.

If your company does not have a computer or does not wish to purchase the computer graphics software and hardware, you could have your graphics done by an independent computer service bureau. Another solution is to buy a microcomputer with graphics capabilities.

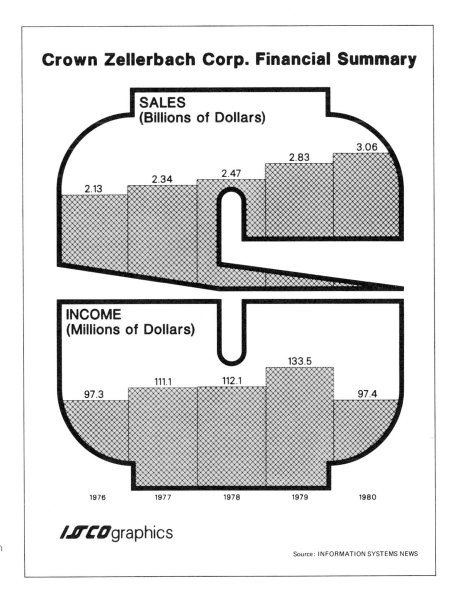

FIGURE 18 A computer-produced visual aid. (Reprinted with permission from ISSCO, San Diego, California)

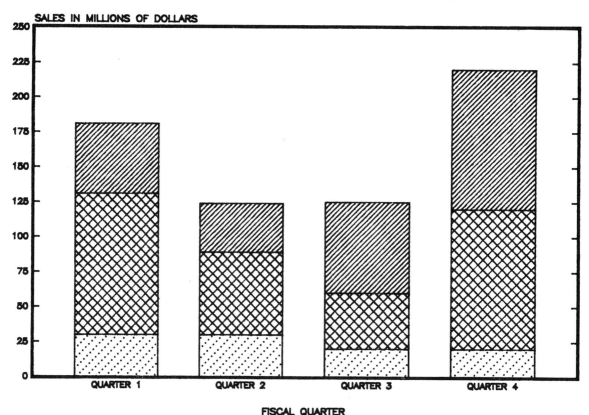

FIGURE 19   A computer-produced visual aid. (Reprinted with permission from Hewlett-Packard Corporation.)

SUMMARY

The purpose of visual aids is to help the report audience understand the meaning of your written data more completely. Visual aids do not take the place of written data, but they can be used to simplify, supplement, and support the overall written presentation. When presenting any visual aid, you should (1) identify it, (2) document it, (3) introduce it, (4) interpret it, and (5) put it in the appropriate place.

Many types of visual aids are available for your use in reports. Basically, these visual aids are categorized as tables, graphs, and miscellaneous. Tables can be either informal or formal. An informal table is used as an alternative to writing a few numbers or a short list of words into the text. Such a table becomes a part of the narrative. A formal table, however, summarizes larger amounts of data, and it needs to be separated from the narrative. Formal tables can be classified as general or special purpose.

Three basic types of graphs are bar, line, and pie or circle. When preparing a bar graph, you might choose one of the following specific types: simple, grouped, or segmented. Three common types of line graphs are single, multiple, and cumulative. Miscellaneous visual aids consist of the following: (1) flow charts, (2) organizational charts, (3) time charts, (4) maps, (5) pictograms, and (6) photographs, drawings, and diagrams.

Today, you can use computers to produce visual aids for your business reports. Called computer graphics, these aids have resulted from recent technological advances.

Additional Readings

Brown, Harry M. *Business Report Writing.* New York: D. Van Nostrand, 1980, pp. 167–186.

Brown, Leland. *Effective Business Report Writing,* 3rd ed. Englewood Cliffs, N.J.: Prentice-Hall, 1973, pp. 115–144.

Himstreet, William C., and Wayne Murlin Baty. *Business Communications: Principles and Methods,* 6th ed. Boston: Kent, 1981, pp. 331–346.

Kolin, Philip C. *Successful Writing at Work.* Lexington, Mass.: D. C. Heath, 1982, pp. 295–330.

Lefferts, Robert. *How to Prepare Charts and Graphs for Effective Reports.* New York: Barnes & Noble, 1981.

Lesikar, Raymond V. *Report Writing for Business,* 6th ed. Homewood, Ill.: Richard D. Irwin, 1981, pp. 183–207.

Lewis, Phillip V., and William H. Baker. *Business Report Writing.* Columbus, Ohio: Grid, 1978, pp. 117–130.

Moyer, Ruth, Eleanour Stevens, and Ralph Switzer. *The Research and Report Handbook: For Business, Industry, and Government.* New York: John Wiley, 1981, pp. 98–112.

Potts, Jackie. "Computer Graphics Systems for Business." *Today's Office,* Vol. 16, No. 9, February 1982, pp. 35–36, 38.

Sigband, Norman B. *Communication for Management and Business,* 3rd ed. Glenview, Ill.: Scott, Foresman, 1982, pp. 238–263.

Treece, Malra. *Effective Reports.* Boston: Allyn & Bacon, 1982, pp. 192–215.

Vinberg, Anders, and James E. George. "Computer Graphics and the Business Executive—The New Management Team." *IEEE Computer Graphics and Applications,* Vol. 1, No. 1, January 1981, pp. 57–71.

Review Questions

1. What is the major purpose of visual aids? Why are they used in reports?

2. Describe the five common requirements for presenting all types of visual aids. Why does each requirement need to be completed when presenting visual aids?

3. Discuss three applications for documenting visual aids.

4. Why shouldn't a visual aid just appear in a report without an introduction? What are three ways of introducing a visual aid? Which way is best?

5. When interpreting the data contained in the visual aid, all you need do is repeat the data in the narrative. Do you agree or disagree with this statement? Explain your answer.

6. Why is it necessary for a visual aid to be placed close to the discussion in the text?

7. What are two types of tabular presentations? When would you use each type?

8. Three general types of graphs are bar, line, and pie or circle. Describe a particular situation in which you would use each type. What are some variations of the bar and line graph?

9. Discuss the circumstances when each of the following miscellaneous visual aids would be used: (a) flow charts, (b) organizational charts, (c) time charts, (d) maps, (e) pictograms, (f) photographs, and (g) drawings and diagrams.

10. What effect have computers had on the preparation of visual aids?

Exercises

1. From the following data, construct a table and label it properly: of the retailing supervisors, 25 were classified as upper-level managers, 47 as middle-level managers, and 38 as lower-level managers.

2. What specific type of bar graph would you use for each of the following situations? Explain your answers.
   a. Comparing the quarterly sales of three regions for the past year
   b. Comparing the dollar value of merchandise returned for the past three years
   c. Showing the net income and net loss for the past five years
   d. Comparing the breakdown of the total number of employees by division
   e. Comparing percentages of the data mentioned in Exercise 2(d)
   f. Comparing the range of employee aptitude test scores for the past five years

3. During the past five years, the following dividends were paid by Wilson Manufacturing Company: $6.20, $5.80, $4.25, $5.70, and $5.95. Prepare a simple bar graph to show these data.

4. What specific type of line graph would you use for each of the following situations? Explain your answers.
   a. Measuring the net income for the past five years
   b. Comparing sales, expenses, and net income for the past five years
   c. Showing the fluctuation in meeting quarterly sales quotas for the past year
   d. Comparing the breakdown of total sales by region for the past six years
   e. Comparing percentages of the data mentioned in Exercise 4(d)

5. During the past six years, the following amounts were spent by each division for research and development—Division 1: $29,000, $40,000, $42,000, $53,000, $62,000, and $75,000; Division 2: $34,000, $44,000, $50,000, $57,000, $64,000, and $70,000. Prepare a multiple line graph to show these data.

6. A department store had total monthly sales of $116,000. A breakdown of the sales by department was

Notions	$ 5,000
Ladies' wear	30,000
Men's wear	28,000
Children's wear	14,000
Sporting goods	20,000
Hardware	9,000
Shoes	10,000
Total	$116,000

Prepare a pie graph to show these data.

7. Prepare a flow chart using the steps necessary for reconciling your checkbook balance.

8. Prepare an organizational chart for a business where you are employed or for an organization where you are a member.

CHAPTER ELEVEN

Presenting the Research Results

The goals in studying the text and completing the activities in this chapter are to know

1. The basic report writing style guidelines
2. The proper format techniques for preparing reports
3. The various parts of a long, formal report
4. How to write a long, formal report

The final step in the research process is writing the report. The writing phase should be just a matter of following through your writing plan by using your final outline and note cards. This chapter contains specific applications of writing principles as they apply to reports. In addition, format procedures and the major parts of a formal report are discussed and illustrated.

APPLYING BASIC WRITING PROCEDURES AND TECHNIQUES

To develop an effective report writing style, as in anything you might aspire to do well, practice is required. The following are some suggestions about how to proceed in writing the report.

1. Select a time of day for writing that will have the fewest distractions.
2. Write those sections with which you feel most comfortable first. Doing this will build your confidence in completing the remaining sections.
3. Write the first draft as rapidly as you can. Worrying about selecting the "right" word or spelling a difficult word at this point will distract you. Get your thoughts down and expect to rewrite the material later.
4. Set goals for writing different parts of the report. This approach is necessary because you will not be able to write a complete report at one sitting. Establish the time that you will complete the report and set intermediate goals. Use a work progress schedule like the one shown in Chapter Seven to keep up with your progress.
5. Document the sources of data you present. The three ways to document data directly within a report are as follows:
   a. With footnotes at the bottom of the page (or with endnotes at the end of the report)
   b. With a full citation within the text at the point you refer to the source
   c. With a reference to a list of sources using a key number and page number(s) within the text at the point where the reference is made

You also can document data with a bibliography of sources related to the report topic. The bibliography may be just a list of sources, or you might annotate the entries. An annotation is a brief summary of the contents of a source.

Documentation is discussed in Appendix C. Also consult a style manual for ways to type and place documentation on the pages of the final draft of your report. Here is a list of several popular style manuals:

Campbell, William Giles, and Steven Vaughan Ballou. *Form and Style: Theses, Reports, Term Papers.* 4th ed. Boston: Houghton Mifflin, 1974.

Modern Language Association. *MLA Style Sheet.* New York: Modern Language Association, 1980.

Moyer, Ruth, Eleanour Stevens, and Ralph Switzer. *The Research and Report Handbook.* New York: John Wiley, 1981.

Publication Manual of the American Psychological Association, 2nd ed. Washington, D.C.: American Psychological Association, 1977.

Turabian, Kate L. *A Manual for Writers of Term Papers, Theses, and Dissertations,* 4th ed. Chicago: University of Chicago Press, 1973.

6. Edit and revise your first draft until you are satisfied with your effort. Then proofread the report using the proofreading techniques discussed in Chapter One. You can use word/information processors to proofread and edit your report copy. Chapter Thirteen contains more information about this subject.

All the writing principles presented in Chapters One and Two apply to writing a report. Perhaps you should review these techniques before you begin to write. The principles that have special application to the report writing process are *writing style, tense,* and *transitions.*

Personal or Impersonal Writing Style

The personal style of writing is informal. When using this style, use the first and second person throughout the report. By using personal pronouns—I, my, me, you, your, we, our, and us—you can convey a rather personal touch to your business writing. On the other hand, the impersonal writing style is more formal. When using this style, write in third person throughout the report. Avoid using personal pronouns entirely. Impersonal pronouns (those that do not refer to a person) may be used.

The best style to use for a particular report depends upon the report audience's requirements and the formality of the situation. Use impersonal style for longer, more formal reports written for people outside your organization or perhaps for executive officers within your organization. Use a personal style for memorandum reports and letter reports. (These latter reports are discussed further in the next chapter.)

The following examples show how the styles differ:

Personal As you can see from the results of the consumer survey, your nonfood departments are an essential part of your grocery store.

Impersonal   As the results of the consumer survey show, nonfood departments are an essential part of the grocery store.

Verb Tense

The proper tense to use is the tense that declares the time at which the event happened which you are discussing. Refer from the present time, the time at which you are preparing the report. For example, the conclusion *is* (present tense), but you *collected* the data (past tense). Use the present tense for all timeless events (those that existed in the past, now exist, and will exist in the future). For example, use present tense in presenting the findings.

Transition Statements

Use transition statements to achieve smooth thought flow in your writing, especially in presenting data. Two types of transition statements are transition sentences and lead-in sentences or paragraphs. Use transition sentences to connect ideas between subsections. Generally, a brief summary of one major section and a short reference to the next major section could be used as a transition sentence. An example of a transition sentence is the following:

> (last sentence of a section)   Input and output qualities are very important in determining which copier to buy, but the prices paid for these qualities also command attention. (A section on prices follows.)

Use lead-in sentences or paragraphs to introduce all the subsections of a major section. An example of how to begin a major section with a lead-in sentence is as follows:

> The cost involved in owning and operating a copier can be subdivided into four categories. These categories are initial cost, maintenance, supply, and depreciation cost. (Sections on four categories follow.)

APPLYING PROPER FORMAT TECHNIQUES

The effectiveness of a report can be enhanced by the way it is presented. Appearance makes a difference from a psychological standpoint. In addition to making sure that your report copy is attractive, use proper headings, margins, indentions, spacing, and page numbering.

Headings

You can use headings to show readers how the parts of a report fit together. If you arranged the headings in your final outline as suggested in Chapter Nine, you might use them in the report as well. The various levels of headings are called degrees. Although several variations of heading formats exist, a commonly used format is shown in Figure 1.

Margins

The first page of the actual report body should have a 2″ top margin. The top margin for the remaining pages of the report should be 1″. For the side and bottom margins, reports have a 1″ margin. If you are going to bind your report at the left or at the top, add $\frac{1}{2}$″ to that margin to allow for the binding. For left-bound reports, the center point of the line of

FIGURE 1 A description and placement of report headings.

COMMONLY USED HEADING FORMATS

FIRST-DEGREE HEADING

Use first-degree headings to identify the main sections of your report. Type these headings in all capital letters centered over the copy as shown. Please note that the title of the report is not a heading although it is typed in the same way as a first-degree heading. Remember also that you need at least two first-degree headings.

Second-Degree Heading

Use second-degree headings as subtopics of the main topics. Type these headings centered and underlined with the first letter of the main words capitalized as shown. Remember that you need at least two second-degree headings for each subtopic.

Third-Degree Heading

Use third-degree headings to identify subtopics of second-degree headings. Type this heading flush against the left-hand margin with the first letter of the main words capitalized as shown. As with the other two headings, you need at least two third-degree headings for each subtopic.

Fourth-Degree Heading. This heading is used to show subtopics under third-degree headings. Type the fourth-degree heading with the first letter of the main words capitalized. The heading is indented with five spaces and underlined on the first line of the paragraph as shown. This heading ends with a period, after which the paragraph copy follows on the same line. As in the other three headings, you need at least two fourth-degree headings for each subtopic.

writing is $\frac{1}{4}''$ to the right of the center of the page. The preliminary pages, such as the table of contents and abstract, and supplementary pages, such as the bibliography and appendix, have the same margin as the first page of the actual report body. Margin requirements are shown in Figure 2.

Indentions, Spacing, and Page Numbering

Generally, you should indent all paragraphs five spaces. The report could be typed either single or double spaced. Leave one blank line between paragraphs.

Number the pages of preliminary parts with small roman numerals. The title page is numbered, but the number should not be typed on that page. Do type numbers on all other pages of the preliminary parts, however. Center the number horizontally a $\frac{1}{2}''$ from the bottom of the page. Number all other pages in the report with arabic numerals. The first page of the report body is "1," and it is centered and typed $\frac{1}{2}''$ from the bottom of the page. On the remaining pages (including the supplementary parts), type page numbers in the right-hand corner. Place the number even with the right margin and $\frac{1}{2}''$ down from the top of the page. If the report is to be top-bound, type these page numbers at the center and $\frac{1}{2}''$ from the bottom of the page.

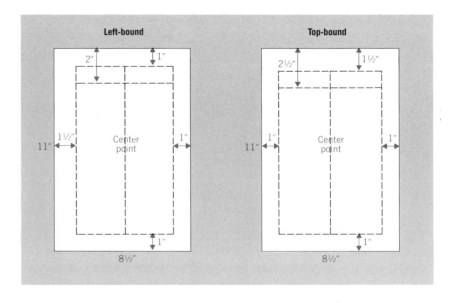

FIGURE 2 Margins for left-bound and top-bound reports.

PRESENTING THE FORMAL REPORT

Generally, any report you arrange in an indirect or logical order is organized inductively. The major parts of inductive organization are arranged in this order: introduction, analysis of data or findings, summary, conclusion(s), and recommendation(s) if you have one. When you arrange a report in a direct order, it is organized deductively. The major parts of deductive organization are arranged in this order: conclusion(s), recommendation(s) (if you include one), analysis of data or findings, and summary. You may add preliminary and supplementary parts; adding these parts lengthens the report and makes it more formal.

Identifying Parts of Long, Formal Reports

The parts you might include is determined by the nature of the report and by the requirements of your audience. Some parts should be included in all reports, however. The following outline shows all the parts that might appear in a long, formal report presented in inductive order. Asterisks are used to show parts that normally are included in any such report.

I. Preliminary parts
    *A. Letter or memorandum of transmittal
    *B. Title page
    C. Letter or memorandum of authorization
    D. Letter or memorandum of acceptance
    *E. Table of contents
    *F. Table of illustrations
    *G. Synopsis

II. Body (or text) parts
    *A. Introduction
        1. Statement of authorization
        2. Background of the problem
        *3. Statement of the problem
        4. Statement of hypothesis
        *5. Scope of the problem
        6. Limitations
        *7. Sources and methods of data collection
        8. Definition of terms
        *9. Report preview
    *B. Data analysis (findings)

*C. Report ending
    1. Summary
    2. Conclusion(s)
    3. Recommendation(s)
III. Supplementary parts
    *1. Bibliography
    2. Glossary
    3. Appendix
    4. Index

Preliminary Parts

Include preliminary parts to prepare your audience for understanding the information in the report body. These parts should be well organized.

Letter or Memorandum of Transmittal The letter or memorandum of transmittal is written to deliver the report in writing to the reader, who is the report authorizer. Write a letter when the report is sent outside the company, a memorandum when sent within the company.

What you will say depends on the research topic and the general situation in which the report topic was investigated. Organize the message using the favorable correspondence plan shown in Chapter Four. Use normal correspondence style and tone and avoid trite openings. Topics you might discuss are cost or time limitations, the report contents (especially the problem), conclusions, and recommendations. Close with an appreciation for the assignment and an offer to discuss the report contents further.

Generally, the transmittal letter or memorandum is not bound with the report. If it is bound, place it either as the first page or before the table of contents. A memorandum of transmittal is shown in Figure 3.

Title Page The title page should contain these sections: the title of the report typed in capitals; the name, title, and address of the individual(s) for whom the report was prepared; the name, title, and address of the report writer; and the date. Each line should be centered horizontally on the page, and each section should have about equal vertical spacing between them. The titles should be descriptive. For example, "The Effects of Price-Level Changes on Asset Valuation for Thomas Chemical Company" is descriptive; "Price-Level Changes" is not. An example of a title page is shown in Figure 4.

Letter or Memorandum of Authorization The letter or memorandum of authorization is sent by the authorizer to the researcher. This gives the researcher written authorization to complete the project. You should include a copy of this authorization in the report.

SIMPSON RESTAURANTS

It's a family affair at Simpson

To: Mr. Thomas Cooper, General Manager

From: Mr. John Hoffman, Regional Manager

Date: October 21, 1983

Subject: Food Spoilage Controls in the Restaurant Industry

The report on food spoilage controls in the restaurant industry that you requested on September 15, 1983, is attached.

The controls presented in this report will provide you with a system for controlling food spoilage, while maintaining increased profit margins. Four basic points of control have been discussed; these points are: purchasing, receiving, storing, and issuing. These controls would apply to all of your restaurant operations, regardless of size or volume.

I appreciate the opportunity to complete this assignment for you. Should you have any questions about the report, please call me at Extension 423. I'll be glad to answer them for you.

FIGURE 3 A memorandum of transmittal.

THE EFFECTS OF PRICE-LEVEL CHANGES ON
ASSET VALUATION FOR THOMAS CHEMICAL COMPANY

Prepared for

Mr. Paul Robinson, Controller
Thomas Chemical Company
Rochester, New York

Prepared by

Mr. Thomas Peters, Staff Accountant
Thomas Chemical Company
Rochester, New York
December 20, 1983

FIGURE 4 A title page.

Letter or Memorandum of Acceptance   The letter or memorandum of acceptance is the researcher's reply to the letter or memorandum of authorization. Basically, the act of signing the acceptance commits the researcher to prepare the report within the requirements of the authorization. Include a copy of this correspondence in the report.

Table of Contents   The table of contents generally should be included in any formal report that has five or more pages in the body. This table should contain the headings or captions of all the major divisions and perhaps subdivisions of the report and the page number where each part begins. Often, a row of periods (leaders) extends from the end of the heading to the page number. The table of contents assists the reader in locating a particular section; thus, the headings used in the table of contents should be the same as those that appear in the report. A table of contents is presented in Figure 5.

Table of Illustrations   The table of illustrations identifies the label, number, and title of the visual aids used in the report and the page number where they are located. You could divide this table into two sections if you prefer: tables and figures. Remember that the title of the visual aid included in the table of illustrations should be the same title used in the report. If you have fewer than four entries, you could include them in the

TABLE OF CONTENTS

FIGURE 5 A table of contents.

table of contents rather than prepare a separate table of illustrations. A table of illustrations is shown in Figure 6.

Synopsis The synopsis is a condensed version of the report body. This part is sometimes called an abstract, epitome, precis, or executive's overview. Include at least the main ideas from all the major sections in the body. Write the synopsis only after the report is completed and limit it to one page if possible. You may single space the synopsis even though the report is double spaced throughout the body. Although your report might be arranged inductively, the synopsis can be written either deductively or inductively. When the report is routed to people other than the authorizer, they may read only the synopsis. Figure 7 contains an example of a synopsis.

TABLE OF ILLUSTRATIONS

iv

FIGURE 6   A table of illustrations.

SYNOPSIS

For the past three years, Delta Manufacturing Company, Houston, Texas, has experienced an absentee rate among operations employees of 10 days per employee per year, or 4 percent. Although this rate is near national averages, the cost of this absenteeism is presently $360,000 per year. The plant manager believes the absentee rate can be reduced. Research shows that when workers are motivated, absentee rates of 1.0 to 1.5 percent are possible.

Approaches to absentee reduction include descriptive, disciplinary, and reinforcement control and other methods such as job enrichment and flextime. Of these approaches, the most widely used is disciplinary control. Disciplinary control is most useful for reducing abnormally high rates of absenteeism. For absentee rates in the 3 to 5 percent range, the most dramatic reductions have come from positive reinforcement programs.

The two types of positive reinforcement plans considered in this study are a lottery-based reward system and a "Christmas bonus" system. In the lottery system, each employee who has no absences for an entire month is eligible for a drawing for cash awards at the end of the month. Ten employees per month are selected to receive $25.00 each. Under the Christmas bonus plan, each employee receives $10.00 at Christmas time for each day his or her absences for the year are less than 10. The maximum amount of the bonus is $50.00 per employee.

Projected figures, based on the success of similar programs, show that the lottery system would reduce absenteeism by 25 percent. This would save about $88,000 per year. The Christmas bonus system would reduce absenteeism by 32 percent. This would save about $107,000. Based on these estimates and other advantages of the Christmas bonus plan, it is recommended that this plan be adopted to reduce absenteeism.

v

FIGURE 7   A synopsis.

Report Body Parts

The body (or text) parts of a report usually are divided into three major sections: *introduction, data analysis* or *findings,* and *report ending.*

Introduction   The purpose of the introductory section is to acquaint the reader with the report problem and to establish the credibility and usefulness of the research. Several of the items included in your research plan, presented in Chapter Seven, are parts of the report introduction.

Statement of Authorization

The statement of authorization is a brief statement that might be included in the report when an oral authorization is made. This statement says who the authorizer is and might state some of the requirements placed on the researcher. If a letter or memorandum of authorization is included in the report, this statement is not needed. See Figure 8 for an example.

Background of the Problem

The background of the problem is designed to provide the reader with the framework within which the research problem is set. You might discuss the larger problem(s) that surrounds the research problem. Also, you might discuss the history of the conditions leading to the current problem. See Figure 8 for an example.

Statement of the Problem

The statement of the problem identifies the problem to be researched. This statement should be clear and specific. See Figure 8 for an example. Also refer to a detailed discussion of problem statements in Chapter Seven.

Statement of Hypothesis

The hypothesis is a technical statement drawn from the problem statement. The hypothesis is to be tested for an answer to the research problem. You can write a hypothesis in either a directed or null form. A discussion and examples of hypotheses are given in Chapter Seven.

Scope of the Problem

The scope of the problem sets the boundaries of the study; in other words, how far reaching is the study? Sometimes, these boundaries are made clear by the discussion of the problem statement. When this occurs, then you could omit the scope. A discussion and an example of a scope statement are given in Chapter Seven.

To: Shirley B. Landry, Director
Corporate Affirmative Action

From: John Galloway, Administrator
Employee Information Systems

Date: February 19, 1983

Subject: Compliance with Equal Employment Opportunity Guidelines

Attached is the report you requested concerning the female hiring practices at Thompson Industries based on Equal Employment Opportunity guidelines.

The historical employment data from the three Thompson Industries divisions were analyzed in this study. A five-year base was selected for analysis: 1978 to 1982.

The analyses of the data show that the Chicago and Dallas divisions were above the compliance requirements; however, the Atlanta Division was below the requirements for the five-year period.

Thank you for the opportunity to conduct this study for you. If you would like to discuss any aspects of this report, Mr. Landry, please call me.

FIGURE 8 A formal analytical report.

AN ANALYSIS OF FEMALE HIRING PRACTICES AT THOMPSON INDUSTRIES, INCORPORATED, BASED ON EEO COMPLIANCE GUIDELINES

Prepared for

Shirley B. Landry, Director
Corporate Affirmative Action
Thompson Industries, Incorporated
New York, New York

Prepared by

John Galloway, Administrator
Employee Information Systems
Thompson Industries, Incorporated
February 19, 1984

FIGURE 8 (*Continued*)

TABLE OF CONTENTS

LIST OF ILLUSTRATIONS

iii

FIGURE 8 *(Continued)*

Limitations

Limitations are outside constraints placed upon the researcher over which he or she has no control. Some common limitations are too small a budget, too little time for conducting the study, and the inability to acquire proper tools or materials. If limitations are too great, you might decide not to conduct the study.

Sources and Methods of Data Collection

The part on sources and methods of data collection tells the reader how the researcher collected the data. If the collection process was purely secondary, it should be identified as such. If any primary research techniques were used, you should discuss the sample selection and the way in which you collected the data. For example, how were questionnaire validity and reliability established and how was the questionnaire administered? In addition, the statistical techniques you used to analyze the data should be presented. See Figure 8 for an example.

SYNOPSIS

On February 12, Shirley B. Landry, director of Corporate Affirmative Action, authorized a study to determine if EEO hiring guidelines for females were being met at Thompson Industries, Incorporated. In addition, the study was to serve as a five-year planning tool in establishing female hiring goals for each of the three Thompson Industries divisional employment offices.

A computer program was developed and used to query the hiring data of each of the three divisions. Employment data for 49,452 past and present employees were searched by the program to determine date of employment, division, and sex. Census Bureau data on the sex mix of the population surrounding each division and sex mix for applicants were used to determine what the EEO guidelines should be.

In highlight, the study resulted in the following findings:

- Dallas and Chicago are 7 percent above the compliance figure for the five-year period.
- Atlanta was 4 percent below the compliance figure for the five-year period.

Based on these findings, the Employee Information Systems Department recommends (1) the development of an intensive recruiting program to bring qualified females into the Atlanta division and (2) the development of a training program to train females for drafting and designing jobs in Atlanta. At the same time, Atlanta should hire 1 female for every 2 males until 32 additional females are hired. This hiring practice will bring Atlanta into compliance.

iv

FIGURE 8 (*Continued*)

AN ANALYSIS OF FEMALE HIRING PRACTICES AT THOMPSON INDUSTRIES, INCORPORATED, BASED ON EEO COMPLIANCE GUIDELINES

I. GENERAL OVERVIEW OF THE PROBLEM
A. Statement of Authorization

On February 12, Shirley B. Landry, director of Corporate Affirmative Action, orally authorized a study to determine if Equal Employment Opportunity (EEO) hiring guidelines for females were being met at Thompson Industries, Incorporated.

B. Background of the Problem

The EEO guidelines published by the federal government in late 1974 state that corporations advertising themselves as equal opportunity employers must maintain a specified relationship between the number of males and females hired. The relationship is expressed as a percentage and is determined by the sex mix of the surrounding population when weighted by the sex mix of the employment applicants.

C. Statement of the Problem

The problem of this study was to determine whether affirmative action goals established by the Corporate Affirmative Action Committee were in

FIGURE 8 (*Continued*)

compliance with EEO guidelines. The results of this study will be used to establish five-year hiring goals for each of the three Thompson Industries divisional employment offices.

D. Sources and Methods of Data Collection

The Employee Information Systems Department (EISD) is an employee service function for the three Thompson Industries divisions. All the data about the employment life cycle of Thompson Industries employees are maintained by the EISD on a computerized data base located at the Chicago Division offices. Data on newly hired employees are sent to the EISD from each divisional employment office. The data undergo both manual and automated auditing before being added to the data base. A breakdown of the current work force for each division is shown in Table 1.

TABLE 1
Divisional Work Force Size for Each Division

Division	Work Force Size	Percentage of Total Work Force
Chicago	12,360	75.83%
Dallas	3,850	23.61
Atlanta	90	0.56
Totals	16,300	100.00%

FIGURE 8 (*Continued*)

3

A computer program was developed to query the data base. The program was designed to select only the employees who were hired in 1978 through 1982. The employees who were included in this control period were defined further by sex, division, and year of employment. The program was processed against the data base on February 5, 1983. Of the 49,452 past and present employee records queried, only 3 were found to contain unidentifiable codes. These records were deleted from the study. The sex mix data that were used for the study were published by the U.S. Census Bureau in 1981.

II. REVIEW OF EACH DIVISION'S HIRING MIX

Each division of Thompson Industries was analyzed for the control period to determine the ratio between females and males hired.

A. Chicago Division Hiring Mix

The Chicago Division employs the most people, almost 76 percent of the total work force. The historical data show that the Chicago office hired 30 percent females and 70 percent males during the control period.

FIGURE 8 (*Continued*)

B. Dallas Division Hiring Mix

The Dallas Division is currently the second largest, employing about 24 percent of the total work force. The historical employment data shows that 35 percent of the people hired between 1978 and 1982 were females and 65 percent were males.

C. Atlanta Division Hiring Mix

The Atlanta Division was established as a specialized division for drafting and designing. Because of this, the division currently employs only 90 people. However, the ratio of people hired during the control period was 18 percent females and 82 percent males. A summary comparison by sex for each division is presented in Figure 1.

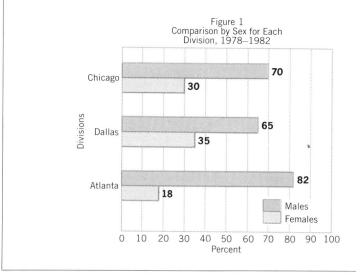

Figure 1
Comparison by Sex for Each
Division, 1978–1982

FIGURE 8 (*Continued*)

Definition of Terms

Any term that the reader is likely to find unfamiliar should be defined. If these terms are too numerous to include in this part, then place them in a glossary at the end of the report. Or you may define each term at the point you use it in the report.

Here is an example of the parts to use in defining terms:

Term   Class   Differentiation
Inventory record is a file that shows the quantity, description, and price of an item in stock.

Report Preview

The report preview is a transition statement from the introductory parts to the data analysis section. In other words, all the main topics that you

III. ACTUAL HIRING PRACTICES COMPARED WITH EEO GUIDELINES

The hiring practices for each division were analyzed and compared with the EEO guidelines to determine whether the divisions were in compliance.

A. Chicago and Dallas Actual Hiring Practices in Compliance

The mix for the Chicago and Dallas divisions is in compliance with the EEO guidelines. When compared with the weighted sex mix of the surrounding population, both Chicago and Dallas are 7 percent above the compliance requirement.

B. Atlanta Actual Hiring Practices Not in Compliance

The Atlanta Division fell short of the EEO guidelines by 4 percent. The variance can be explained, however. The Atlanta Division employs only high-level drafting and designing employees. A review of the pre-employment testing statistics at Atlanta shows that only 1 in 20 applicants were qualified for the jobs for which they applied. A comparison of actual hiring practices with EEO guidelines for each division is illustrated in Figure 2.

FIGURE 8 (*Continued*)

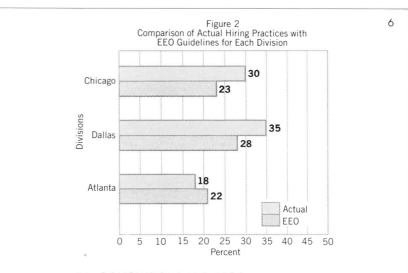

Figure 2
Comparison of Actual Hiring Practices with
EEO Guidelines for Each Division

6

IV. CONCLUSIONS AND RECOMMENDATIONS

No action is needed at the Chicago and Dallas divisions because they are in compliance with EEO guidelines. However, to bring the Atlanta Division into compliance, 32 females should be hired.

Based on the conclusions of this study, the recommendation is made that an extensive recruiting program be pursued to bring qualified female applicants into the Atlanta Division. In addition, a training program should be developed to train females for the drafting and designing positions. The EEO goals for Atlanta should be set to hire 1 female for every 2 males hired until 32 females are hired.

FIGURE 8 (*Continued*)

will discuss in the remainder of the report should be presented in this part.

Data Analysis   You should discuss the findings in the data analysis section. Remember to explain each finding in its relationship to how the research problem was solved. If you perform statistical analyses, you should present the data resulting from the analyses through some type of visual aid. See Chapters Nine and Ten for more information on how to prepare the data analysis section.

Report Ending   The last main section of the report body is the ending. Generally, you should divide this section into three parts: summary, conclusions, and recommendations. The nature of the report will determine what items you should include in this section. For example, if the report is purely informational, then you probably will include only a summary. But if the report is analytical, then you will need to draw conclusions and perhaps make recommendations.

Summary

The summary is designed to draw together the main points of the data analyses. This part gives the reader an overview of the research findings. Remember not to include the introductory parts in the summary. This summary is not the same as the synopsis, which some report writers call a summary.

Conclusions

The conclusions are answers to the problem statement. You may draw only one conclusion, depending on the nature of the problem. Each conclusion should be based on your findings. Therefore, you should never introduce new data in this part (or any part of the report ending). If you have several conclusions, you could number and list them with an appropriate lead-in sentence. An example of such a sentence is the following: "Based on the findings of this study, the following conclusions are drawn." A statement of conclusions is shown in Figure 8.

Recommendations

You should draw the recommendations directly from the conclusions. If you have several recommendations to make, you might number and list them with an appropriate lead-in sentence. An example of a lead-in sentence is the following: "Based on the conclusions of this study, the following recommendations are made."

The recommendations and conclusions might be combined under one heading. Whether you should do this depends upon their number and complexity. If you combine them, present the conclusions first. A sample of recommendations is shown in Figure 8.

Supplementary Parts

Supplementary parts provide additional related material about the report for the reader. These parts consist of the bibliography, glossary, appendix and index.

Bibliography   The bibliography provides the reader with the data sources consulted during the research. See Appendix C for an example.

Glossary   The glossary is an alphabetical list of technical or otherwise specialized terms that you define for the reader. Generally, when you have six or more terms to define, include them in this part of the report rather than in the introduction.

Appendix   The appendix (or appendices) contains material such as general tables or graphs, sample questionnaires, covering and follow-up letters or memorandums, computer program printouts, and the like. Include these items as appendices whenever including them in the body would interrupt the thought flow of the reading matter.

Give a title to each appendix ("Questionnaire," "Follow-up Letter") and list each in the table of contents. When you have more than one appendix, label them with capital letters. Examples of a label and title for an appendix are the following: "Appendix A: Questionnaire" and "Appendix B: Follow-up Letter."

Index   The index provides a cross-reference by name, subject, or both to the content of the report. Usually, research reports that are extremely long and detailed might benefit from an index. In this situation, the index is a detailed extension of the table of contents.

Illustrating a Formal Analytical Report

A formal analytical report written in an inductive or indirect order is shown in Figure 8, which begins on page 256. Today, employees of some companies have reports typeset on photocomposition equipment. (These reports will look similiar to the one in Figure 8, except that all pages will be the same size.) While this report does not include all the parts discussed in this chapter, remember to include all appropriate parts in each report that you write.

SUMMARY

The final step in the research process is writing the report. If you have completed all the preceding steps, the writing phase just should involve following through your writing plan.

Whether you use a personal or impersonal writing style depends upon the situation and the requirements of the audience. Use the tense that reflects the time at which an event happened. Also, you use transitions to provide coherence to the thought flow of the data.

Applying proper format techniques will improve the overall quality of the report from a psychological standpoint. Use proper headings, margins, indenting, spacing, and page numbering for best results.

When presenting the research results, the report writer should know how to put together the specific parts of a long, formal report. Generally, you should divide such a report into three main sections: preliminary, body (or text), and supplementary. The possible parts that might go in each section are listed on pages 279–280. Every report will not contain all possible parts, however. Instead, you should use those parts that will aid the audience's understanding of the problem you are discussing in the report.

Additional Readings

Brown, Harry M. *Business Report Writing*. New York: D. Van Nostrand, 1980, pp. 225–261.

Brown, Leland. *Effective Business Report Writing*, 3rd ed. Englewood Cliffs, N.J.: Prentice-Hall, 1973, pp. 72–104, 271–336.

Dawe, Jessamon. *Writing Business and Economic Papers*. Totowa, N.J.: Littlefield, Adams, 1975, pp. 125–172.

Haggblade, Berle. *Business Communication*. St. Paul, Minn.: West, 1982, pp. 168–169, 193–243.

Himstreet, William C., and Wayne Murlin Baty. *Business Communications: Principles and Methods*, 6th ed. Boston: Kent, 1981, pp. 380–420.

Lesikar, Raymond V. *Report Writing for Business*, 6th ed. Homewood, Ill.: Richard D. Irwin, 1981, pp. 119–181.

Lewis, Phillip V., and William H. Baker. *Business Report Writing*. Columbus, Ohio: Grid, 1978, pp. 89–98, 103–115, 133–140.

Moyer, Ruth, Eleanour Stevens, and Ralph Switzer. *The Research and Report Handbook: For Business, Industry, and Government*. New York: John Wiley, 1981, pp. 113–189.

Murphy, Herta A., and Charles E. Peck. *Effective Business Communications*, 3rd ed. New York: McGraw-Hill, 1980, pp. 623–663.

Treece, Malra. *Effective Reports*. Boston: Allyn & Bacon, 1982, pp. 66–105, 218–293.

Wilkinson, C. W., Peter B. Clarke, and Dorothy C. M. Wilkinson. *Communicating Through Letters and Reports*, 7th ed. Homewood, Ill.: Richard D. Irwin, 1980, pp. 468–476, 488–541.

Wolf, Morris Philip, Dale F. Keyser, and Robert R. Aurner. *Effective Communication in Business*, 7th ed. Cincinnati: South-Western, 1979, pp. 393–406.

Review Questions

1. Discuss the effects of the report writing suggestions presented in this chapter on your particular situation. What changes do you plan to make in the way you prepare reports as a result of this information? Explain your answer.

2. What is the difference between the personal and impersonal writing styles? Give an example of each. Which style is best for report writing?

3. What are two types of transitions? What are the benefits of using transitions?

4. Explain the use of headings in a report.

5. What are the three major parts of the long, formal report? What purpose does each major part serve?

6. What is the difference between the synopsis (or summary) that appears in the preliminary parts of a report and the summary that appears in the body?

7. Explain the difference between conclusions and recommendations.

8. What is an appendix? Where should you place an appendix in a long, formal report?

Exercises

1. Top Brand Grocery Stores, Inc., has grocery stores in the suburbs of Portland, Oregon. During the past year, the company has expanded the health and beauty aids departments in each store. The merchandise in these departments is priced slightly higher than is similar merchandise in drug and discount stores. The managers are developing a marketing and pricing plan for the departments. To plan well, they need to know how many and what types of customers purchase health and beauty aids in the departments.

   The following data were gathered from a questionnaire given to those customers who purchased these items. These questionnaires were administered at two stores between 9 A.M. and 5 P.M.

   Total customers purchasing health and beauty aids: 967

   Ages: 21 and younger, 22 percent; 22 to 30, 48 percent; 31 to 40, 18 percent; over 40, 12 percent

   Sex: females, 94 percent; males, 6 percent

   Marital status: married, 76 percent; single or divorced or widowed, 24 percent

   Employment: full-time, 72 percent; part-time, 21 percent; unemployed, 7 percent

   Frequency of purchasing items: always, 60 percent; often (every other time), 12 percent; sometimes (every third time), 20 percent; rarely (when needed), 4 percent. Two main reasons why items purchased: time and convenience

   Write a report to the company's managers describing your findings.

2. You have just been promoted to the position of director of training and development at Denworth Industries. As one of your first assignments, the president of the company has asked you to prepare a training program for first-line supervisors in the areas of leadership, motivation, and communication skills. Write a report to the president that includes the rationale of the new program and outlines the topics that will be presented.

3. Deca Motel has a popular, high-quality, economy motel. However, during the past six months, the motel has experienced a decline in room occupancy. The price of room rates rose slightly during the period. However, company managers thought that there might be other reasons for this decline in occupancy. Write a report for the motel's managers discussing the possible reasons for this decline. Recommend a course of action.

4. Assume that you are the supervisor of the

data processing department at Owens Systems, Inc. The data processing department operates 24 hours a day, and your employees work rotating shifts. You are concerned about the mental and physical effects that the rotating shifts have on the employees and their families. Some of the mental effects mentioned by several of your employees were insomnia, stress, irritability, depression, and lack of concentration. Some of the physical effects mentioned were headaches, upset stomachs, and loss of appetites. Write a report to the vice president in charge of operations. Analyze the effects of rotating shifts on employees and their families and recommend possible solutions.

5. Generic products have been available in the Orchard Park area grocery stores for about a year. A variety of generic goods can be purchased that are packaged with plain labels and contain no brand names. These goods are offered by retail grocery stores at prices below those of brand-name products. As the regional director of a grocery store chain, you wanted to determine if consumers are responding to generic products as an acceptable alternative to brand-name products in your Orchard Park store. Questionnaires were distributed to customers during a two-day period from 9 A.M. to 9 P.M. each day. The data gathered with the questionnaires are as follows:

Total number of questionnaires completed: 85

Customer purchasing habits: bought generics, 67 percent; not bought generics but familiar with them, 27 percent; not familiar with generics, 6 percent

Background of customers who bought generics:

    Sex—females, 77 percent; males, 23 percent

Age—under 20, 3 percent; 20 to 30, 52 percent; 31 to 40, 28 percent; 41 to 50, 12 percent; over 50, 15 percent

Average savings to customers who bought generics: 25 percent

Customers who believe that quality of generic products compares well with that of brand-name products: 82 percent

Write a report to the vice president of marketing.

6. Compile a list of 20 common generic products that are available at two or three grocery stores in your area. Record the price of each product and then record the price of a comparable name brand. Write a report to your instructor in which you evaluate your findings.

7. A cosmetics buyer for a local department store wanted to determine the type of customer who purchases cosmetics. The factors involved are occupations, income levels, ages, and brands of cosmetics purchased. The buyer conducted a survey by administering questionnaires to 50 customers. The following data were gathered:

Age: under 20, 6 percent; 20 to 29, 37 percent; 30 to 39, 32 percent; 40 to 49, 10 percent; 50 and older, 15 percent

Family income levels: under $10,000, 34 percent; $10,000 to $20,000, 46 percent; over $20,000, 20 percent

Occupations: professional, 29 percent; administrative, 43 percent; students, 6 percent; homemakers, 18 percent; unemployed and retired, 4 percent

Daily use of cosmetics: 80 percent

Average purchase range: less than $5.00, 10 percent; $5.00 to $10.00, 52 percent; $10.01 to $20.00, 32 percent; over $20.00, 6 percent

Brand "status": extremely important, 29 percent; important, 48 percent; not important, 18 percent; no opinion, 5 percent

Write a report to the department store manager.

8. A new company restaurant opened recently at Baxter Industries. As manager of food services, you wanted to determine the level of satisfaction that the employees had with the new restaurant. The factors that concerned you were as follows: (a) physical attributes (comfort, cleanliness, overall appearance), (b) food (quality, portions), (c) price, (d) food service workers (courteous, neat, helpful), and (e) overall satisfaction

You conducted interviews with 75 employees to determine their reactions to the new restaurant. The following data were drawn from the interviews:

Physical Attributes
Outstanding, 65 percent
Very satisfied, 22 percent
Satisfied, 10 percent
Not completely satisfied, 3 percent
Not satisfied, 0 percent

Price
Outstanding, 25 percent
Very satisfied, 30 percent
Satisfied, 22 percent
Not completely satisfied, 15 percent
Not satisfied, 8 percent

Food
Outstanding, 40 percent
Very satisfied, 50 percent
Satisfied, 8 percent
Not completely satisfied, 0 percent
Not satisfied, 2 percent

Food Service Workers
Outstanding, 80 percent
Very satisfied, 20 percent
Satisfied, 0 percent
Not completely satisfied, 0 percent
Not satisfied, 0 percent

Overall Satisfaction
Outstanding, 40 percent
Very satisfied, 28 percent
Satisfied, 32 percent
Not completely satisfied, 0 percent
Not satisfied, 0 percent

Write a report to the vice president of finance.

CHAPTER TWELVE

Understanding Special Applications of Report Writing

The goals in studying the text and completing the activities in this chapter are to know

1. The general characteristics of short, informal reports
2. The proper format techniques for preparing short, informal reports
3. The situations that require a specific type of short, informal report
4. How to prepare the types of short, informal reports to solve specific report problems

The report research and writing process described in Chapters Seven through Ten apply to all types of reports. The long, formal report presented in Chapter Eleven is not the most common business report. However, writing this report is the most effective way in which to learn what goes into a report and how to put it together. Short, informal reports are commonly written in business today. The general characteristics and basic formats of these reports are discussed in this chapter.

GENERAL CHARACTERISTICS OF SHORT, INFORMAL REPORTS

As do formal reports, informal reports transmit meaningful data to the report audience for either informational or decision-making purposes. Usually, they are not more than five pages long. General characteristics of these reports are

1. *Uses the personal writing style.*   If you wish, use a personal, conversational writing style for these reports. The first and second person is acceptable and very common. Follow the writing principles given in Chapters One and Two. Be careful to limit the use of self-references (I, me, my).

2. *Could be either informational or analytical.*   Informal reports may be either informational or analytical. The kind of report needed depends on the nature of the problem to be solved. In informal analytical reports, the data analysis might not be as detailed as that in formal analytical reports. But the overall approach to the problem analysis should be the same. Also, visual aids might be used in either type to support your findings.

3. *Uses the deductive organizational plan frequently.*   Busy managers often prefer to know the major solutions for a problem before reading the details. For this reason, a deductive plan often is used in informal business reports. However, depending on your analysis, you may use other plans.

4. *Uses few preliminary, introductory, and · supplementary report parts.*   When the person who authorizes the report is very familiar with the problem situation, you might be able to omit many of the introductory parts of the report. No clear rule exists saying how many introductory items you should include. The number used depends upon the audience's requirements, including their backgrounds in the subject area of the report discussion. Because informal reports are shorter and less detailed than are formal reports, some preliminary

and supplementary parts may be omitted as well. The decision about what to include depends upon the nature of the report and the audience's needs.

FORMAT OF SHORT, INFORMAL REPORTS

Generally, short, informal reports are written in one of three formats: memorandum, letter, or manuscript. These reports might contain headings, footnotes, tables and figures, and perhaps some supplementary items. Usually, they are typed single spaced.

Memorandum Reports

The memorandum is probably the most common format for short, informal reports. The reason for this is that informal reports are used widely for communicating data within companies, where the memorandum is the appropriate format. An example of an analytical memorandum report written in a deductive organizational plan is shown in Figure 1.

Letter Reports

You should use the letter format when preparing a report for readers who are outside your company. Include a subject line after the salutation that describes clearly the report title. The content of this report is much the same as if it were a memorandum report. However, be sure to include the customary goodwill opening and closing statements that letters normally have. An example of an analytical letter report written in an inductive organizational plan is shown in Figure 2.

Short Reports in Manuscript Form

You could write a short report in manuscript form if you prefer this format. However, making this choice should meet the requirements of your report audience. The overall structure of this report follows that of the long, formal report discussed in the last chapter. However, the letter or memorandum of transmittal and title page are the only preliminary parts that normally are included. Most of these short reports are organized either inductively or deductively.

your friendly bank . . .

THE FIRST NATIONAL CITY BANK

MEMORANDUM

To: Vince Simpson, Senior Vice-President

From: Paula Miller, Supervisor

Date: July 15, 1983

Subject: Effect of the SEI Computerized Accounting System
           on Trust Administration

Recommendations

Based on my analysis of the SEI system, I believe additional
training should be given to trust administrators. They need
to understand better the reports and other system information generated by this computerized accounting system.
Also, the input forms should be reviewed to determine if
revisions can be made to reduce the amount of clerical work
by our trust administrators. Although these areas should be
improved in the future, I feel that our bank should remain
on the SEI system.

These recommendations resulted from interviews you authorized on June 11, 1983. The interviews were held with
seven trust administrators who have experience with both
the SEI system and the old manual system. For the purpose
of making this study, the administrators' responsibilities
were separated into four major categories: (1) establish-
ment of new accounts, (2) account administration, (3) asset
administration, and (4) reports.

Establishment of New Accounts

All of those interviewed said that establishing a new
account is more complex and time consuming under the SEI
system. However, the administrators thought the data that
are available through the system are more beneficial and
complete.

FIGURE 1 A memorandum report in deductive organizational plan.

Account Administration

Receipts

Receipts of income and principal were perceived to be more dependable under the SEI system by all those interviewed, except one administrator who thought there was no change.

Disbursements

The opinions regarding disbursements were almost divided equally. Three of those interviewed thought that the increased clerical work required was too time consuming. The other four did not mention this clerical work as a negative factor for handling disbursements. All the administrators liked the increased dependability and accuracy of disbursements under the SEI system.

Tax Accounting

All the administrators believe that when transactions were coded correctly, income tax information could be obtained more readily and would be more accurate.

Asset Administration

Investment Reviews

All of those interviewed said that the investment data were equally clear under both systems. However, they also noted that the integrity of the investment data was far superior to that of a manual system. Three administrators mentioned a problem with pricing tape.

Cash Management

All the administrators cited the benefits to the customers and the accuracy of the investments as highly beneficial when the cash management function is computer controlled.

FIGURE 1 (*Continued*)

<u>Reports</u>

<u>Internal</u>

Each administrator found the computerized reports to be both useful and timely. However, some of the reports were difficult to interpret and understand.

<u>Customer</u>

All the administrators reported that customer statements were more attractive, but they were more difficult for the customer to understand. In addition, they thought the statements were being prepared on a timely basis.

FIGURE 1 *(Continued)*

MARKETING
RESEARCH
UNLIMITED
INCORPORATED

4251 TAMIAMI TRAIL
MIAMI, FL 33010
TELEPHONE: (305) 754-1234

August 24, 1983

John R. Tabor, General Manager
Benson Manufacturing Company
645 State Street
Florida City, FL 33034

Dear Mr. Tabor

Subject: Interest in Company Supported Financial
          Cooperative

On July 8, 1983, you authorized Marketing Research
Unlimited to sample several of your employees' responses
to determine whether they might support a financial cooper
ative.

Background

Several factors were considered to determine whether Benson
Manufacturing Company employees could benefit from the
savings and loan services that a company cooperative could
offer. These factors were satisfaction of service received
from present financial institutions, employee interest in
borrowing money, and personal investment habits.

Method

To find out the amount of interest in establishing a financial cooperative, I interviewed a sample of 25 employees.
Of the 25, 11 presently are working as managers while 14
are not managers.

General Banking Service Favorable

Area banking services appear to be satisfactory. The

FIGURE 2 A letter report in inductive organizational plan.

John R. Tabor
Page 2
August 24, 1983

employees described the services they received as prompt,
courteous, dependable, and efficient. Convenience is a
major factor in choosing where to get banking services.

Interest Keen in Borrowing Money

Even with the high interest rates charged by financial
institutions, employee interest in borrowing money remains
high. Fifty-six percent of the employees reported that
changing interest rates on consumer loans have had little
or no effect on their decisions to borrow money.

Even though fluctuating interest rates have affected fewer
than half of the employees, the number of outstanding loans
is high. Also, 10 of the 25 employees interviewed seek
financial assistance every four years.

Investment Habits Irregular

With the cost of living increasing almost daily along with
the fluctuations in the prime lending rate, it is not sur-
prising that your employees' investment habits are unstable
as well.

Only 44 percent of the employees have savings accounts.
The high interest rates paid on money market certificates
have contributed to the lack of interest in having savings
accounts. The remaining 56 percent of the employees would
be willing to invest in a savings account which would offer
them a return of at least 7 percent.

If a 7 percent return were offered to the employees on their
savings, almost one half of them would be willing to invest
between $50 and $100 monthly. The employees' monthly
savings investment is shown in Table 1.

FIGURE 2 (*Continued*)

John R. Tabor
Page 3
August 24, 1983

Table 1

Dollar Distribution of Monthly Savings Investment

Monthly Investment	Number of Employees	Percent
Over $200	1	4
100 - 200	2	8
50 - 100	12	48
Under 50	10	40
Total	25	100

Recommended Action

Based on my analysis of the sample of 25 employees, there seems to be a definite interest in establishing a company supported financial cooperative. However, before a decision is made, I recommend that you conduct a company-wide survey to determine whether most employees would support a cooperative.

Should you need any explanation of any part of this report, Mr. Tabor, please call me at 754-1234. Also, if you want to pursue the company-wide survey, I would be happy to conduct it for you.

Sincerely yours

Linda White

Linda White
Research Associate

Enclosure

FIGURE 2 *(Continued)*

SPECIFIC TYPES OF SHORT, INFORMAL REPORTS

Many different types of short, informal reports exist in business today. On the one hand, these may be one-page printed forms for special-purpose reporting (performance appraisals, for example). On the other hand, they may be more complex and detailed (proposals, for example). You may present these latter types of reports in memorandum, letter, or manuscript format. Other than proposals, examples of these reports are feasibility, justification, periodic, progress, and process or procedure description reports.

Proposals

Two reasons to write proposals are to (1) get projects, products, or services accepted either within or outside the business and (2) seek money by obtaining grants for research or special projects. Proposals may be solicited in some cases. An example of this is a request for proposal (RFP), as when a governmental agency or professional foundation requests competitive proposals for funding of a project. Also, they could be unsolicited. For example, an individual may write a proposal to upper-level managers in a company to suggest a course of action that might benefit company operations.

When you write a proposal based on an RFP, follow the requirements as closely as you can. These requirements vary from case to case. The following plan shows all the parts you could include in a proposal. Whether you use all these items depends on the nature of the proposed action and the report audience's requirements.

1. *Title page.* The title page should include the title of the proposal, name of the granting body or individual, name of the preparer, and the date.
2. *Abstract or summary.* The abstract or summary tells the reviewer exactly what you plan to do and how it will be done. Limit this part to about 100 to 300 words, depending on the length of the proposal.
3. *Background.* The background section includes a discussion of the situation that surrounds the problem or need. This may include a review of the literature to show the relationship of the current proposal to the literature areas that exist on the subject.
4. *Statement of the problem or need.* The problem or need statement makes clear what you intend to investigate.
5. *Objective(s).* The objective statement(s) reveals to the proposal reviewer the parts of the specific plan. This includes the kind of data

you will collect and how you will apply these data to the problem or need.

6. *Procedures or methodology.*   The procedures or methodology section will show how you will gather and analyze your data.

7. *Time requirements.*   In the time requirements section, tell what time period is needed to complete the research or project. You could use visual aids to show your planned activities. Time charts and flow charts are especially useful in proposals.

8. *Personnel.*   You should include the names and backgrounds of the principal researchers or investigators in the personnel section. You might place a résumé for each investigator in the appendix of the proposal.

9. *Cost requirements.*   The cost section should provide an estimate of all the costs of the project or research. These costs should include such items as supplies, typing, duplicating, computer time, and travel.

10. *Appendix.*   All supporting documents that might interest the proposal reviewer should be included in the appendix.

Feasibility Reports

You might conduct a feasibility study to determine whether a particular project, equipment, or program procedure might help to resolve a specific problem. The report might involve primary or secondary research or both. The feasibility report is an analytical report that presents solutions or evaluates alternatives. The purpose is to determine whether you can accomplish and put into effect the solutions or alternatives. An example of a feasibility report is to present the results of an investigation into the possible purchase of a new type of equipment.

Most feasibility reports are internal and are written in the memorandum format. Major emphasis should be placed on the analysis, conclusion, and recommendation. Some of the parts you might include in a feasibility report follow. This arrangement is inductively organized.

1. Background of the problem

2. Statement of the problem

3. Scope of the problem

4. Analysis (should include all the areas investigated and perhaps the cost benefits)

5. Conclusion

6. Recommendation

Justification Reports

Justification reports are similar to feasibility reports in cases where feasibility reports support a particular action. A feasibility report might recommend that an action be taken or not be taken. However, a justification report always recommends taking an action and then justifies it. You might write a justification report to justify buying a new copying machine, hiring a new sales representative, or installing a new cost accounting system. When writing these reports, focus the major part of your discussion on the benefits of taking the action you recommend. For best results, use the deductive organizational plan. You might arrange the report parts in the following order:

1. Recommendation
2. Conclusion
3. Analysis and discussion (should contain all factors that might favor the recommendation, such as cost, quality, and use)
4. Summary
5. Appendix (might include product literature, equipment specifications, and like materials)

Periodic Reports

Periodic reports usually are written to tell managers what activities have taken place for a certain time period. The time period might be daily, weekly, monthly, or even yearly. These reports may be external or internal. Probably the most familiar periodic report to you is the corporate annual report to stockholders. Generally, the organizational plan for an annual report might be as follows:

1. Financial and/or corporate highlights (usually includes visual aids)
2. Letters to shareholders from corporate chairman of the board or president
3. Various discussion sections (may be about products, new developments, future directions, and so forth, and usually includes visual aids)
4. Financial statements
5. Discussion notes about financial statements
6. Auditor's report
7. Names and titles of company directors and officers

Where the annual report is an external periodic report, the daily, weekly, or monthly reports are internal. These internal reports usually are written in memorandum format. Because the periodic report generally is written to the same person each time, introductory and concluding remarks are not necessary. All that is necessary is a brief discussion of the activities that took place during the reporting period.

Progress Reports

You should write progress reports to let the reader know about the status of a particular project. For example, you might be putting in a new computer system or constructing a new building and wish to report on your progress. Generally, progress reports are written during the various stages of the project. The information they contain helps managers to monitor each phase of the project.

You can write a progress report after a project is completed to show the effects the project has had on operations. A basic organizational plan that the progress report could follow is

1. *Introduction.* The introduction could include the purpose of the report, a brief background statement, and perhaps an overview of the project.
2. *Work completed.* If you have a series of progress reports, divide the work completed section into two parts: (a) a summary of the work completed during the previous periods and (b) a summary of the work completed since the last progress report.
3. *Work to be completed.* The work to be completed section should contain an overview of the remaining work. Include the dates when work will be completed.
4. *Conclusion.* Make comments in the concluding section on whether time and budget requirements can be met. Also, if any part of the project is put into operation, evaluate its effectiveness.

An example of a progress report written after a new computer system was installed in a company is shown in Figure 3.

Process or Procedure Description Reports

In business and industry, many situations require you to complete some process or procedure. Examples are handling inventory, operating a microcomputer, preparing a tax return form, and hiring an employee. To complete such processes or procedures successfully, you must be able to follow directions carefully. If you should write the instructions for others

C.A.P. CRANFORD AUTOMOTIVE PARTS, INCORPORATED
MEMORANDUM

To: John Williams, President

From: Peter Jackson, Controller

Date: April 30, 1983

Subject: Progress Report on Computerized Parts Inventory
          Control System

Introduction

The purpose of this progress report is to determine the
effects of our new computerized inventory control system on
the overall business operations.

Before we installed this new system on January 7, 1983, we
used a manual system for parts inventory control. Some of
the problems we encountered with the manual system were as
follows: (1) using too much time to operate the system and
(2) carrying more inventory than was needed. Also, there
was a lack of coordination in maintaining inventory control
among the three stores located in Buffalo, Lackawanna, and
Orchard Park.   Therefore, I will report on the progress
made during the first quarter of this year.

Work Completed

This new system required the installation of one display
terminal and modem at the Buffalo store. This terminal is
connected to our distributor's computer in Syracuse. We
receive our inventory reports by mail from there.

Before installing the new system, each store had one full-
time employee who posted each part purchase and sale
manually. This process took eight hours a day to complete.
However, with the new system, we have only one full-time
employee located at the Buffalo store who completes the
process in three hours. We now send all the daily activity data to the Buffalo store for processing.

FIGURE 3 A progress report.

A problem that we had was that we carried more inventory than was actually needed. The parts manager from each store had to place monthly and quarterly orders. They had to go through every inventory card in the manual system to check its sales history. The parts manager then took a week to decide how many of each part to purchase. With the new system, only special orders from a different distributor requires manual processing.

The new system has a reorder point. The computer will look at the sales history and the cost of the parts. Then it will run these data through the economic order quantity (EOQ). This procedure will determine the optimum quantity of parts to order.

We have improved the coordination in maintaining the inventory control among the three stores. The new system requires one general parts manager to control the purchasing processes of the three stores. In addition, this system provides a listing of all parts located in each store. Thus, if one store needs a part that is not on hand, the sales clerk can consult the list to determine if the other two stores have the part. Parts availability for our customers has increased from 79 percent to 90 percent as a result of having this new system.

Work to be Completed

Removing remaining problems from the system and the computer program is work that is yet to be completed. We plan to have these problems solved by June, 1983.

Conclusion

With this new system, we now have a method of preventing excess inventory. This system will maintain a balanced assortment of inventory which will provide our customers better service. We will be able to carry more of a variety rather than an excess quantity. Also, this system will save the parts manager's time. From a financial viewpoint, working capital will be freed and our return on investment will increase.

FIGURE 3 *(Continued)*

to follow, prepare a detailed, step-by-step narrative in report form. Include visual aids such as flow charts, drawings, and pictures when they will help.

When you write this type of report for a nontechnical audience, write the description in simple, nontechnical language. Explain any unfamiliar terms that you use. The following suggested plan shows all the parts that you might include in a process or procedure report:

1. *Introduction.*   The introduction section should include the purpose of the report.

2. *Rationale.*   The rationale statement gives an overview of the importance of understanding the process or procedure. Also, include any background information needed by the audience to understand the process or procedure.

3. *Description of the functions.*   A description of the functions includes a list of them along with a short description of each.

4. *Instructions.*   Instructions should be given in a step-by-step way so that the reader can complete the activity correctly. You may wish to list these instructions. Use the imperative mood, active voice, and simple sentences. Also you might key them to a visual aid that shows the entire process or procedure.

5. *Conclusion.*   The concluding comments could include a brief summary of the process or procedure. You might also include any other information that might help the user to complete the activity. For example, additional readings may help.

SUMMARY

Short, informal reports are characterized as (1) using a personal writing style, (2) being informational or analytical, (3) frequently using deductive organizational plan, and (4) using few preliminary, introductory, and supplementary report parts.

The format of short, informal reports can be memorandum, letter, or manuscript. The selection of the proper format depends upon the audience's requirements and the report's nature. Many different types of these reports exist. The most common are proposals and fea-

sibility, justification, periodic, progress, and process or procedure description reports.

You will write proposals to get projects, products, or services accepted either within or outside the business. Also, the proposal is written to seek money by obtaining grants for research or special projects. You might write a feasibility report to show whether a particular project, equipment, or program procedure might help to resolve a specific problem. A justification report is similar to a feasibility report, except that a justification report always recommends taking a specific action and justifies it. The feasibility report explores the question more fully from all sides.

You will write periodic reports to managers to report on activities that have taken place for a certain time period. A progress report will let the reader know about the status of a particular project. A process or procedure description report will instruct others about how to proceed to complete an activity.

Additional Readings

Brown, Harry M. *Business Report Writing.* New York: D. Van Nostrand, 1980, pp. 265-285.

Brown, Leland. *Effective Business Report Writing,* 3rd ed. Englewood Cliffs, N.J.: Prentice-Hall, 1973, pp. 19-52, 343-394.

Dagher, Joseph P. *Technical Communication: A Practical Guide.* Englewood Cliffs, N.J.: Prentice-Hall, 1978, pp. 62-70, 214-246, 264-272.

Himstreet, William C., and Wayne Murlin Baty. *Business Communications: Principles and Methods,* 6th ed. Boston: Kent, 1981, pp. 350-371.

Kolin, Philip C. *Successful Writing at Work.* Lexington, Mass.: D. C. Heath, 1982, pp. 335-381.

Lannon, John M. *Technical Writing,* 2nd ed. Boston: Little, Brown, 1982, pp. 152-227, 400-472.

Lesikar, Raymond V. *Report Writing for Business,* 6th ed. Homewood, Ill.: Richard D. Irwin, 1981, pp. 109-117.

Moyer, Ruth, Eleanour Stevens, and Ralph Switzer. *The Research and Report Handbook: For Business, Industry, and Government.* New York: John Wiley, 1981, pp. 36-50, 64-77.

Pauley, Steven E. *Technical Report Writing Today,* 2nd ed. Boston: Houghton Mifflin, 1979, pp. 28-72, 141-148, 171-220.

Treece, Malra. *Effective Reports.* Boston: Allyn & Bacon, 1982, pp. 30-61.

Weisman, Herman M. *Basic Technical Writing,* 4th ed. Columbus, Ohio: Charles E. Merrill, 1980, pp. 64-87, 287-294.

Wilkinson, C. W., Peter B. Clarke, and Dorothy C. M. Wilkinson. *Communicating Through Letters and Reports,* 7th ed. Homewood, Ill.: Richard D. Irwin, 1980, pp. 551-572.

Review Questions

1. Discuss the four general characteristics of short, informal reports.

2. Three common formats for short, informal reports are memorandum, letter, and manuscript. Discuss the situations in which you would use each format.

3. What is a proposal? What are two reasons to write proposals? How does a proposal differ from the research plan presented in Chapter Seven?

4. What is the purpose for writing a feasibility report?

5. What is a justification report? How does it differ from the feasibility report?

6. Periodic reports provide information about activities during a time period. How are periodic reports used by their audiences? What value do these reports serve?

7. Discuss the importance of progress reports. What benefits do they provide managers?

8. Why would you write a process or procedure description report? What role do visual aids play in these reports?

Exercises

1. The following sentences are written in formal, impersonal writing style. Rewrite them in an informal, personal style.
   a. "The data analysis indicate the trend toward flexible work hours."
   b. "Interviews were conducted with a representative sample of bank branch managers."
   c. "Based on the findings of this study, the following conclusions are made:"
   d. "Based on the conclusions of this study, the following recommendations are drawn:"
   e. "Further research should be conducted to determine the effects of change on new employees."

2. Locate an old research paper or perhaps a report from the place where you work. Then write a memorandum report detailing the highlights of the report. Organize your report in a deductive organizational plan.

3. Write a letter report to your instructor or to your employer that outlines the effect of technology on the office of the future.

4. The division of research at Mobjack University is requesting proposals for research grants to study the effect of electronic mail and teleconferencing on university operations. Prepare a proposal outlining your study.

5. Using one of the following topics, prepare a feasibility report in a memorandum format:
   a. Adopting a management by objectives (MBO) program

   b. Changing inventory methods from FIFO (first-in, first-out) to LIFO (last-in, first-out)
   c. Adding a new exercise unit to an existing building
   d. Moving a shoe store to a new location in a shopping mall
   e. Buying a microcomputer for the office

6. Keep a record of both your work and personal activities for two weeks. Then prepare a periodic report about these activities in a memorandum format. Remember to classify your activities into various sections and to use report headings.

7. Find a business or other organization that has recently begun a new construction project or installed a new computer or word processing system or some other equipment or procedure. Then interview a representative of the organization. Determine what work was completed, what work needs to be completed, and perhaps what reactions the representative has about the project. Then prepare a progress report about your findings.

8. Choose one of the following topics and prepare a process or procedure description report. Remember to include a visual aid to support your description.
   a. Buying or selling merchandise and updating inventory
   b. Preparing a Form 1040A federal income tax return
   c. Operating a microcomputer
   d. Hiring new employees
   e. Filing a grievance with an employer

UNIT 4

Communication Systems in Organizations

CHAPTER THIRTEEN

Word/Information Processing

THE COMMUNICATOR'S NEW TOOL

The goals in studying the text and completing the activities in this chapter are to know

1. The types of word/information processing equipment
2. How dictation equipment is used by business communicators
3. How to dictate effectively
4. How managerial work stations and optical character recognition equipment are used
5. The types of keyboarding equipment used in processing messages electronically
6. How to store messages on word/information processing equipment
7. How to prepare short and long documents on word/information processing equipment
8. How to prepare form documents on word/information processing equipment
9. The correct printer to use for a particular purpose when using word/information processing equipment
10. The advantages and disadvantages of physical and electronic distribution systems

INTRODUCTION

Changes in office automation technology in recent years have brought much needed help for business communicators. Using what is called *word/information processing equipment* to automate many functions, the entire process of producing and delivering business messages is now greatly improved. This includes help with *every* step in the process: *composing messages, editing and revising them, producing final copy, and even distributing messages to receivers.* You can perform simple tasks automatically with this equipment, for example, adding or deleting information or moving ideas about in a message you are composing. Once your message is prepared, you can check your work for spelling and grammatical errors before producing the final copy. The result is that you can now compose a *more accurate message faster and easier* than with conventional methods. The equipment is easy to learn to use (called "user-friendly"), so many executives are now producing their own messages and distributing them without any assistance from others.

Two types of equipment are now used widely. One is the *word processor*, which is designed specifically for performing language functions such as preparing correspondence and reports, including visuals such as tables. Leading manufacturers of word processors include International Business Machines and Lanier Business Products. The other type of equipment being used is the *personal computer*, which is designed primarily for performing statistical functions. However, personal computers can be used to perform language functions as well, given the appropriate program (software) package. Among the leading manufacturers are Commodore, Radio Shack, and Apple.

Word processors are sold primarily for business use, but personal computers are now being sold widely for both home and business use. Personal computers have been accepted so well in the marketplace that they are now advertised in magazines for general readership, such as *Time* and *Newsweek*. Labeling them a product of the year, *Fortune* magazine reports that the number of personal computers sold jumped from 850,000 in 1981 to 3.1 million in 1982.[1] Harold C. Kinne, senior vice president of Future Computing, a marketing research company, estimates that units sold will grow by 50 percent annually through 1986.[2]

Basically, word/information processing is a systematic approach to storing, revising, and printing documents. This system begins with the person who originates the ideas or information and ends with the dispatch

[1]"Products of the Year," *Fortune*, December 27, 1982, p. 42.

[2]Harold C. Kinne, "Personal Computers: An Executive's Best Friend?" *Today's Office*, November 1982, p. 72.

of the typed document or typed copy. In other words, a word/information processing system includes input, processing, output, and distribution of messages.

MAKING THE INPUT

The information that is entered into a word/information processing system for processing is called the *input*. For longer, more complex documents, such as business reports and statistical data, you might provide this input as a handwritten draft. The typist (transcriber) will then prepare the information in mailable form on the word/information processor using your handwritten draft as the source. For shorter, simpler documents such as letters and memorandums, you might use some form of dictation equipment to provide the input.

Dictation Equipment

The two types of dictation equipment available are called *endless loop media* and *discrete media*. All endless loop media equipment uses magnetic tape to store the information and does not have to be replenished. The typist can begin typing (transcribing) the information before the dictator finishes dictating it. Figure 1 shows how an endless loop dictation system operates. Endless loop equipment is used in centralized dictation systems.

Discrete media equipment employs a recording unit with a removable storage medium—usually a cassette tape—that is placed manually into the "playback" (transcribing) unit when the dictated information is typed. Figure 2 shows a transcribing unit that uses a cassette tape for recording dictation. Three types of discrete media equipment are *centralized systems*, *portable units*, and *desk-top units.*

The two types of centralized dictation systems are *telephone line* and *private wire*. With the telephone line system, you use a telephone handset or some other dictation device to dial the telephone number of the word/information processing center. The recording unit in the center switches on automatically, and the dictator then may begin dictating the message. With the private wire system, you make the connection to the recording unit in the center by flipping a switch located on a microphone or control box on the dictator's desk. The control box is wired directly to the recording unit in the center. Figure 3 shows a centralized dictation system that uses cassette tape as the recording medium.

Portable dictation units are especially useful for people who travel frequently or who spend time away from the office for other reasons.

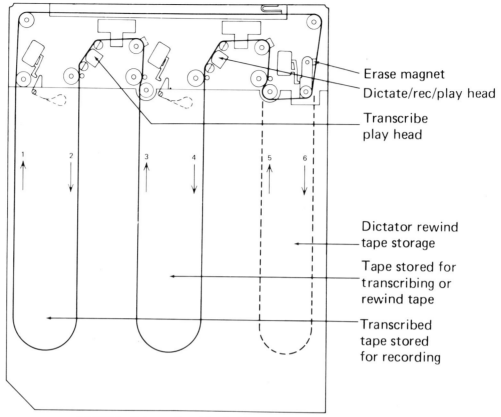

Erase magnet
Dictate/rec/play head

Transcribe
play head

Dictator rewind
tape storage

Tape stored for
transcribing or
rewind tape

Transcribed
tape stored
for recording

FIGURE 1 Schematic of the inside of a Dictaphone Thought Tank System 193. The tape drops from the head (4) and is pulled by the opposite transcribe head (3) when transcribing. (Courtesy of Dictaphone Corporation)

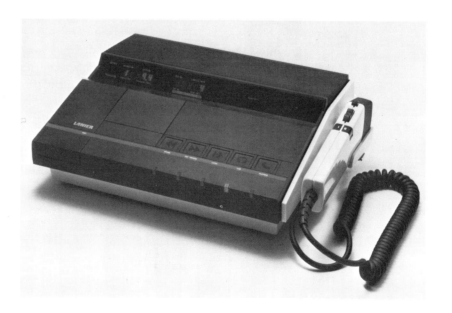

FIGURE 2 Desk-top transcribing unit that uses cassette tape to store dictation. (Courtesy of Dictaphone Corporation)

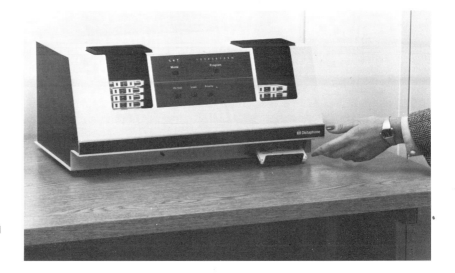

FIGURE 3 Dictaphone's Nucleus System. A central recording system with an automatic media changer that uses standard cassettes. Designed especially for large central systems. (Courtesy of Dictaphone Corporation)

The magnetic recording media used in the portable unit can be mailed easily to the office for transcription into mailable copy. A typical portable unit uses some type of cassette tape, and the units are available in a variety of sizes. A portable dictation unit is shown in Figure 4.

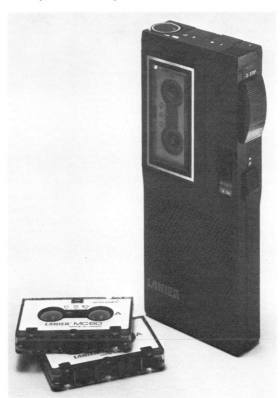

FIGURE 4 Lanier's Pocket Caddy, a portable dictation unit that uses microcassettes. (Courtesy of Lanier Business Products, Incorporated)

A desk-top dictation unit provides an alternative to the portable unit. To use this system, you dial a telephone number and are connected directly to the recording unit. You then can dictate your message, which will be recorded for transcription by a typist. The types of desk-top units vary according to the function(s) they perform. For example, some units will only record dictation, while others can be used only to play back recorded information. Another type is a combination dictation/transcription unit, where dictation and playback can take place on the same machine. In most companies where desk-top units are used, they perform only a single function. When information has been recorded on a single function unit, the dictation medium is removed and is sent to the typist who then transcribes whatever has been dictated. Figure 5 shows dictation being recorded with a desk-top dictation unit. Then, Figure 6 shows a typist transcibing dictation from a desk-top unit.

FIGURE 5 Dictaphone's Dictamation desk-top dictation system. Composed of desk-top unit that uses standard cassettes. (Courtesy of Dictaphone Corporation)

FIGURE 6 Lanier's Insight. Desk-top dictation/transcription system that uses microcassettes. (Courtesy of Lanier Business Products, Incorporated)

Regardless of the dictation system and devices you use, knowing how to prepare for dictation and how to dictate effectively make use of the system more efficient. The result will be more effective messages.

Dictation Techniques

Knowing how to communicate effectively with the person who will transcribe the information you dictate can help to prevent confusion. Many managers do not know how to dictate properly, however. When dictating information directly to a secretary who takes shorthand notes, you can answer immediately any questions about the intent of the message or how the message is to be prepared for mailing. But when you record dictation, this interchange is less direct. Therefore, any garbled dictation or missing instructions, for example, can take time to clarify.

Because machine dictation is used widely as a method of input into a word/information processing system, managers today should know how to operate dictation equipment. Recorded dictation can be processed faster and costs less to process than dictation done directly to a secretary. Instructions for operating specific brands of equipment are provided by the vendors who sell the equipment. With proper instruction and practice, however, you can improve your ability to dictate. The first step is to organize yourself for dictating before you actually begin to dictate. The following instructions will help you in this preparation stage.

CHECKLIST OF PREPARATION STEPS FOR DICTATION

1. *Gather all necessary reference materials.*
   a. Materials to be gathered include the letter or memorandum you are answering, previous correspondence or reports needed for reference, and names and addresses.
   b. For certain kinds of communication, you may need a membership directory of an organization or trade association or a foreign language dictionary.
2. *Establish a purpose for the communication.* You should have clear in your mind the precise reason that the dictation is necessary. For example,
   a. Are you trying to get, give, or record information?
   b. Are you going to acknowledge receipt of any information?
   c. Are you going to tell someone about something that might require immediate action?
   d. Are you going to make a recommendation or a referral?
3. *Make some type of outline.* An outline helps you to organize your thoughts and decide what ideas to communicate and how best to present them. Be sure that your outline is adequate before starting to dictate.
   a. Jot down an outline on a piece of paper *or*
   b. Underline important points in the letter or memorandum you are answering that you plan to respond to *or*
   c. Jot down marginal notes on the letter or memorandum to which you will refer while dictating.
4. *Consider your reader.*
   a. What background and experience does the reader have?
   b. Will the reader react to your message as you wish?

      c. Will you satisfy the reader's needs for information, or will he or she have more questions after reading your response?

5. *Have an extra recording medium available.* If you are using a desktop unit for dictation, have an extra recording tape ready for use in case you fill the first tape.

Once you are organized completely, you are then ready to dictate. The instructions in the following checklist will help you with the dictation itself.

CHECKLIST OF DICTATION TECHNIQUES

1. *Identify yourself*—name, position, and department, for example.
2. *Name the type of document*—letter or memorandum, for example.
3. *Name the type of stationery to be used*—letterhead or plain paper, for example.
4. *Give special instructions.* Include letter and punctuation style and spacing to be used if other than those of a standardized style already agreed upon.
5. *Give the number of copies needed.*
6. *Identify the priority for processing*—rush or routine.
7. *Name the type of copy being dictated*—rough draft or final copy.
8. *Give and spell out receiver's name and address.*
9. *Dictate the material in the order in which it should be transcribed.*
10. *Spell all proper names, unusual and technical words, and words that sound alike.*
11. *Give special instructions.*
    a. Capitals: say "all caps" if entire word(s) is (are) to be capitalized, "initial cap" if only the first letter in a word is to be capitalized.
    b. Indentions.
    c. Paragraphs.
    d. Tabulations: give format to be used. For example, "arrange this in three-columned headings; type in initial caps and underline each heading."
    e. Underlining.
12. *Note any unusual punctuation.*
    a. Hyphens, especially in hyphenated words.

    b. Commas used to set off words such as those in a series or in quotations.

    c. Other marks: semicolon, colon, exclamation point, dash, slash, or parenthesis, for example.

13. *Give closing information.* Include name, title, and/or department.
14. *Describe any enclosures.*
15. *Note any distribution of copies.*
16. *Give any deferred corrections or changes.*
17. *Give instructions for retaining the recording medium used to store the dictation.*
18. *Identify the end of document.*

Users of most word/information processing systems still use hand-written copy or dictation as the primary method for getting information into the system. However, new technology is providing a way to end this time-consuming step and to use some other method of input.

Other Methods of Input

Managerial work stations and optical character recognition equipment (OCR) are now being used to transfer information directly to word/information processing systems. A keyboard similar to a typewriter keyboard and a screen that looks like that of a television set can serve as a managerial work station. This equipment allows you to enter words and statistical data directly into the system. This information then can be communicated electronically either inside or outside the organization. Using this type of work station, you can create correspondence and reports yourself without the aid of a secretary. Also, you can use this equipment (sometimes called a multifunction work station) to read incoming mail and to file and retrieve stored documents electronically. You can also use it to set up a reminder file of appointments and deadlines, create new documents, and send and receive messages. Figure 7 shows the different tasks that can be done at a managerial work station.

An optical character recognition reader is a machine that can scan or read pages of documents. An OCR reader can send information from these documents to a word/information processing system (or to a computer) at 25 times the speed of manual typing. As these new methods for information entry are improved in the future, business communicators will be able to produce usable typescripts of documents without any assistance from other people.

After the word/information processing system receives the input, processing of the information, the next step, can begin.

MULTIFUNCTION WORKSTATION

Date: March 2, 1983

APPOINTMENTS

8:30 Return phone calls
9:00 Meeting w/J. Jones
10:15 Conference w/Smith, Peterson & Stenjem
12:30 Lunch w/G. Gusell
2:00 Complete Oil Report
3:00 Meeting w/D. Hucker
5:00 Home/get ready for dinner party at C. & J. Friel's.

TICKLER FILE

1. Send reminder letter to Larry Bergerud.
2. Call Raymond Lamb re file #48.2.
3. Reissue statement to Doug Welch.
4. Prepare oil report for Ecology Impact Committee.
5. Begin gathering tax file for personal income tax return.
6. Prepare visuals for Board of Directors 4/4/83 presentation.

CALENDAR OF ASSOCIATES

	L. J. Arntson	D. Woodman	J. Kupsh	J. LeCompte	D. Busche	J. Morton	R. Fisher	M. Sorenson	M. Salas	M. Taylor	R. Johnson	L. Mattingly
8:00								N				
9:00								O				
10:00								I				
11:00								T				
12:00								A				
1:00								C				
2:00								A				
3:00								V				
4:00												
5:00												

INCOMING MESSAGES

3:42 a.m.
Hi Paul: Will meet you at 12:30 at Francois today. G. Gusell.

7:15 a.m.
Paul: Thanks for the report on ecological patterns of the Suder area. Helps me very much. See you at racquetball on 3/10/83. HJS

7:20 a.m.
Your Conniejean's stocks are up 8 points. Please return your order by 9 a.m. today if you wish a change. Winnie Balsukot.

7:21 a.m.
Please advise re itinerary for East coast June trip ASAP. Nancy at Travelmakers.

8:02 a.m. Call me. C. Freer.

REVIEW FILES

File requested: #48
—Other identifiers:
Schick, Charlene
Schick & Associates
File requested: #1204
—Page 98 of Complaint.

DOCUMENT ASSEMBLY

Revise quarterly P & L statement. Delete last quarter figures, insert new quarter figures from File 84. Delete pages 5, 18, 94 in Dictation Procedure Handbook. Add new definitions into glossary, realphabetize and communicate to all branch offices.

INCOMING MAIL

(Directions: Please have any hard copy OCR scanned and entered into system.)
ENTER: 3/2/83 mail.

TEXT REVISION

March 2, 19//

Mr. Fred Wallace
Data Processing Director
NOCCC District
1000 North Lemon
Fullerton, CA 90638

Dear Fred:

Please include the telecommunications, OCR, and phototypesetting options on our word/information processing bid specifications. We consider these vital components on any equipment system we will consider.

Sincerely,

CHRISTEN ERIK & ASSOCIATES

Paul A. Watkins, Manager
Information Systems

FIGURE 7 View of the functions served by a managerial work station. (From Marly A. Bergerud and Jean Gonzalez, *Word/Information Processing: Concepts of Office Automation,* 2nd ed. (New York: John Wiley, 1981).)

PROCESSING THE MESSAGE

When you transmit information directly through an OCR reader, the processing begins when the words or data received are converted to electronic characters for storage. If the input is longhand or dictated information or originates at a managerial work station, processing begins when the typist "keyboards" (types) it. Generally, keyboarding is done on an automated typewriter keyboard. Once the information is keyboarded, you can save or store it so that additional processing can be done later if needed.

Keyboarding Equipment

Keyboarding on word/information processing equipment is similar to typing done on standard typewriters. The two types of keyboards are *membrane* and *full stroke*. A membrane keyboard has a flat surface without raised keys; key locations are touch sensitive, so you merely press the key location area to enter information for processing. Touch typing, typing without looking at the keyboard, is difficult to do on membrane keyboards, so speed is a problem. Inexpensive personal computers such as Timex' Sinclair models have membrane keyboards.

A full-stroke keyboard has keys that actually move down when you press them. These keys activate in the same way that those on a regular typewriter do. You can type by touch on these keyboards, so they are more efficient for word/information processing than the membrane keyboards.

Most word/information processing equipment has certain automatic features that are important for business communicators because they make the job of composing and editing messages easier than does any other method now used. For example, you can end a typed line and return to a new line without stroking a carriage return key; the machine does this automatically at a certain point on the line. You can delete or add characters, words, lines, or entire paragraphs at the push of a button, features that especially are important for revising messages. In addition, you can merge paragraphs, change margins, and hyphenate words merely by pressing keys on the keyboard.

In recent years, software packages have been marketed that will check your spelling automatically for errors. One, called *Electric Webster* from Cornucopia Software, contains a dictionary of 50,000 words to which you can add the spelling of other words. Software programs are now under development that can be used to correct grammatical errors automatically as well. One that is already being marketed is called *Gram-*

matik. These new software packages are especially useful for business communicators.

Keyboarding on the automated keyboards is faster than on standard keyboards. Keyboard equipment is classified as *stand-alone* or *shared systems* with either *display* or *nondisplay work stations*.

Display Work Stations

Today, many word/information processing keyboards are connected to a screen similar to a television screen. Called a VDU (visual display unit) or CRT (cathode ray tube), you can produce a letter, report, or other message on these screens without using paper. As you keyboard the information into the machine, an image of what you enter appears on the screen. You can see the message while you create it. Proofreading, corrections, and revisions can be done on the screen as you compose the message or afterward. When the copy on the screen is error free, you can store it for later use or print it onto paper. Figure 8 shows a work station with a display screen. Business communicators can work more efficiently on equipment that has a visual display unit than on nondisplay equipment.

FIGURE 8 Work station with display screen. IBM's Displaywriter is a text processing system with an electronic ''dictionary'' that checks the spelling of about 50,000 words. The machine can transmit mail electronically. (Courtesy of International Business Machines Corporation)

Nondisplay Work Stations

Nondisplay or blind work stations do not have a visual display screen. Instead, a copy of the information you enter for processing appears on paper inserted into the machine. Therefore, the paper itself is the screen. While you can see what you enter into a nondisplay unit, you cannot see an entire page of a document as you make revisions. Therefore, the ability to make corrections is limited. The nondisplay work station looks like a standard typewriter, except that the keyboard has special keys that allow you to edit messages and perform other functions automatically. Figure 9 shows a nondisplay work station.

Stand-alone System

A stand-alone word/information processing system consists of a single work station that is used by one person. The equipment is self-contained in that it is not connected to a central computer; therefore, information is processed completely within the system itself. This system will have a keyboard and a printer, and in some systems, a separate console to hold the storage media. A stand-alone display system is composed of a visual display unit (VDU), a keyboard, and a printer. Unless you wish to do so,

FIGURE 9   Nondisplay work station. IBM's Electronic 75 has an upgradable capacity of 7,500 to 15,000 characters of working memory. (Courtesy of International Business Machines Corporation)

you do not need to place the printer in the area where the VDU and keyboard are located. Through communication links (usually telephone lines), you can send messages from one system to another, an especially attractive feature for business communicators who need to send messages rapidly. Figure 10 shows stand-alone systems with display and non-display work stations.

Shared System

Equipment that uses a central computer to process messages is part of a shared system. Several work stations or terminals can be connected to one central computer. The two types of terminals used in a shared system are called *dumb* and *intelligent.* Dumb terminals will not operate if the computer is not operating because these work stations rely completely on the computer for logic and computing power, for storage, and for printing final copy. An intelligent terminal has its own logic and computing power and therefore will operate regardless of whether the computer is operating. In this case, the computer provides central support and access to greater storage capacity, processing power, and other equipment. A single shared system can have a combination of intelligent and dumb terminals connected to a computer. Figure 11 shows how a shared system can work.

Storage Media

An important part of using a word/information processing system for business communication is the storage and retrieval of information that you have entered into the system. Storage is the ability to keep what has

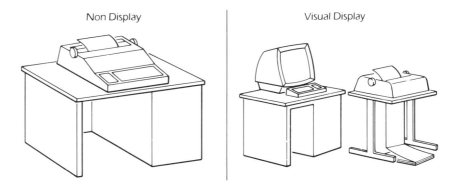

Non Display   Visual Display

FIGURE 10 Diagrams of display and nondisplay stand-alone systems. (From Marly A. Bergerud and Jean Gonzalez, *Word/Information Processing: Concepts of Office Automation,* 2nd ed. (New York: John Wiley, 1981).)

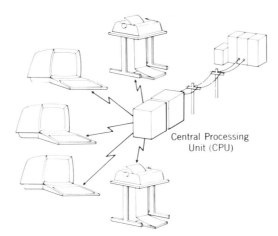

FIGURE 11 Diagram of a shared system. (From Marly Bergerud and Jean Gonzalez, *Word/Information Processing: Concepts of Office Automation,* 2nd ed. (New York: John Wiley, 1981).)

Central Processing Unit (CPU)

been keyboarded so that it can be recalled and used at a later time. Information may be stored either within the word/information processor itself or outside the machine. When using the internal storage, the information is stored electronically in a buffer or working storage section of the machine as you keyboard it into the system. While the information is in the working storage area, changes and corrections can be made. To keep information for an indefinite time, you must transfer it from the working storage medium.

Some word/information processors have an internal memory for long-term storage use. Other machines, however, require an external storage media. Most word/information processors available today use a magnetic disk called a "floppy" disk for external storage. The standard size 8″ floppy disk looks like a small phonograph record. You can store from 70 to 130 pages of text on one disk. Some machines do use a smaller $5\frac{1}{4}$″ floppy "diskette" that will store 30 or more pages. A photograph of a floppy disk is shown in Figure 12.

A Winchester disk (hard disk) also can be used to store information. This disk is harder than a floppy disk and can hold 10 times the infor-

FIGURE 12 A floppy disk used for storage. (Courtesy of Verbatim Corporation)

mation. A Winchester disk cannot be handled, however, but because it is packaged in a boxlike container, it is less likely to be damaged than a floppy disk. A photograph of a Winchester disk is shown in Figure 13.

Because word/information processors do have storage media, business communicators can use them effectively to retain files of information that have been communicated already or to retrieve information for editing or other types of changes. Regardless of the type storage media used, the ability to recall previously typed information helps to reduce the time required to produce final copy.

Document Preparation

The greatest advances in ease and efficiency of producing messages with word/information processing equipment are in the preparation of messages themselves. As mentioned earlier in the chapter, you can correct errors and revise messages easily without retyping an entire message.

Short Documents

For short documents such as letters and memorandums, you can type them faster by using the automatic features of the equipment. These features include

1. An automatic return to the left margin without striking a carriage return key
2. A backspace key that "erases" errors you have made
3. Special keys that allow you to delete, add, or move information— characters, words, or lines, for example
4. Special codes (using two or more keys in combination with one another) that will close up blank spaces left by deletions, adjust margins, and hyphenate words at line endings

FIGURE 13 A Winchester disk used for storage.

Long Documents

Correcting and revising long documents such as reports is easier and less time consuming, too. Really, there are no restrictions on the amount of information you can add, delete, or move about from place to place in the message. For example, you can manipulate paragraphs or entire pages, merge text to eliminate space left by deletions, or move text to make room for additions. Examples of how the deletion and addition process works are shown in Figures 14 and 15. In addition, the following are

Before

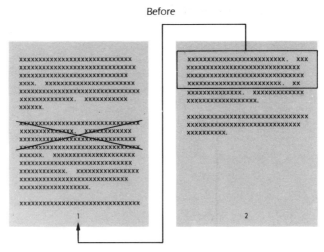

Document with Paragraph Deleted

After

FIGURE 14 The deletion process. (From Marly A. Bergerud and Jean Gonzalez, *Word/ Information Processing: Concepts of Office Automation,* 2nd ed. (New York: John Wiley, 1981).)

New Document

Before

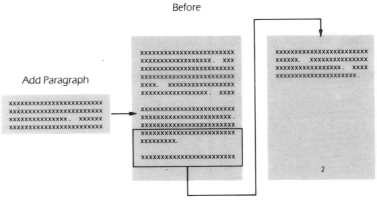

Add Paragraph

Document with Paragraph Added

After

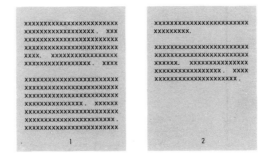

FIGURE 15 The addition process. (From Marly A. Bergerud and Jean Gonzalez, *Word/ Information Processing: Concepts of Office Automation,* 2nd ed. (New York: John Wiley, 1981).)

New Document

other tasks that you can perform automatically in producing long documents with a word/information processor:

1. Divide a long document into pages of a fixed number of lines
2. Number or renumber pages
3. Adjust the bottom margin on a page to allow space for footnotes or other reference notes
4. Place information such as chapter numbers and title names at the top or bottom of pages
5. Prevent "widow lines"—single lines of a paragraph at the top or bottom of a page
6. Search an entire document for a character or group of characters and replace them one by one with new characters or groups

Form Documents

With word/information processing equipment you can produce form documents with ease and economy. Form documents are those that you use over and over again but send to different people each time you use them. These may be letters, memorandums, reports, contracts, or leases, for example. Using the storage media, you can store these messages and retrieve them whenever needed. After a list of names and addresses is typed and stored, you can then combine these data automatically with a stored form message to get a final copy ready for mailing. If you need to change some part or parts of the message on a form document for a particular use, that can be done too. As the final copies of the form letters are produced, the information that differs on each copy can be inserted automatically in the proper place. Then, you can prepare envelopes with the equipment as well. Figure 16 shows a form letter designed for repetitive use along with "variable" information (information that will change from copy to copy) that will be inserted automatically as the final copies are produced.

FIN #9
Revised 10/9/78
Orig: Laura Keeton

Start on line 13

Envelope with letter
One Copy

DATE

____
____
____

Dear __________:

Thank you for your telephone call offering your commercial banking facilities for the new Sambo's store in ____________. We normally do not open our commercial bank accounts until approximately thirty days before the opening of our restaurant, and should your bank be chosen as our depository, our Territory Manager in your area will be contacting you prior to that time.

Prior to the opening, the local Territory Manager and/or District Manager for your area will be notified by this office that a bank is required for the new Sambo's. At this time, the Territory Manager/District Manager will be contacting all the local banks, and should your bank be chosen as our depository, the Territory Manager/District Manager will let this office know and we will send the necessary paperwork to your bank.

If you have any comments or questions, please do not hesitate to contact this office.

Yours very truly,

Laura Keeton
Cash Management
Sambo's Restaurants, Inc.

Enclosure

Sambo's Restaurants, Inc. 6410 Cindy Lane Carpinteria, California 93013 805 681-6…
Mailing Address P.O. Box 538 Carpinteria, California 93013

Review Date	Dept	Name	Position	Supervisor	Salary	Emp #
03-18-78	Acct	Abbott, S. C.	Acct. I	McKnight	13,788	1234
05-18-78	Legal	Adams, T. O.	Lawyer	Wheaton	28,500	4928
06-13-78	Finance	Anderson, R. L.	Typist	Atkinson	9,800	4837
04-24-78	Legal	Anderson, S. A.	Typist	Mills	11,800	4837
09-26-78	Admin	Anderson, T. R.	Sec II	Lombarli	12,400	2938
10-22-78	Sales	Andrews, R. R.	Sales Rep	Beamer	40,000	4029
10-21-78	Sales	Amster, T. O.	Manager	Nelson	59,920	3857
02-11-78	Marketing	Astro, R. A.	Sales Rep	Williams	32,770	1029
04-18-78	Legal	Awskri, E. M.	Lawyer	Campbell	19,500	3847
12-31-78	Personnel	Barber, E. O.	Typist	O'Donnell	9,000	3928
01-08-78	Purch	Birdett, T. O.	Acct. I	Anderson	13,940	5572
02-09-78	Marketing	Berberet, R. W.	Lawyer	Dakan	66,000	6384
07-17-78	Acct	Bergerud, M. K.	Typist	Ritter	11,290	2495
02-19-78	Admin	Boston, W. A.	Sec II	Rider	12,400	8273
05-18-78	Acct	Bottles, R. S.	Sales Rep	Ehmann	23,788	6401
11-02-78	Legal	Carno, M. K..	Manager	Schick	34,500	9283
09-11-78	Finance	Carno, L. A.	Sales Rep	Franklin	29,800	7492
07-12-78	Admin	Carno, R. J.	Lawyer	Freer	32,400	9938
06-29-78	Sales	Castoria, K. L.	Typist	De Nova	11,000	5737
03-18-78	Sales	Catski, R. Y.	Acct. I	Cleveland	19,920	4359
04-18-78	Marketing	Ceastor, P. K.	Lawyer	Sears	32,770	4928
06-13-78	Legal	Church, R. S.	Typist	Tyrrell	14,500	7364
09-26-78	Personnel	Chusted, T. O.	Sec II	Webb	19,000	8201
10-22-78	Purch	Claffey, P. R.	Sales Rep	Gorno	23,940	9828
10-21-78	Marketing	Claffey, W. J.	Manager	Riedel	66,000	3474
02-11-78	Acct	Cusot, Y. P.	Sales Rep	Dianesen	19,290	[illegible]
04-18-78	Admin	Dapple, L. J.	Lawyer	Griffin	22,400	8753
12-31-78	Acct	Datro, L. Q.	Typist	Parnell	13,788	8234
01-08-78	Legal	Daza, T. Z.	Acct. I	Wheaton	14,500	6238
02-09-78	Finance	Derrty, O. O.	Lawyer	Hucker	29,800	7625
07-17-78	Admin	Desten, R. A.	Typist	Lombarli	12,400	8363
02-09-78	Sales	Dirck, A. S.	Sec II	Wilde	11,000	4739
05-18-78	Sales	Distenati, C. O.	Sales Rep	Johnson, R.	59,920	5745
11-02-78	Marketing	Dorset, T. W.	Manager	Williams	32,770	7382
09-11-78	Legal	Duffer, T. Y.	Sales Rep	Thomas	19,500	6438
07-12-78	Personnel	Dugin, K. W.	Lawyer	Jones	59,000	2734
06-29-78	Purch	Eaton, R. J.	Typist	Anderson	13,940	6452
03-18-78	Marketing	Eaton, T. J.	Acct. I	Ennuso	16,000	9463
04-18-78	Acct	Ebert, A. M.	Lawyer	Le Compte	19,290	4739
06-13-78	Admin	Emington, R. M.	Typist	Rider	22,400	0134
09-26-78	Acct	Ester, W. A.	Sec II	Johnson, C.	13,788	4628
10-22-78	Legal	Ettinger, J. P.	Sales Rep	Light	24,500	6281
02-11-78	Admin	Franke, A. S.	Sales Rep	Lombarli	32,400	8348
04-18-78	Sales	Franklin, R. R.	Lawyer	Wilde	40,000	2634
12-31-78	Sales	Fudge, T. W.	Typist	Mattingly	9,920	8345
01-08-78	Marketing	Gage, C. A.	Acct. I	Williams	12,770	3875
02-19-78	Legal	Gavarski, T. O.	Lawyer	Thomas	11,500	1469
07-17-78	Acct	Gonzalez, J. E.	Typist	McCandless	9,000	3473

FIGURE 16 Form letter and list of variable data for repetitive use. (From Marly A. Bergerud and Jean Gonzalez, *Word/Information Processing: Concepts of Office Automation,* 2nd ed. (New York: John Wiley, 1981).)

Form documents such as contracts and leases can be prepared in a similar manner to that shown in Figure 16. First, you would type the basic message and store it. Then when you need to prepare and mail a copy of the message, you would type as needed any additional information— names, addresses, dates, amounts of money, for example. The equipment then will merge automatically the two sets of information as you have directed to produce the final copy.

Another method that companies can use instead of entire form messages is to prepare standard (form) paragraphs and store them for later use. To produce a letter or some other document in this way, "tell" the machine what paragraphs you want and in what order. The machine will then assemble the paragraphs as you instructed to create the new document. If needed, changes in wording, additions, or deletions can be made in form paragraphs before the final copy is produced.

GETTING THE OUTPUT

The final printing of a document produced on a word/information processing system is called *output*. Today, work produced on this equipment is high quality; each document looks like an original copy. With some types of equipment, you can keyboard and print copy with the same machine. With other types, you must keyboard on one piece of equipment and print on another. Two types of printers are available: *impact* and *nonimpact*.

With impact printers, characters are transferred by a typebar, a typing element, or a print wheel striking an inked or carbon ribbon against the paper. Impact printers produce good-quality copy but are noisy and relatively slow.

A nonimpact printer has no printing device striking the paper, so it prints quietly. Also, printing with this type printer is faster. The two types of nonimpact printers used today are *inkjet* and *laser*. Inkjet printers form characters by spraying a stream of ink onto the paper. Laser printers use a light beam to shape characters on a light-sensitive surface; a toner then transfers the image to paper. Both types print rapidly. Inkjet printers can print up to 2200 words a minute, whereas laser printers can reach speeds up to 600 pages a minute.

Currently, you can buy intelligent copier/printers (ICP) that combine laser, computer, and photocopying technologies. A document that is stored in a word/information processor can be transferred through a communication link to an ICP for copying. When using an ICP to produce output, you have a choice among different type styles and print sizes. In addition, you can store company logos, letterheads, business forms, and even signatures in the memory of an ICP.

As you have been able to see thus far in reading the chapter, you can produce high-quality messages in less time and with less effort with word/information processing equipment. So much of the work is done automatically at the input, processing, and output stages that the entire writing process becomes faster and easier. Once you have produced the final copy of a document, the next step is to distribute it. Advances in technology in recent years have brought reform to this procedure as well.

DISTRIBUTING THE MESSAGE

Sending copies of documents to addresses or to files is called *distribution.* To be effective, distribution must be timely. The two methods currently used to distribute correspondence, reports, and other business documents are *physical* and *electronic.*

Physical Distribution Methods

The two physical methods used to distribute business messages are *file* and *mail carrier systems.*

File Systems
File systems are organized procedures for classifying documents for storage. The traditional file system is that stored by hand in filing cabinets. Because many companies today need to store and retrieve millions of messages every year, this traditional system works poorly. As a result of the need for a better method and changes in technology in recent years, two new file system methods are now being used: *micrographics* and *video disks.*

FIGURE 17 Microfilm roll used in micrographics. (Courtesy of Bell & Howell Corporation)

Micrographics   A file system in which miniature visual images of messages are stored on microfilm is called micrographics. You can keep these images in far less space than paper copies require. The two types of microfilm commonly used are roll film, shown in Figure 17, and microfiche, shown in Figure 18. Most often, cameras are used to photograph the microfilm images directly from the original paper documents; the film is then developed and stored. However, a process called computer output microfilm (COM) is now available that will produce the microfilm directly without first producing a paper copy. When COM is used to pro-

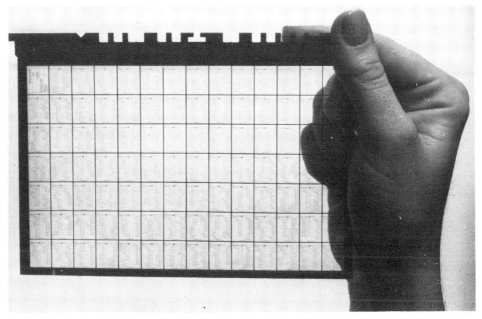

FIGURE 18 Microfiche used in micrographics. (Courtesy of Image Systems, Incorporated)

duce microfilm for filing, computer-assisted retrieval (CAR) helps to retrieve stored records when needed; these computer files can be retrieved at rapid speeds. A CAR system is shown in Figure 19.

Video Disks   A video disk is a plastic disk that looks like and is about the size of a long-playing phonograph record. You can store both visual images and sound on a video disk. As many as 54,000 visual images can be stored on a single disk. When you need to retrieve the stored file, you can do so with a video disk player, which can locate an image within 5 seconds and display it with sound on a television screen.

Mail Carrier Systems
Several mail carrier systems are still being used by companies to distribute business documents. The internal company mail service is still used widely to distribute interoffice communications by hand to offices or mailboxes within a company. Also, mail is delivered manually by the United States Postal Service and some private mail service companies. However, the increasing cost and slow service of using mail carrier systems have brought many company executives to seek other means for sending messages. As a result of these needs and advances in technology, electronic mail distribution methods are gaining acceptance today.

FIGURE 19   Computer-assisted retrieval (CAR) Micrographics system. The microimage terminal allows the user to view one image, store it in a memory, and recall it by pushing a button. (Courtesy of Eastman Kodak Company)

Electronic Distribution Methods

Methods called *telecommunications* are available now to send business messages as electronic signals over telephone wires or through space using microwave technology or satellite networks. In using one of these systems, you would keyboard your message into the system at one location and then transmit it electronically to another location. At the other location, the message can be displayed on a visual display unit (VDU) or a paper copy can be printed. This type distribution of messages is being called *electronic mail.*

The information you send as electronic mail may be words, statistical data, or graphics, including pictures. If you wish, you can take pictures at one location and send them to a VDU or printer at another location. Graphic information sent electronically in this way is called *facsimile* (FAX). A facsimile machine will scan the copy of the message in one location and send the information to another location, where another facsimile machine will reproduce a copy of the message.

Electronic distribution methods give fast delivery compared with mail carrier systems. You can measure distribution time in minutes rather than in days. A variety of methods that you could use to send your business messages electronically are shown in Figure 20. The technology

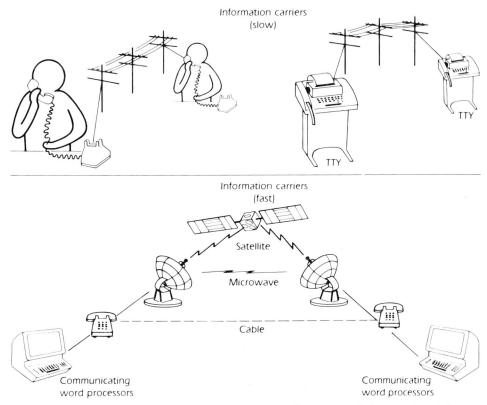

FIGURE 20 Electronic distribution methods. (From Marly A. Bergerud and Jean Gonzalez, *Word/Information Processing: Concepts of Office Automation*, 2nd ed. (New York: John Wiley, 1981).)

used in telecommunications also can be used in teleconferencing, conducting electronic meetings where the participants are in different locations.

SUMMARY

You can use word/information processing equipment to automate many of the tasks in producing business communication of all types. This includes automated assistance with composing messages, editing and revising them, producing final copy, and even distributing messages to receivers. Two basic types of equipment now used widely in word/informa-

tion processing are word processors and personal computers.

Information that is entered into a word/information processing system is called input. The source for input may be handwritten draft or dictation. Two types of dictation equipment are endless loop media and discrete media. Using endless loop media, you can begin typing information before the dictator finishes dictating it. Discrete media most often uses a cassette tape for storage. Three types of discrete media equipment are centralized systems, portable units, and desk-top units.

The best dictators are those who prepare carefully before dictating and then use good techniques while dictating. Five steps in the preparation stage are listed on pages 296 and 297. Eighteen steps to follow while dictating are given on pages 297 and 298.

Managerial work stations and optical character recognition equipment are now being used to transfer information directly to word/information processing systems. Using this equipment, business communicators can produce usable final copies of messages ready for mailing without any assistance from others.

After input, the next step in producing mailable messages with word/information processing equipment is processing the message. The two types of keyboards now being used are membrane and full stroke. Full-stroke keyboards are better for producing business messages. Keyboard equipment is classified as stand-alone or shared systems with either display or nondisplay work stations. A display work station is more useful in producing business messages than a nondisplay unit. A stand-alone system can process information within the system itself, while a shared system depends upon a central computer for processing. Both dumb and intelligent terminals can be used with shared systems.

Information can be stored in a word/information processing system or in an external storage medium. Most types of equipment use a "floppy" disk for storage, but some types use a Winchester disk. Information stored on these disks can be retrieved when you need it.

Special functions of word/information processors make document preparation easy and efficient. These include a backspace key that "erases" your errors and special keys for adding, deleting, and moving information, for example. Both long and short documents are easy to prepare. Also, form documents can be prepared and stored with ease for later use.

Output is the final printing of a document produced on a word/information processing system. The two types of printers used to print the final copy are impact and nonimpact. Impact printers use a typebar, a typing element, or a print wheel striking an ink or carbon ribbon against the paper to print copies. Nonimpact printers use either an ink jet to spray characters onto the paper or a laser to shape characters on paper that has a light-sensitive surface. Nonimpact printers are much faster than impact printers.

Sending copies of documents to addresses or to files is called distribution. Two distribution methods now used by business communicators are physical and electronic. Two physical methods are file and mail carrier systems. File systems include the traditional storage by hand in filing cabinets and storage on microfilm (micrographics) and video disks. A mail carrier system is the traditional method of delivering mail manually as does the United States Postal Service.

Electronic methods, called telecommunications, can send messages almost instantly from one location to another using telephone wires, microwave technology, or satellite networks. You can send words, statistical data, and graphics, including pictures, as "electronic mail."

Additional Readings

Bergerud, Marly, and Jean Gonzalez. *Word/Information Processing Concepts: Careers. Technology and Application.* New York: John Wiley, 1981.

————, and Jean Gonzalez. *Word Processing Concepts and Careers.* 2nd ed. New York: John Wiley, 1981.

Casady, Mona J. *Word Processing Concepts.* Cincinnati, Ohio: South-Western, 1980.

Cecil, Paula B. *Word Processing in the Modern Office.* 2nd ed. Menlo Park, Calif.: Benjamin/Cummings, 1980.

Halpern, Jeanne W. *Paper Voices: How Dictation and Word Processing Are Changing the Way College Graduates Write.* Washington, D.C.: Educational Resources Information Center (ERIC), U.S. Department of Education, National Institute of Education, Document Number CS20633/ED203318, 1981.

"Information Systems: The Management Challenge." *Review.* October 1981, pp. 53–69.

Kleinschrod, Walter A. *Management's Guide to Word Processing.* Chicago, Ill.: The Dartnell Corporation, 1977.

————, Leonard B. Kruk, and Hilda Turner. *Word/Information Processing: Operations, Applications, Administration.* 2nd ed. Indianapolis, Ind.: Bobbs-Merrill, 1983.

Lewis, Stephen D. "The Effect of Word Processing on Business Letter Writing." *The Delta Pi Epsilon Journal.* Vol 21, No. 2, April 1979, pp. 26–32.

Mason, Jennie. *Introduction to Word Processing.* Indianapolis, Ind.: Bobbs-Merrill, 1979.

Mayer, Kenneth R., and Bella G. Clinksdale. *Synthesis of Word Origination Research and Application for Business Communication Curricula.* Washington, D.C.: Educational Resources Information Center (ERIC). U.S. Department of Education, National Institute of Education, Document Number CE027996/ED198319, 1980.

Quible, Zane K., and Margaret H. Johnson. *Introduction to Word Processing.* Cambridge, Mass.: Winthrop, 1980.

Rosen, Arnold, and Rosemary Fielden. *Word Processing.* 2nd ed. Englewood Cliffs, N.J.: Prentice-Hall, 1982.

Unley, Shirley M. "What's on the Market: WP Equipment Review." *Management World.* April 1981 (published annually).

Uris, Auren. *The Dictation Book.* Willow Grove, Penn.: International Word/Information Processing Association, 1980.

Waterhouse, Shirley A. *Word Processing Fundamentals.* San Francisco: Canfield Press, 1979.

Review Questions

1. Name and discuss the two types of equipment on which you can perform word/information processing functions.

2. List and describe the four major steps in word/information processing.

3. Explain the differences between endless loop media and discrete media dictation equipment.

4. List and explain the five major steps in preparing to dictate a message.

5. Look at the first five steps on the checklist of dictation techniques given in the chapter. Then assume that you are writing a letter and write down the information needed for these steps.

6. List and explain the major tasks that you can perform at a managerial work station.

7. What is the difference between a membrane and a full-stroke keyboard? Which is better for preparing business communications?

8. Describe a stand-alone word/information processing system and compare it with a shared system.

9. List at least five special features of word/information processing equipment that help to make document preparation easier to do.

10. Give the difference between impact and nonimpact printers.

Exercises

1. Make a list of the types of letters, memorandums, reports, and other documents that you now have to produce on the job or for classes. Then visit stores where word processors and personal computers are sold to study the features of available equipment. Compare the needs you listed with the features of the equipment you examine. Then write a report about what you have learned. Explain which type and brand of equipment you would prefer to buy and defend your choice.

2. Compare the time it takes to write a longhand draft to the time it takes to dictate the same information. To do this, time yourself while you write and then dictate the following letter:

   Dear Ms. Jarvis:

   Thank you for sending the current catalog of merchandise you sell at Indigo Products. I received it only two days after you shipped it.

   The catalog you sent does have several types of carved and painted Peruvian gourds that I like. However, the available colors are unsuitable for the color scheme in my newly redecorated living room, where they would be used. You have listed that you have red, yellow, and brown shades, but I need blue or purple shades to match the color scheme in the room. Do you have gourds in shades of either color? The specific design on the gourds does not matter, but the color is important.

   If either color is available, will you please send a description of it so that I can place an order. I'd appreciate receiving the information by April 1 so that I can order and receive the merchandise by May 1, the date my home will be shown on the La Mesa Tour of Homes.

   Sincerely yours,

3. Assume that you are the manager at Balton's Books, a local bookstore. You received a telephone inquiry from J. Fred Magici who lives in a small town 45 miles from your city. You agreed to order a book for him entitled *What You Should Know About Personal Computers*. Your supplier just wrote you that the book is out of print, but a similar book entitled *How to Use Personal Computers Effectively* is available at the same price. You decide to dictate a letter to Mr. Magici to explain the situation and ask if he will accept the available book as a substitute. You can have the book shipped directly to him from the publisher with overnight delivery by express mail if he wishes.

   Now, consult the checklist of preparation stages for dictation in the chapter. Then follow the 5 steps to prepare to dictate the letter. Perform the tasks in each step as required for this situation.

4. Assume that you have prepared to dictate the letter to J. Fred Magici in Exercise 3. Now dictate the letter on whatever type of dictation equipment is available to you. In doing so, follow the 18 steps in the checklist of dictation techniques given in the chapter.

5. Using whatever type of dictation equipment is available to you, dictate the following memorandum. In doing so, follow the steps in the checklist of dictation techniques given in the chapter.

   To: Sally Bernois, Inventory Supervisor
   From: (Your Name), Word/Information Processing Center Supervisor

   Will you send me a checklist of our inventory of software packages held in stock for our Apple II and TRS-80 personal computers.

   We are considering buying several new types of software packages but first need to know what we have in stock and how many of each.

   Can you send the checklist by Friday,

Sally? If we receive it by then, we can take advantage of a 20 percent discount now being offered by the vendors.

6. Using word/information processing equipment, please enter the memorandum in Exercise 5 into the system and store it. Once you have done this, perform the following tasks:

    a. Add the word *please* after the second word in the first line of the message. The copy should read as follows: *Will you please send me. . . .*

    b. Add the following words and punctuation in the first sentence of the second paragraph after the words *software packages:* *, including a spelling checker program,.* The copy should read as follows: *. . . software packages, including a spelling checker program, but first. . . .*

7. Using word/information processing equip-

ment, please delete all changes you made in the memorandum while performing Exercise 6. The memorandum should now read as it did in Exercise 5.

8. Enter the letter in Exercise 2 into your word/information processing system. Now make the following changes:

    a. Change the first paragraph to read as follows: *The catalog of Indigo Products' merchandise that I requested last week arrived today. Thank you for sending it so quickly.*

    b. In the second paragraph, move the last sentence to the point where it follows the second sentence in the paragraph.

    c. Check your spelling for errors with a spelling checker software program if one is available. Also, check your work for hyphenation errors with a software program if that feature is available.

UNIT 5

Employment Communication

CHAPTER FOURTEEN

Finding Employees
WHAT DO EMPLOYERS DO?

The goals in studying the text and completing the activities in this chapter are to know

1. **How the hiring process works**
2. **Legal requirements employers must meet**
3. **The nature of and relationship between advertising and job descriptions in standard recruiting situations**
4. **Methods employers use to screen job applications**
5. **The purpose and structure of various types of job interviews**
6. **How employers conduct job interviews**
7. **How employers evaluate the results of job interviews and make recommendations**
8. **How job offers are made and negotiated**

Managers of successful companies recognize that their continued success depends on the type of people they hire. Those who have the responsibility to recruit, screen, and hire applicants probably appreciate this the most. While doing their jobs, they use just about every communication principle discussed in this book.

Study the series of steps that applicants and employers take in the hiring process which is shown in Figure 1. The major steps are:

1. Prepare job description and advertise the opening.
2. Review applications and résumé packages.
3. Interview selected applicants and review the interviews.
4. Make final selection and notify applicants.

Most applicants never complete the entire process. Instead, they are eliminated from contention by the employer or they stop pursuing the job themselves. As a prospective employer yourself, you will need to learn each step in the process so that you can hire the best qualified applicants. Also, studying the employment process will help you to prepare your own job search.

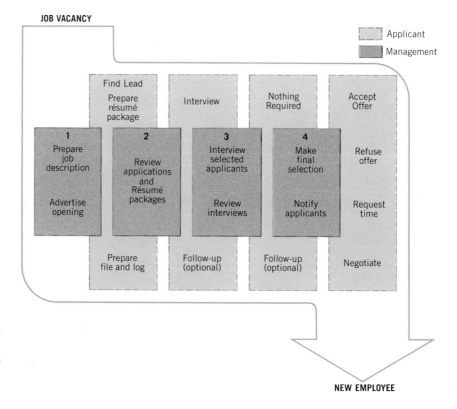

FIGURE 1 Composite flow chart of the messages in the hiring process for both management and applicants.

Employers hire applicants to fill new positions and to replace those who vacate positions for one reason or another. To do these jobs, they must know how to plan, analyze, and make decisions and should have good oral and written communication skills. Their duties include acting as liaison, advertising jobs, writing job descriptions, conducting interviews, screening applicants, and negotiating wages and salaries. The goal is to hire the best qualified applicant at the most reasonable cost. This task calls for monitoring the total process as steps are being taken to fill available positions.

HIRING AND THE LAW

Employers must know how to follow the provisions of the Federal Fair Labor Practices Codes to protect themselves and to avoid discriminating against applicants. The two major laws affecting hiring are the Equal Pay Act of 1963 and the Civil Rights Act of 1964. These acts and the supplementary legislation that followed protect both applicants and employees of any company that employs more than 15 people. Basically, these laws prohibit an employer from using any potentially discriminatory information as a basis for refusing employment. This includes information about a person's age, sex, race, religion, birthplace, ancestry, skin color, or medical condition. Whether the information was gathered directly or indirectly does not matter.

Most employers follow the "Bona Fide Occupational Qualifications" procedure to protect themselves. That is, they ask applicants only for information that directly affects a person's ability to perform a job satisfactorily. This information is considered, but none other. Therefore, when you prepare a job description, a job specification, design an application form, write a job advertisement, or interview applicants, stick to job-related factors. You can get copies of federal employment laws and guidelines by writing or calling the U.S. Department of Labor. Also, a good idea is to ask a lawyer to review documents you prepare before using them.

RECRUITING APPLICANTS

Recruitment is the first hiring task—finding people who want jobs and who can perform the duties of the jobs you have available. The first step in recruitment is to clarify what jobs are to be filled from the outside and what the job duties are. Job titles can deceive the person who does the hiring, so the first thing to do when a job opens is to meet with the person who will supervise the new employee. For instance, when a job as junior accountant needs filling, meet with the head of the accounting department to find out just what duties a new employee must perform. What does a person do who holds the position and how does the job fit with others in the department and the company? Make a list of these duties and compare them with the *job description* you have on file, if one is on file. By doing this, you can avoid hiring from an outdated job description.

Job Description

A standard job description is shown in Figure 2. While job descriptions vary in length from a few paragraphs to several pages, they should describe job duties, working conditions, and benefits. From the job description, you then develop specifications, which are qualifications an applicant must have to perform the job.

In addition to its use in job assessment, a job description can be sent to employment agencies, college recruiting offices, and applicants to help you find the right person for the job. But treat job descriptions as guidelines, not as molds that applicants must fit. Sometimes the best qualified applicant for a job may not meet all the listed requirements. (The section on screening applications that follows contains more information about how to choose the best qualified person for a job.)

When writing a job description yourself, follow the principles given in Chapters One and Two. Divide the information into easy-to-follow categories. Then use short sentences, descriptive adjectives and adverbs, and active verbs to describe the job interestingly. After writing the first draft, check it to see if it answers all the questions an applicant might have about the job. A well-worded job description will tell a person whether to apply. In this way, it acts as a preliminary screening device.

Job Advertisements

A *job advertisement* is a direct solicitation for applications for a job, and there are two types: *display* and *classified*. Display advertisements appear in professional and trade journals and newspapers but not always in the classified section. They are larger than classified advertisements and include the company's logo or other artwork. Display advertisements cost more than classified advertisements because a graphic artist must prepare them for publication. A sample display advertisement is shown in Figure 3.

Career Opportunities

General Telephone Company of California

September 26, 1983

Position Title: Marketing Management Associate

Location: General Headquarters
             General Telephone Company of California
             100 Wilshire Boulevard
             Santa Monica, California 90400

Start Date: December, 1983

Duration of Program: One Year

Salary: $24,000 per year

Job Responsibilities:

The marketing management associate will have an initial six-month assignment
which will consist of establishing an overall marketing plan for the telephone
answering services market. Subsequent assignments within the marketing
department for the following six months will be geared to the associate's
interest in developing either as a specialist or generalist. Following
successful completion of the program, the Associate will be eligible for
permanent placement within the GTC organization.

Program Purpose:

This program is geared toward the development of high potential employees
interested in long-term managerial careers within the marketing department
of GTC.

Qualifications Sought:

Recent graduates with a bachelor's degree in marketing or an MBA with a
marketing emphasis are eligible for this program. Candidates must possess strong
written and oral communications and presentation skills, plus analytical
planning and organizational abilities. Candidates must have the ability
to work independently in project completion with limited supervision. Prior
experience (paid or unpaid) in financial/marketing activities such as pricing
analysis, capital management, and cost flow layouts would be desirable.

Application Procedure:

Applicants may forward a complete resume by November 1, 1983, to:

                    Management Staffing Office
                    General Telephone Company of California
                    P.O. Box 889, RC 3221 A
                    Santa Monica, CA 90406

                    AN EQUAL OPPORTUNITY EMPLOYER

FIGURE 2 A Job Description for Entry Level Position.

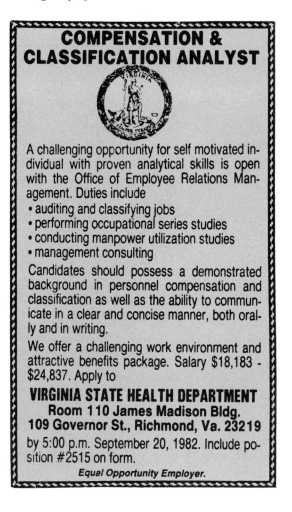

FIGURE 3 A display advertisement.

Classified advertisements always appear in the classified section of a newspaper or professional or trade journal. They usually contain a brief statement (four to six lines) about the job duties and tell applicants how and where to apply. Because classified advertisements are easier to prepare for publication, they cost less.

Consider carefully where to place an advertisement to get the right kind of applicants. Generally, an advertisement in a trade or professional journal will attract fewer but better qualified applicants than will one placed in a newspaper. However, journals are published less often than are newspapers, so it takes longer to fill a job advertised in a journal. Because most newspapers sell more copies of Sunday editions than daily editions, an advertisement in a Sunday edition usually will attract more applicants.

When you write a job advertisement, do it in the same style and tone as you write job descriptions. Describe the job interestingly and as completely as space will allow. Your purpose should be to attract "good" applicants, those who are well qualified and who want the job. Measure your success by the quality of the applicants your advertisement attracts, not by the quantity. Balance the writing tone between being persuasive and being realistic. Whenever possible, avoid abbreviating and omitting words, a practice that can result in confusion. Use the job advertisement in Figure 3 as a guide.

Company literature supports job advertisements by giving an applicant a broader look at an organization. This literature includes pamphlets, brochures, newsletters, flyers, and magazines and gives general information about the company, its employees, and its operations. Serious applicants will appreciate a chance to look at these publications.

How much should you spend on advertising a job? The answer depends on how many applicants are available. Usually, the more skilled an applicant must be, the harder it is to find qualified people to fill the job. As a result, you normally will have to spend more time and money to fill skilled than unskilled jobs. When applicants are very hard to find, you may have to advertise through employment agencies or computer matching services, both of which are more expensive than newspaper and journal advertising. Also, you can send company representatives to recruit on college campuses and at meetings of professional organizations and unions. Therefore, spend as much as you must to "get the word out" in the right places that you have jobs available. Employers do have advertising budgets, though, and must limit spending accordingly. Following a successful recruitment campaign, the next step that managers face in the hiring process is that of selecting the best qualified applicant from among those who apply. To reach this goal, most managers screen or "cut" the applicants after each of three points: reading the application package, holding a personal interview, or holding additional interviews.

SCREENING PRACTICES

Most companies begin the selection process by asking each applicant to prepare a standard application. The application forms may differ from firm to firm and even within a company, but differences in format usually exceed those in content. While different jobs do sometimes require that you ask different questions on application forms, all forms should comply with the Equal Employment Opportunities Commission guidelines. In addition to filling out application forms, professional and managerial applicants usually include a résumé. They also may write an application letter to get the process started and provide recommendation letters and examples of their work when appropriate. As a rule, the more a firm plans to pay for a person's services, the more information it will require before making a decision.

Another general practice is that the more complex a job or the more responsibility the successful candidate must assume, the more time a firm will spend evaluating applicants' credentials. For example, managers may spend a great deal of time deciding which of two applicants to hire for a key sales position when both have successful sales records but quite different backgrounds. On the other hand, they may spend little time deciding between two applicants for a turret lathe operator's job if both are qualified.

Initial Screening Steps

Screening usually begins with reading the application packages. The first step is to eliminate all applicants who lack the *basic* qualifications listed in the job description; these are qualifications that a candidate *must* have to perform the job duties satisfactorily. This initial screening is a search for *negative* information, and about half of all applicants are eliminated at this point in a normal situation. Once the unqualified applicants are screened, the focus shifts to *positive* factors in an attempt to determine who is the best qualified. The manager seeks to answer the question, "Among those who have the basic qualifications, which one has the potential to do the best job?"

When you evaluate applications and compare job applicants' credentials, follow the procedure shown in Figure 1, keeping in mind the company's overall employment objectives. Screening requires good reasoning ability, and you will improve greatly with experience. When you first look through an application package, ask yourself these basic questions: "Does it look carefully prepared?" "Is it complete?" "Is this an example of the quality of work I would like an employee to produce on the job?"

Next, look at career aspects: "How far has the person advanced?" "How well has this person progressed compared with his or her peers?" "What career direction is this person taking and is this job compatible with that direction?" Look for key information: "Are any statements incorrect, missing, overstated, or understated?" "Are there any unexplained 'gaps' or time lapses in the record?" Look for patterns like a large number of jobs held during a short time period. Being thorough is important at this point, so check everything.

When you question information, call to verify it; you can learn a lot about qualifications and personality by doing this.

Classifying Applicants

When the initial screening is done, applications should be organized into three files: *qualified, undecided,* and *unqualified.* Reject the unqualified candidates at this point and begin further screening of the undecided file. How much time you spend with this file depends on the number of applicants, the time available to fill the job, and the questions you have for which you can get answers. Reclassify all candidates in the undecided file as qualified or unqualified. To be fair and to abide by the law, reclassify candidates as unqualified only for cause. Remind yourself that you are looking for the best qualified applicant. An unqualified applicant probably would be unsuccessful on the job, so everybody gains when you reject this type of application.

Notifying Applicants

The final step in the initial screening process is to notify applicants about your decisions. While this can be done by telephone, writing letters is better. By writing you can evaluate what you have said before mailing it. *Interview invitation letters* go to qualified candidates and *refusal letters* go to the unqualified ones. The invitations should include all information needed for the applicants to get to the interviews: time, place, and name of the person conducting the interview. Write in a positive tone, yet do not sound so encouraging that an applicant will assume that he or she has been hired already. Close the letter by asking the applicant to confirm the interview. Follow the favorable message format in Chapter Four when writing these invitations.

Refusal letters are among the worst written correspondence in business today. Some writers take the "don't call us, we'll call you" attitude and build a lot of ill will for the company by doing this. Others send impersonal and ill-fitting form letters that do the same thing. The best refusal letter is an original that contains a personal explanation of why the applicant is being rejected. These take more time to write, however. So if you must use a form letter, write a personalized form message; make sure that it fits the situation precisely, and sign each one yourself. Word/information processing equipment produces original-looking form letters, and you can substitute or insert information in form letters using this equipment. See Chapter Thirteen for details on word/information processing equipment and form letters. Write refusal letters in a sympathetic but reserved tone and follow the unfavorable message format covered in Chapter Five. A sample refusal letter is shown in Figure 4.

INDUSTRIES

117 South Englewood Drive
Centennial, CO 80110

May 7, 19--

Mr. Cecil Magnum
Apartment 3B
7881 Kiowa Ridge
Steamboat Springs, CO 80477

Dear Mr. Magnum:

Thank you for applying for a position with us at FHS
Industries.

We have reviewed your application carefully along with
several others. Based on an analysis of how all
applicants' qualifications fit the duties of this particular job, we have made a decision to hire another candidate. While your qualifications do meet the basic requirements for the job, the person we have elected to hire is
both fully qualified and has six years' experience in this
type work.

We appreciate your interest in working at FHS Industries
and invite you to make another application when we again
have a position open for which you qualify.

Yours truly,

Janet Gerard

Janet Gerard
Personnel Officer

rff

FIGURE 4 An application refusal letter.

Employment Interviews

In the next stage of the screening process—employment interviewing— you begin to learn more and more about fewer and fewer people. The purpose here is to narrow the field of candidates so the focus shifts from those who can do the job to the individual who can do the best job. The initial or screening interviews give a manager the first chance to meet face to face with the applicants who were sent interview invitation letters. The main objective of these interviews is to appraise the "fit" between the job description and each applicant being interviewed.

Rarely will a person receive a job offer after the first interview. That decision usually is deferred until after a second interview, or even a third or fourth. In fact, the person who conducts the first interview usually will be a professional interviewer but may not have the authority to hire anyone. Instead, that interviewer will gather additional information and make a recommendation about whether to interview a person a second time. Those who will supervise the new employee will attend or perhaps conduct further interviews. The supervisor usually makes the decision about whom to hire.

Successful professional interviewers are skilled at listening, asking questions, evaluating answers to questions, and making recommendations based on the results of interviews. As far as an interviewee is concerned at this point, this interviewer is the company itself, not just the company's representative. Here, the interviewer acts as liaison between the applicant on the one hand and the supervisor on the other. Therefore, the professional interviewer must be professional, even in minor ways. For example, a well-qualified applicant may have serious doubts about accepting a job if he or she is made to wait too long in an outer office before an interview or if he or she is treated in any other rude or insensitive manner. An interviewer should act interested in the applicant, express a desire to know more about the applicant's background, and avoid rushing through the interview. Making an applicant feel comfortable, welcome, and respected can make a person want the job.

What questions do professional interviewers ask in these screening interviews? What do they want to know? While the specific questions do vary to fit different situations, they should be designed to reach these four goals:

1. Learn which applicants have the best qualifications to perform the job duties

2. Get answers to questions that arose from reading the application packages

3. Get all the basic information about the qualifications of each employee so that his or her qualifications can be compared with those of others

4. Learn about each applicant's personality and explore any additional information that might support a candidate's basic qualifications for the job

To get the best answers, an interviewer should attempt to detect and reduce an applicant's anxieties so that the applicant can peform well in the interview. The interviewer should be ready to answer questions about the job itself and the company's history, goals, philosophy, employee policies, and work procedures. Also, the applicant may want to know when the company will hire someone for the job and how well she or he is competing for it.

Structuring an Interview

Interviews range from highly structured to unstructured. Some interviewers like to maintain full control of an interview, so they write down all the questions they will ask in the order they will ask them. Tightly structured interviews allow all participants to respond to the same questions, which makes later comparison and analysis of qualifications easier. This procedure also saves time.

Here is a typical sequence of questions an interviewer might ask in a structured interview:

1. How did you find out about this job opening?
2. Would you be willing to relocate if hired?
3. Why did you leave your last position?
4. What is the best professional journal in your field?
5. How did you spend your spare time when in school?

Notice that these are closed questions that call for specific answers and invite little explanation.

Other interviewers believe that structured interviews give an applicant too little opportunity to communicate freely. They also believe that these interviews are stressful and that they will not get the best answers to questions by using this procedure. These interviewers prefer a more open format, one that allows and encourages the applicant to talk more freely.

Here is a typical sequence of questions that an interviewer might ask in an unstructured interview:

1. Tell me how you think your education prepared you for this job?
2. What motivates you most to do a job well?
3. How would you define a successful career?
4. If I asked you for three or four words that best describe yourself, what words would you choose?

5. What is the most important question I could ask you about your ability to perform the duties of this job?

These open questions call for thoughtful answers and invite explanations. Should an applicant give a short reply to one of these questions, the interviewer will ask "Why?" and encourage further comments.

Some interviewers mix both procedures, asking some closed and some open questions. In fact, the best approach to most interviews is to do just that. This balanced approach to questioning saves time compared with an unstructured interview; yet it gives the interviewer a chance to explore an applicant's personality and job qualifications.

Handling Stress in Interviews

Most applicants are bothered by stress during interviews. It often causes them to perform poorly. When this happens, you cannot measure fully an applicant's qualifications. For this reason, you should try to get the applicant to relax before the interview begins and watch for signs of stress throughout. The best way in which to do this is to emphasize your own humanity. Act friendly and as though you feel comfortable in the situation. Offer the applicant a cup of coffee or make some similar gesture at the beginning of the interview. Do not overdo it, but do assume that an applicant is feeling at least some stress and that you need to compensate for it with your own behavior.

Because some jobs require people to work in stressful conditions, some interviews are intentionally stress oriented. In such cases, the interviewer will allow normal tension to develop unchecked and, if necessary, will build on that tension by asking probing questions and perhaps by acting cold and unfriendly. This procedure is really a test of skill in handling stress that the applicant must pass—the job requires the ability. Stress interviews are used most often in business for hiring managers, salespersons, and complaint adjusters—people who must work well in stressful situations. A few interviewers always conduct stress interviews regardless of the type job to be filled. These people believe that applicants reveal more meaningful things about themselves when placed under duress.

Planning Interview Formats

An interview, like a speech, should have a beginning, a middle, and an end. You can use this general plan to separate the interview goals into elements that will define what should be done when.

The Beginning   The most charged moment in an interview occurs when the interviewer and the applicant first meet each other. At that moment, first impressions form and the general climate for the meeting is set. Tension is greatest at the beginning of an interview, so that is the right time for the interviewer to try to establish a calm, relaxed mood. A comfortable setting helps do this, and so does "small talk"—general conversation. You can get ideas about how to get started from a résumé. An example is to talk about a city you have both lived in or a hobby you share. However you do it, your purpose is to establish a supportive climate and a friendly start.

The Middle   The second part of the interview, the middle, focuses on the interview questions and answers. Remember when conducting this portion that a good question makes a good answer possible. The most successful interviewers not only know what questions to ask but also know how and when to ask them. This situation requires a flexible format and calls for the interviewer to monitor the total situation as the interview progresses. Professional interviewers try to develop a keen sense of pacing so that they will know when to listen and when to move on to another question. Here are 12 guidelines for conducting the question-and-answer part of the interview:

1. Ask leading questions to encourage more than a specific yes-or-no response when appropriate.
2. Pace the questions so that the applicant has enough time to respond completely, but avoid long pauses. If the applicant wanders from the subject, gently but firmly bring the conversation back to it.
3. Use only the amount of time you reserved for the interview. Given the time you have available, gather as much information as you can that will help you to make the right recommendation or decision later.
4. Rephrase a question or move on to another one when the applicant is unable to give you an answer. Long, awkward pauses are embarrassing.
5. Avoid asking questions for which you already know the answers because this practice wastes time.
6. Ask follow-up questions when exploring an issue. For example, if you learn that the applicant had a personality conflict with his or her last supervisor, you might say, "What did your supervisor do that you found to be most bothersome?"
7. Avoid tricky questions or those that might entrap the applicant. Instead, maintain an atmosphere of trust.
8. Keep a record of what is said so that you can review it later. However, avoid letting your note taking interfere with the interview.

9. Remain neutral when you hear or respond to the applicant's answers to your questions. Be pleasant and encouraging, but avoid overt agreement or disagreement with the applicant's opinions.

10. Speak distinctly and avoid mumbling while writing.

11. Ask the applicant to clarify any answers that are unclear to you.

12. Be flexible. You can get the answers you need in many ways. Do not expect one interview to duplicate another.

The questions you ask should not violate the laws that govern fair employment practices. Some questions may be discriminatory in some situations but not in others. You may ask questions that will help you to determine if an applicant meets a job requirement. For example, you may ask a person's age when the job requires that the holder be bonded and you have reasonable doubt that the applicant is old enough. When doing this, remind the applicant of the job requirement before asking his or her age. To hire the best qualified people, you should ask appropriate questions and expect to get truthful answers.

The End   Once the applicant answers all your questions, begin to close the interview. But before doing this, check your notes thoroughly to make sure that you have all the information you need. Then, you might ask if the applicant has any questions for you. When these questions are answered, tell the applicant what to expect next. For instance, explain that you are conducting interviews with other applicants or that another interview with this person might be needed. Or if the next step is to decide who will get the job, say so. Also, remember to tell the applicant when another interview or the hiring decision will be made. Try to speak positively about the interview as you close, but remain neutral about a hiring decision. Being too positive can give the applicant false hope; being too negative can be discouraging.

A plan for designing and executing an interview is shown in Figure 5. Based on a 30-minute time limit, the plan shows how to proceed to develop the activities and reach the goals of a job interview.

Planning Other Interview Formats

Besides the basic interview format described in the preceding sections, companies hold employment interviews in other formats on occasion. The reasons for conducting other types of interviews range from efficiency, to necessity, to trying out new managerial ideas. The four other primary interview formats are campus interviews, group interviews, panel interviews, and role playing and simulation sessions.

THE INTERVIEWER'S PLAN

Objectives of the Interviewer: 1. Evaluate the Candidate
2. Stimulate the Candidate's Interest in the Firm
3. Maintain the Goodwill of the Candidate

Structure of a Good Interview (30 min.)

Time	Interviewer's Activity	Interviewer's Purpose
4–5 min.	1. Reading résumé	1. Notice grades, academic achievement, extracurricular activities
	2. General comments Résumé Weather "Why did you decide to study at ____?"	2. Establish rapport Put candidate at ease Ask questions candidate can answer easily so he or she gains confidence
	3. Information gathering	3. Decide whether to ask the candidate back for a second interview
	a. Open questions—requiring explanatory answers "How do you spend your leisure time?" "Tell me about your college experience." "What courses did you like?"	a. Determine candidate's motivations and habits
	b. Closed questions—requiring short factual answers How does a candidate act in certain situations? Focus on past behavior	b. Determine if candidate's apparent attributes are reflected in reality
16 min.	c. Listening techniques Echo (repeat phrases) Eye contact Silence	c. Show acceptance
	d. Behavior observations Interested? Enthusiastic? Poised? Assertive?	d. Pierce through candidate's nervousness to substance of what the candidate is like
5 min.	4. Answer questions	4. Sell the organization
1 min.	5. Summary and close	5. Tell the candidate when and how he or she will hear from the organization
4 min.	6. Write up evaluation	6. Write while impression is fresh

FIGURE 5 The interviewer's plan. (Joan W. Rossi, "Make Your Students Interview Ready," *The ABCA Bulletin,* September 1980, p. 3.)

Campus Interviews   Some personnel officers conduct employment interviews on college and university campuses. These recruiters travel to campuses to interview graduating students for jobs with their companies.
Those who spend the extra money to do this think that interviewing on
campus gives them a chance to hire talented applicants before they graduate. But a problem with the campus interview is that the interiewer has
little control of the situation. For one thing, the interviewer may have little
time to study an applicant's application package before the interview.
For another, the interview setting and facilities are controlled by campus
officials. Also, these interviews last for shorter time periods than do those
held at the company, often for no more than 15 or 20 minutes.

Because of these problems and because the applicants are often
unfamiliar with the interviewer's company, more time in the interview
must be spent building goodwill for the company and orienting applicants
to it. Therefore, the interviewer has to rely heavily on company literature
to sell the firm. The result is that these sessions are usually prescreening
interviews, an additional step in the hiring process. Despite the problems
involved, many companies continue the job search on campuses because
of the pool of professional and managerial applicants there.

Group Interviews   Sometimes, company officials interview candidates in
groups when so many people apply for a job that individual interviews
are impractical. A single interviewer may talk with as many as four to
six applicants at the same time. One problem with this format is that the
interviewer can spend little time getting in-depth responses from a single
person. Another is that the dynamics of the group often interferes with
the interview goals. For example, if you as the interviewer select three
people from a group to begin talking with, each applicant will respond
as a member of the group, not just as an individual. Also, personalities
emerge in group interviews and affect the outcome. For instance, one
person may attempt to dominate the group; two people might form a
bond to oppose a third; or everyone may respond only when spoken to
directly.

Group interviews save both time and money and they can be effective. They require highly skilled interviewers, however. A group interviewer must be a discussion leader who can extract specific information
about applicants as an interview proceeds.

Panel Interviews   Some companies conduct panel interviews, where a
group of company officials interviews a single candidate. As a result,
these interviews are more stressful for an applicant than are any other
type. In fact, the stress interviews discussed earlier in the chapter are
often held in panel formats. In this approach, the group shares the session

time, so each interviewer has little time for individual questioning. A panel interview should be led by one member of the managerial group who must know how to control stress and group dynamics.

Personalities may emerge in panel interviews. Panel members may seek power, recognition, or some other individual goal that is contrary to the interview goals. These interviews are expensive, largely because of scheduling problems and the high cost of the interviewers' time. Therefore, they are held most often when an important job in the company is to be filled.

Role-Playing and Simulation Sessions   Role-playing and simulation sessions are held to measure how skilled an applicant is at handling joblike situations. An example is to ask an applicant to exchange roles with an interviewer to measure the applicant's managerial skills. Another way of measuring these skills is to ask an applicant to talk to an empty chair as though a sullen employee were sitting in it. In a combined group interview/role-playing format, applicants might be asked to role play as employers and employees. For instance, one applicant might be asked to settle a dispute between two other applicants.

An advantage of role-playing and simulation sessions is that company officials can see applicants perform job skills before hiring them. A disadvantage is that a lot of time is required to prepare for, set up, and administer these sessions and to evaluate the results afterward. A second problem is that interviewers in these sessions should have professional training in human behavior and analysis; they must be able to determine which behavior is significant and which is not. Also, while these situations do simulate realism to some extent, they do not duplicate actual job performance.

Recording Interview Results

A problem with taking notes during an interview is that it can interrupt information flow. An interviewer may stop too often to take notes, may talk while writing, or may indicate the special importance of a remark by reaching for a pen or pencil. All such tactics are distracting. To help reduce the effects of these type problems, many companies use *applicant evaluation forms* such as the one in Figure 6. Rather than take notes, an interviewer can mark his or her impressions of an applicant during an interview and then complete the form after the interview. Using these forms saves time and prevents distractions.

Although application evaluation forms can give objective evidence, the makeup of such a form does not always fit every interviewing situation. Also, even when the forms are well designed, they gather a limited amount of information. For these reasons, some companies record job

---

APPLICANT EVALUATION FORM

Applicant's Name _____   Position _____

Overall Appraisal	Poor		Average		Good
1. Initial impression	1	2	3	4	5
2. Personal demeanor	1	2	3	4	5
3. Preparation for interview	1	2	3	4	5
4. Ability to express self	1	2	3	4	5
5. Level of maturity	1	2	3	4	5

Total _____

Career Qualifications					
1. Academic preparation	1	2	3	4	5
2. Professional experience	1	2	3	4	5
3. Knowledge of job	1	2	3	4	5
4. Leadership ability	1	2	3	4	5
5. Career potential	1	2	3	4	5

Total _____

Personality Impressions

These judgments are not absolutes, merely impressions. You do not have to completo ovory ono, or, if you wish, you may expand your responses on the back.

Dominance:	Aggressive/passive
Self-regard:	Positive/negative
Self-confidence:	Strong/weak
General behavior:	Friendly/shy or hostile
Interactions:	Spontaneous/guarded or reticent
Feelings about change:	Accepts or enjoys/negative or fearful
Endurance:	Sticks to tasks/gives up
Overall evaluation:	Consider abilities to perform job tasks, form relationships with peers and future career success. Use back of sheet if required.

Would this person be an asset to the company?
What should this applicant's hiring priority rating be on a 1 to 10 scale?

Interviewer _____   Date _____

FIGURE 6 An applicant evaluation form for interviewer.

interviews on audio or video tapes. These methods allow interviewers greater freedom while interviewing and provide permanent records for later review and documentation. Video tapes are especially good for reviewing an applicant's behavior later with other company officials before making a hiring decision. To be fair, get the applicant's consent before using audio or video equipment to record an interview. While recording, keep the equipment in the background to avoid making an applicant self-conscious.

Some companies use polygraph machines, commonly called lie detectors, to record applicants' physical responses to tension. Normally, these machines are used when interviewing candidates for high-security positions, as when employees are required to keep financial records or handle money. The use of these machines is regulated by state right-to-work laws, so verify the legal restrictions on the use of these machines in your state before using them in employment interviews. Some firms consider it unethical to use polygraph machines, even though their use might be legal. When used, they should be operated only by trained personnel because the data they provide are subject both to error and misinterpretation. These data cannot be used as evidence if a legal dispute arises.

Holding Follow-up Interviews

If you are unable to make a hiring decision after the initial interview, the next step is to hold follow-up interviews with the top candidates. (Occasionally, you may eliminate all candidates after initial interviews, in which case you will start the hiring process over at this point.) Companies almost always hold second interviews when filling top managerial positions because of the importance of those jobs. For these meetings, you will need to invite the manager who will supervise the successful candidate. You may decide to ask this supervisor to conduct the interviews or at least to participate actively in them. Follow-up interviews give the supervisor a chance to meet the applicants, talk with them about the job, and ask more specific questions about their qualifications.

A follow-up interview should not merely repeat the initial interview for a new audience. Instead, seek additional information about the applicant's job qualifications. For example, focus on each applicant's job knowledge if you still question which applicant knows the most about the work.

EVALUATING INFORMATION AND MAKING RECOMMENDATIONS

Once you gather all the appropriate information about the applicants for a job, the next step is to evaluate each applicant's qualifications. All decisions made should be based on written, oral, or observed evidence. Written evidence includes application forms, résumés, application and recommendation letters, work samples, and aptitude and skills tests. Oral evidence includes the answers to interview questions. Observations are made about the way in which an applicant behaves and answers questions. While observation is as valid as other types of evidence, interpreting it takes skill. Written evidence is easiest to evaluate unless the information in recommendations is not clear.

People who know an applicant write *recommendation or reference letters* to companies about the person's job qualifications. Normally, an applicant furnishes names and addresses of these reference sources to a company. Then, someone in the company asks for the recommendation letters.

Recommendation letters are quasi-official documents that can be used as evidence in legal disputes. Therefore, modern practice calls for writing favorable reference letters. You might be saying, "If no one is going to be critical, why should an interviewer ask for recommendation letters?" This position has merit, but a well-written recommendation letter can supply valuable insights about an applicant's qualifications. Compare these helpful descriptions furnished by a past employer about two applicants:

> Janice enjoys working in an active environment. She accepts responsibility and likes to get involved with solving ongoing production problems. Because she works well with others, Janice can direct other employees' work without creating bad feelings.

> George is a quiet man who is happiest and most productive when working alone. He is patient and responsible and requires little supervision. When working on long-term projects and on those requiring meticulous thinking, George is at his best.

Descriptions such as these actually help employers to match applicants to jobs.

For employers, recommendation letters either support or raise questions about an applicant's qualifications. When you receive a recommendation letter about an applicant that you are considering for a job, evaluate its credibility first. If it sounds insincere, downplay its importance in making your hiring decision. But if it sounds sincere, use the letter as a starting point for gathering other information.

Based on the information you have evaluated, you will now make a recommendation to hire or not to hire the person. Making the recommendation should be drawn from a logical conclusion that is based on objective information. The recommendation report is usually sent to the person who will supervise the applicant who is hired, so that person normally makes the decision. On the one hand, your report may be just a copy of a completed applicant evaluation form (see Figure 6). On the other hand, you may write a formal report as detailed as those discussed in Unit 3. How much you will say about an applicant depends on the number of applicants, the time available to fill the job, and the importance of the job itself. The format for presenting these evaluative reports is normally dictated by company policy.

Legally, employers must provide objective criteria to job candidates and must base hiring decisions on these criteria. So if you include your opinions in your recommendation report, remember to include the evidence that led you to form these opinions.

MAKING AND NEGOTIATING JOB OFFERS

After making the hiring decision, the next step is to notify the successful applicant. You may decide to telephone or telegraph the news, but follow this with a job offer letter to confirm the offer and provide details.

Open the job offer letter with the offer itself following the favorable correspondence plan discussed in Chapter Four. The details in this letter should include the position title, salary and fringe benefits, the starting date and time, and the name and location of the person to whom to report on the first workday. Also include a telephone number to call for further information and any other necessary details. Check to be sure that all you say in this letter complies with the job advertisement and description as well as with statements made during the interviews. Because a job offer letter commits the company legally, phrase the letter carefully. Close with a statement that encourages the candidate about working for the company and ask for acceptance by a certain date.

Sometimes applicants are willing to accept a job, but not on the terms you offer. This situation leaves you with the choice of either negotiating the offer with the candidate or refusing to negotiate. Negotiations involve telling the candidate what you can do and communicating this effectively. For instance, if you can accept an applicant's counterproposal or can offer a reasonable compromise, write a persuasive letter following the plan given in Chapter Six. If you cannot, write a refusal letter following the unfavorable correspondence plan given in Chapter Five.

Before writing refusal letters to the unsuccessful candidates, wait for written acceptance from the first person to whom you offered the job. Should the best qualified applicant turn down your offer, you might want to offer the job to the second best qualified person. When the job is filled, write refusal letters to the unsuccessful applicants. A sample job refusal letter is shown in Figure 4, which follows the plan discussed in Chapter Five.

WELCOMING NEW EMPLOYEES

After an applicant accepts a job offer but before he or she reports for work, company officials usually write letters welcoming the new employee to the company. When writing these letters, follow the favorable correspondence plan discussed in Chapter Four. Begin with the welcome itself and try to bring the new employee into the situation. Details in these letters include information about job opportunities, pride, and rewards. Be positive but sound realistic; remarks that sound too glowing may be disregarded as propaganda. Close these letters positively by looking forward to a good working relationship with the new employee.

If you have a job orientation program for new employees, the welcoming letter should include information about the program, including when and where to report for it. If not, include basic orientation information about the job in this letter.

SUMMARY

The process of hiring job applicants includes recruiting, screening, and making hiring decisions. Negotiating job offers and welcoming new employees is also part of the process. Laws that control hiring procedures include the Equal Pay Act of 1963, the Civil Rights Act of 1964, and the Equal Employment Opportunities Act of 1972. These laws prevent companies from discriminating arbitrarily among job applicants.

The first step in filling a job is to examine the job description to see what the job requirements are. The next step is to write either a display or classified job advertisement and place it in a newspaper or professional or trade journal. Many companies also advertise jobs with company literature.

After a job is announced and people apply for it, the next step is to screen the applicants. The first part of the screening process is to examine the application packages to select the most qualified applicants for interviews. At this point, write interview invitation letters to those you wish to interview and refusal letters to the other applicants. Screening interviews are held

to get information that will help you decide who is best qualified for a job. These interviews may be structured or unstructured, but most are at least loosely structured. As is true for a speech, an interview has a beginning, a middle, and an end.

Other interview formats include campus, group, panel interviews, and role-playing and simulation sessions. When recording interviews, take notes, use application evaluation forms, or record the interviews on audio or video tapes.

If no one is hired after the screening interviews, the next step is to hold follow-up interviews with the top candidates. After this, evaluate the results of the follow-up interviews and make employment recommendations. The next step is to write a job offer letter to successful applicants. When you must negotiate the terms of a job offer, be positive, clear, and persuasive. Once a candidate is hired, remember to write refusal letters to the remaining applicants.

The last step in the hiring process is to write letters welcoming successful job candidates to the company.

Additional Readings

Downs, Cal W., G. Paul Smeyak, and Ernest Martin. *Professional Interviewing.* New York: Harper & Row, 1980.

Equal Employment Opportunity Act of 1972. Washington, D.C.: Government Printing Office, 1972.

OFCC Affirmative Action Guidelines. Washington, D.C.: Bureau of National Affairs, 1972.

Pell, Arthur R. *Recruiting and Selecting Personnel.* New York: Simon & Schuster, 1969.

Roger, Jean L., and Walter L. Fortson. *Fair Employment Interviewing.* Reading, Mass.: Addison-Wesley, 1976.

Stewart, Charles J., and William B. Cash. *Interviewing: Principles and Practice.* Dubuque, Iowa: W. C. Brown, 1978.

Timm, Paul R. *Managerial Communication: A Finger on the Pulse.* Englewood Cliffs, N.J.: Prentice-Hall, 1980.

For additional reference sources, check the reference section at the end of Chapter Fifteen.

Review Questions

1. What are the major steps in the hiring process? List and describe them.

2. Explain why employers cannot discriminate arbitrarily against applicants in the hiring process. Then make a list of the types of discriminatory practices that are illegal.

3. Explain the difference between a job description and a job advertisement. What is each used for when recruiting applicants?

4. What is company literature? How is it used in the hiring process?

5. Explain the initial steps in screening job applicants for the screening interviews. Also, how are applicants classified in this procedure.

6. What should the interviewer do in the beginning, middle, and end portions of a standard job interview? Give the purpose for each of the three parts and explain how to fulfill the purpose.

7. Why do personnel officers interview on college and university campuses?

8. Why do companies hold group and panel interviews? Give the purpose of each.

9. List the ways of recording interviews. Then explain the advantages and disadvantages of each method.

10. When should you decide to hold follow-up interviews? Under what conditions? What does an interviewer try to achieve in follow-up interviews?

Exercises

1. Obtain three current job descriptions from companies, employment agencies, or your campus library or placement office. Look for those in your preferred employment field. Compare the information on the job descriptions and list all the common job qualification requirements. Are you preparing yourself now to meet these requirements? List any

common requirements that you are not now meeting or planning to meet.

2. Make a list of six places where prospective employers in your field advertise for jobs. Then rank the employers according to their appeal as a place for you to work.

3. Set up a simulated employment interview in your class. You could do this in one of two ways: (a) ask an employer to come to your class and conduct an interview with students or (b) ask students to role play as interviewers and interviewees. Record the interviews on video tape if possible. Evaluate the success of the sessions afterward. You might even give grades to interviewers and interviewees. As a part of the evaluation, make a list of changes needed to improve the interviews.

4. Visit your campus job placement center and make a list of the services offered there. Which of these services can you use? List them and also state a date at which you can make the most use of each service.

5. Make a list of five people you would ask to write a recommendation letter for you. State why you chose each person. Also, list three jobs you would like to apply for. Now, if you could ask only three of the five references to recommend you for each of the three jobs, which three would you ask to recommend you for each job?

6. Assume that you work for EmCee Micro-

phonics Company as the personnel manager. In this job, you use the hiring process discussed in this chapter. Assume that you have just hired Bennett Budd as a new accounting assistant in the payroll department. Write a letter welcoming Mr. Budd to the company. Follow the favorable correspondence plan presented in Chapter Four.

7. Clip two job display advertisements and two classified job advertisements from your local newspapers. Explain how well you think each of the four advertisements presents the job. Compare the display and classified advertisements with each other and then the two types with each other. Discuss your comparison in your explanation.

8. Assume that you work for R. E. Penter Group, a local manufacturer of robots for industrial use that are sold throughout the country. You have just finished screening six applicants for a job as district sales supervisor for a three-state area. You want to interview three of the applicants, but the other three do not have the five years of sales experience required for the job. Write an interview invitation letter for use as a form to invite the three to a screening interview. Then write a refusal letter that can be used as a form to notify the three unsuccessful applicants. Remember to design the letters so that some personal information can be placed in each form when desired.

CHAPTER FIFTEEN

Finding a Job

WHAT DO APPLICANTS DO?

The goals in studying the text and completing the activities in this chapter are to know

1. Methods for seeking qualified job leads
2. How to prepare a professional job application package
3. What applicants do before, during, and after interviews
4. How to present job qualifications to meet prospective employers' expectations
5. Methods for handling job offers

Looking for a job is a challenging but rewarding experience. The challenge is in finding the right job, and the reward comes through the benefits of having that job. Almost everyone looks for a job at least once, and most people seek to change jobs several times during a career. Too many people consider job hunting a nuisance and a temporary setback rather than an opportunity to improve their lives.

Some applicants today are entering the job market for the first time, others want to change employers, and others want to change careers. All can benefit from the information in this chapter. The discussion takes the job applicant's viewpoint and examines ways in which to conduct a successful job search. With this information and that in Chapter Fourteen, you will know how the employment process works from both the employer's and the applicant's perspectives.

To succeed in searching for a job, you will rely heavily on your speaking and writing skills and your ability to research and analyze information. In chronological order, the five steps in the job seeking process are

1. Finding job leads
2. Preparing a professional application package
3. Keeping mailing logs and writing follow-up letters
4. Interviewing with the employer
5. Responding to a job offer

FINDING JOB LEADS

The first step to take in finding a job is to look around to see who is hiring now. Two goals to pursue at this point are (1) to evaluate the general job market and (2) to seek several jobs for which you qualify. Begin by checking the classified section of your Sunday newspaper, the biggest single source of jobs in general. The fewer the jobs available, the better your strategy must be and the more vital it is that you know how to emphasize your job qualifications.

As you clip job advertisements, be thorough but selective. For example, if you collect 25 advertisements and then reject 20 of them, you probably are discriminating well. The 5 you select will most likely be good job prospects.

Locating Sources of Job Leads

Sources that provide good job leads include newspapers and other publications, placement agencies and services, letters of inquiry, and personal contacts and networks.

Publications

Newspapers are the most popular source of job leads, and a good one. Begin with the classified section but also look for job display advertising in other parts of the paper. In addition, articles in the business section can give you ideas about which companies are hiring. As you read, look for information about company goals to guide you in choosing the right company. Also jot down the names of company officials mentioned in the articles for later use when you begin to make applications.

Local newspapers usually carry announcements for jobs in a particular geographical area. On the other hand, large city daily newspapers often announce jobs in distant locations. National papers such as *The Wall Street Journal* advertise jobs in the entire country and abroad. If you want to move to another place to work, the names of the country's newspapers are listed by location in the *Working Press of the Nation*, Vol. 1, and in *Ayer's Directory of Publications*.

Professional journals are sometimes overlooked as sources for job leads. Some professional journals have job placement columns and even classified sections. Also, most of them print articles about prospective employers and the general job market. They also print announcements of professional activities, including meetings, workshops, seminars, and conferences. All are good places to meet company officials and working professionals. You can locate professional journals in your field in one of two ways: (1) look for them in *Ayer's*, the *Working Press*, or the *Business Periodicals Index* if you know their names; or (2) look for them in an encyclopedia of associations if you know the group's name or that of a related organization. These encyclopedias include the *Career Guide of Professional Associations* and the *Directory of National Trade and Professional Associations* in the United States.

Both industrial groups and individual companies publish *trade journals* and *in-house publications*. While these publications generally do not advertise for employees, they do provide timely information about industries and companies. Stories on retirements, new plant and office locations, plant expansions, and relocations of plant facilities all mean that jobs are available. Trade journals are listed in standard periodical indexes and are usually available on request.

Placement Agencies and Services

Placement agencies and services where you can get job leads include *college placement services, governmental agencies, professional organizations,* and *private employment agencies*. Most colleges have placement services that help graduates find jobs. These services act as go-betweens for applicants and employers. They provide services ranging all the way from job referrals to career counseling. So visit the placement office on your campus to find out what they can do for you. While there, ask for a copy of the *College Placement Annual,* a publication containing information on more than 1500 employers.

Governments have placement agencies at all levels—federal, state, and local. Together, they form the biggest single group of employers in the nation. The largest, the federal government, operates 10 regional and hundreds of area employment offices through the U.S. Office of Personnel Management (OPM). OPM hires applicants for all types of federal jobs, including managerial jobs. A managerial job applicant must take the Professional and Administrative Career Examination (PACE) to get a federal job. To qualify to take PACE, you must hold a baccalaureate degree. Veterans get preference in hiring for federal jobs; so if you are a veteran and want to pursue a federal job, begin by visiting your local Veterans Administration office.

State governments operate quite differently from the federal government—which only hires for itself. Federal law requires that a state government must furnish placement services for all its citizens. This means not only that state governments hire for themselves, but also that they must furnish information about jobs in other sectors.

Local governments offer a greater variety of placement services than either federal or state governments. Most, however, are interested only in filling jobs they have available themselves. While local governments are not a prime source for job leads, they may have just the right job for you. So it may be worth your time to visit local city or county offices to see what they have available.

Professional organizations are a valuable source of job leads. They assist in one or more ways by offering placement services, publishing announcements of job openings, and offering opportunities to meet people who are hiring. If you do not know the right organization for you, ask a professional in your field or look it up in an encyclopedia of associations in the library.

Private employment agencies are in business to find jobs for their clients, so their services do cost money. For some jobs, employers pay all or part of the agency's fee; for others, they pay nothing. Because these agencies differ one from another, take the time to find the one that suits your needs best. When you contract with a private employment agency, read your contract carefully or consult a lawyer before signing it.

Inquiry Letters

A more assertive way in which to find a job than anything mentioned thus far is to ask prospective employers if they can use someone with your credentials. "Knocking on doors" in this way can expand your job search dramatically. Rather than waiting for an employer to advertise a job, this approach calls for you to get things started. Although you may be turned down often, many employers appreciate initiative. Consider writing inquiry letters to prospective employers whenever you (1) are having problems getting job leads in other ways, (2) want to work for a particular company or in a particular location, or (3) are seeking a job with greater potential. Write these letters as favorable messages of the direct request type as discussed in Chapter Four. A sample is shown as Figure 1.

Personal Contacts and Networks

Your telephone is a valuable tool for uncovering job leads. If used well, you may even be able to track down job openings before they are advertised. The networking principle covered in the chapter on group communication can be applied to telephone job hunting in either *personal* or *indirect contact*. When using personal contact, begin by calling people you know who may be able to help you find job leads. Explain to them what you want and ask for their assistance. Whenever people cannot help, ask if they know someone who can. Then when you call the person to whom you are referred, start by explaining who made the referral. Using this networking pattern almost certainly will result in finding job leads.

Indirect contact works on the same principle as personal contact. But instead of calling people you know, begin by calling companies that may have jobs available. Ask if they have job openings just as you would in an inquiry letter. If a company is not hiring, ask if someone in the firm can suggest the names of other companies that might be. If possible, get the names of the right people to call in the companies to which you are referred.

Keep good records when using these network approaches. Find out what jobs are available and get the correct spelling of people's names. The keys to success in using these job hunting methods, though, are endurance and timing. Keep making calls and keep looking for referrals. Use the names of people you already have talked with to introduce yourself to the next person you call. The number of people you call is not important. What is important is that sooner or later your inquiry will be met with, "Yes, we are looking for someone."

Qualifying Job Leads

When you become satisfied that you know what jobs are available, the next task is to screen the job leads to discard those you do not want. If you do not do this, you may find yourself giving too much time and effort

331 Fleming Drive
New Ross, IN 47968
January 27, 19--

Mr. E. V. Morse, Personnel Manager
Solar Tech Industries
535 North Brand Avenue
Fort Wayne, IN 46811

Dear Mr. Morse

Would your company be interested in hiring an auditor who
knows how to save money?

For the past four years I have worked for Indiana Home
Developers as manager of internal audits at field locations. While here, I have assisted the controller with
handling complex accounting and financial systems problems.
In this work, I helped save money on major financial transactions, $555,000 in one case.

Now, I would like to join a smaller firm in a related
building field, one like Solar Tech. This would allow me
to help the company while using my experience and educational preparation (a B.S. degree in Accounting from
Indiana State University at Terre Haute). I can bring
expertise in advanced accounting and problem-solving
ability to the job. Also, I can serve effectively as a
communication liaison between production and management.

If my background interests you, I will gladly send you a
résumé. Then if you think my credentials suitable, I shall
appreciate an interview to discuss ways in which my abilities might be put to good use at Solar Tech.

Sincerely yours

Leslie Blanchard

Leslie Blanchard

FIGURE 1 An inquiry letter.

to following through on unproductive leads. Worse yet, you may accept the wrong job.

The procedure for qualifying job leads is similar to what managers experience when they screen applications. The purpose differs, however. Employers screen applications to find the best qualified person for a job on the best terms for them. On the other hand, you are looking for a job that you will feel comfortable doing, that pays well, and that has the best fringe benefits for you. Therefore, you should focus on (1) whether you meet the job qualifications and (2) what you want in a job.

To qualify a job lead according to job qualifications, divide the qualifications into "hard" and "soft" requirements. "Hard" requirements are those that you must have to do the job; "soft" requirements are those that will be helpful but are not required. If you lack some of the "hard" requirements, disqualify the job lead. On the other hand, if you do have all the "hard" requirements, consider pursuing the lead. If you have all the "hard" requirements and some of the "soft" ones, definitely pursue the lead. The closer your qualifications fit what employers say they are looking for, the better.

Once you reduce the available job leads to those you qualify for, begin to weigh your interests. For each job, ask yourself if you would like the job if you had it. Would it give you the opportunity, status, security, and other benefits you want now and in the future? The answers to these questions will start you thinking about what you want from a job rather than just wondering whether you can find one. To be objective about your interests, make a list of what you expect from your job and career. Then find out whether each employer you are considering can meet these personal requirements.

Learning about employers may require some research. Three ways in which to do this are through reading published materials, receiving answers to inquiry letters, and conducting interviews. Information about large companies is found in business indexes, for example, *Thomas' Register of American Manufacturers, Moody's Manuals,* and *Dun & Bradstreet's* reports. If you cannot find the right information in these indexes, look in either the *Guide to American Directories* or *Trade Directories of the World.* These works list all the major trade and financial guides.

Inquiry letters and telephone or personal interviews are less formal sources of information than publications. Chambers of Commerce, local service clubs, professional organizations, rival companies, and telephone directories are all good sources of information about employers. The networking technique works well here too. If one person does not know about a company, ask for the name of someone who might know. The more people you write or call, the more complete your information will be.

PREPARING THE APPLICATION PACKAGE

The single most important message to get across to any prospective employer is that you are the best qualified applicant for the position being offered. You will have two opportunities to do this: when you submit your application and when you meet the employer for an interview. While all stages in the employment process are important, the application package is especially so because it will determine if your application will be processed.

When faced with finding a job, many people take literally the instructions, "send résumé." They assume that that is all there is to it: type your qualifications on a sheet of paper and send it forward. Much more is involved in the successful process, however. Preparing a résumé is a chance to use your communication skills to show the reader you are right for the job. The complete "package" involves three different sources of information, all focusing on the same goal:

1. *Résumé*—an objective description of qualifications
2. *Application letter*—a statement of reasons why the applicant is qualified for and would do well in the position
3. *Recommendation letters*—statements about an applicant's qualifications, abilities, and potential by people who know the applicant

You are responsible for writing the résumé and application letter. Although you do not write recommendation letters yourself, you should prepare to have them ready at the time you apply for a job.

Because most companies require applicants to complete standard application forms, you might ask, "Why bother with résumés, too?" While there are many reasons to do so, the two most important are (1) they save the employer the time and effort spent in sending out application forms and waiting for responses, and (2) they present a clear picture of an applicant's qualifications.

Information can take many forms in résumés, depending on how you want to present your qualifications. For instance, you have choices about what to emphasize and how to organize and phrase information. As a result, the résumé differs from an application form, where questions and space available for answers are predetermined. For example, an application form may have just a few lines to answer a question about your college preparation. About all you can get in the space is your degree, major, date of graduation, and alma mater. On the other hand, you can devote a half page of detailed description to this item in a résumé if you wish.

A résumé is a tool—not a task—that can be used to sketch your background in a way to convince an employer to hire you. This should be done ethically and credibly, though. Personnel officers are accustomed to screening résumés, so they are not naïve. The employer's job is to screen applicants until only the best qualified remain in contention for a job. Therefore, your job is to design a résumé that will get you past the screening process to an interview.

The Résumé

The first step in writing a résumé is to decide what information to include in it. Once this is done, layout and preparation are easy to do. The core content of a résumé is (1) the employer's requirements for the position and (2) your qualifications that best prepare you for the position. In theory, these two should be the same, but in practice they often differ. Employers always view academic qualifications and employment experience as the two most critical areas to examine closely on a résumé. Other information can only support these two areas.

Academic qualifications usually appear under a heading labeled *education.* They include degrees, courses, seminars, scholarships, internships, and certifications received from or through colleges and universities. Awards, honors, grants, and other academic recognition received may be listed here as well. Include whatever information is needed to get across your scholastic aptitude and talent.

Employment experience is usually labeled as *experience* and generally includes a listing of previous employers, job titles, and dates of service on these jobs. You may wish to add a brief description of job duties and the names of your supervisors. Some applicants, especially those who entered college immediately after finishing high school, have little to put under this heading. If you find yourself in this position, consider adding a heading called *related experience* and include any unpaid work experience you have had. Listing volunteer work shows that you have some experience that will help you do the job.

Reference information also should be included in résumés. This information includes your name, address, and telephone number and those of people who will recommend you for the job.

Layout and Preparation of a Résumé

Most of the information about yourself that you will include in a résumé fits easily into subject clusters. These clusters form the "information blocks" needed to build a résumé.

Here are the five subject clusters that usually appear in a standard résumé:

1. *Heading.*   Your name, address, and telephone number. You may include your job title, career objectives, and date of availability.
2. *Education.*   Your educational preparation given in chronological order. Begin with the most recent information.
3. *Experience.*   Your employment background that supports your ability to perform the job successfully. List this in chronological order beginning with the most recent information.
4. *Related experience.*   Your unpaid work experience that may substitute for paid work experience. Including this is optional.
5. *References.*   Names, titles, addresses, and telephone numbers of people who will recommend you for the job. These people should know about your job skills, aptitudes, and experience. Instead of listing these references, you may just say that "references will be furnished upon request." When you do this, though, notify your reference people to be prepared if the employer does call on them.

Use these five subject clusters as guides, not as rules. You may wish to present some information that does not fall neatly into one of these clusters. If so, just add new headings. Several appropriate examples are *military record, community service, memberships in organizations, publications,* and *special skills.*

When starting your career, your résumé probably will fit on one page without looking crowded. After you have worked for several years, however, you may need more than one page to show your qualifications properly. Giving too little information, say, half a page, looks as though you are quite inexperienced or did not care enough to prepare a complete résumé. Giving too much information can cause more important items to get lost among less important ones.

If you have too little information, here are ideas to consider: (1) What extracurricular activities were you involved in while in college? Were you on the debating team? Did you work for the school newspaper? Were you active in a professional organization? These activities improve your communication skills, and employers are interested in that. (2) What specific skills have you acquired that might be useful on a job? Did you work as a waiter or waitress? If so, you learned to deal with people, handle money, and solve interpersonal problems. Do you know a foreign language or can you use a personal computer? If so, you have skills that may be useful on some jobs. This type of sorting through your background can help you to come up with valuable information to put in your résumé.

Developing the format of a résumé takes time, but it is easy to do. Begin by typing the basic subject clusters as information blocks. Use headings and indentation to show how the information is divided. Then cut out the information blocks with scissors and arrange them on a piece of paper in the way you think they look best. Tape the cutouts to the paper and use this model as a guide for typing the résumé you will use. Unless you decide to spend extra money to have your résumé printed, copy it on a photocopying machine. Keep the original and send clean, sharp copies to prospective employers.

Two standard or traditional résumés are shown in Figures 2 and 3. A functional résumé that emphasizes job skills is shown in Figure 4.

Tips on Writing Résumés

People have different opinions about what makes a "good" résumé. The best practical measure is whether the résumé you submit leads to a job interview, the next step in the employment process.

Here are several suggestions to follow that will increase your likelihood of getting a job interview:

1. *Look at models.* Study sample résumés wherever you can find them. Your friends may have résumés, and some books are devoted entirely to them.

2. *Allow enough time.* Take enough time to do a complete job. Normally, this takes several weeks.

3. *Avoid novelty.* Being different in novel ways detracts from the emphasis placed on your credentials. Pink paper, script typefaces, and odd-sized paper are novelties. Cartoons, ransom notes, wanted posters, and the like are "cute" but unprofessional.

4. *Be accurate.* Proofread for typographical, spelling, blocking, and content errors. Be especially careful to spell names and addresses correctly.

5. *Use only relevant information.* Include only information that supports your candidacy for the job. If you doubt whether to include an item, don't.

6. *Include a job objective.* Employers often look for this statement. It helps them to organize applications for jobs and gives them a personal statement about your employment goals. (Notice that the job objective is mentioned in the heading of the sample résumé in Figure 3.)

ANTHONY WINDFELDER   Telephone: (309) 779-1090
117 Carbon Cliff Road   After 5:00 P.M.
Rock Island, Illinois 61201   Availability Date: June 20

JOB OBJECTIVE

To obtain an entry-level position with a progressive microcomputer development company. To acquire experience in software technical writing and to advance into a management position in software development systems.

EDUCATION

June 1983	**B.S. Degree in Information Systems**
	Southern Illinois University; Carbondale, Illinois
	Completed advanced courses in BASIC and
	Pascal languages, systems analysis,
	and report writing for industry.
June 1976	**A.A. Degree in English and Foreign Languages**
	Chicago City College; Chicago, Illinois

EXPERIENCE

Data Communications Technician	Central Bank; Peoria, Illinois, 1981 to present
	Responsible for operating the Hewlett-Packard
	minicomputer and data network

MILITARY SERVICE

May 1976 to June 1981	Air Traffic Controller
	United States Air Force
	Completed special schools in basic computer
	technology and conversational Spanish

HONORS AND ACTIVITIES

President	University Computer Chess Society, 1981–1982
Dean's List	Grade-point average of 3.0 on 4-point scale, 1982
Editor	*Alumni Bulletin* for School of Business, 1981
Member	Associated Business Writers of America, 1981 to present

REFERENCES

Will be furnished on request.

FIGURE 2 Standard résumé for a graduating senior.

EXPERIENCE WHICH QUALIFIES ALICE LEROUX
FOR THE POSITION OF OFFICE MANAGER

3456 Princeton Drive
Baton Rouge, LA 70805
Telephone: (504) 364-2179

PERSONAL INFORMATION

Date of Birth: May 1, 1960   Marital Status: Single

ACADEMIC PREPARATION

1978-1982   Louisiana State University, Baton Rouge, LA;
               graduated with bachelor's degree in
               business administration with major in
               office administration and background in
               computer sciences; final grade point
               average 3.5 on 4 point scale

1974-1978   Rex High School, Baton Rouge, LA; general
               course work with emphasis in mathematics
               and computer programming

JOB TRAINING

June, 1980 to West Baton Rouge Parish Summer Youth Program,
August, 1980   Baton Rouge, LA; job duties included
               typing, filing, and answering telephone

July, 1979 to Secretary (part time) for Inver Auto
June, 1980   Repairs, Baton Rouge, LA; job duties
               included transcribing, typing, filing,
               scheduling repairs, billing, pricing
               merchandise, and answering telephone

HOBBIES AND INTERESTS

Sewing, cooking, fishing, water skiing, basketball, and
   chess

PEOPLE TO CONTACT FOR REFERENCES

Ms. Janet Theou   Mr. Ray D. Brix   Dr. Jim Duhe
Clariot High School   21 Bixby Lane   621 South Street
Baton Rouge, LA 70861 Lafayette, LA 70502   Baton Rouge, LA 70031
(504) 388-0987   (504) 876-4443   (504) 777-9321

FIGURE 3 Standard résumé for a graduating senior.

ROBERT M. UCHIMURA
73 South Locust Street
Rowland Heights, California 91748
(213) 964-8090

General Qualifications

Marketing and Business Planning
Program Management and Control
Financial Planning Management
Proposal Preparation and Management

Marketing and Business Planning

Developed, monitored, and controlled product line/business plans for a major division of a medium-sized company. Detailed business plans are prepared each year and monitored, controlled, and updated each month. Top-level five-year business plans also are prepared each year. Plans included market analysis, sales forecast, sales strategy and tactics, expected profit margins, and resource requirements.

Program Management and Control

Managed R&D programs ranging in value from $20,000 to $2,000,000, varying from two months to eighteen months in duration, concerned with development of data processing and sensor systems. Performed program scheduling, cost estimating, and control of these programs.

Financial Planning and Management

Responsible for recommending allocation of company discretionary resources (Bid & Proposal and IR&D funds) to top management. Monitored, controlled, and periodically reallocated funds as required. Also monitored capital expenditures necessary to satisfy marketing objectives. Performed RO1 analysis for each business area from historical and forecasted sales to determine allocation of resources.

Proposal Preparation and Management

Involved in writing, organization, and direction of proposals for development of advanced data processing systems and sensor systems.

Education

M.B.A.	Business Administration	1971
M.S.	Electrical Engineering	1967
B.S.	Electrical Engineering	1964
B.S.	Mathematics	1963

Firms

1971–1974	Market Planning: ElectroSystems; Azusa, California
1964–1971	Project Engineering: Ryan Aircraft; Fullerton, California

Personal

Birth date: June 3, 1942

Security Clearance: Secret   References are on file.

FIGURE 4 A functional résumé. (From *Technique of Job Search* by Ross Figgins, Harper & Row, 1976, p. 36. Used with author's permission.)

The Application Letter

Whether to write an application letter to accompany a résumé is an issue today among authorities in the placement field. Those who think that you should write a letter disagree about what to say in it; those who think that you should not write a letter contend that employers rarely read them. Normally, an employer will pick up an application package, skip over the letter, and browse through the résumé to see if the applicant qualifies for the basic job requirements. If an applicant has the basic qualifications for the job, the employer will then read the application letter — if it is there! As a result, an application letter has excellent *potential* to help you get a job.

So if an application letter is read *after* the résumé is read, the letter should not request the employer to read the résumé. This letter gives you a second opportunity — the résumé is the first — to persuade an employer that you are right for the job. When done well, an application letter works in conjunction with a résumé to form a persuasive message. The résumé presents your qualifications and the letter draws conclusions about them, explaining why you should be hired.

Rarely is an applicant hired on the strength of the application package. Instead, this package can persuade an employer to call you in for an interview, and you may be hired as a result of what takes place in the interview. So the application letter is an important bridge between the résumé and an interview. To make the letter convincing, keep in mind two goals: (1) the need to arouse the employer's interest in you and (2) the need to interpret the information on the résumé.

Follow the persuasive correspondence plan presented in Chapter Six when writing your application letter. Sample application letters are shown in Figures 5 and 6. The letter in Figure 5 is written to accompany the résumé in Figure 2.

Recommendation Letters

Most employers ask job applicants to submit recommendation letters to support their job candidacy. These letters are prepared by people who can supply supplementary information about the applicant's skills, experience, personal attributes, and career potential. As the applicant, you should arrange to have these letters written on your behalf. Also, furnish or be ready to furnish the names, addresses, and telephone numbers of these references.

The first step in the process is to select the references. Avoid any urge to just choose people who will say nice things about you. Instead, seek out those whose support will carry the most weight. The best ref-

117 Carbon Cliff Road
Rock Island, IL 61201
August 7, 19--

Mr. Aubrey Wheeler
Apex Microcomputer Company
711 Hansen Avenue
Chicago, IL 60111

Dear Mr. Wheeler

Will you please consider my application for the job as a
microcomputer technician that you advertised in the August
issue of Computer World.

For the past two years, I have been working as a data
communications technician for Central Bank of Peoria. In
this work, I have operated a Hewlett-Packard minicomputer
to record and monitor customer accounts. The Hewlett-
Packard is similar to the Max 2000 minicomputer series that
you manufacture, so this experience will help me do a
better job with Apex. Also, I noted that you specialize
in sales to banks, and my knowledge of banking computer
operations will be an advantage as well.

While in the United States Air Force, I worked as an air
traffic controller. This job gave me experience in
working under stressful conditions, which can be put to
good use in the competitive environment of the microcomputer industry. In addition to the work experience, I
hold a bachelor's degree in information systems and have
completed advanced courses in Basic and Pascal languages
and systems analysis.

May I have an interview to discuss this application, Mr.
Wheeler? I will be in Chicago September 5-17 and would
like to meet with you at that time if possible. Will you
please write or call me at (309) 779-1090 to set up an
appointment.

Sincerely yours

Anthony Windfelder

Anthony Windfelder

AW/ps

Enclosure

FIGURE 5   An application letter to accompany a résumé.

```
881 Walnut Park Drive
Rowley, MA  01969
January 21, 19--


Ms. Carroll Haynes, Personnel Manager
Matlock Publishing Company
Chicago, IL  60610

Dear Ms. Haynes:

Can you use an energetic young woman who is interested in
building a career in publishing?

At age 26 I have earned a university degree with honors in
business management and have gained work experience as a
research assistant, newspaper copy editor, and legal
assistant.  As a management trainee with Matlock, I would
be able to put my education and skills to use in helping
meet the company's goals.

My special skills are in motivation and communication.  In
the past my supervisors have noted my abilities to act as
a liaison between clients and office personnel and to write
effective reports and correspondence.  Also, my adminis-
trative background includes preparation of legal documents,
delegation of work assignments and arrangement of work
schedules, recruiting and training, and research and
clinical studies.

If you were to ask me in an interview for three adjectives
that best describe me as an employee, Ms. Haynes, I would
answer capable, enthusiastic, and ambitious.  Do you look
for these traits in job applicants?

A telephone call to 617-444-8886 or a letter to set up an
interview will be appreciated.  I would enjoy meeting
with you to discuss how I might fit in at Matlock.

Sincerely,

a. T. Lee

(Mrs.) A. T. Lee

ATL/lt

Enclosure

P.S.  I will relocate and can travel as required.
```

FIGURE 6 An application letter to accompany a résumé.

erences are people who have worked with you or who are working in the field in which you are applying for a job. Employers will view these people as having the professional credentials needed to make sound judgments about your qualifications and potential.

Once you know who you want to write recommendation letters for you, the next step is to ask them to do it. Some applicants in their enthusiasm forget to do this, and then the employer's request for a letter comes as a surprise to the reference. This practice is both discourteous and dangerous; the reference can refuse to write a letter or guess about what to say. So call your prospective references and make an appointment with them to discuss your application in person or by telephone. A face-to-face discussion is better. References need information about the job to give you an appropriate recommendation. Should a prospective reference decline to take time to discuss the application fully with you, drop the matter there. Instead, ask someone else to do it.

The next step is to meet with each of your references. Take a copy of the job description and résumé to the meetings and leave them for reference. During the meetings, explain what has happened to date, ask for their advice, and tactfully try to reach agreement about how their letters will best fit the situation. These letters should be written as favorable correspondence following the plan given in Chapter Four.

When someone agrees to write recommendation letters for you, keep the individual informed afterward. Tell the person how many letters he or she may have to write and when. Also, let the person know when changes along the way affect him or her. When you do get a job, call your references to share the good news. Then, consider sending each of them a thank you note to express your gratitude.

Placing an application and arranging for recommendation letters are the most important steps in job hunting, but not the only ones. Successful applicants try to keep things happening; they understand that when things are standing still, nothing can happen. Keeping things happening calls for monitoring the process along the way to see that everything is done when it should be done. Two tools to help you do this are (1) *mailing logs* and (2) *follow-up letters.*

KEEPING MAILING LOGS
AND WRITING FOLLOW-UP LETTERS

A mailing log provides a record of the status of your job hunting activities. When different job applications are at different stages of development, a record helps you to keep up with dates and periods between messages and alerts you about what to do when. For example, if you make an application but do not get a response for two weeks, you will know to inquire about it. The position may have been filled, your application may have been mislaid or never have been received, or the employer may have been too busy to respond. Whatever the problem may be, you will need to know what is happening to keep your job hunt going. Keeping a mailing log makes it easy to monitor a job hunt. A sample log is shown in Figure 7. Also, you might wish to keep extra copies of résumés, sample inquiry letters, transcripts, and so forth along with this log. This way, all your employment materials will be organized and easily accessible.

Follow-up letters are not a required part of a job search, but they can make a difference in whether you get a job in some cases. These letters (or telephone calls) can help to get the next move started, can reinforce earlier messages, and can solve problems that occur. For exam-

Employer	Initial Contact	Follow-up	Response	Special Notes
Lockheed	Application package 9/1	Send letter 9/15	Job filled 9/20	Will be hiring again in January. Contact: W. Ely.
Northrop	Application package 9/2	Send letter 9/16	Yes	Interview to be scheduled. If not, letter 9/20.
Aero-Jet	Inquiry 9/5	Send letter 9/20		If no response by 10/10, drop lead.
Grumman	Inquiry 9/6	Application package 9/12	Favorable 9/10	Received job description. May be hiring November.
Boeing	Application package 9/6	Call 9/15	Interview on 9/18	Spoke with Grace Levering. Research company further.
Aero-Nutronics	Résumé only 9/9		No 9/16	Not hiring now. Could have opening in March.
Marquart	Application package 9/10	No Follow-up		

FIGURE 7 A mailing log illustrating the kind of information recorded.

ple, a follow-up letter after mailing an application package or after having an interview gives you a chance to clarify misunderstandings or provide more information, if needed. Write this letter in the favorable correspondence plan given in Chapter Four. A sample follow-up letter is shown in Figure 8. This letter follows an interview, the occasion most likely to call for follow-up. Use the same approach for writing follow-up letters, though, including the one written after an application is made.

PARTICIPATING IN INTERVIEWS

If your job lead was a good one and your application package was effective, the next step is an interview with the prospective employer. Having passed the major screenings, you are now a finalist for the job. An applicant's part of an interview involves preparation for three stages: before, during, and after.

Before the Interview

The first thing to do before the interview is to gather all the information you have about the company. The information you gathered while qualifying job leads will be useful during the interview. Anything else you need to know can be gathered using the same research methods. Answers to such questions as "How many people work for the company?" and "What is the company's organizational structure?" will be useful. Think about what might be discussed in the interview, and then gather information on those topics.

The interview is a two-way process. You will be able to ask and answer questions and offer other information as well. Questions you may be asked are discussed in Chapter Fourteen. Be ready to discuss those, and also prepare yourself for those times when you will need to ask questions or offer relevant information that was not requested. Examples of topics you should prepare to discuss are your career goals, advancement opportunities, job duties and responsibilities, salary, and company benefits and programs.

Once you are certain about how to handle your part, begin getting ready the things you will need to take to the interview. Remember to take one or two copies of your résumé to use during the interview and perhaps to leave with the employer. Most job candidates can take a portfolio of work samples. For example, a professional photographer or com-

567 South Albertson Street
Pomona, CA 91767
March 10, 19--

Mr. Michael Kennedy
Chief Personnel Officer
Parsons Chemical Corporation
2444 North Wabash Avenue
Los Angeles, CA 90745

Dear Mr. Kennedy

Thank you for the opportunity to interview with you last
week for the job as Assistant Personnel Benefits Administrator.

I thoroughly enjoyed our tour of the laboratory and testing
facilities and appreciate your explanation of the duties
and responsibilities of the job. The job does seem to be
the right challenge for me, and the benefits and incentive
programs at Parsons are excellent.

You mentioned during our conversation that you want to
review my salary record. Because this information is not
included on my résumé, I am sending it with this letter.

Mr. Kennedy, the visit with you left me feeling positive
about the possibility of working for Parsons. I would
appreciate an opportunity to join your staff and look
forward to hearing from you.

Sincerely yours

Janice Sugiki

Janice Sugiki

JSS/kw

Enclosure

FIGURE 8 A follow-up letter after an interview.

mercial artist would always take along a portfolio. A district sales manager might take an incentive program that he or she developed on another job. A training officer might take sample lesson plans.

Because you will want to be in your best frame of mind during the interview, begin removing any barriers that might distract you the day of the interview. Decide what you will wear and get it ready. Also, remember to put together your portfolio of work samples. You might want to avoid drinking or eating anything that might make you nervous or otherwise upset you physically the day of the interview—coffee, for example. Give yourself enough time to get to the interview without rushing. Try to get there about five minutes early so that you will have time to compose your thoughts before the interview begins. You are ready now for the interview itself.

During the Interview

Your primary responsibility in an interview is to act professionally. Try to answer all questions thoroughly and accurately. Be natural. When you have the opportunity, expand on your responses to include those ideas you want to bring into the conversation. If you do not know or have forgotten the answer to a question, don't panic. Just explain that you do not know or that you have forgotten; then if it seems important at all, offer to find the answer and furnish it later. The interviewer will decline your offer if the information is not needed.

As explained in Chapter Fourteen, the interview might be highly structured, unstructured, or some combination. That will be determined by the interviewer. During the interview, you will ask or be asked either open or closed questions, probably both. Open questions invite you to discuss your answers, giving explanations; they are thought questions. Closed questions call for brief responses. Open and closed questions are discussed also in Chapter Fourteen. Regardless of the structure of the interview or the type question with which you are dealing, focus your answers and questions on the job and your qualifications.

The Fair Labor Practices Code governs the type of information that an employer can require of you, so keep that in mind. What can be asked is covered in the previous chapter, but remember that you can volunteer any relevant information that you think might help you get the job. Generally, the idea to stay away from areas covered in the Fair Labor Practices Code is a good one—religion, national origin, marital status, and so forth.

People are sometimes so serious about interviews that they do not do their best in them. It might help you be more natural if you treat it as a game—one of the "games of life." A game requires a game plan, so you will need one. Your game plan can be a list of items that you want to make sure to cover in the interview. For example, you will want to make sure that the interviewer understands all the reasons that you are right for the job. Make a list of these and bring it to the interview. Then as you have an opportunity, clarify the items on your list; most of them will be covered without your having to bring them up. Monitor the interview as it progresses: How is it going? What needs to be said? When should I make a point? If you are not able to make all the points on your list or game plan, don't force them on the interviewer. Most applicants aren't able to make all relevant points, but then not everything has to be said to have a successful interview.

When the interviewer begins to bring the interview to a close and offers you a chance to make final points, use that opportunity to summarize your qualifications and ask questions for which you still need answers. If it looks as though you are running out of time, explain that you want to make certain points that could affect the hiring decision. That usually will get you the few minutes you need.

Beyond all else, be sure to maintain your composure during the interview. The best way to avoid being anxious is to simply realize your own value. You can handle the job and you are ready to explain how and why you can handle it. If you find yourself feeling anxious or rushed, take a deep breath silently. If you face an unusually difficult question and need to consider your response, ask for a moment to think it over. Concentrate on succeeding; then you'll be so busy doing it that you won't have time to worry about how well you're doing.

The interviewer will close the interview, but your job is to follow the lead. Close cordially without lingering. If you have a last-minute point to make or question to ask, do it quickly. The interviewer probably has a schedule to keep and will appreciate your thoughtfulness about it. Exit on cue with a smile and a handshake. Now you have completed the interview.

After the Interview

Remember to take time during the same day of the interview to reflect on how it went. Sit down in a quiet place and replay what transpired. Make a list of things that went well and those that did not go so well. Ask yourself, "How well did I do? Was it a good interview? What are my chances for getting the job—fair, good, or excellent?" Also begin to think about whether you want the job if offered. Making the list helps you to decide objectively about what further action to take if any. Also, the list can help you do a better job in future interviews.

If you want to pursue the job further, write a follow-up letter similar to the one shown in Figure 8.

RESPONDING TO A JOB OFFER

What should you do after you get a telephone call or letter telling you that you can have the job? The answer depends on two questions: (1) Do you want to work for this firm? (2) Are the terms of the offer satisfactory? If you received a telephone call, do not answer the offer immediately. In the same way, do not answer a letter the minute you have read it. Give yourself enough time to consider your answers to the questions just mentioned. You can respond in one of four ways: (1) accept as offered, (2) reject, (3) ask for additional time for consideration, or (4) negotiate the terms.

If you accept the offer, write an *acceptance letter* even if you also telephone your acceptance. Follow the favorable correspondence plan given in Chapter Four when writing the letter. If you reject the offer, write a rejection letter. Follow the unfavorable correspondence plan given in Chapter Five when writing this letter. Be professional, and assume that you are dealing with professionals. A sample refusal letter is shown in Figure 9.

If you need more than a day or two to consider a job offer, make a telephone call to request the time. When it is impractical to do this, write a *request for more time letter*. Sometimes you may have more than one offer to consider at the same time, or you may be expecting another offer shortly. Another reason to delay is to give yourself more time to investigate unresolved issues that came up in an interview. Write this letter following the unfavorable correspondence plan given in Chapter Five.

If you would like to accept the offer but do not agree with the terms, write a *negotiation letter*. Follow the unfavorable correspondence plan presented in Chapter Five when writing this letter because you are refusing the initial offer. To get ideas about what to say, study the section on negotiations in Chapter Fourteen. A sample negotiation letter is shown in Figure 10.

December 12, 19--

Mr. Gerald M. Waite, Manager
Tacoma Investment Industries
1112 Seahurst Place
Seattle, WA 98104

Dear Mr. Waite:

I appreciate very much your job offer which arrived yesterday and want to respond quickly so as not to delay you.

When we met last week to discuss the position you have
available as a junior accountant, I did not know that
Pacific Stamp Services in Vancouver was planning to offer
me a position. That offer arrived yesterday also, and the
terms of their offer are about the same as yours. Because
I would like to work for a small company, I have decided
to accept Pacific's offer. That job will enable me to gain
diversified experience quickly. Also, they offer a lot
of opportunity for advancement as a result of their
practice of promoting from within the company.

Had Pacific not made the offer, I would have gladly accepted
the position with you on the terms you offered. Again, your
consideration of my application is appreciated, and I look
forward to meeting you again as we go about our business
activities here in the Northwest. Until then, you have my
best wishes for success in your efforts at Tacoma Investment.

Yours truly,

David Roche

David Roche

P. O. Box 164
Arnada Park Annex
Vancouver, WA 98611

FIGURE 9 A letter refusing a job offer.

513 Twin Knolls
Flagstaff, AZ 86001

July 2, 19--

Ms. Maria Delgado
Personnel Manager
Abbott and Abbott Agencies
900 Wilshire Boulevard
Los Angeles, CA 90012

Dear Ms. Delgado

Thank you for your offer of employment as an information
officer trainee with Abbott and Abbott. Your offer is
fair for market conditions, and I do appreciate it.

While in college during the last two years, I have incurred
debts through student assistance loans that I must begin to
repay through installment payments this year. So when I
figured my personal budget based on the salary you offered,
it became clear that I would not have enough income to pay
my basic living expenses and also begin to repay the loan.

In reading the brochure you enclosed about the company, I
saw that trainees are given a ten percent salary increase
after three months. Since I have already had three years
of part-time experience with a local public relations and
advertising firm, I feel qualified to begin at that more
advanced stage in the trainee program. The salary paid at
that stage would be enough to cover all my expenses. Would
you please consider reviewing my résumé and work samples to
see if you agree that I qualify as a stage-two trainee? If
you can agree, then I am ready to accept such an offer and
very much want to do so.

I shall appreciate your reconsideration of the situation,
Ms. Delgado. If you can agree with this proposal, I am
ready to move to the West Coast and am excited about the
possibility of working for Abbott and Abbott.

Sincerely yours

Caryn McDowell

Caryn McDowell

FIGURE 10 A letter negotiating a job offer.

SUMMARY

Finding job leads is the applicant's first step in the job search. Publications such as newspapers, professional and trade journals, and in-house publications are good sources of job leads. Placement agencies and services include college placement services, governmental agencies at all levels, professional organizations, and employment agencies. Job leads also can come through inquiry letters and personal contacts. When looking for job leads, screen them so that you only apply for jobs that you have the qualifications to hold.

After finding and screening job leads, prepare an appropriate package. A résumé contains information on academic qualifications, employment experience, and references, and other information may be added as needed. When writing a résumé, look at models and allow yourself enough time to do a thorough job. Avoid novelty and be accurate. Also, use only relevant information in it and remember to include a job objective. Take advantage of the opportunity to write an application letter to go along with the résumé. This letter gives you a chance to explain why you are the right person for the job.

Recommendation letters are written by people who support an applicant's job candidacy. The best references are people who have worked with an applicant or who work in the field in which the application is being made. Ask these people ahead of time if they will serve as references. Then give their names to employers with whom you are applying, and they will request recommendation letters from the references.

To keep up with your job search, keep a mailing log. Along with keeping a log, consider writing follow-up letters.

The interview follows a successful job application. Before an interview, spend time getting ready for it. Plan carefully and make it to the interview on time and be fully prepared. During the interview, plan to ask and answer both open and closed questions. Be yourself, and try to get and give all the information needed by you and the employer. Reflect on the interview afterward, and then continue to pursue the job if you are still interested in it.

When responding to a job offer, you can accept the job offered, reject it, ask for more time to consider it, or negotiate the terms. In each case, you can usually do this with a letter, although calling employers may be appropriate also.

Additional Readings

Career Guide to Professional Associations. Cranston, R.I.: Carroll Press, 1976.

Dictionary of Occupational Titles. Washington, D.C.: U.S. Bureau of Labor, Government Printing Office.

Encyclopedia of Careers and Vocational Guidance. Garden City, N.Y.: Doubleday, 1975.

Encyclopedia of Associations. Detroit: Gale Research Company. Published every second year with interim annual updates.

Figgins, Ross. *The Job Game: Winning the Job That's Right for You.* Englewood Cliffs, N.J.: Prentice-Hall, 1980.

Medley, H. Anthony. *Sweaty Palms: The Neglected Art of Being Interviewed.* Belmont, Calif.: Wadsworth, 1978.

Merchandising Your Talents. Washington, D.C.: Government Printing Office.

Occupational Outlook Handbook. Washington, D.C.: U.S. Bureau of Labor, Government Printing Office.

Preparation for PACE. Chicago: Henry Regenry, 1978.

Review Questions

1. Where do most companies advertise job openings?

2. What is a letter of inquiry? When would you use one in a job search?

3. Explain the importance of networking in finding job leads.

4. How should job leads be qualified? Why is this important to do?

5. What goes into an application package? How does each part function in the process?

6. What is included in a résumé? How is the decision of what to leave in or out made?

7. Why keep mailing logs?

8. How would you prepare yourself physically and mentally for an important job interview?

9. Would you bring anything along with you to the interview? What, if anything?

10. If you were offered a job, what are your four basic options? Describe the kinds of messages you could send. Under what conditions would you send each?

Exercises

1. Invite a professional who is experienced in interviewing job applicants to a class meeting. You might ask a personnel officer, someone from your college placement center, or someone from a local business. Using role playing, ask this person to interview members of your class. Class members who are not interviewed should prepare critiques for an evaluation session to follow each interview. If possible, continue the interviewing by conducting stress and nondirected interviews. Videotape these interviews for later analysis if possible.

2. Clip a promising job advertisement from the newspaper and prepare a résumé of your credentials to suit the requirements of the job.

3. Write an application letter to accompany the résumé you prepared for Exercise 2.

4. Make a list of six job openings in your field for which you are qualified. Then learn what you can about the companies. Note how you would use specific information you uncover to prepare your application package.

5. Go on a "blind" job interview, one in which you just walk into a company you know nothing about and ask for a job. If you get the interview, keep a record of your experiences. Compare what you learned with the experiences of others in your class.

UNIT 6

Oral Communication

Chapter 16 Speaking and Listening

CHAPTER SIXTEEN

Speaking and Listening

The goals in studying the text and completing the activities in this chapter are to know

1. The purpose and use of the four most common speech styles
2. How to define a topic for an oral presentation, analyze the audience, and develop a speech plan
3. Techniques for developing the introduction, body, and conclusion for an oral presentation
4. How to prepare an outline for an oral presentation
5. What to do before, during, and after an oral presentation
6. The importance of good listening habits
7. Six steps to becoming an effective listener

A corollary of business life is that as soon as you complete a good written report or proposal, someone will walk up to you and say, "I read your material and would like you to explain it to the board (or some other group)." This form of positive feedback is more than a compliment; it is a natural and expedient procedure to share information orally and, by extension, to receive it in the same manner. Speaking and listening do not change the basic communication process, although some of the strategies and techniques differ. These next few pages explain just how information is processed in the oral medium—when we talk, rather than write—and when it is advantageous to know how to speak and to listen well.

EXAMINING SPEECH STYLES

The overall considerations in deciding on a proper speech style are audience size and membership, the occasion, the type of information, and the media to be used. The four speech styles to choose from are impromptu, extemporaneous, manuscript, and memorized.

Impromptu speaking takes place when you are called upon to "say a few words" without warning. Therefore, you have no time to prepare. Strengths of impromptu speaking are that it is spontaneous and informal. On such occasions, the speaker talks about a topic of interest to a group, and therefore feedback, while the speech is being delivered, becomes important to its success. Because of the spontaneous nature of the impromptu speech, you should avoid taking unneeded risks while giving them. For example, avoid making dramatic statements, announcing policy changes, or making long-term commitments when giving an impromptu speech.

Extemporaneous speaking takes place when the speaker has time to study and prepare for the speech. However, few notes or other material are used in the delivery. Using this format allows a speaker to be natural and make changes during the presentation according to how the audience is responding.

Manuscript speaking takes place when the speaker prepares completely for a presentation right down to choosing the exact words to say. Phrases are polished in writing and practice, and the audience and situation are studied carefully. The advantage of manuscript speaking lies in the chance to use the best possible language and delivery style. A disadvantage is that changes are hard to make while speaking; therefore, immediate feedback has little value. Another disadvantage is that these speeches often lack spontaneity and therefore sound "canned." Winston Churchill, a gifted speaker, was able to speak spontaneously from manuscript, however. He could do this because he had full command of the language, the issues, and the audience.

Memorized speaking takes place when the manuscript speech is presented without a manuscript in hand. The speaker memorizes the speech and therefore can give complete information to the audience. Nonverbal communication such as gestures and full eye contact can enrich the presentation. Speakers giving memorized information sometimes fall victim to what actors call "going up on the line." That is, they forget for a moment where they are in the speech because they forget what they have just said. The likelihood that this will happen increases as the extent of memorization increases. Why? The more you commit to memory, the less attention you pay to it as you speak what you have memorized. Another disadvantage is that a memorized speech often sounds too formal. Further, the chance to respond to feedback is limited; making adjustments is difficult because every word, sentence, and illustration is fixed in place.

Generally, the best choice of speech styles is extemporaneous speaking. However, the other types are *good* when the occasion fits. For example, when a precise message involving media such as radio or television must be given, manuscript or memorized speaking is best. Once you choose a speech style, preparation can begin.

PREPARING THE SPEECH

Adlai Stevenson said this about preparing a speech:

> If you would make a speech or write one
> Or get an artist to indite one
> Think not because 'tis understood
> By men of sense, 'tis therefore good.
> Make it so clear and simply planned
> No blockhead can misunderstand.

Preparing a good speech does require planning well enough that your message can be understood fully by the audience. Once a topic is chosen, the next step is to define the objective and the problem statement.

Defining Objective and Problem Statement

What is the topic of the speech to be? Is the goal to inform? to raise issues? to offer solutions? to persuade? Defining this objective for an oral presentation will keep you on course during the preparation. The measure of what to include in the presentation is the *problem statement,* one sentence that clearly describes what the talk is about. The statement of the problem is to a speech what the topic sentence is to a paragraph—the main idea. Once it is defined, selection of material, organization, and focus will follow logically.

You may or may not actually speak the words of the problem statement, but you should imply the problem statement throughout the talk. When preparing the problem statement for a speech of your own, remember that the idea should go beyond a mere statement of the subject. It should tell the audience what the subject should mean to them after the presentation. Assume that you are making a 10-minute talk on the company's credit union to new employees. You plan to cite a list of short-term loan services offered. "How your credit union works for you" is too broad a statement to guide the audience properly. A better one is, "How a new employee can apply now for a short-term loan." Such a clearly defined statement allows you to focus on the services offered and will interest listeners by showing them how the services can work for them. When writing the problem statement, avoid abstract language that will broaden the focus.

Therefore, a good problem statement restricts the subject. The first example just cited forces the speaker to talk about a wide range of subjects, many of which may be in the company's handbook or credit union brochures. Were this the first of a series of talks on the subject, such a broad beginning might be proper. But with limited time, focus on the few ideas you can get across and relate these directly to the listener's interests.

When the problem statement is defined, you are ready to research the topic and adapt the material to the audience.

Doing Research and Audience Adaptation

Research your oral presentation in the same way you do written reports. Consult Chapter Seven for information on planning for research and Chapter Eight for research methods and procedures. When gathering information, try to have more on hand than you plan to use. Having more information than you need will help you to do a better job with the presentation itself and with answering questions afterward.

While conducting research on your topic, also gather *relevant* quotations, anecdotes, or stories to create interest in the speech. Your local library holds a wealth of such material. For example, *Bartlett's Familiar Quotations* contains thousands of quotations on hundreds of subjects. Also consult special speakers' and toastmasters' handbooks. You can use such interest getting material, called "brights," throughout a speech—in the introduction, body, and conclusion.

When you begin to organize the material collected through research, select a *general format* in which to pattern the material for good information flow.

Selecting a General Format

Patterns are useful to help an audience follow the information flow of your topic. Because a spoken plan is harder to follow than a written one, use one of these common patterns to make your presentation:

Time	Employs a chronological sequence of events. Presents items as they happened, as is done in a story, history, or diary.
Space	Follows a physical arrangement of some type. An example is to describe an office layout by beginning with a key location, such as with the receptionist's desk at the entrance.
Cause and Effect or **Effect and Cause**	Works on the assumption that events contribute to other events in various ways. Giving proof that shows a valid link between events is crucial to the effectiveness of this pattern. An example is using medical data to link cigarette smoking to lung cancer.
Problem Solving	Follows the plan: identify a problem, analyze data about it, and then derive a solution from the data. This pattern follows the research plan discussed in Chapter Seven. An example in industry is to (1) discover that an assembly-line method is slowing production in the plant (identifying a problem), (2) study methods that might resolve the problem (analyzing data), and (3) choose the best method to resolve the problem (deriving a solution).
Specific to General or **General to Specific**	Uses an inductive or deductive format as discussed in Chapters One and Nine. Specific-to-general format (inductive) begins with details and leads to the main idea, while general to specific reverses this arrangement (deductive).
Basic Components	Employs a parallel division of major parts of a topic. For example, a talk on food stores may

be divided into three general areas: meat, produce, and canned and packaged goods. A list may be used to clarify the sequence of ideas.

Comparison and Contrast (sometimes called "Advantages and Disadvantages") Shows two sides of a subject or issue evaluating the "pros" and "cons" or similarities and dissimilarities. Use this format in either analytical or persuasive presentations.

Once you decide to use a particular pattern, stick with it throughout the presentation. Mixing the patterns will confuse an audience. However, you may organize minor points differently from the general format to make them clearer.

After you select the appropriate format, you are ready to begin the basic development of the speech itself—the introduction, body, and conclusion.

Putting Together the Basic Development

Aristotle, the ancient Greek philosopher, first suggested dividing messages into three basic elements: *a whole, which has a beginning, a middle, and an end.* In *The Poetics* he explained that the beginning is that part that nothing precedes, but something follows. The middle is that part between the beginning and the end. The end is that part that grows out of what precedes it, but nothing follows. The greatest value of this organization is that it divides speeches into critical segments for analysis. Writers use this basic plan just as speakers do, as shown by the advertising copy editor's *Rule of Three:* tell them what you're going to tell them, tell it to them, and then tell them what you just told them. This translates to speech as *introduction, body,* and *conclusion.*

The Introduction

Getting off to a good start is crucial to speaking success. You have read about the effect of first impressions at various times while reading this book. These impressions are formed in speech during those initial moments before an audience. When a speaker appears before an audience, members quickly evaluate him or her for competence, interest, and general merit. Therefore, a presentation that begins well usually continues well with little effort. On the other hand, a bad start can frustrate your efforts no matter how good the remainder of the speech.

The introduction serves a number of *information* functions. To turn a "collection of people" into a "group of active listeners," the beginning should

1. Clearly introduce the subject (and the problem statement if using deductive organization).

2. Bring the audience to a level of common knowledge about the topic. Doing this provides a basis for understanding what follows. Information such as historical background, definitions of terms, and a review of events that led to the speech itself can bring an audience to a level of common knowledge.

3. Set the mood for the presentation. Moods range from that of light entertainment at a retirement party to a grave explanation of an executive decision to lay off workers.

4. Arouse audience interest in the topic. To do this, show that what is to follow is worthwhile to them. Ideally, interest grows out of a speaker's credibility.

5. Establish a personal or professional rapport between speaker and audience.

6. Preview the organization of the presentation. Remember that listeners cannot reread information as readers can. Once confused, an audience cannot follow well the remainder of the speech until their sense of organization is re-established.

7. Create smooth transition into the body.

Normally, the opening of a speech is the most difficult part to write. For this reason, you may wish to write it last, after everything else is in order. Consult the following checklist of introductory techniques for ideas on getting started.

CHECKLIST OF INTRODUCTORY TECHNIQUES

Quotation A word, phrase, or passage phrased especially well or relevant enough to the topic to be quoted directly. Quotations from authorities on the topic work nicely.

Humor An appropriate story or anecdote to please the audience.

Novelty A surprise statement to grab attention quickly. May come from the topic itself or from a relevant outside source.

Mystery An unanswered question to build intrigue.

Conflict	An opposition of ideas that leads to comparison and contrast.
Journalism	A "real-life" incident such as describing an event, including names, dates, and other factual information.
Statistics	Significant numerical data on the topic.
Visual Aid	A graphic aid to introduce the subject.
Occasion	A reference related directly to either the audience or the occasion.
Colleagueship	A direct appeal to a problem or situation shared by all members of an audience.
Motivation	An appeal to common human needs like physical needs, safety, love, and self-esteem.

When using humor, which is risky, try not to force it or make its use obvious. Humor should grow naturally out of a topic and underscore a basic point of the presentation. When an audience senses that a speaker is building from gag to gag, for example, the speech becomes a source of entertainment rather than of information. Then, the audience stops listening for facts and ideas and begins waiting for the next punch line.

Therefore, the goal of the opening is not so much to entertain an audience as to interest them in the topic by involving them with it. Creative writers call this a "hook," as shown in Frederic Brown's opening in a story called "Knock": "The last man on earth sat alone in a room. There was a knock at the door . . .".[1] What audience could resist such an opening—as long as it relates well to the topic?

In moving from the introduction to the body (and from body to conclusion), the *transition* must be smooth. The transition statement links the two. What is said must be relevant, of course, and may be made more effective when supported by visual aids. Also, the tone of voice will cue the listener that transition is taking place. The goals of transition are to direct the audience forward, emphasize important points, and unify the development of the problem statement.

The Body

The body contains the major amount of information in a speech. While what is said here does depend on the situation, this information should support the problem statement. When developing the body, pay particular attention to the complexity of the material, the amount of time available, and the audience's preknowledge of the subject.

The body of a good speech develops from idea to idea in a logical

[1]Robert Bloch, ed., *The Best of Frederic Brown* (New York: Balantine Books, 1977), p. 14.

manner following one of the general formats presented earlier in the chapter. The following simile shows the function of the body. Liken the development of an oral presentation to building a bridge across a river. The introduction is the first abutment on the one shore, the starting point. The conclusion is the last abutment on the other shore, the goal to be reached. The body is composed of the major spans in between, the problem statement development; they hold the weight of the bridge by getting across the main points of the speech. The trestles and underpinnings of the bridge are the supporting points in the body of the speech. Just as you add cross-bracing, planking, flags, and even toll gates to the bridge, you add clarifying statements, humor, and audiovisual materials to complete the structure of the speech.

The Conclusion

Just as members of an audience form first impressions during the introduction to a speech, they form last impressions during the conclusion. Those closing statements linger in the listeners' minds and help to shape their thinking about the topic afterward. A well-prepared conclusion should

1. Prepare the audience for the end of the presentation. Do this with the words you use and through your tone of voice.
2. Review the major points of the presentation and draw conclusions from these points.
3. (if a persuasive talk) Urge the members of an audience to take action or alter their opinions.
4. Leave room for feedback from the audience. A question-and-answer session can provide this opportunity.
5. Tie together any "loose ends" remaining at this point.
6. Disengage the speaker from the audience gracefully.

Here is a checklist of concluding techniques:

CHECKLIST OF CONCLUDING TECHNIQUES

Summary	A recap of major points of the speech.
Quotation	A word, phrase, or passage quoted from a relevant source, especially if said by someone who is well known in the field. Use the quotation to draw together the ideas presented in the body.
Illustration	A real or fictitious event that shows a vivid example of the problem statement.

Appeal	Either a suggestion to take action or an appeal to change a belief.
Charge	A challenge to change future events through direct involvement.
Statistics	A summary of relevant data on a topic.
Motivation	An inducement based on an audience's psychological needs.

Once you know what will go into the introduction, body, and conclusion of a speech, the basic development is complete. The next step is to prepare the speech outline.

Drafting the Speech Outline

Speakers use outlines to remind them of what points to make and the order in which to make them. Most of your speeches will be extemporaneous. An outline of them should be typewritten on paper or cards. When using paper, choose the more efficient standard size ($8\frac{1}{2}'' \times 11''$). When using cards, choose either $5'' \times 4''$ or $7'' \times 5''$; the small $5'' \times 3''$ card often slips from nervous hands while speaking. Whichever you choose, be sure to type the material in outline form so that you can read and follow it easily.

A speech outline may take any of three forms: *topical, phrase,* or *sentence.* Topical form employs simple nouns to direct the speaker from point to point. This form is shortest and can be put together more quickly than can either of the others. However, the brevity forces a speaker to rely more heavily on memory. The phrase form contains more information about the subject than does topical form and usually employs verbs and direct objects; yet all but essential words are deleted. Sentence form employs complete, grammatically correct sentences. Both the sentence and phrase forms give more information than does the topical form, but sometimes transition statements sound awkward when speaking from sentence outlines. For this reason, phrase form is probably the best all-around choice.

Putting Together the Speech Outline

For most of your presentations, you will need to prepare a complete outline. Type the outline in capital letters and, if possible, on a typewriter that has a special large type called *orator.* Be sure to number the pages or cards; and if you wish, highlight important points with colored felt-tipped pens. Type both major and minor points in vertical columns leaving wide margins for any special notes you might want to add about delivery. Such a special note was discovered on a company president's outline for a speech given to stockholders after a year of record low sales: "Argument weak here. Yell!"

You may prefer an alternative format that joins a full narrative style with an outline form. It contains enough material to keep the speaker from feeling at a loss for information but still allows for a great deal of control. This format is flexible enough to allow you to rearrange points, shift emphasis, or even lengthen or shorten the time of delivery during presentation. Composed of a written introduction and conclusion that bracket an outline form, this combination format can be complemented easily by support and reference material as needed.

A sample of an alternative form outline is shown in Figure 1. Note that the introduction and conclusion appear verbatim as they will be delivered but that the body is in phrase outline form. Among all options, this format is best for most speeches, especially extemporaneous ones. Using this outline, you can lengthen or shorten a presentation as needed. For example, assume that you are giving a 20-minute speech using the outline in Figure 1. Suddenly, you get a signal that you have 5 minutes left just as you begin part II in the body. You are still in control; you could either spend less time on each remaining point or cover only major points. This way, you will finish on time with the integrity of the speech intact and without becoming flustered.

Giving Written Reports Orally

The following is a typical communication problem arising in modern business practice. You have researched a problem and have prepared a written report of the results. Now, you must present the results orally to a committee or some larger group.

To prepare for such a presentation, follow these steps:

1. *Clarify the assignment.* What is the objective of the presentation? to inform? to persuade? Will the audience be making a decision about whether to act on your report findings? Is your presentation part of a program? How much time do you have? Must you answer questions?

2. *Analyze the audience.* Gather any needed information about members of the group and do an audience analysis of them. Consider preknowledge about the topic, demographics, and psychographics in this analysis.

3. *Analyze the report information.* Using the information gathered in the first two steps as a guide, divide the presentation into three cat-

WHY WORD PROCESSING NOW?

Objective:

To explain the development of word processing as a technology and a procedure.

Problem Statement:

Word processing will influence how offices are managed as well as how information is handled.

Introduction:

A hundred years ago typewriters revolutionized the world of business! Today word processors are having much the same effect. But, for many people, they are still strange and somewhat frightening. This problem will not just disappear. The purpose of this presentation is to show how WP is simply a natural development of modern office procedures in combination with improved technology.

Body:

   I. Defining Word Processing:
      A. Definitions—central elements involved
      B. Effect on Personnel
      C. Cost Effectiveness and Efficiency
  II. Historical Perspective:
      A. Development and Impact of Typewriter
      B. Social Office Structure
      C. Emergence of Word Processing
 III. Changing Office Organization:
      A. Traditional Organizational Chart (Slide 1)
      B. Word Processing Center Organizational Chart (Slide 2)
      C. Comparison

Conclusion:

So you see, word processing is not new. Neither is it a gadget nor a fad. WP is part of an evolutionary process in handling information. It is also the creative and efficient merging of existing procedures and emerging technology.

Sources:

Kleinschrod, Walter, Leonard B. Kruk, and Hilda Turner. *Word Processing: Operations, Applications and Administration.* 2nd ed. Indianapolis, IN: Bobbs-Merrill, 1983.

Mason, Jennie. *Introduction to Word Processing.* Indianapolis, IN: Bobbs-Merrill, 1980.

Equipment:

Overhead projector.

FIGURE 1 Speech outline for short presentation.

egories of information: *essential, nonessential,* and *support.* Plan to use all the essential information, none of the nonessential, and as much of the support as needed to reach your objective. Is any additional information needed?

4. *Plan the presentation.* Choose the general format that seems most appropriate for the subject matter and the audience. Also decide whether the speech style will be extemporaneous, manuscript, or memorized and what audiovisual aids are needed.

From this point, prepare an outline as you would for any other type of speech. Then you will be ready to make the presentation itself.

MAKING THE PRESENTATION

Your speech is now researched, outlined, and organized. You know what you are going to say and the way in which you are going to say it. Consider the following suggestions when making the presentation.

Before the Presentation

A practice run-through of your presentation will give you an idea about how good your speech is. You might start practicing alone to get an idea about your pace, timing, voice qualities, and the thought flow; try this with a tape recorder. Then practice before a mirror to get an idea about when and how to use gestures and facial expressions. If you lack experience as a speaker, practice the presentation before friends or family members to get reactions.

Rehearsals give feedback about where to vary your regular speaking tone. When speaking to a large group, for example, pitch your voice to reach that person in the last row. Practice also gives you a chance to work out little problems that occur — your speed of delivery, for example. How long does it take you to read a manuscript page aloud? How many words a minute do you speak? This will tell you how much you can say in the time allotted.

Correct any problems that show up in practice before giving the presentation.

During the Presentation

The moment is here, the time to stand up and give your speech. The audience is waiting. You're a little nervous. Calm yourself. Take a few deep breaths and concentrate on the most important thing you have to do next: *get your message across to these people.* Focus on them and let all else fade into the background. You are ready to start.

Getting Started

An audience's first impression of you equals and may even surpass their interest in your topic. Recognize that your audience is curious about you. They want to know right away what kind of person you are. Show them. You dressed to fit the occasion and now will show poise and speak confidently. As you begin the introductory remarks, remember to follow your note cards or paper.

Using Delivery Techniques

Listening to a trained public speaker teaches us that the human voice is a remarkable instrument. You can produce hundreds of inflections with your voice, and your voice has a wide range. Use it to deliver a smooth but emphatic message. Add interest and stress points with your voice— the audience needs the guidance.

Posture, gestures, and facial expressions must be right for the occasion. Large and small body movements give visual clues about your command of the situation and the subject. Body movements should underscore your words and image. Your posture, gestures, and facial expressions should complement your words; if members of the audience become conscious of them, they will be distracted. For example, a slouching posture and crossed arms can defeat an otherwise confident appeal for "all of us to pull together," as can exaggerated tugging on an imaginary rope or an overstated grimace.

Watch the audience and listen to them for feedback as you speak. If you project enough to overcome self-consciousness and focus the talk on the audience's interests, they will give you support. Watch their facial expressions, attentiveness, body movements, and eye contact for clues. Early in the presentation, you might choose one or two people to talk to directly or exchange an idea with. This will give you a measure of how things are going. While presenting a point, check audience reactions and then make needed adjustments in what you say next.

If those in the front row start fidgeting or looking at their watches, they are not yet interested in what you are saying. If your listeners begin to fall asleep, what can you do? The one thing not to do is to continue doggedly on the way you are going. Change directions. You have to get their attention now before going on.

Avoiding Slander

Unless the content of your speech requires that you do so, avoid saying or implying negative ideas about others while speaking. In cases where you must make such statements, be objective and document what you say. Even careless statements can provide a basis for a lawsuit for slander. Slander is committed through spoken words or with gestures, and it is a type of defamation of a person's character done without good reason. To slander a person is to violate his or her right to keep a good reputation. An example is to accuse someone of cheating on his or her income tax return to a third person in a case where the accused person is not guilty.

Handling Stage Fright

Call it jitters, apprehension, weak knees, chicken, sweaty palms, or just stage fright. The fear of speaking before a group is pervasive. In *The Book of Lists,* David and Irving Wollechinsky reported that fear of speaking before a group is the greatest common fear among Americans; 41 percent of the respondents in a survey reported having this fear. If you have a slight case of stage fright, then you are not alone.

What to do, then? Some say simply to ignore it, that it will go away with experience. But some may suffer too much from it to get the experience needed. A more sensible approach is to work at overcoming anxiety by (1) reaching out to become more confident and (2) reducing your apprehensions about your ability.

Confidence comes from knowing that you are well prepared and are ready to face whatever may arise. Thus, careful speech preparation is a large factor in determining how confidently you will deliver the speech. Having a good speech to deliver and knowing it well give reason to be confident. You should be able to answer questions about the subject, and remember, audiences almost always want you to do well. After you have done everything necessary to make the speech successful, defuse your stage fright by comforting yourself with the thought that you are well prepared.

You can reduce your fears about your ability by giving an audience-centered presentation. Think about what they need to know and how to tell it to them. Concentrate on getting across your ideas. Watch for signals that interest is lagging or that points are unclear; correct these problems as they arise. If you can shift your concern from what they think about you to how well you are getting the message across, you can thwart self-consciousness, the major cause of self-doubt.

You will have stage fright because you want to perform well. A small amount of it will keep you alert, so you should not fear some stage fright. Try to keep it in proportion, though, as it comes and goes during your presentation. When you feel it coming, take a deep breath or two and move your head around to release the tension in your neck. When you make a mistake, concentrate on what you are doing and you will recover quickly and naturally. If someone else makes a mistake, such as spilling coffee on your charts or pulling the plug on your microphone, acknowledge the situation, readjust, and then go on. These occasions can actually make an audience more attentive and more receptive to you and your ideas.

Using Audiovisual Aids

Audiovisual aids are mechanical devices that appeal to our visual or auditory senses. They can make your words more articulate, describe your ideas more clearly, increase how much you can say without increasing the time needed, and add interest to a presentation. These aids include samples or models, chalkboards and flip charts, handouts, illustrations, projected material, and audio tapes and recordings.

When deciding whether to use an audiovisual aid, consider *appropriateness* first. Will it add to content or interest, or will it be just a novel digression? No audiovisual aid substitutes for the speaker; rather, it enriches the presentation by complementing what the speaker is doing or saying. A simple slide illustration can dominate a speech if it is emphasized too much. Instead of giving an oral presentation highlighted with illustrations, you can wind up giving a slide show highlighted with oral captions. Manage your audiovisual aids discreetly and put them in a proper relationship to other parts of the presentation. Learn to use them when needed and to keep them in the background when not needed.

Samples or Models   Samples or models are the easiest visual aid to use. As you describe something to an audience, show it as well. If the samples or models are small and inexpensive, pass them out to let the audience look at and hold them while you speak. If they are large or delicate and expensive, or if you have only one, use them as models to make your points. Keep them out of sight until needed, and then hold them in your hands or place them in the audience's view and yours.

Chalkboards and Flip Charts   Chalkboards and flip charts are versatile and easy to use. Use them to show how a process or procedure works. For example, you can work a mathematical equation or develop an accounting process on a chalkboard or flip chart. Remember, though, that the time you spend writing is lost time for your audience. They must wait while you write, and you have your back to them. Also, an audience may continue looking at a chalkboard after you have gone on to another point. With a flip chart, turn over a blank page when ready to go on.

Handouts   Outlines, illustrations, and reference or supplementary notes are the three types of speech handouts. Outlines show the audience the organization and content of the speech. This reduces the need to take notes. Pass out your outline before the presentation begins. Illustrations clarify confusing or difficult material in the speech. Pass them out at the time during the speech that you are ready to present the content they illustrate. Reference or supplementary notes add information about the speech topic beyond that given in the presentation. Pass them out at the conclusion of your speech. While handouts have many advantages, disadvantages are that they take time to pass out and they can distract your audience.

Illustrations   Illustrations include tables, charts, graphs, drawings, diagrams, photographs, pictograms, and so on. Use them in speeches as you would in a written report, at the point that a visual dimension is needed to support your words. The subject matter and layout depend on the topic itself and your way of presenting it. The best illustrations, though, are large enough to read easily and are laid out simply. Use a pointer or ruler to point to the place on an illustration you are covering and so that you do not block the view. Consult Chapter Ten to learn how to prepare illustrations and how to select the right type illustration.

Projected Material   Any type of written, drawn, or computer generated material can be shown on one or another type of projection equipment if properly prepared. The types of projection equipment you might use in making oral presentations are opaque, overhead, slide, filmstrip, motion picture and video tape projectors. For best results, this equipment requires a darkened room and a large screen. The key to successful use of projected material lies in good coordination. First, learn to use the equipment well, including how to correct common malfunctions. Next, practice using the equipment beforehand; for example, actually use your aids on the overhead projector or play the motion picture. When you are ready to make the speech, get all the equipment together in the right place and make sure both aids and equipment are ready to use. Operate the machines yourself if possible, working the aids into the total presentation smoothly. Projected material should not dominate a presentation.

Audio Tapes and Recordings   Audio aids can explain ideas, but they can also set or change a mood. For example, the voice and words of an authority on your subject can add credibility to your presentation.

Another person should operate audio equipment for you when possible because you may need to interact with the material while it is playing. Just as you need to make a dramatic point, you may also need to lower the volume or change tapes.

While a speech is not a multimedia event, audiovisual aids can help to make a speech clear and interesting. You should use these aids rather than have them use you. Select carefully from among available aids to find those that fit your situation. Create your own aids when appropriate ones are not available. Work them into the speech as an integral part of the total presentation.

After the Presentation

A question-answer session often follows a presentation. This gives the members of the audience a chance to clarify points in their minds and to seek further information. For the speaker, this provides a chance to get feedback on both the subject and the manner of presentation. So allow time to encourage questions and try to give concise, meaningful responses to them.

As you are being questioned, listen on two levels: (1) what responses are needed and (2) how well was the idea presented initially. For instance, *Where did you get that information?* could be a direct challenge to your credibility and show disagreement with your problem statement. *Where could I get more information about this subject?* may be a compliment and show an aroused interest in the subject. Interpret the nonverbal signals sent along with the questions themselves, and you will know how best to respond.

A checklist for evaluating your oral presentations is shown in Figure 2.

Effective speaking depends upon effective listening, the other side of the communication process. Everyone does both in business. A good listener can help a speaker be effective or can prevent him or her from doing so. Likewise, a good listener can learn much from an oral presentation regardless of how good a job the speaker does.

DEVELOPING GOOD LISTENING HABITS

Hearing is the first step in listening, the physical act of recognizing sounds. Listening begins with hearing but also involves processing sounds and assigning meaning to them. Rudolph Verderber stated in his book, *Communicate!*, that "Research studies have shown that most of us listen

Name _____ Topic _____

Section 1: Audience Rapport with Speaker (check only if used effectively)

Eye contact _____   Hand control _____

Enthusiasm _____   Facial expression _____

Voice variation (inflection) _____   Use of notes _____

Speaker's interest in subject _____   Gesturing _____

Body movement _____   Positive humor _____

Speaker identity with audience _____

Comments _____

Section 2: Speech Structure	Excellent	Good	Acceptable	Needs Improvement
Introduction				
Gained my immediate attention	_____	_____	_____	_____
Stated purpose clearly and early	_____	_____	_____	_____
Sounded clear, stayed on topic	_____	_____	_____	_____
Implementation (body)				
Supported statements with facts	_____	_____	_____	_____
Documented facts where necessary	_____	_____	_____	_____
Sounded believable	_____	_____	_____	_____
Sounded persuasive	_____	_____	_____	_____
Conclusion				
Used smooth transition from body	_____	_____	_____	_____
Summarized major points	_____	_____	_____	_____
Closed smoothly	_____	_____	_____	_____
Organization				
Was coherent, easy to follow	_____	_____	_____	_____
Was concise	_____	_____	_____	_____
Was clear	_____	_____	_____	_____
Was correct and appropriate	_____	_____	_____	_____

Comments _____

Figure 2   Checklist for evaluating oral presentation.

Section 3: Visual Aids (check only if appropriate)

Used appropriate aids _____

Used aids effectively _____

Comments _____

Section 4: Credibility (check only if done effectively)

Content   *Overall*

  Extent of coverage _____   Convincing _____

  Difficulty level of coverage _____   Interesting _____

  Clarity of coverage _____   Positive _____

Delivery

  Diction _____

  Semantics (word usage) _____

Comments _____

Figure 2   (*Continued*)

with only 25 to 50 percent efficiency—that means that 50 to 75 percent of what we hear is never processed."[2] Such inefficient listening results from poor listening habits. These habits range from simply not paying attention to subconscious rejection of certain information for personal reasons.

Can you think of anyone who needs to listen well more than business executives do? Yet these and other professionals whose very careers depend upon good listening habits often do a poor job of it. Carl Rogers noted that a person's inability to communicate is a result of his or her failure to listen effectively, skillfully, and with understanding to another person. He said, "The one who consistently listens with understanding, however, is the one who eventually is most likely to be listened to."[3] You can learn to listen better because listening skills are *learned*. Through analyzing problems and following guidelines, you can learn to hear and to understand what is said every hour of every day.

To become better listeners, follow the Six P's or six steps to more effective listening habits.

1. *Preparing.*   Preparing, the first step in becoming a better listener, is to set your mind to the task. Listening is an active communication

[2]Rudolph Verderber, *Communicate!* 3rd ed. (Belmont, Calif.: Wadsworth, 1981), p. 107.

[3]Carl R. Rogers and Richard E. Farson, "Active Listening," in Richard C. Huseman et al., eds., *Readings in Interpersonal and Organizational Communication*, 2d. ed. (Boston: Holbrook, 1973), p. 549.

skill, not a passive process. Preparing to listen well involves becoming conscious that you are surrounded constantly by sounds and therefore the opportunity to practice always is available. Becoming conscious of the sounds around you can make you aware that you must be selective in attending to some of them while ignoring others. The rewards are clearly worth the effort. Preparing, then, is the first part of the listening readiness stage.

2. *Perceiving.*   Perceiving is the second step in becoming a better listener and the second part of the readiness stage. This calls for recognizing how people thwart even the best speaker's efforts through sloppy perception. They "tune out" much of what is said to them. People practice selective perception by listening with bias; they hear what they choose to hear. Are these excuses for poor listening familiar to you:

"George doesn't know what he's talking about!"

"I can't follow all these figures and junk!"

"Oh brother, this old gaffer is a real bore!"

"Why did they pick Sally? Nobody likes her!"

"I'll bet I know more about this topic than that 'turkey' up there!"

"I've heard this before . . . wonder what I'll do this weekend?"

With these practices, many people mentally stuff cotton in their ears, setting out not to listen by rejecting the speaker as a source of information. Or they become bored and disinterested. Or they simply refuse to accept information that runs counter to their present beliefs and attitudes. Referred to as *blocking,* these habits keep them from listening objectively. Blocking may be triggered by anything from the speaker's personality, to past associations with ideas you hear, to the speaker's choice of words. But the result is the same in each case— poor or selective listening. The secret to perceiving well is to listen *objectively.* To do this, avoid confusing the message with the source or with unrelated experiences. In doing this, focus on listening for the meaning behind the words—the ideas themselves. *Withhold judgment* until you have heard the entire message.

3. *Participating.*   Participating, the third step, requires that you become actively involved in listening, that you work at it. Listening time is no time to conserve energy because good listening takes effort. Concentration is needed to follow difficult directions, for example; but it is also required to screen noise and other distractions. Also, attention

spans are short—after 20 to 30 seconds of concentration, attention lapses, at least briefly.

How then can you participate better with the speaker? One method calls for a conscious commitment as described in steps 1 and 2—preparing and perceiving. A second method calls for being more responsive to both the speaker and the subject—involvement creates interest! To do this, be brave by reacting openly (verbally and non-verbally as appropriate) to give the speaker feedback. For example, nodding in agreement is a powerful act of active listening and a fine cue to help the speaker do a better job.

4. *Processing.*   The fourth step, processing, involves *thinking.* While someone is speaking to you, think about the message; that is, process the information in your own mind to make sense of it. The ability to process information is much greater than is the ability to speak rapidly. A normal speech rate ranges from 125 to 175 words a minute, but you can comprehend at a normal rate of 300 to 400 words a minute. While your comprehension rate does vary according to how much you know about the topic and how complex it is, usually you are left with extra thinking time when you listen.

How do people use extra thinking time? Often, they jump ahead and assume that they are going to hear what is not then said to them. Sometimes, they simply let their minds wander. At other times, they hear something that gets them thinking along parallel lines while they digress from the speaker's next point. What then can you do to keep listening attentively? The answer is to turn inward by focusing your thoughts on the topic. Use the free seconds between ideas to recap what has been said so far. Then attend to the next point as it is being made. Do think about the direction a speaker's topic is taking, but then follow the speaker's ideas to see if you are correct.

5. *Probing.*   The fifth step is probing. This involves making sense of what is said by fitting the facts given to you into the context of the speaker's main idea. Then probing involves evaluating ideas to make a complete message from bits of information given you—fitting the parts to the whole. When you do not understand an idea or how it fits into the larger theme, ask questions at opportune times. In an interpersonal setting, usually you can ask questions immediately. In group settings, you may have to wait until a complete division of the information is presented or until the end of the presentation.

Good speakers organize speeches well and therefore make it easy or unnecessary to probe. But many people are not good speakers, so you must become a good listener to understand clearly what is said to you. Ask the speaker to repeat a section that is unclear or ask a specific question about a point that is unclear: "What do you mean by point A?" or "How does point A relate to point D?"

6. *Personalizing.* The sixth step, personalizing, is to direct the information you hear toward your own benefit. How can what is said help you meet your own wants and needs? professionally? financially? socially? Fit the information into your experience to help in pursuing your own goals. This self-interest is a real motivator to listen well by listening actively. As Wilson Mizner has said, "A good listener is not only popular everywhere, but after a while he (or she) knows something."[4] Knowing something is a powerful tool for building a successful business career.

SUMMARY

Effective speaking and listening skills are essential to success in business. Good speakers help listeners to do a better job, and the reverse is also true. The discussion in this chapter focuses on how to build good speaking and listening skills and on how they relate to each other.

The basic speech styles are impromptu, extemporaneous, manuscript, and memorized. Most speeches are extemporaneous. After choosing a speech topic and style, develop a problem statement. This statement gives the main idea of the speech. Then, research the topic and analyze the audience. Next, select a general format. The general format is the overall organization the presentation will take—cause to effect or problem solving, for example.

After selecting the general format, develop the introduction, body, and conclusion of the presentation. Once you complete this basic development, draft a speech outline and put it on note cards or paper. When giving written reports orally, clarify the assignment first; then analyze the audience and report information and plan the presentation.

Always practice a speech before giving it. During the presentation, try to get a good start and to use effective delivery techniques. Avoid slander and handle stage fright by reaching out to become more confident and reducing apprehensions about your ability. Use appropriate audiovisual aids to complement your presentation; integrate them into the presentation where needed, but do not allow these aids to dominate your presentation. During the question-answer session, listen to questions on two levels: (1) what responses are needed and (2) how well was the idea presented initially.

Good listening habits call for applying the Six P's of effective listening. Preparing and perceiving form the readiness stage. Participating calls for active involvement with the speaker and message. Processing involves thinking about the message, and probing calls for making a complete message of the parts. Personalizing focuses on the self-interest in a message.

[4]H. L. Mencken, ed., *A New Dictionary of Quotations* (New York: Knopf, 1966), p. 700.

Additional Readings

Brown, J. W., and R. B. Lewis. *Audio-Visual Instruction: Technology, Media, and Method,* 5th ed. New York: McGraw Hill, 1976.

Capps, Randall, et al. *Communication for the Business and Professional Speaker.* New York: Macmillan, 1981.

Hunt, Gary T. *Public Speaking.* Englewood Cliffs, N.J.: Prentice-Hall, 1981.

McCroskey, James C. *An Introduction to Rhetorical Communication,* 2nd ed. Englewood Cliffs, N.J.: Prentice-Hall, 1972.

Montgomery, Robert L. *Listening Made Easy.* New York: AMACOM (American Management Association), 1981.

Nadeau, Ray E., and John M. Muchmore. *Speech Communication: A Career Education Approach.* Reading, Mass.: Addison-Wesley, 1979.

Ross, R. *Speech Communication: Fundamentals and Practice,* 5th ed. Englewood Cliffs, N.J.: Prentice-Hall, 1980.

Schniff, Roselyn L., et al. *Communication Strategy: A Guide to Speech Preparation.* Glenview, Ill.: Scott, Foresman, 1981.

Severin, Werner J., and James W. Tankard. *Communication Theories: Origins, Methods, Uses.* New York: Hastings House, 1979.

Sussman, Lyle, and Paul D. Krivonos. *Communication for Supervisors and Managers.* Sherman Oaks, Calif.: Alfred, 1979.

Verderber, Rudolph F. *The Challenge of Effective Speaking,* 4th ed. Belmont, Calif.: Wadsworth, 1979.

————. *Communicate!* 3rd ed. Belmont, Calif.: Wadsworth, 1981.

Wollechinsky, David, and Irving Wallace. *The Book of Lists.* New York: William Morrow, 1977.

Review Questions

1. List and explain two or three situations in which giving a memorized presentation is appropriate.
2. Explain briefly how to begin a presentation, what to put in the middle part, and how to close it.
3. Explain how to prepare and use note cards or an outline for an extemporaneous presentation.
4. Compare the feedback that a speaker gets to that that a writer of reports or correspondence gets.
5. Should audiovisual aids be used in every oral presentation? Explain your answer.
6. Compare the problem statement in an oral presentation with that of a written report.
7. What role does hearing play in the listening process?
8. List and define the Six P's of good listening.
9. Explain how good speakers can help listeners do a better job of listening and how good listeners can help speakers do a better job of speaking.

Exercises

1. Prepare and deliver an eight-minute persuasive presentation on a business subject. Use an extemporaneous format and an outline. Examples of topics are "How to Get a Small Business Loan" and "Investing in Stocks and Bonds."

2. Practice speaking before groups by giving a four-minute impromptu speech on one of the following topics (or choose your own topic):

country music	taxes
agriculture	TGIF's (Thank Good-
auto repair	ness It's Friday)
orchids	OPEC (Organization
cooking	of Petroleum
elevators	Exporting
mutual funds	Countries)
the 1960s	truck drivers
mobile homes	health clubs

3. Select three of the topics listed in Exercise 2 and write a problem statement for each. Then develop *two* introductions for one of the topics.

4. Visit the audiovisual or media center on your campus. Find out what equipment is available and learn to operate each type if possible. Then list one way that you could use each type in a presentation. If you prefer, visit the center in small groups. Another option is to ask an audiovisual specialist from the center to visit your classroom to discuss the equipment.

5. Prepare an informative speech outline describing the characteristics of a new product that has been marketed recently. Explain how you could change the outline to make a persuasive speech. Examples of appropriate topics are "Preparing Computer Graphics," "Working for a Large Company," and "Making Money in Your Spare Time."

6. This problem on listening involves you as the source of information. Spend one day listening. Take a conversation, speech, or lecture from the day's experience and analyze it according to the Six P's. Write down your analysis and be prepared to share it with the class.

Appendices

APPENDIX A

Elements of Grammar

Clarity and correctness are two essential elements of communication. Using grammar properly is necessary for being clear and correct in business communication. Follow the guidelines in this appendix when you have questions concerning correct grammatical usage.

PARTS OF SPEECH

Words are the building blocks of communication. These words form the seven basic parts of speech: nouns, pronouns, verbs, adjectives, adverbs, prepositions, and conjunctions.

Nouns

A noun is the name of a person, place, thing, quality, or concept.

> Jim   town   dog   truth   universe

Classifications
Nouns can be classified in two ways:

1. *Proper nouns:* name of a specific person, place, or thing. Proper nouns are capitalized (see "Capitalization").

> Mary Smith   St. Louis   Ford

A

2. *Common nouns:* name used to refer to any one of a number of persons, places, things, qualities, or concepts. Common nouns are not capitalized.

boys   cities   animals   honesty   mathematics

Number

Nouns may be singular or plural in number. Collective nouns usually name something composed of two or more items. These collective nouns are usually considered singular in number.

family   staff   faculty   committee

Concrete/Abstract

A *concrete noun* names something that can be seen, smelled, tasted, touched, or heard *(dog, flower, cake, desk, whistle)*. Concrete nouns are emphatic.

An *abstract noun* names something that cannot be seen, smelled, tasted, touched, or heard *(happiness, idea, religion)*. Abstract nouns are not as emphatic as concrete nouns.

Pronouns

Pronouns take the place of nouns. Therefore, they serve the same purposes as nouns.

Classifications

Pronouns can be classified in several ways:

1. *Personal pronouns:* refer to specific persons or things *(I, you, them)*.

2. *Indefinite pronouns:* do not refer to specific persons or things *(all, few, none, some, each, several, somebody, no one, everyone)*.

3. *Demonstrative pronouns:* point out or identify *(this, that, these, those)*.

4. *Interrogative pronouns:* introduce a question *(who, whom, whose, which, what)*.

5. *Relative pronouns:* join a dependent clause to an antecedent in an independent clause *(who, whom, whose, which,* and *that)*. These pronouns may introduce restrictive or nonrestrictive clauses (see "Punctuation—Comma").

6. *Reflexive/intensive pronouns:* direct action back to antecedent or emphasize an antecedent. Reflexive pronouns are made by adding *self* or *selves* to the pronoun "one" or to the following personal pronouns: *my, our, your, him, them, her,* and *it*.

Person

A personal pronoun may have one of three persons; that is, personal pronouns may refer to the person speaking (first person: *I, me, my*), the person spoken to (second person: *you, your),* or the person(s) or thing(s) spoken about *(third person: they, it, them).*

Case

A pronoun may take one of three cases: subjective (or nominative), objective, or possessive. Case refers to the relationship of a pronoun and other words in the sentence, clause, or phrase. The subjective case is used when the pronoun is a subject or a predicate nominative.

The objective case is used when the pronoun is the object of the verb or preposition or the subject or object of an infinitive phrase.

> *Mary wants us to leave with her at 5:00 p.m.* (*us* is the object of the verb and subject of the infinitive "to leave." The object of the preposition "with" is *her*)

The possessive case is used when the pronoun shows ownership. Common pronouns in the possessive case are *mine, yours, his, theirs, ours.*

Verbs

A verb expresses action, condition, or state of being. Verbs tell what the subject does, what the subject is doing, or what is done to the subject. Without a verb, a group of words cannot be a clause or a sentence.

Classes

The two classes of verbs are transitive and intransitive. Transitive verbs show physical or mental action between a subject and a direct object. Intransitive verbs also show physical or mental action but do not have a direct object.

Voice

The way in which a subject and a verb interact in a sentence is termed "voice." The two types of voice—active and passive—are directly related to the type of verb used.

In active voice, an action verb is used resulting in the subject of the sentence performing the action indicated by the verb.

> The stockholders elected a new president.

In this example, the subject (stockholders) is performing the action indicated by the verb (elected).

A

Passive voice is less direct and less emphatic than active. When a sentence is written with a passive verb, the subject no longer performs the action; rather, the subject now receives the action.

A new president was elected by the board of directors.

Notice that the subject (president) is receiving the action of the verb (was elected).

You can easily determine if a sentence is written in passive voice by answering three questions:

1. Is the subject doing the action indicated by the verb?

2. Does the verb consist of at least two words, one of which is the form of the verb "to be" (is, being, am, are, was, were, will be, has been, had been, have been, or will have been)?

3. Is the word "by" expressed or implied ("by whom" or "by what")?

Mood

The manner in which a verb shows action is termed "mood." The three forms of mood are indicative, imperative, and subjunctive.

A verb in the indicative mood states a fact or asks a question:

The applicant was hired for the position.
Was the applicant hired for the position?

A verb in the imperative mood expresses a command or makes a request:

Hire the applicant today.
Please call me about the vacancy.

A verb in the subjunctive mood expresses something contrary to fact, a wish, or a command or request in a "that" clause. The subjunctive verb "were" is used for all three persons to indicate a condition known to be contrary to fact or to indicate a wish.

If he were here, he would know how to handle this complaint.
Sometimes I wish I were head of this company.

The verb "be" is used for all three persons when a command or request is presented in a "that" clause.

The personnel manager recommended that the new clerk be assigned here.
The customer demanded that the clerk be fired for inconsiderate behavior.

Tense

The tense of a verb is the form taken to express distinctions in time. Regular verbs form their past tenses and past participles by adding "d" or "ed" to the present tense: *manage, managed, managed.* Irregular verbs do not follow such a set rule when forming their past tenses and past participles: *do, did, done; lie, lay, lain.*

Adjectives

Adjectives modify or describe nouns and pronouns. Adjectives answer questions such as which? what kind? how many? whose? how much?

In addition, adjectives may be used to compare persons and things: comparative degree compares two persons or things; superlative degree compares three or more persons or things. There can be regular forms and irregular forms for these degrees:

    tall   taller   tallest   (regular degree)
    good   better   best   (irregular degree)

Adverbs

Adverbs modify verbs, adjectives, and other adverbs. Adverbs answer the questions when? where? how? how often? how much?

Adverbs may also be used to compare persons and things; these forms also may be described as regular and irregular:

    late   later   latest   (regular degree)
    badly   worse   worst   (irregular degree)

For adverbs ending in "ly" the comparative and superlative degrees are made by adding "more" ("less") or "most" ("least"), respectively:

    more (less) quickly   most (least) quickly

Prepositions

A preposition relates a noun or pronoun to another word in the sentence. The word related is the object of the preposition in the prepositional phrase.

> The head of the department interviewed the applicant. (*of* is the preposition; *department* is the object of the preposition. The prepositional phrase *of the department* serves as a modifier of the noun *head.*)

A

Conjunctions

Conjunctions join words, phrases, or clauses in a sentence (see "Punctuation—Comma" and "Punctuation—Semicolon"). Types of conjunctions are the following:

Coordinating Conjunctions

Coordinating conjunctions connect two or more words, phrases, or clauses of equal importance and of equal grammatical construction. The most common coordinating conjunctions are *and, but, or, nor, for,* and *yet.*

Correlative Conjunctions

Correlative conjunctions are coordinating conjunctions used in pairs to connect and relate words, phrases, or clauses. The common pairs of correlative conjunctions are *neither-nor, either-or, not only-but also,* and *both-and.*

Subordinate conjuctions

Subordinate conjunctions connect a dependent clause with an independent clause. Words that can serve as subordinate conjunctions include *after, although, as, because, when, if, whether, before, since, though, while, whenever,* and *unless.*

Conjunctive Adverbs

Conjunctive adverbs connect two independent thoughts of equal importance and grammatical construction in a sentence. In addition, since these words are adverbs, they show a relationship between the clauses. The common conjunctive adverbs include *however, moreover, therefore, furthermore, then, consequently, besides, accordingly, also, nevertheless,* and *thus.*

PUNCTUATION

Whenever you use a mark of punctuation, your sole purpose should be to achieve clarity. Omitting needed punctuation usually results in ambiguity.

Period

1. Use a period at the end of a statement or command.

> The personnel office is on the third floor.
> Sign all letters before mailing them.

2. Use a period at the end of a courteous request for action.

> Won't you please let us know your decision as soon as possible.

3. Use a period in various abbreviations (see "Abbreviations").

Question Mark

Use a question mark after a direct question where the intent is to obtain a direct answer.

> Do you market your product through a retailer or do you sell directly to the consumer?

Exclamation Mark

Place an exclamation mark after an interjection or an exclamation.

> Yes! Sell the stock immediately!

Comma

1. Use a comma to set off a parenthetical expression. Parenthetical expressions are words or groups of words that may be removed from a sentence without affecting the meaning or clarity of the sentence. When such an expression comes at the end of a sentence, only one comma is necessary, whereas two commas are needed when the expression is in the middle of a sentence.

> The report, however, is not complete.
> The applicant is not qualified for the position, in my opinion.

2. Use a comma to set off an appositive. An appositive is a word or group of words immediately following another word or expression that explains or modifies the first expression. Some appositives are essential for clarity; no commas are used. Other appositives are not essential and should be set off by commas before and after the appositive. Only one comma is needed when the appositive ends a sentence.

> My sister Claire was hired for the position of chief accountant.
> (Claire is the essential appositive; no comma is used.)
> John Jenkins, our sales manager, will be happy to meet with you.
> Please send your order to Miss Mary Cummings, our order manager.

A

The following are additional expressions in apposition:

a. State when city precedes it.

> Our transportation center has been moved from Springfield, Missouri, to Kansas City, Missouri.

b. Year when month or month and date precede it.

> He was elected president of Exmore Company on January 3, 1982, and promoted to Chairman of the Board on July 7, 1983.

c. Titles and degrees following a person's name.

> Please send all correspondence to John James, Jr., in care of this office.

d. Inc. and Ltd. in company names.

> Our parent corporation, Mitchell, Inc., changed its name to Mitchell, Ltd.

3. Use a comma to set off an introductory expression, series of prepositional phrases, participial phrase, or dependent clause at the beginning of a sentence.

> However, your order is being processed at this time.
> To be of better service to you, we have just installed a toll-free "800" line.
> Knowing that you would need the goods now, we immediately shipped them to you.
> When it is necessary to place a last-minute order, simply use our toll-free service.

4. When three or more items are listed in a series with the last item separated from the others by a conjunction, place a comma after all items except the last.

> You are assured of quick, efficient, and courteous service.

> *Note:* Some business writers suggest omitting the comma before the conjunction. If you choose to omit it in one series in a document, omit it in all series in that document. If a conjunction is placed between all items in a series, no commas are used.

> Our itinerary takes us to Chicago and Phoenix and Los Angeles.

If "etc." is used in a series, the word "and" does not precede it, but a comma does follow the "etc."

> Include direct costs, equipment, personnel, etc., in your proposal.

5. Use a comma to join two independent clauses of a compound sentence when a comma does not appear elsewhere in either of the two clauses (see "Sentence Structure—Compound Sentences").

> Will you attend the sales meeting, or will you send a substitute?

> *Note:* Some business writers place a comma between independent clauses even though a comma appears elsewhere in the compound sentence.

6. Use a comma to set off a nonrestrictive clause or phrase. A nonrestrictive clause is not essential to the completeness of the sentence. A restrictive clause, however, is essential to the clarity of the sentence.

> Send your questions to Mary Adams, who is director of Public Relations, for a quick reply. (nonrestrictive clause)
> Companies that develop employee training programs have reported excellent results. (restrictive clause)

7. Use a comma in numbers containing four or more digits. The comma separates thousands, millions, and so on.

> 7,193   342,961   4,805,977

> *Note:* Some business writers omit using a comma with four-digit numbers (for example, $1200).

Commas are not used in the following numbers: serial numbers, house numbers, policy numbers, page numbers, volume numbers, zip codes, telephone numbers, and digits of a year.

Semicolon

1. Use a semicolon to join two closely related independent clauses when no conjunction has been used.

> The ability to communicate is essential; the ability to communicate on the job is critical.

2. Use a semicolon before a conjunctive adverb that joins two closely related independent clauses.

> Expenses have increased drastically; consequently, next year's budget has been prepared carefully.

> *Note:* A comma follows the parenthetical conjunctive adverb (see "Punctuation—Comma," rule 1).

3. Use a semicolon before a coordinating conjunction in a compound sentence when one or both of the independent clauses contain a comma (see Comma rule 5 note).

    > Our order was for paper, ribbons, and envelopes; but you sent only paper and envelopes.

4. Use a semicolon instead of a comma in a series when commas appear within the various elements of the series.

    > Our offices are located in Atlanta, Georgia; Memphis, Tennessee; Birmingham, Alabama; and Jackson, Mississippi.

5. Use a semicolon before expressions such as *for example* and *namely* when the words that follow these expressions seem to have been added as an explanation.

    > When greeting callers on the telephone, always identify your department and give your name; for example, Accounting, Miss Smith.

Colon

1. Use a colon before expressions (such as for example, namely, and thus) that connect ideas when they introduce ideas alluded to earlier in the sentence.

    > There are three requirements for the job: namely, speaking knowledge of the German language, five years' working experience, and a bachelor's degree in business administration.

2. Use a colon to introduce a list, either in sentence form or on separate lines.

    > Three persons were suggested for Sales Representative of the Year: Gladys Ortiz, Samuel Bigelow, and Joanne Strait.

3. Use a colon to separate hours and minutes when expressing time.

    > Our hours are from 8:30 a.m. to 4:30 p.m.

Quotation Marks

1. Use quotation marks to
    a. Set off a direct quotation.

        > The personnel manager stated, "We only hire persons with an M.B.A. degree for that type of position."

    b. Set off a slang expression, coined expression, or technical term.

A

When questioned about a conflict of interest, the consultant replied that the allegations were "hogwash."

c. Set off titles of songs, magazine and newspaper articles, chapters in published works, and unpublished works.

The research report, "Sexual Harrassment in the Office," is due for distribution next month.

2. When combined with quotation marks,
   a. Always place a period or comma inside the ending quotation mark.

   The accountant stated, "Our taxable income is at an all-time high."
   He labeled the report on our hiring practices as "garbage," and I must agree.

   Note: When a quoted statement begins a sentence, place a comma inside the ending quotation mark and a period at the end of the sentence.

   "We provide our new employees with a two-week paid vacation after twelve months," replied the interviewer.

   b. Place question and exclamation marks outside the ending quotation mark if the question or exclamation is the entire sentence. Place these marks inside the ending quotation mark if the quoted material is the question or exclamation.

   Did she say, "I can go"?
   "What type of vacation policy does your company have?" she asked.
   He exclaimed, "I accept the offer!"

   Note: When the question mark or exclamation mark is placed inside the ending quotation mark, no additional punctuation is necessary immediately outside the ending quotation mark (see second example above).

   c. Always place semicolons and colons outside the ending quotation mark.

   You stated, "I'll pay the bill by the end of the week"; however, we still haven't received payment.

Apostrophe

1. Show omission of letters in contractions by inserting an apostrophe at the exact point of omission.

   It's time for the appointment; he'll represent me.

A

2. An apostrophe is used to show possession in

    a. Singular nouns not ending in "s." Add an *'s* at the end of the noun: *manager's report.*

    b. Singular nouns ending in "s." Add an *'s* at the end if a new syllable is formed: *boss's remarks.*

    c. Singular nouns ending in "s." Add only an apostrophe if pronunciation would be difficult if the *'s* rule were applied:

        President Hastings' speech

    d. Regular plural nouns (those ending in "s"). Add an apostrophe:

        committee members' reports

    e. Irregular plural nouns (where the form of the word changes — *man-men, child-children*). Add an *'s:*

        men's hats

3. Do not include an apostrophe with possessive pronouns:

    ours   yours

Hyphens

1. Use a hyphen when dividing a word at the end of a typewritten line (see "Word Division").

2. When two adjectives precede a noun, the two adjectives may jointly modify the noun. In this instance, the two adjectives should be hyphenated.

    The well-known consultant received a large fee for his work.
    The up-to-the-minute news is that the stock will be sold.

    Note: If the compound expression follows the noun it is modifying, the expression is not hyphenated.

    The consultant they hired is well known.

3. If the first word in a compound expression ends in "ly," do not hyphenate the expression even if it precedes the noun.

    He edits a widely read magazine.

CAPITALIZATION

Some business writers differ on some of the rules of capitalization. The rules that follow apply to most situations where you might have a question.

Abbreviations

Capitalize abbreviations as you would normally capitalize the words for which the abbreviations stand.

First Words

Capitalize

1. The first word of a sentence.

2. The first word of a direct quotation regardless of its location in the sentence.

   > The recently posted sign read, "Unauthorized persons are prohibited."

3. The first word of each item in a listing.

   > 1. Storage disks
   > 2. Continuous feed paper

4. The first word of a complete statement following a colon if such a statement is a formal rule, a direct quotation, or a statement introduced by a single word.

   > *Note:*   All visitors must register with the receptionist.
   > Murphy's law states as follows: "If anything can go wrong, it will."

5. The first word of a complimentary closing.

   > Sincerely yours   Very truly yours

Proper Nouns

Always capitalize proper nouns. Several specific rules relate to particular categories of proper nouns.

1. Titles.

   a. Capitalize a title that precedes a name, but do not capitalize a title that follows a name unless it is the title of a high government official.

> President Reagan
> Ronald Reagan, President of the United States
> Jane Smith, president of the P.T.A.

b. Unless it is a title of a high-ranking government official, foreign dignitary, or international figure, do not capitalize a title that is used as a substitute for a specific person's name.

> The Pope will visit our country this month.
> The president of the corporation will speak to the stockholders.

c. When used as substitutes for names, capitalize words showing family relationships or when the title precedes the name.

> Please call Father when you get home. (used as a name)
> Please call your father when you get home. (used to designate family relationship)
> Your Uncle Phillip and your two cousins will be visiting next month.

d. Capitalize all words in the titles of books, magazines, and other publications, except articles (a, an, the), prepositions of four or fewer letters, and conjunctions, unless these are the first or last word in the title.

> The Peter Principle   Management Organizational Theory

2. Place names.
   a. Capitalize the official names of cities and their "coined" or imagined names.

   > New York City   the Big Apple
   > Philadelphia   the City of Brotherly Love

   b. Capitalize "city" when it follows the name of the city; do not capitalize "city" when it precedes the name of the city unless it is part of the corporate name of the city.

   > New York City is a major financial center of the world.
   > Wall Street is in the city of New York.

   c. Capitalize "state" when it follows the name of the state; do not capitalize "state" when it precedes the name of the state.

   > The Grand Ole Opry is in the state of Tennessee; however, Carnegie Hall is in New York State.

   d. Capitalize the names of streets, buildings, rivers, and mountains. Also capitalize the words "street" or "river" when they are part of the proper name. Do not capitalize the generic term when it stands alone or plural generic terms when used with the proper nouns.

> Maymont Park is located off Byrd Avenue.
> The Mississippi River is the largest river in the United States; however, the Missouri and Ohio rivers are also very large.

3. Organizations.
   a. When referring to a specific organization, such as a business, capitalize the major words in the name.

   > We completed a major sale of computer software to Glasgow Controls Company last week.
   > The Wharton School of Business is a part of the University of Pennsylvania.
   > The annual blood drive will be conducted by the American Red Cross.

   b. Generally, only capitalize terms such as personnel department, maintenance division, and board of directors when they are actual units within your own organization. When referring to someone else's organization, do not capitalize these terms.
   c. Do not capitalize generic terms that are used in place of the full name of an organization unless special emphasis is intended.

   > When you enroll in the M.B.A. program at our university, you will study a comprehensive, up-to-date curriculum.

4. Brand names. Capitalize the brand name or trademark associated with a product; however, do not capitalize the generic product following the brand name.

   > Orion International purchased only Ford automobiles for its sales fleet.

5. Days of the week, months of the year, events, and holidays.
   a. Capitalize the names of days, months, holidays, events, and religious holidays.

   > On the first Monday in September, we celebrate Labor Day; other days we celebrate include Thanksgiving, Christmas, and Memorial Day.

   b. Do not capitalize the names of the seasons unless personified or used to designate a special event.

   > The annual fall stockholders' meeting will be held in San Francisco. As the Spring Fling will be sponsored by our organization, all employees are encouraged to attend.

A

Derivatives of Proper Nouns

1. Capitalize a word derived from a proper noun.

   > The Spanish Ambassador visited our company to discuss our products.

2. Capitalize all names derived from races, people, tribes, religions, and languages.

   > The Afro-American League has requested it be allowed to use our auditorium.

Miscellaneous

Do not capitalize

1. Points of the compass unless they designate a definite region or are part of a proper noun.

   > Several major companies have moved their headquarters to the South because of favorable labor laws and climate.
   > The West Coast has become known for its electronics industry; many of these electronics companies moved west early in the 1950s.

2. Names of subject areas except for proper nouns or specific course titles.

   > She completed several courses in accounting, for example, Tax Accounting I and II and Auditing I.
   > A business English course is very beneficial to students majoring in business administration.

3. First words in indirect quotations or interrupted quotations.

   > The personnel manager said he could attend the meeting.
   > "Let's come to order," exclaimed the president, "so that we can quickly finish this meeting!"

ABBREVIATIONS

Generally, avoid abbreviations in your writing as they may not be clear to the reader. When you find you must abbreviate, there are several widely accepted rules to follow:

1. If a term has a common abbreviation that will be used throughout the document, write out the word in full the first time and place the abbreviation in parentheses.

Ms. Mary Constantine will head the Word Processing (WP) Department.

2. Always abbreviate courtesy titles when used with a person's name. The regular courtesy titles are Dr., Mr., Mrs., and Ms. Always abbreviate Jr., Sr., and Esq. when they follow a full name. No courtesy title precedes a name when Esq. is used.

3. In general, do not abbreviate military, political, or religious titles.

    Governor McCormick, General Patton, Reverend King

4. Generally, do not abbreviate the points of the compass when used with street names.

    134 South Main Street rather than 134 S. Main Street.

5. Generally, do not abbreviate Incorporated, Company, Corporation, Manufacturing, and other similar terms in business names unless the company does so in its letterhead.

6. In general, do not abbreviate the names of the days of the week and months of the year.

7. Write the following without periods.

   a. Acronyms:

      COBOL   LASER   LOX

   b. Names of well-known businesses or other organizations.

      IBM   AT&T   NAACP

   c. Radio and television stations and television networks.

      WQXR   CBS

   d. Names of well-known government agencies and international organizations.

      FCC   IRS   UN

   e. Time zones.

      EST   MDT   PST

8. Write the following with periods.
   a. Academic degrees.

      B.A.   M.Ed.   Ph.D.   D.D.S.

      Note: CPA, CPS, CAM, and so on have no periods when they stand alone but have periods when used with academic degrees.

A

    b. Expression of time.

        a.m.   p.m.

    c. Geographic abbreviations consisting of single initials.

        U.S.   U.S.S.R.

    d. A.D. ("in the year of our Lord") and B.C. ("before Christ"). These two abbreviations should always be written in all capitals. A.D. should be written in front of the year; B.C. after the year.

        A.D. 7   231 B.C.

NUMBERS

The following rules will assist you in writing numbers:

1. Generally, spell out numbers from one to nine and use figures to express numbers of 10 and above.

    The manager interviewed three candidates for the position.
    Please order 75 reams of letterhead paper.

2. Avoid starting a sentence with a number. If you must, spell out the number in words.

    Twenty-three employees are on vacation this week.

3. When one number immediately precedes another number, express the smaller of the two in words.

    He made six 10-minute phone calls to close the sale.

4. Use figures with a.m. and p.m. Use figures with o'clock in informal writing (such as business writing).

    Our hours are from 9:00 a.m. to 5:30 p.m.
    The accountant left for the meeting at 10 o'clock.

    Note: If all times are on the hour, the colon and zeros are not necessary when using a.m. or p.m.

    We left for the board of directors meeting at 10 a.m.

5. Use figures to express exact or approximate amounts of money but spell out indefinite amounts of money.

    The invoice amounted to $1,200, but we were allowed nearly a $7 discount.

Current starting salaries for persons with M.B.A. degrees are several thousand dollars over those of beginning teachers.

Note: Use a "$" (with figures) instead of writing out dollars. Express whole dollar amounts without a decimal point and two zeros.

6. Use figures and the word "cents" for expressing amounts under a dollar except when related amounts require a dollar sign.

Photocopies on this machine cost only 3 cents each.
These audio tapes are on sale for $1.25 each or $.75 each if bought in quantity.

7. Use cardinal numbers (1, 2, 3) when the day follows the month; use ordinal numbers (1st, 2nd, 3rd), either as words or figures, when the day precedes the month.

The data processing convention will begin on the 21st of September.
She was hired as the personnel manager on July 7.

8. Use figures and the word "percent" spelled out when expressing percentages in sentences.

The interest rate was quoted at 15 percent on the bond issue.

9. When the street name is a number, spell out the name if nine or below. Use figures for street names of 10 and above. Cardinal numbers may be used if preceded by a point of the compass; for clarity, use ordinal numbers if no word precedes the street name.

Send the order to 231 Fifth Street; however, send the invoice to our office at 147 East 52 Street.
All applications can be mailed to our personnel department at 749 65th Street.

WORD DIVISION

As a general rule, avoid dividing words at the end of typewritten lines. However, when you must divide, follow these simple rules.

1. Divide words only between syllables. Thus, no matter how long a word, if it has only one syllable, it cannot be divided:

through   chrome

A

2. Divide only words of six letters or more regardless of the number of syllables:

   let-   ter   order   prior

3. Do not separate a one-letter syllable at the beginning of a word. Do not separate a two-letter syllable at the end of a word. Do not separate a syllable that does not contain a vowel:

   enough (not e-nough)   poorly (not poor-ly)   wouldn't (not would-n't)

4. Hyphenated compound words should be divided only at the point of the hyphen:

   self-control (not self-con-trol).

5. Avoid dividing proper names. If necessary, place the person's first name at the end of one line and surname at the beginning of the next:

   Sandra Smith (not San-dra Smith).

6. Do not use a hyphen when placing part of a date on the next line. Attempt to put month and day together on the same line.

7. Do not divide the last word on a page.

SENTENCE STRUCTURE

Four types of sentences are simple, compound, complex, and compound-complex. The advantages of using various sentence structures is discussed in Chapter One.

Simple Sentences

A simple sentence contains one complete thought. The sentence may contain a compound subject or a compound predicate but the result is one thought.

The committee approved the report.

Compound Sentences

A compound sentence contains two complete but related thoughts. Each thought could stand by itself as a separate sentence.

The sales department accepted the report, but the collection department rejected it.

The two independent clauses can be joined with a coordinating conjunction, a conjunctive adverb, or a semicolon (see "Parts of Speech—Conjunctions" and "Punctuation—Comma and Semicolon").

A

Complex Sentences

A complex sentence contains an independent clause (a complete thought) and a dependent clause (a thought that cannot stand by itself).

> Because you already have an account with our bank, the procedure for authorizing us to handle your payroll deposit is simple.

In complex sentences, the dependent clause starts with a subordinate conjunction (see "Parts of Speech—Conjunctions"). The dependent clause may be at the beginning or at the end of the sentence.

Compound-Complex Sentences

A compound-complex sentence contains at least two independent clauses and one dependent clause.

> Although sales have increased, our company's profits have continued to decline; but management has developed a new marketing strategy.

Common Sentence Errors

Six common errors are committed when constructing sentences: sentence fragment, run-on sentence, comma splice, misplaced phrase, subject/verb agreement, and pronoun/noun antecedent agreement.

A sentence fragment is a group of words that does not form a complete thought.

> After he delivered his speech

A run-on sentence usually contains two or more complete thoughts that have not been joined with a conjunction or appropriate punctuation mark.

> The employee evaluations arrived the follow-up interviews were held.

A comma splice occurs when two independent clauses are joined by a comma without an accompanying conjunction.

> The ability to communicate clearly is essential, the ability to communicate on the job is critical.

A

A misplaced modifying phrase results in a phrase being separated from the idea it modifies.

We can sell you this desk at a very reasonable price, which has a leather top.

The number of the subject and verb must agree—singular subjects take singular verbs; plural subjects, plural verbs. This type of error can result from many situations, the most common of which is intervening phrases.

The sales manager, as well as her three assistants, are attending the meeting in St. Paul.
The evaluations of the employment procedure is on your desk.

Since pronouns take the place of nouns, they should agree in number with the nouns they are replacing.

The salesmen should take care in the preparation of his report.

Another problem with pronoun/noun antecedent is the ambiguity that exists when there is not a clear indication of what the pronoun refers to.

The sales manager and his assistant finished the report but he made several errors in it.

PARAGRAPH CONSTRUCTION

Paragraph construction is discussed in Chapter One, Fundamental Writing Techniques.

APPENDIX B

Business Reference Sources

Because information is the basis for decision making, knowing the types of published materials that are available is important. Many reference sources exist for the business student to use in researching problems, preparing cases, and writing reports. This appendix contains names and descriptions of the basic business reference sources. Remember that public, academic, and corporate libraries often have a variety of materials. Whenever you are unable to locate the materials you need, ask your librarian for help.

PERIODICALS AND FINANCIAL NEWSPAPERS

Periodicals and newspapers offer both current information and specialized studies. The following is an annotated list of the most important ones.

Accounting Review. American Accounting Association, Evanston, Illinois (quarterly).

Advertising Age. Crain Communications, Chicago, Illinois (weekly). Major source of advertising statistics and current news on market strategies, product lines and brands, and advertising firms.

Barrons. Dow Jones & Company, New York (weekly). National business and financial weekly with articles on investment companies, industries, trends, companies, and other business topics. Stock and bond prices are given.

Business Week. McGraw-Hill Book Company, New York (weekly). Essential reading for business students regardless of particular area of interest. Gives important

B

business indicators, surveys of corporate performance, investment outlook and articles on new business developments and trends in all aspects of business, government, environment, management, marketing, and foreign affairs.

Dun's Review. Dun & Bradstreet Corporation, New York (monthly).

Forbes. Forbes, Inc., New York (semimonthly). First issue each year contains "Annual Report on American Industry."

Fortune. Time, Inc., New York (monthly). Articles on various companies and company executives, new products, and discoveries. Also contains the famous *Fortune* list of largest corporations.

Harvard Business Review. Graduate School of Business Administration, Harvard University, Boston (bimonthly). Business management journal. Articles written for the practitioner.

Journal of Business. University of Chicago Press, Chicago (quarterly). Scholarly articles on business, economic methodology.

Journal of Marketing. American Marketing Association, Chicago (quarterly). Scholarly articles on themes and practices in marketing.

Management Review. AMACOM (American Management Association), New York (monthly). Articles on current management literature.

Monthly Labor Review. U.S. Department of Labor, Washington, D.C. (monthly). Articles providing current statistics on unemployment, employment consumer prices, wholesale prices, earnings.

Nation's Business. Chamber of Commerce of the United States, Washington, D.C. (monthly). Popular articles on business, economics, and politics.

Personnel Journal. Personnel Journal, Inc., Santa Monica, Calif. (monthly). Short articles on various issues in personnel management and industrial relations.

Sales and Marketing Management. Sales Management, Inc., New York (semimonthly). Trade journal that publishes annual statistical issues: survey of buying power, survey of industrial purchasing power, and survey of selling costs.

The Wall Street Journal. Dow Jones & Company, New York (daily Monday–Friday). Contains business and financial news and articles on mergers and other corporate strategies. Also contains stock and bond prices.

Washington Post. The Washington Post Company, Washington, D.C. (Monday edition). Monday edition has section on business that provides an overview of the week's activities and features on companies and business issues.

ABSTRACTS AND INDEXES

Abstracts are short, concise summaries of articles provided to give readers a clear indication of the contents of the articles. Indexes give the access points for articles. Some indexes are general (such as *Reader's Guide to Periodical Literature);* others are specialized (such as *Accountants Index).* General business and economic indexes are listed here. You may wish also to consult abstracts and indexes in other fields—for example, psychology, education, engineering.

Abstracting and Indexing Services Directory. John Schmittroth, ed., Gale Research Company, Detroit, Mich. 1982 to present (three times a year). New publication giving detailed information on about 1500 abstracts, indexes, digests, serial bibliographies, and catalogs. Title announcement bulletins in all subject areas. Title, publisher, and key word indexes.

Business Index. Information Access Corporation, 1979 to present (monthly, with monthly cumulation). Coverage includes 640 journals, *The Wall Street Journal,* and *The New York Times* Business Section. Arranged by Library of Congress Subject Heading, with some modification. Microfilm, easy-to-read indexing, pre-loaded.

Business Periodicals Index. H. W. Wilson Company, New York, 1958 to present (monthly, except July, with annual cumulation). Cumulative subject index covering accounting, marketing, taxation, industries, trade, finance, and all aspects of business. The primary business periodicals index.

Funk and Scott (F & S) Europe. Predicasts, Inc., Cleveland, Ohio, 1978 to present (monthly, with quarterly and annual cumulations). Indexes articles on business developments and operations in Europe and the Soviet Union. Arranged by Standard Industrial Classification (SIC) number or product, region and country, and company.

Funk and Scott (F & S) Index of Corporations and Industries. Predicasts, Inc., Cleveland, Ohio, 1960 to present (weekly, with monthly and annual cumulations). Covers U.S. company, industry, and product information included in journals, business oriented newspapers, trade magazines, and special reports. Arranged by industry, product and corporate name.

Funk and Scott (F & S) International. Predicasts, Inc., U.S. companies with foreign offices and industry and product information. Arranged by SIC number, region and country, and company.

Journal of Economic Literature (formerly *Journal of Economic Abstracts).* American Economic Association, Nashville, Tenn., 1963 to present (quarterly). Contains review articles, book reviews, annotations of new books, and abstracts of selected journal articles.

Public Affairs Information Service. Public Affairs Information Service, Inc., New York, 1915 to present (biweekly with quarterly and annual cumulations). An index to economic, social, and political affairs covering all types of materials published internationally in English.

Social Sciences Citation Index. Institute for Scientific Information, Philadelphia, 1973 to present (triannually with annual cumulations). A citation index with author, corporate, permuterm subjects (key word index), and source indexes. Allows user to see the association of ideas between author and those that the author cites. Covers over 1000 journals in the social sciences. Useful for studies in economics, organization, and behavioral management.

The Wall Street Journal Index. Dow Jones Books, Inc., Princeton, N.J. 1957 to present (monthly, with annual cumulations). Index to *The Wall Street Journal.*

BUSINESS AND FINANCIAL SERVICES

Business and financial (subscription) services give the latest information on stock prices, developments in industries, current evaluations of companies, and changes in laws and/or their interpretations. Some are published in looseleaf format to allow for constant updating. Many times, the same information is covered by two or more services.

> *Directory of Business and Financial Services*, edited by Mary M. Grant and Norma Coté, 7th ed. Special Libraries Association, New York, 1976. Describes business, economic and financial services issued on a regular basis. Title arrangement with subject and publisher indexes.

> *Federal Taxes.* Prentice-Hall, Englewood Cliffs, N.J. (looseleaf with weekly supplements). Gives complete information about all federal tax laws, regulations, court decisions, and administrative rulings. Also covers tax planning. Comes with supplemental guides.

> *Industry Surveys.* New York: Standard & Poor's Corporation. Gives summaries of industry activities (number of shipments, and so forth), trends, and outlook for future. Useful in case analyses.

> *Investment Companies.* Wiesenberger Services, New York (annual with supplements). Provides information on mutual funds and investment companies. Covers United States and Canada.

> *Labor Relations Reporter.* Bureau of National Affairs, Washington, D.C. (looseleaf with weekly supplements). Very comprehensive. Covers current labor relations, state laws, fair employment practices, wages and hours, and labor arbitration.

> *Moody's Handbook of Common Stocks.* Moody's Investors Service, New York (quarterly). Contains price charts and financial data for over 1000 common stocks.

> *Moody's Manuals.* Moody's Investors Service. New York (six volumes, published annually with semiweekly supplements). Manuals cover United States and Canada and foreign companies listed on U.S. exchanges. Gives company information, including brief history, financial statements and ratios, products, officers, and subsidiaries. Similar to Standard & Poor's *Standard Corporation Records.* Individual titles are as follows:

Moody's Bank and Finance Manual

Moody's Industrial Manual

Moody's Municipal and Government Manual

Moody's OTC Industrial Manual

Moody's Public Utilities Manual

Moody's Transportation Manual

> *Standard Corporation Records.* Standard & Poor's Corporation, New York (looseleaf with bimonthly supplements). Similar to *Moody's Manuals,* but company names are listed alphabetically rather than by type. Covers companies having listed and unlisted securities.

Standard Federal Tax Reports. Commerce Clearing House, Chicago (looseleaf with weekly supplements). Gives complete information about federal tax laws, regulations, court decisions, and administrative rulings. Covers tax planning. Includes supplemental guides.

Value Line Investment Survey. A. Bernhard and Company, New York (looseleaf with weekly supplements). Excellent investment service giving information about stocks. Describes trends in industries as they relate to investors. Gives statistical data on individual companies, such as price-earnings ratios, profit margins, and quarterly sales. Also gives betas, stock price averages, and ratings.

DIRECTORIES

Directories are systematic listings of companies, associations, agencies, organizations, products, or individuals. They may have alphabetical, geographical, or subject arrangements.

Directory of Corporate Affiliations. National Register Publishing Company, Inc., Skokie, Ill. (annually). Contains listings of parent companies and their divisions and subsidiaries. Includes name and geographical indexes.

Dun & Bradstreet's Principal International Businesses. Dun & Bradstreet Corporation, New York (annually). Covers over 50,000 businesses in 133 countries. Lists country, product lines, sales volume, number of employees, chief officers, and address. Has geographical, product classification, and alphabetical access.

Encyclopedia of Associations. Gale Research Company, Detroit, Mich. (annually with periodic supplements). Covers labor unions; public affairs organizations; chambers of commerce; trade, business, and commercial organizations; and scientific, engineering and technical organizations. Includes name, address, divisions, purpose, publications, and trade associations.

Kelly's Manufacturers and Merchants Directory. IPC Business Press Ltd., East Grinstead, West Sussex, England (annually). Lists British and European companies by classified trade, company name, and exporting service.

Million Dollar Directory. Dun & Bradstreet Corporation, New York (annually). Directory of over 120,000 companies with net worth over $500,000. Gives officers, product line, SIC number, approximate sales, and number of employees. Has division index, alphabetical listing of officers, and geographical and industrial indexes.

National Trade and Professional Associations of the United States and Canada and Labor Unions. Columbia Books, Washington, D.C. (annually). Lists 5800 trade and professional associations; has geographic, association, and subject index.

Reference Book. Dun & Bradstreet Corporation, New York (annually). Very comprehensive geographical listing of U.S. and Canadian firms for which estimated financial strength and credit appraisal are given. Also given are SIC number and product line.

Standard & Poor's Register of Corporations, Directors and Executives. Standard & Poor's Corporation, New York (annually). This national "directory of direc-

B

tors" lists corporations, officers, directors, and trustees. Has SIC, geographical, and corporate family indexes.

Standard Directory of Advertisers. National Register Publishing Company, Skokie, Ill. (annually). Guide to over 17,000 corporations. Has geographical and classified indexes. Gives number of employees, basic product line, approximate sales, advertising agency, and type of media and distribution.

Thomas' Register of American Manufacturers and TOMCAT File. Thomas Publishing Company, New York (annually). Comprehensive listing of American manufacturing firms. Lists arranged by specific product and alphabetical name with index to product classification. Also has list of trade names and catalogs of some companies.

United States Government Manual. Office of the Federal Register, General Services Administration, Washington, D.C. (annually). Directory of governmental agencies and key personnel with addresses and telephone numbers.

Industrial and manufacturers' directories for states are published by *McRae's Blue Book Company* and by state chambers of commerce.

BIBLIOGRAPHIES

Bibliographies are publications designed to bring together all material that has been published on a topic or at least the most significant works. They include descriptions and attributes of the publications arranged by subject or author. Some are comprehensive recurring bibliographies, retrospectives, or literature guides. Literature guides include source lists and describe the characteristics of the literature of the field as well; they also include explanations of differences among the types of sources and the information provided.

Brownstone, David M., and Gorton Carruth. *Where to Find Business Information: A Worldwide Guide for Everyone Who Needs the Answers to Business Questions.* New York: John Wiley, 1979. Describes major sources.

Daniells, Lorna. *Business Information Sources.* Berkeley: University of California Press, 1976. Describes major sources in broad areas of business—finance, personnel, and so forth.

Economics Information Guide. Detroit, Mich.: Gale Research. Specific volumes are as follows:
  Vol. 2 *Economics of Minorities: A Guide to Information Sources,* edited by Kenneth Gagala, 1975.
  Vol. 3 *History of Economic Analysis,* edited by William Hutchinson, 1976.
  Vol. 4 *Russian Economic History: A Guide to Information Sources,* edited by Daniel R. Kazmer and Vera Kazmer, 1976.
  Vol. 5 *Transportation Economics: A Guide to Information Sources,* edited by James P. Rakowski, 1976.

Vol. 6 *Economic Education: A Guide to Information Sources,* edited by Catherine A. Hughes, 1977.

Vol. 7 *Health and Medical Economics: A Guide to Information Sources,* edited by Ted J. Ackroyd. 1977.

Vol. 8 *Labor Economics: A Guide to Information Sources,* edited by Ross Azevedo, 1976.

Vol. 9 *Mathematical Economics and Operations Research: A Guide to Information Sources,* edited by Joseph Zaremba, 1977.

Vol. 10 *Money, Banking and Macroeconomics: A Guide to Information Sources,* edited by James M. Rock, 1977.

Fletcher, John, ed. *The Use of Economics Literature.* Hamden, Conn.: Archon Books, 1971. Information source for research and development.

Harvard University, Graduate School of Business Administration, Baker Library. *Business Reference Sources: An Annotated Guide for Harvard Business School Students,* rev. ed. Compiled by Lorna Daniells. Boston: Baker Library, Graduate School of Business Administration, Harvard University, 1979.

Hills, William G., André W. Van Rest, Richard C. Kearney, and Stephen T. Smith. *Administration of Management: A Selected and Annotated Bibliography.* Norman: University of Oklahoma Press, 1975.

International Bibliography of Economics—Bibliographies International de Science Economique. New York: International Committee for Social Sciences Documentation, UNESCO, 1959 to present.

Jablonski, Donna M., ed. *How to Find Information About Companies,* 2nd ed. Washington, D.C.: Washington Researchers, 1982. Excellent guide designed for the practitioner.

Management Information Exchange Business Services and Information: The Guide to the Federal Government. New York: John Wiley, 1978.

Management Information Guide. Detroit, Mich.: Gale Research. Specific guides are as follows:

1. *Real Estate Information Sources,* edited by Janice B. Babb, 1963.
2. *Building Construction Information Sources,* edited by Howard B. Bentley, 1964.
3. *Public Finance Information Sources,* edited by Vera H. Knox, 1964.
4. *Textile Industry Information Sources,* edited by Joseph V. Kopcinski, 1964.
5. *Developing Nations: A Guide to Information Sources,* edited by Eloise Re Qua, 1965.
6. *Standards and Specifications Information Sources,* edited by Erasmus J. Struglia, 1965.
7. *Public Utilities Information Sources,* edited by Florine E. Hunt, 1965.
8. *Transportation Information Sources,* edited by Kenneth M. Metcalf, 1965.
9. *Business Trends and Forecasting Information Sources,* edited by James B. Woy, 1965.
10. *Packing Information Sources,* edited by Gwendolyn Jones, 1967.
11. *Government Regulation of Business Including Antitrust Information Sources,* edited by Beatrice S. McDermott, 1967.

12. Systems and Procedures Including Office Management Information Sources, edited by Chester Morrill, Jr., 1967.

13. *Electronic Industries Information Sources*, edited by Gretchen R. Randle, 1968.

14. *International Business and Foreign Trade*, edited by Lora J. Wheeler, 1968.

15. *Computers and Data Processing Information Sources*, edited by Chester Morrill, Jr., 1969.

16. *Food and Beverage Industries: A Bibliography and Guidebook*, edited by Albert C. Vara, 1970.

17. *Commercial Law Information Sources*, edited by Julius J. Marke, 1970.

18. *Accounting Information Sources*, edited by Rosemary Demarest, 1970.

19. *Investment Information: A Detailed Guide to Selected Sources*, edited by James B. Woy, 1970.

20. *Research in Transportation: Legal, Legislative and Economic Sources and Procedures*, edited by Kenneth U. Flood, 1970.

21. *Ethics in Business Conduct: Selected References from the Record: Problems, Attempted Solutions, Ethics in Business Education*, edited by Portia Christian, 1970.

22. *Public Relations Information Sources*, edited by Alice Norton, 1970.

23. *American Economics and Business History Information Sources*, edited by Robert W. Lovett, 1971.

24. *Insurance Information Sources*, edited by Roy Thomas, 1971.

25. *Communication in Organization: An Annotated Bibliography and Sourcebook*, edited by Robert M. Carter, 1972.

26. *Public and Business Planning in the United States: A Bibliography*, edited by Martha B. Lightwood, 1972.

27. *National Security Affairs: A Guide to Information Sources*, edited by Arthur D. Larson, 1973.

28. *Occupational Safety & Health: A Guide to Information Sources*, edited by Theodore P. Peck, 1974.

29. *Chemical Industries: A Guide to Information Sources*, edited by Theodore P. Peck, 1974.

30. *Purchasing: A Guide to Information Sources*, edited by Douglas C. Basil and others, 1977.

31. *Executive and Management Development for Business and Government: A Source Book*, edited by Agnes O. Hanson, 1976.

32. *Management Principles and Practice: A Guide to Information Sources*, edited by K. G. Bakewell, 1977.

33. *Management and Economics Journals: A Guide to Information Sources*, edited by Vasile Tega, 1977.

34. *Agricultural Enterprises Management in an Urban-Industrial Society: A Guide to Information Sources*, edited by Portia Christian, 1977.

35. *Human Resource Development in the Organization: A Guide to Information Sources*, edited by Jerome L. Franklin, 1978.

Small Business Bibliographies. Washington, D.C.: U.S. Small Business Administration. A series of annotated bibliographies on various aspects of small business management.

The Source Directory. Cleveland, Ohio: Predicasts, Inc., 1973 to present (annually with quarterly supplements).

Wasserman, Paul, and others. *Encyclopedia of Business Information Sources: A Detailed Listing of Primary Subjects of Interest to Managerial Personnel, with a Record Sourcebooks, Periodicals, Organizations, Directories, Handbooks, Bibliographies, and Other Sources of Information on Each Topic,* 4th ed. Detroit, Mich.: Gale Research, 1980.

Woy, James B. *Investment Methods: A Bibliographic Guide.* New York: R. R. Bowker, 1973.

Woy, James B. *Commodity Futures Trading: A Bibliographic Guide.* New York: R. R. Bowker, 1976.

GOVERNMENT DOCUMENTS AND STATISTICS

The federal government is one of the world's largest publishers, spending over $800 million yearly to gather and publish statistical data. Governmental publications range from pamphlets on child care to specialized research treatises. Most libraries have selected governmental publications. However, certain libraries throughout the United States are full or partial depositories for these publications. State, provincial, and local governmental publications also are data sources.

American Statistics Index: A Comprehensive Guide and Index to the Statistical Publications of the United States Government. Washington, D.C.: Congressional Information Service, 1973 to present (annually with supplements).

Andriott, John L. *Guide to United States Government Publications.* McLean, Va.: Documents Index, 1973 to present.

Andriott, John L. *Guide to United States Government Statistics,* 4th ed. McLean, Va.: Documents Index, 1973 to present.

Bureau of the Census Catalog. Washington, D.C.: U.S. Bureau of the Census (annually). The Census Bureau is the largest publisher of federal statistical data. Its catalogs give descriptive lists of publications. The Bureau publishes both census data and projections based on sampling. The following is a partial list of these catalogs:

Census of Agriculture

Census of Construction Industries

Census of Governments

Census of Housing

Census of Manufacturers

Census of Mineral Industries

Census of Population

B

Census of Population and Housing (contains "Census Tract Reports" for each Standard Metropolitan Statistical Area)

Census of Retail Trade

Census of Selected Service Industries

Census of Transportation

Census of Wholesale Trade

Country Business Patterns, annually (good source for local data)

Enterprise Statistics

Checklist of State Publications. Englewood, Colo.: Information Handling Services, 1977 to present.

Congressional Information Service. Washington, D.C.: Congressional Information Service, 1970 to present (annually with supplements).

Economic Report of the President. Washington, D.C.: United States Office of the President (annually). Included with *Annual Report of the Council of Economic Advisers.* Gives state of economy and outlook for future as seen by the president of the United States.

Handbook of Basic Economic Statistics. Washington, D.C.: Economic Statistics Bureau (monthly). Issued by a private research organization. Contains compact compilation of more than 1800 statistical series about all aspects of national economy. Material is selected and condensed from federal governmental sources. Often publishes information before federal government publishes it.

Handbook of Labor Statistics. Washington, D.C.: U.S. Department of Labor (biennially). Compiles major series produced by the Bureau of Labor Statistics into one volume. Covers labor force, employment, unemployment, productivity, compensation, prices and living conditions, earnings/employment by industrial relations, occupational injuries and illnesses, and selected foreign labor statistics.

Index to United States Government Periodicals. Chicago: Infordata International, Inc., 1970 to present (quarterly). Contains many lay and research-oriented periodicals not indexed in major abstracts and indexes.

Monthly Catalog of United States Government Publications. Washington, D.C.: U.S. Superintendent of Documents, 1896 to present (monthly). Index to all governmental publications. Arranged alphabetically by agency with subject and title indexes.

Standard Industrial Classification Manual (SIC). Washington, D.C.: Office of the President, Office of Management and Budget. 1972. The SIC defines industries according to the composition and structure of the economy and covers entire field of economic activity. Used by businesses to classify customers and suppliers. Helps make easier comparison of statistics describing the economy.

Statistical Abstract of the United States. Washington, D.C.: U.S. Bureau of the Census, 1878 to present (annually). Standard summary of statistics on social, political, and economic organization of the United States. Appendix IV has the *Guide to Sources of Statistics* and the *Guide to State Statistical Abstracts.*

Statistical Reference Index. Washington, D.C.: Congressional Information Service, 1980 to present (annually with supplements). Indexes nongovernmental statistics such as those from trade associations.

Survey of Current Business. Washington, D.C.: U.S. Department of Commerce (monthly). Most comprehensive source for current business statistics. Contains business indicators and information on employment and earnings, labor force, finance, foreign trade, commodities, products, and industries. Also contains articles and special statistical reports such as "Corporate Profits" and "Balance of Payments." *Business Statistics* is biennial supplement to this publication; it contains statistics recorded in the monthly issues.

United States Industrial Outlook. Washington, D.C.: U.S. Department of Commerce (annually). Provides economic outlook for five years for over 200 industries. Based on state of economy at time of writing and likely future directions.

Wasserman, Paul. *Statistical Sources,* 7th ed. Detroit, Mich.: Gale Research, 1982.

SUBJECT HANDBOOKS, SUBJECT DICTIONARIES, AND ATLASES

Some other helpful sources for business references are subject handbooks, subject dictionaries, and atlases. Examples of useful subject handbooks are *Handbook of Financial Management* and *Handbook of Marketing Research.* The *Dictionary of Economics and Business* is an excellent subject dictionary. An outstanding atlas is Rand McNally's *Commercial Atlas and Marketing Guide.*

COMPUTER-ASSISTED INFORMATION SERVICES

Much useful information is available today through machine-readable data bases. Some of these data bases are primarily bibliographical, but others contain actual data that can be analyzed for specific purposes. Libraries, companies, information brokers, and some individuals use these services. A fee is usually charged for these services, and they can be expensive.

ABI/Inform. Abstracted Business Information Company, Louisville, Ky. A bibliographical data base service for management, marketing, finance, personnel and other business-related journals.

Compustat. Investors' Management Service, Standard & Poor's Corporation, Denver, Colo. A statistical data base of financial information. Many business schools have these files for use in conducting research projects.

Management Contents. G. D. Searle and Company, Skokie, Ill. (biweekly). Covers 200 business and economics journals. Offers an "on line" computerized database service that many libraries use in searches. Also published in paper format.

B

Predicasts Terminal System. Predicasts, Inc., Cleveland, Ohio. Combined bibliographical and statistical data base covering many Predicast publications, such as the *Funk and Scott (F & S) Index to Corporations and Industries* and *Source Directory.* Excellent for searching current articles and statistics on a particular industry.

Social Sciences Citation Index. Institute of Scientific Information, Philadelphia. A bibliographical data base. Also available in paper format.

APPENDIX C

Standard Bibliographic Citations

Preparing documentation is a part of both primary and secondary research. In primary research, you generate your own data. In secondary research, you gather data prepared elsewhere. Presenting documentation of primary research includes discussing the primary research procedures you used to gather your data. Presenting documentation of secondary research procedures involves giving credit to those who originated the data.

Three standard types of reference citations are footnotes, full citations within the report text, and references to a list of sources. You should select one procedure and use it consistently throughout your report. Also, you might include a bibliography as documentation and to cite sources for further study.

FOOTNOTES

The main purpose of footnotes is to give credit to the source that has supplied data for your report. The data may be ideas, concepts, opinions, or direct quotations, for example. This type is called a *source footnote*. A second purpose for using footnotes is to give details about ideas that might be related indirectly to the topic being discussed. This type is called a *discussion footnote*. You also can use footnotes to refer to related sources or to cross reference other report parts. This type is called a *reference footnote*.

Numbering and Indenting

Number each footnote consecutively with arabic numerals. Generally, the number is raised slightly above the writing line. This raised number is called a superscript. The superscript numbers in the footnotes correspond to those in the report text. Indent the first line of each footnote five spaces, and then start any other lines flush against the left margin. Single space the footnote lines.

Content and Arrangement—Source Footnotes

For source footnotes, usually the footnote includes the name(s) of the author(s) or editor(s), publication title, publication facts, publication date, and page number(s). The publication facts and date are placed in parentheses. Because first-time reference is complete, later references to the source can be shortened. The examples that follow are common types of source footnotes for references made the first time you cite the source in a report.

1. *Book with one author:*

   [1]Sandra E. O'Connell, *The Manager as Communicator* (San Francisco: Harper & Row, 1979), p. 51.

The author's name, book title, publication facts (city of publisher, publisher's name, and publication date), and page number are given in book citations. Do the same thing for handbooks and pamphlets. Also, you may type the book title in all capital letters rather than underline it.

2. *Book with two authors:*

   [2]Ronald L. Applbaum and Karl W. E. Anatol, *Effective Oral Communication for Business and the Professions* (Chicago: Science Research Associates, 1982), pp. 184–185.

3. *Book with three authors:*

   [3]C. W. Wilkinson, Peter B. Clarke, and Dorothy C. M. Wilkinson, *Communicating Through Letters and Reports,* 7th ed. (Homewood, Ill.: Richard D. Irwin, 1980), pp. 135–139.

When a book is in an edition other than the first, you should include the edition number. Also, when the city of the publisher might not be known by the reader, then include the state, which is abbreviated.

4. *Book with four or more authors:*

> [4]Craig E. Aronoff and others, *Getting Your Message Across: A Practical Guide to Business Communication* (St. Paul, Minn.: West Publishing Company, 1981), p. 214.

When a book has a subtitle, you should include it in the footnote. Use a colon or a dash to separate the title from the subtitle. This colon or dash might or might not appear in the actual title of the book. Also, you could use the Latin form "et al." instead of "and others."

5. *Book with no author but with an editor or editors:*

> [5]Kevin J. Harty, ed., *Strategies for Business and Technical Writing* (New York: Harcourt Brace Jovanovich, 1980), pp. 3–4.

Note that this book is a collection of works by various authors but that the reference is to a page not written by one of the authors.

6. *Book with one author identified in a collection of works but with an editor or editors:*

> [6]Vincent Vinci, "Ten Report Writing Pitfalls: How to Avoid Them," in *Strategies For Business and Technical Writing,* Kevin J. Harty, ed. (New York: Harcourt Brace Jovanovich, 1980), pp. 250–253.

Notice that the author's work is placed within quotation marks.

7. *Article in a magazine or journal with author given:*

> [7]Joseph A. Boyd, "A Manager's Guide to Specialized Networks," *Administrative Management,* Vol. 43, No. 5, May 1982, p. 27.

The author's name, article title placed within quotation marks, magazine name, issue volume and number, publication date, and page number are given. Instead of underlining the magazine name, you could type it in capital letters.

8. *Article in a magazine or journal with no author given:*

> [8]"Computers Create Picture-Perfect Graphics," *Modern Office Procedures,* Vol. 27, No. 4, April 1982, pp. 56–57.

9. Article in a newspaper:

> [9]Thomas Petzinger, Jr., "Double Talk Grips Business Reports as Firms Try to Sugarcoat Bad News," *The Wall Street Journal,* March 31, 1982, p. 25.

If you footnote a newspaper that your report audience may not know, then you could put the newspaper's city in parentheses after the title.

10. *Government publication:*

> [10]Library of Congress, *LC Classification Outline*, 3rd ed., (Washington, D.C.: Government Printing Office, 1975), pp. 7–9.

Notice that the name of the governmental body is placed in the author's position.

11. *Unpublished material:*

> [11]Andrew H. Barnett, "Communication in Auditing: An Examination of Investors' Understanding of the Auditor's Report," Unpublished D.B.A. dissertation, Texas Tech University, 1976, pp. 51–54.

12. *Interview:*

> [12]Personal interview with John Sampson, Controller, Babon Manufacturing Company, Las Vegas, Nevada, June 21, 1982.

An interview is the only primary research source that you would include in a footnote.

Content and Arrangement—Discussion and Reference Footnotes

A discussion footnote explains an idea in complete sentences. The following is an example:

> [1]Although the LIFO and FIFO methods of inventory evaluation are used in this analysis, other methods, such as weighted average and specific invoice, could be used as well.

A reference footnote can refer to related sources or cross-reference another report part. A related source reference footnote follows:

> [2]For an additional discussion of inventory procedures, see Glenn A. Welsch and Robert N. Anthony, *Fundamentals of Financial Accounting*, rev. ed. (Homewood, Ill.: Richard D. Irwin, 1977), pp. 259–279.

A cross reference footnote is the following:

> [3]See Table 5, "Perceptions of Real Estate Brokers Regarding the Impact of High Interest Rates in the Housing Market," p. 15.

Short Forms of Source Footnotes

You might need to footnote a particular source more than once in a report. After you present the complete citation in the first footnote, you can shorten later references. Two ways to do this are to use either traditional Latin abbreviations or author's name and page number.

If using the traditional Latin abbreviations, you would use abbreviations as shown in the three following situations:

1. *Ibid.* Ibid. is an abbreviation for *ibidem*, meaning "in the same place." You would use this term when you wish to reference the immediately preceding footnote. If you want to reference the same page as did the preceding footnote, then just use the word Ibid. If you wish to reference a different page, then you would use Ibid. and the page number(s). Examples of these are as follows:

> [1]Paul R. Timm, *Managerial Communication: A Finger on the Pulse* (Englewood Cliffs, N.J.: Prentice-Hall, 1980) p. 201.
> [2]Ibid.
> [3]Ibid., pp. 205–206.

2. *Op. cit.* Op. cit. is an abbreviation for *opere citato*, which means "in the work cited." Use this term when you want to refer to a previous source in cases where there has been another footnote(s) since you first footnoted this one. The author's last name precedes op. cit.; then the page number(s) follows. Continuing with the previous example, op. cit. is used as follows:

> [4]Delmar Fisher, *Communication in Organizations* (St. Paul, Minn.: West Publishing Company, 1981), p. 285.
> [5]Timm, op. cit., p. 202.

3. *Loc. cit.* Loc. cit. is an abbreviation for *loco citato*, which means "in the place cited." You would use this term only to refer to the same page of a previous footnote. The author's last name precedes the term. Again continuing with the previous example, loc. cit. is used as follows:

> [6]Timm, loc. cit.

When using these abbreviations in documenting information, you can either italicize them (in typing use an underscore) or not.

Abbreviating Latin terms can be confusing. Therefore, another way to cite later references is to use the author's last name and page number(s). Here is an example using the same six citations that were used to illustrate Latin abbreviations.

[1]Paul R. Timm, *Managerial Communication: A Finger on the Pulse* (Englewood Cliffs. N.J.: Prentice-Hall, 1980), p. 201.
[2]Timm, p. 201.
[3]Timm, pp. 205–206.
[4]Delmar Fisher, *Communication in Organizations* (St. Paul, Minn.: West Publishing Company, 1981), p. 285.
[5]Timm, p. 202.
[6]Timm, p. 202.

Placement of Footnotes

Place footnotes at the bottom of the same page where the superscript numbers appear in the report text. Once the reader sees the superscript number in the report, he or she can look at the bottom of the page for the source citation. Use a $1\frac{1}{2}$-inch horizontal line begun at the left margin to separate the footnote entries from the report text. Indent the first line of each footnote five spaces and type the remaining lines flush against the left margin. Use single spacing but leave one blank line between footnotes. The following excerpt from a report shows the placement of the footnotes:

> The importance of identifying communication barriers or breakdowns within an organization is beginning to focus. Rogers stated that, by the year 2000, organizations will be "giving as much attention to the quality of interpersonal relationships and the quality of communication as they currently do to the technological aspects of their business."[3] Rogers went on to say that organizations "will pay more attention to breakdowns in personal communication that to breakdowns of the circuitry in their computer."[4]

-----

[3]Carl R. Rogers, "Interpersonal Relationships: U.S.A. 2000," in *Psychosocial Dynamics of Effective Behavior,* Harold W. Bernard and Wesley C. Huckins, eds. (Boston: Holbrook Press, 1971), p. 586.
[4]Rogers, p. 586.

Some report writers place the footnotes on one or more pages at the end of the report. Type these footnotes in the same order as they appear in the report text and entitle them *endnotes.*

Placement of Long, Direct Quotations

Short, direct quotations, paraphrases, and summaries are placed directly in the text of the report without using any special indentions. However, when a direct quotation is four or more lines long, the quotation should be set out from the text, indented five spaces on both sides, and single spaced. The following report excerpt is an example of this situation:

... define what it is expected to do. Thompson stated,

A business should buy equipment that can be expanded easily with new programming features as they become available. Any equipment purchased must be compatible with other manufacturers' equipment already owned.

In addition, the servicing of the equipment should be considered ...

FULL CITATIONS WITHIN REPORT TEXT

Another procedure for acknowledging the source is to enclose the complete citation within parentheses at the point you make reference to the source in your report. For example, consider the following illustrations of this procedure:

One objective of office systems planning, according to Mark A. Lieberman, Gad J. Selig, and John J. Walsh [*Office Automation: A Manager's Guide for Improved Productivity* (New York: John Wiley & Sons, Inc., 1982), p. 37], is "to integrate the functional areas of information systems, telecommunications, and office technology within the organization."

Lou Pilla ("New Directions in Telecommunications," *Management World,* Vol. 11, No. 3, March 1982, p. 12) noted that "advances in communications technologies now allow computer systems to transmit greater quantities of information, faster, to more locations."

REFERENCES TO A LIST OF SOURCES

A third procedure for acknowledging a source is to insert a key number and page number(s) in parentheses where the reference to the source appears in the report text. The key number will refer the reader to a numbered list of sources at the end of the report. Arrange this list in alphabetical order by author's last name or in the order the references appear in the report text. The page number(s) identifies the specific page(s) location of the original source. A colon generally separates the key number and page number(s). An example of this procedure follows:

One objective of office systems planning, according to Lieberman, Selig, and Walsh, is "to integrate the functional areas of information systems, telecommunications, and office technology within the organization" (1:37).

Pilla noted that "advances in communications technologies now allow computer systems to transmit greater quantities of information, faster, to more locations" (2:12).

List of Sources (at end of report)
1. Mark A. Lieberman, Gad J. Selig, and John J. Walsh, *Office Automation: A Manager's Guide for Improved Productivity* (New York: John Wiley & Sons, Inc., 1982).
2. Lou Pilla, "New Directions in Telecommunications," *Management World*, Vol. 11, No. 3, March 1982, pp. 11–12.

BIBLIOGRAPHY

The bibliography lists the sources you used or consulted during the entire report process. Very often, you might compile a tentative bibliography of sources about a particular topic during the report planning phase. Then you might add sources as you gather additional data.

Placement and Indention

The bibliography is a supplemental part of the report that is placed at the end. Place the first line of each bibliographical entry flush against the left margin. Indent the second and other lines five spaces. Remember to single space the lines and leave one blank line between entries.

Content and Arrangement

The content of the bibliography is similar to those of footnotes and other references. The last name is presented first, followed by the first and middle name or initials. Periods instead of commas separate the various sections of the entry. Also, include the total number of pages in the periodical citations rather than the specific page number(s) cited in footnotes. However, do not give page numbers for books and other sources.

You could type the word *bibliography* in capital letters as the main heading of this list. The sources that follow the heading could be organized in one of two ways. First, the entire bibliography could be presented in alphabetical order based on the author's last name. Second, the bibliography could be organized into categories of books, periodicals, and miscellaneous sources. Within each category, however, the sources should be alphabetized. An example of an entire bibliography in alphabetical order is shown in Figure C-1. The 12 sources used in this example are the same sources shown as source footnotes earlier in the appendix.

BIBLIOGRAPHY

← ———————— (2 blank lines)

Single spaced { Applbaum, Ronald L. and Karl W. E. Anatol. *Effective Oral Communication for Business and The Professions*. Chicago: Science Research Associates, 1982.

← ———————— (1 blank line)

Aronoff, Craig E., Otis W. Baskin, Robert W. Hays, and Harold E. Davis. *Getting Your Message Across: A Practical Guide to Business Communication*. St. Paul, Minn.: West Publishing Company, 1981.

Barnett, Andrew H. "Communication in Auditing: An Examination of Investors' Understanding of the Auditor's Report." Unpublished D.B.A. dissertation, Texas Tech University, 1976.

Boyd, Joseph A. "A Manager's Guide to Specialized Networks." *Administrative Management,* Vol. 43, No. 5, May 1982, pp. 26–28, 50, 54, 56.

"Computers Create Picture-Perfect Graphics." *Modern Office Procedures,* Vol. 27, No. 4, April 1982, pp. 56–58.

Harty, Kevin J., ed. *Strategies for Business and Technical Writing.* New York: Harcourt Brace Jovanovich, 1980.

Library of Congress. *LC Classification Outline,* 3rd ed. Washington, D.C.: Government Printing Office, 1975.

O'Connell, Sandra E. *The Manager as Communicator.* San Francisco: Harper & Row, 1979.

Petzinger, Thomas, Jr. "Double Talk Grips Business Reports as Firms Try to Sugarcoat Bad News." *The Wall Street Journal,* March 31, 1982, p. 25.

Sampson, John, controller. Babon Manufacturing Company, Las Vegas, Nevada. Personal interview, June 21, 1982.

Vinci, Vincent. "Ten Report Writing Pitfalls: How to Avoid Them." In *Strategies for Business and Technical Writing.* Keven J. Harty, ed. New York: Harcourt Brace Jovanovich, 1980, pp. 249–255.

Wilkinson, C. W., Peter B. Clarke, and Dorothy C. M. Wilkinson. *Communicating Through Letters and Reports,* 7th ed. Homewood, Ill.: Richard D. Irwin, 1980.

Indented 5 spaces

C

FIGURE C-1 A bibliography.

Annotated Bibliography

An annotated bibliography includes a brief overview or summary of the contents of a bibliographical entry in addition to the basic citation. Usually, the first line of the annotation is indented five spaces, and the lines are single spaced. An example of an annotated bibliographical entry is as follows:

> Ferguson, Stewart and Sherry Devereaux Ferguson, eds. *Intercom: Readings in Organizational Communication.* Rochelle Park, N.J.: Hayden Book Company, 1980.
>
> This book contains 39 articles dealing with various organizational communication areas, such as interviewing, conferencing, small-group decision making, problem solving, and managing conflict.

APPENDIX D

Correspondence Format and Layout

You should use a standard layout for letters mailed outside the company and for memorandums routed within the company. Using a standard layout helps in two ways. First, the reader will recognize the layout and will be able to follow it easily and quickly. Second, employers can hold down costs by standardizing their systems for handling correspondence. The layout and format of letters involves letter parts, salutations and complimentary closes, letter styles, punctuation styles, margins, and addressing procedures. The layout of memorandums involves memorandum parts, styles, margins, and addressing procedures.

LETTERS

Letters have both *major* and *minor* parts. Major parts are those you would normally include in any letter. Minor parts are those you include as needed or preferred. Descriptions of letter parts follow.

Major Letter Parts

The major parts of letters described in the order that they appear in the typewritten copies are as follows:

Letterhead (Writer's Return Address)

The letterhead includes the company name, address, and zip code. It may contain the company logo, slogan, or telephone number as well.

Dateline

Type the complete date in one of these three ways: June 19, 1983; 19 June 1983; or 1983 06 19. The third method is called the *international standard.*

Inside Address (Receiver's Address)

Include the name and title; department, branch, or division; company name; street number and name; city; state or province abbreviation; and zip code.

Salutation

Use a greeting such as "Dear Mr. Jax" to introduce the message.

Message

Include the entire body. (If you include a postscript, then that too is part of the message even though a postscript is a minor letter part.)

Complimentary Close

Close the message with a statement such as "Sincerely yours."

Signature Block

Include both signed and typed signatures and the position the writer holds in the company.

Reference Initials

Include the typist's initials. You may also include a code number when a letter is typed on word/information processing equipment.

    The major letter parts appear in Figures D-1, D-2, D-3, and D-4. Notice that both the salutation and complimentary close are omitted when using the simplified letter style shown in Figure D-4.

Minor Letter Parts

Minor letter parts appear in some letters but not in others. Use them *when needed.* For example, if you enclose materials with a letter, include an enclosure notation in the letter. You may sometimes use minor parts *when preferred.* An example is the use of a subject line. The minor parts of a letter in the order in which they should appear are as follows:

Attention Line

Use an attention line to name the person (or perhaps the position) to whose attention you are calling the message. Do this in cases where the letter itself is addressed to a company or a division within a company.

Subject Line

The subject line names the letter topic. If you prefer, you may place the subject line before the salutation rather than after it.

Company Name

Use the company name in the signature block whenever the writer prefers to sign the letter directly under the company name or when the employer requires it.

Enclosure Notation

Use an enclosure notation to denote that you included some other material with a letter. Whenever more than one enclosure is included, write either the number or names of the enclosures.

Copy Distribution Notation

Use a copy distribution notation to name those people who will receive a copy of the letter. Use one of these three methods: "c: Julia Jones" or "cc: Julia Jones" or "pc: Julia Jones." (Use of the colon is optional.) The letter "c" represents *copy;* the letters "cc," carbon copy; and the letters "pc," photocopy. Do not denote file copies.

Blind Copy Distribution Notation

Use the blind copy notation instead of the copy distribution notation whenever copies are sent to others without the knowledge of the person receiving the original letter. Now and then, you may send both copies and blind copies. Remember not to put the blind copy notation on the original. As with the copy distribution notations, choose one of these methods: "bc: Julia Jones" or "bcc: Julia Jones" or "bpc: Julia Jones." (Use of the colon is optional.)

Postscript

Use a postscript to add comments at the end of the letter. A postscript might contain an idea that you wish to emphasize by placing it at the bottom of the letter.

Additional Page Notation

Use an additional page notation at the top of each page other than the first page of the letter. Include the name of the person receiving the letter, the page number, and the date.

Examples of all minor letter parts appear in Figures D-1, D-2, D-3, and D-4.

Salutations and Complimentary Closes

You may choose your own salutations and complimentary closes or use those designated by your employer. When addressing a firm, you may use the word *Gentlemen* or the nonsexist terms *Ladies and Gentlemen, Gentlemen and Ladies, Dear Madam or Sir,* or *Dear Sir or Madam.* When using the simplified letter style shown in Figure D-4, omit both the salutation and the complimentary close.

Here is a list of commonly used salutations arranged in order of decreasing formality:

Sir

My dear Sir

Dear Sir

My dear Mr. Victors

Dear Mr. Victors

My dear George

Dear George

The formality of the complimentary close in a letter should agree generally with that of the salutation. Here is a list of commonly used complimentary closes arranged in order of decreasing formality:

Yours respectfully

Very respectfully yours

Respectfully yours

Yours truly

Very truly yours

Yours very truly

Sincerely yours

Sincerely

Cordially yours

Cordially

Letter and Punctuation Styles

The major standard letter styles are *block, modified block with blocked paragraphs, modified block with indented paragraphs,* and *simplified.* Punctuation styles are *open* and *mixed.* Descriptions of these letter and punctuation styles follow.

Block Letter Style

When using block style, begin all lines of the letter on the left margin. A letter arranged in this format is balanced visually toward the left side of the page. Block format letters can be typed in less time than either of the modified block styles. A sample block letter style with vertical spacing cues is shown in Figure D-1.

Modified Block with Blocked Paragraphs Letter Style

When using the modified block with blocked paragraphs style, begin the dateline, complimentary close, and each line of the signature block at the horizontal center of the page. Begin all other lines on the left margin. A letter arranged in this format is balanced visually toward the center of the page. A sample modified block with blocked paragraphs letter style with an additional vertical spacing cue is shown in Figure D-2.

Modified Block with Indented Paragraphs Letter Style

When using the modified block with indented paragraphs style, begin the dateline, complimentary close, and each line of the signature block at the horizontal center of the page. Indent the first line of each paragraph in the message (usually five spaces). Begin all other lines of the letter on the left margin. A letter arranged in this format is balanced visually toward the center of the page. A sample modified block with indented paragraphs letter style with additional vertical spacing cues is shown in Figure D-3.

Simplified Letter Style

When using the simplified letter style, begin all lines on the left margin. This style contains no salutation or complimentary close. A subject line is placed in capital letters where the salutation is placed in the other letter styles. Place the writer's name and position in capital letters below the last line of the body. A letter typed in this style is balanced visually toward the left side of the page. A sample simplified letter style with additional vertical spacing cues is shown in Figure D-4.

3415 Holton Boulevard
Hyattsville, MD 23161
↕ (1 blank line)
December 5, 19--

↕ (3 to 6 blank lines)

Sales Department
Finest Goods Department Stores
4123 Northampton Way
Arlington, VA 21146
↕ (1 blank line)
Attention Ms. Jane Ciccariaco
↕ (1 blank line)
Ladies and Gentlemen
↕ (1 blank line)
Please replace the Model Number 64 Sunrise electric toaster
I bought on October 2 at Finest Goods' Laburnum Avenue
store.
↕ (1 blank line)
The drop lever broke on the toaster after one month's use.
A copy of the one-year guarantee which defines the terms
of our agreement is enclosed. Also, the broken toaster
will arrive tomorrow by Speedy Delivery Service.
↕ (1 blank line)
Your Sunrise brand toaster has been a joy to use because it
browns evenly every time. Can you please deliver the
replacement within two weeks as I am now having to make
toast in the oven.
↕ (1 blank line)
Yours sincerely

Henry Becker III ↕ (3 blank lines)

Henry Becker III
↕ (1 blank line)
sw
↕ (1 blank line)
Enclosure
↕ (1 blank line)
P.S. Will you please send me a copy of your new summer
      catalog.

(leave at least 6 blank lines at bottom)

FIGURE D-1 Letter typed in block style with open punctuation. (Includes these
minor letter parts: attention line, enclosure notation, and postscript.)

BETA SPORTSWEAR COMPANY

1891 RAINBOW CIRCLE / PHILADELPHIA, PA 10245
Telephone: (215) 542-6125

15 March 19--

Miss Celia Bonevac
Credit Supervisor
Ace Wholesale Sporting Goods
11897 Lackawanna Avenue
Erie, PA   11302

Dear Miss Bonevac:

Subject: Request for Credit Information

Please send us credit information on Alpine Sporting Goods
Company. The firm applied for credit with us and gave your
company as a credit reference.

Mr. Jose F. Rodriguez of Alpine asked that the company be
allowed to charge $1,000 monthly on open account for goods
purchased from us. Because this is their first such
application with us, we shall appreciate as much information as you can give us.

Alpine requested that the first order be shipped by
April 10. So that this request can be met, can you complete and return the attached credit information form to
us by April 5?

                                   Yours truly,

                                   BETA SPORTSWEAR COMPANY

                                   John M. Bentley, Jr.

                                   John M. Bentley, Jr.
                                   Credit Supervisor

som
  ↕ (1 blank line)
bc: Janice Loxley, Sales Department

FIGURE D-2 Letter typed in modified block style with blocked paragraphs and
mixed punctuation. (Includes these minor letter parts: subject line, company
name, and blind copy distribution notation. Note: The blind copy distribution
notation does not appear on the original.)

WEYGANDT HOME FOR CHILDREN

52888 BROADWAY STREET
LUBBOCK, TX 77523

December 5, 19--

Mrs. Joyce Xavier
888 Madison Street
Lubbock, TX   77532

Dear Mrs. Xavier:

Helping children grow up happily can be a joyful experience.

When a young child smiles at you or calls your name, it makes you feel special.

Feeling special to someone else is something that all of us can appreciate, especially when that someone is a child.

How many times have you thrown away your children's clothing thinking it a waste that they outgrew them before they wore them out? Here at the Weygandt Home, our children's needs are basically provided for through generous donations by the citizens of Lubbock. But right now, some of them do need warm clothes for the winter.

You can help in a special way by donating some of the used clothing (sizes 3-12) that your children have outgrown. We especially need overcoats, gloves or mittens, and pants and skirts. The clothes that your children outgrew last year would serve our children well this year.

Donations to the home are tax deductible and receipts will be provided. But these donations will provide more than tax deductions. They provide an opportunity to feel the warmth that comes from being special in a child's world.

We will gladly pick up your donations any weekday between 9 a.m. and 5 p.m. If you prefer, you are welcome

FIGURE D-3 Modified block letter style with indented paragraphs and mixed punctuation. (Includes an additional page notation. If you prefer, block the additional page notation on three lines flush with the left margin. Also includes a filing code number with the reference initials.)

(6 blank lines)

Mrs. Joyce Xavier   2   December 5, 19--

(2 blank lines)

to bring them to the home at 18 Cross Lane and meet the
children while you're here. Please call us at 732-6570
before November 5, the closing date of the appeal.

                              Sincerely yours,

                              Robert E. Carter

                              Robert E. Carter
                              Director

pjs: S1/Z03

D

457

ACE WHOLESALE SPORTING GOODS
11897 Lackawanna Avenue
Erie, PA 11302

THE "ACE" IN SPORTING GOODS SINCE 1928

December 5, 19--

Mr. John M. Bentley, Jr.
Credit Supervisor
Beta Sportswear Company
1891 Rainbow Circle
Philadelphia, PA 10245

↕ (2 blank lines)

CREDIT INFORMATION

↕ (2 blank lines)

As the enclosed credit information form shows, Alpine
Sporting Goods Company has our highest recommendation for
credit purchases from your firm.

Alpine always pays us on time. Also, they seem eager to
maintain a sound business relationship with us. Therefore,
we think you will enjoy doing business with them.

Just write or call us at 843-0098 when we can supply you
with credit information again.

Celia Bonevac ↕ (3 to 4 blank lines)

MISS CELIA BONEVAC, CREDIT SUPERVISOR

tsm

Enclosures: Credit information form
             Business card
             ↕ (1 blank line)
pc Prince Hawley, Sales Department

FIGURE D-4 Simplified letter style. (Includes these minor letter parts: multiple
enclosures notation and copy distribution notation.)

Open Punctuation Style

The open punctuation style includes no punctuation after the salutation and complimentary close. A sample of open punctuation style is shown in Figure D-1.

Mixed Punctuation Style

The mixed punctuation style includes a colon after the salutation and a comma after the complimentary close. Samples of the use of mixed punctuation style are shown in Figures D-2 and D-3.

Letter Margins

For eye appeal, you should frame letters in white space (margins). The letterhead appears in the top margin of most business letters. However, when typing a letter on a blank page, leave a 1- to $1\frac{1}{2}$-inch top margin. The width of the side margins depends on the length of the letter, but they should be at least 1 inch. The bottom margin should be at least 1 inch.

Many companies use a standard length horizontal writing line for all letters. When this is done, the side margins are predetermined. This practice has increased with the increased use of word/information processing equipment to produce letters.

Letter and Envelope Addressing Procedures

You should typewrite business envelopes to get the fastest delivery service for mail sent through the federal government's postal service. The postal services of most industrialized countries use machines called optical character recognition readers to "read" addresses on envelopes automatically. The mail then is sorted automatically for routing. Use a two-letter state or province abbreviation and a zip code in both the mailing address and the return address on an envelope. (A list of two-letter abbreviations for the United States and Canada is given in Figure D-5. An explanation of the standard five-digit zip codes used in the United States is shown in Figure D-6, and the new nine-digit zip codes—zip + 4—are explained in Figure D-7.) Use the same information in the letter address that you use on the envelope.

Letter Addresses

The return address in a letter usually is printed on a letterhead. This address probably will contain a two-letter state or province abbreviation

Two-Letter Mailing Abbreviations for the United States and Canada

State	United States Abbreviation	State	Abbreviation
Alabama	AL	Montana	MT
Alaska	AK	Nebraska	NE
Arizona	AZ	Nevada	NV
Arkansas	AR	New Hampshire	NH
California	CA	New Jersey	NJ
Colorado	CO	New Mexico	NM
Connecticut	CT	New York	NY
Delaware	DE	North Carolina	NC
District of Columbia	DC	North Dakota	ND
Florida	FL	Ohio	OH
Georgia	GA	Oklahoma	OK
Guam	GU	Oregon	OR
Hawaii	HI	Pennsylvania	PA
Idaho	ID	Puerto Rico	PR
Illinois	IL	Rhode Island	RI
Indiana	IN	South Carolina	SC
Iowa	IA	South Dakota	SD
Kansas	KS	Tennessee	TN
Kentucky	KY	Texas	TX
Louisiana	LA	Utah	UT
Maine	ME	Vermont	VT
Maryland	MD	Virginia	VA
Massachusetts	MA	Virgin Islands	VI
Michigan	MI	Washington	WA
Minnesota	MN	West Virginia	WV
Mississippi	MS	Wisconsin	WI
Missouri	MO	Wyoming	WY

Province	Canada Abbreviation	Province	Abbreviation
British Columbia	BC	Nova Scotia	NS
Labrador	LB	Ontario	ON
Manitoba	MB	Prince Edward Island	PE
New Brunswick	NB	Quebec	PQ
Newfoundland	NF	Saskatchewan	SK
Northwest Territories	NT	Yukon Territory	YT

FIGURE D-5 Two-letter mailing abbreviations for United States and Canada.

and a zip code. Examples of how these letterhead addresses look are shown in Figures D-2, D-3, and D-4. Examples of return addresses as typed on a blank page (without letterhead) are shown in Figure D-1 and as follows:

Scott Swallenberg
4213 Massen Lane
Springfield, MO 60112

Examples of how to typewrite the address (inside or reader's address) in a letter are shown in Figures D-1, D-2, D-3, and D-4.

HOW ZIP CODE® WORKS

ZIP Code is a 5-digit geographic code that identifies areas within the United States and its territories for purposes of simplifying the distribution of mail by the U.S. Postal Service. It should appear on the last line of both the destination and return addresses of mail, following the name of the city and State. The ZIP Code alignments do not necessarily adhere to boundaries of cities, counties, States, or other jurisdictions. The following example illustrates how 5-digit ZIP Codes are formulated and what the significance of each digit is:

ZIP CODE NATIONAL AREAS

The first digit of a ZIP Code divides the country into 10 large groups of States numbered from 0 in the Northeast to 9 in the Far West.

EXAMPLE

■ SCF
● LARGE CITY
○ POST OFFICE

Within these areas, each State is divided into an average of 10 smaller geographic areas, identified by the 2nd and 3rd digits of the ZIP Code.

WHAT YOUR ZIP CODE MEANS

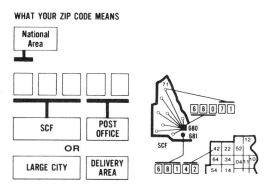

The last 2 digits identify a local delivery area.

FIGURE D-6 Explanation of five-digit Zip Codes. (From *Louisiana Zip Code Directory,* United States Postal Service, August 1979, p. 3.)

Envelope Addresses

The two standard types of business envelopes are Number 6 ¾ (small envelope) and Number 10 (large envelope). The United States Postal Service suggests that the mailing address on an envelope be typed in

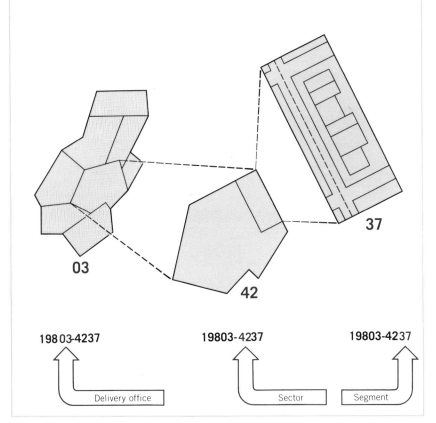

What the new numbers mean

The first five numbers of the ZIP + 4 code will be the same as your present ZIP Code. These numbers are followed by a hyphen and four new numbers. The first two of the new numbers will identify a specific sector of a delivery zone which may consist of several blocks, a group of streets, large buildings or a small geographic area. The last two numbers divide sectors into even smaller areas called segments: one side of a city block or both sides of a particular street, one floor in a large building, specific departments within a firm, a cluster of mailboxes, sections of post office boxes, or other similar geographic groupings.

FIGURE D-7 Explanation of nine-digit Zip Codes (Zip + 4). (From *Zip + 4: What's in It for Business Mailers,* United States Postal Service, Notice 186, January 1982.)

capital letters and without punctuation, but this practice is not yet widely used. Examples of how to address both small and large envelopes are shown in Figure D-8. Notice that the mailing address on the small envelope is shown as recommended by the Postal Service. Also, note that placement notations are given in both examples.

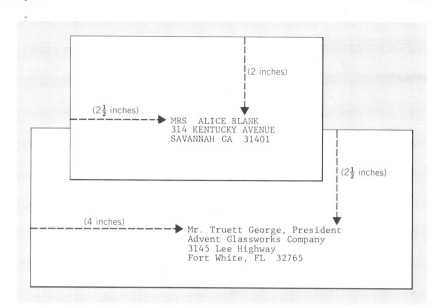

FIGURE D-8 Mailing addresses on small (above) and large (below) envelopes.

MEMORANDUMS

Typewritten memorandums have standard parts just as letters do. In fact, some memorandum parts serve the same function as they do in letters. Addressing memorandums is somewhat different from addressing letters, however.

Memorandum Parts

Memorandums have both *major* and *minor* parts. Major parts are those you would normally include in any memorandum. Minor parts are those you include as needed or preferred. Memorandums also have a *heading* section and a *body* section.

Memorandum Heading Section

The following are the parts of the heading section of a memorandum. All those listed are major parts in a typewritten memorandum.

Memorandum Heading   The memorandum heading includes the company name and may include the company logo and slogan as well.

To   Type the name and position of the person who is to receive the memorandum after the word *To.*

From   Type the name and position of the writer after the word *From.*

Date   Type the complete date after the word *Date* in one of these three ways: December 5, 1983 or 5 December 1983 or 1983 12 05. The third method is called the *international standard.*

File or Reference Number   Type a file or reference number whenever you assign a number for filing or cross referencing.

Subject   Type the title of the topic discussed in the message of the memorandum after the word *Subject.*

Memorandum Body Section

The following are the parts of the body section of a memorandum. Major and minor parts are noted.

Message (major part)   The message is the discussion of the topic of the memorandum.

Signature Block (minor part)   Include a signature block only if you wish to sign the memorandum and do not wish to sign or initial it beside the writer's typed name in the heading section.

Reference Initials (major part)   Include the typist's initials. You may also include a code number when typing a memorandum on word/information processing equipment; when doing this, do not include a file or reference number in the heading section.

Enclosure Notation (minor part)   Use the enclosure notation to show that you included some other material with the memorandum. Whenever you include more than one enclosure, type either the number or the names of the enclosures after the word *Enclosures.*

Copy Distribution Notation (minor part)   Use the copy distribution notation to name those people who will receive a copy of the memorandum. As in letters, you may use the notations *c* (copy), *cc* (carbon copy), or *pc* (photocopy). You also may use the word *Distribution.*

Postscript (minor part)   Use a postscript to add comments at the end of the memorandum. A postscript might contain an idea that you want to emphasize.

Additional Page Notation (minor part)   Use an additional page notation at the top of each page of a memorandum other than the first page. Include the name of the person receiving the memorandum, the page number, and the date.

Examples of all memorandum heading and body section parts except the additional page notation are shown either in Figure D-9 or D-10. The additional page notation is typed like the one in the letter shown in Figure D-3.

Memorandum Styles

Memorandum styles are not as standardized in business practice today as are letter styles. However, to improve efficiency and cut costs, adopt a style and use it consistently. Two popular styles that are easy to use are *blocked* and *modified blocked.*

Block Memorandum Style
When using the block style, align all parts of the heading section on the left margin except the memorandum heading. The memorandum heading usually is printed on the page, and often the names of the other heading section parts are too *(To, From, Date, File, Subject).* All lines of the body section begin at the left margin. A sample block memorandum is shown in Figure D-9, including vertical spacing cues.

Modified Block Memorandum Style
When using the modified block style, align the *To* and *From* entries of the heading section on the left margin. Then, begin the *Date, File* (if included), and *Subject* entries at the horizontal center. The memorandum heading usually is printed on the page, and often the names of the other heading section parts are too. All lines of the body section begin at the left margin except the signature block, which begins at the horizontal center. A sample modified blocked memorandum is shown in Figure D-10.

Memorandum Margins

Often the memorandum heading will be printed at the top of the page. When this is done, the top margin is fixed before you begin to type the memorandum. When typing a memorandum on a blank page, however, type the word *memorandum* in capital letters centered horizontally 1 to $1\frac{1}{2}$ inches from the top of the page. When a standard writing line length

To: J. Stuart Laws
      Corporate Legal Counselor
        ↕ (1 blank line)
From: Amanda R. Loos *ARL*
        Personnel Assistant
        ↕ (1 blank line)
Date: August 4, 19--
        ↕ (1 blank line)
Subject: Preparation of Equal Employment Opportunity Report
        ↕ (2 blank lines)
Will you please help me prepare the state requirements
section of our annual equal employment opportunity report?
        ↕ (1 blank line)
As a result of changes in the state legal code this year,
we must meet additional requirements. Therefore, I need
your legal assistance in preparing Section 6 of the report.

This will take only about 15 minutes of your time. I can
meet you any day this week or next, whatever suits you
best. The report must be mailed to the Equal Employment
Opportunity Commission within three weeks.
        ↕ (1 blank line)
st
        ↕ (1 blank line)
Enclosure: Copy of Section 6 of EEO Guidelines
        ↕ (1 blank line)
cc Tibbet Arns, Legal Assistant

FIGURE D-9 Memorandum in block style. (Includes these minor parts: enclosure
notation and copy distribution notation.)

To: Amanda R. Loos   Date: August 5, 19--
      Personnel Assistant   ↕ (1 blank line)
                                 File: CX 11.21
From: J. Stuart Laws   ↕ (1 blank line)
        Legal Counselor   Subject: Meeting for Equal
                                            Employment Oppor-
                                            tunity Report
                                            Preparation

Let's meet in my office (Suite 245) this Friday at 10:30
a.m. to complete Section 6 of your annual equal employment
opportunity report.

This year, you will need to report how you advertised
available jobs to minority races. Also, you will need to
report the procedure you followed to assure that an applicant's place of residency was disregarded in hiring practices. Please bring this information with you to the
meeting in addition to information that you normally
include in this section of the report.

I look forward to meeting with you on Friday, Amanda.

                                    ↑ (3 to 4 blank lines)

                          J. Stuart Laws

tc
 ↕ (1 blank line)
P.S.   Thanks for sending the copy of Section 6 of the EEO
       Guidelines.

FIGURE D-10 Memorandum in modified block style. (Includes these minor parts:
signature block and postscript.)

467

is used throughout a company, the side margins are predetermined. Be sure to leave at least 1-inch side margins, however. The use of standard writing lines for memorandums has increased with the increased use of word/information processing equipment to produce memorandums.

Leave at least a 1-inch bottom margin for memorandums. When a memorandum is short and several inches of blank space are left at the bottom of the page, just leave the space blank.

Addressing Memorandums

The two most common ways that memorandums are packaged for routing are to place them in either a letter envelope or a reusable manila or paper envelope. When using a letter envelope, type the words *Interoffice Correspondence* or *Interoffice Mail* across the space where a stamp is placed usually. Type the sender's name in the upper left corner and the receiver's name and location where the letter address normally is placed.

When routing a memorandum in a reusable envelope, draw a line through the last name on the envelope and type or write the name of the receiver on the next available line. Sample letter and reusable envelopes are shown in Figure D-11.

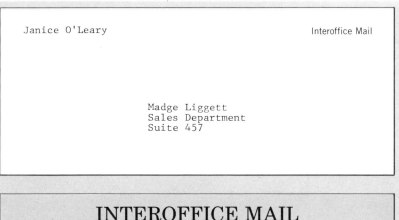

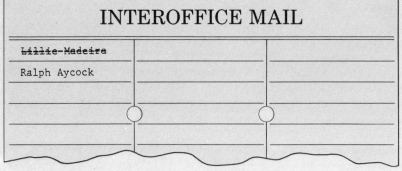

FIGURE D-11 Letter envelope (upper) and reusable envelope (lower) for routing memorandums.

APPENDIX E

Reading Skills in Business Communication

E

Throughout this book, continuing emphasis is placed on your responsibility as a writer to establish a *specific purpose* whenever you prepare a business communication of any kind. For example, see the comment in Chapter One that step 1 in organizing a writing plan is to "identify the purpose for writing." Another example is the observation in Chapter Three that "Before writing a letter or memorandum (you should) first identify the general objective you wish to achieve." When you shift roles from writer to reader of business messages, you will still need to think about *purpose.* But now, in addition to recognizing the writer's objective, you will need to be very much aware of your own purposes as a reader.

Sometimes the two purposes clash. For example, in Chapter Three you learned (or will learn) that a persuasive letter or memorandum should open with a statement designed to attract the reader's attention. But sometimes such a statement can backfire. The editors of *The New Yorker* have a feature that they call "Letters We Never Finished Reading" or, sometimes, "The Ho Hum Department." If, as the overworked senior partner of a CPA firm, you received the following letter (from the Institute for Business Planning, Englewood Cliffs, N.J.), would you react as *The New Yorker* editors did? They put it in their "Ho-Hum Department," which is their way of dismissing it:

> Dear Accountant: It's not easy to excite the accounting profession—but the staff of the Institute for Business Planning has done it with their expanded Fourth Edition of the *Accounting Desk Book.* Rarely does some-

thing come along to warrant the adjective "apocalyptic." We use the word to describe the manual and we use it without apology.[1]

Probably you would discard the letter, too, as soon as you came to the ridiculous word *apocalyptic*—especially if you had on your desk four or five memorandums to react to, six or seven important letters to answer, and three lengthy reports to go through as well as three or four letters on the order of this one that your secretary had somehow let slip through. Your correspondent's purpose of luring you with exaggerated claims for a product would be no match for your purpose of clearing your desk of all but the essentials.

D

LEARNING TO COPE WITH THE COPIOUS: BEGINNING WITH SQ3R

If your working life becomes like that of most men and women in business, you will face daily a formidable stack of printed pages on your desk, even after you have cast aside obviously irrelevant items (like the letter). To solve the perennial problem of "getting through the material," many business people take speed reading courses, and you may want to consider doing that sometime, too. But another way you can begin right now to cope with the problem when it comes is to master a *study skills* technique that you will find helpful in your present and future course work and that you can then adapt to other kinds of reading, including the reading of business communications. The technique works as well as it does because it encourages you to read *purposefully*—with continuing attention to both the writer's purpose and your own.

The method is called SQ3R for *survey* (or *skim*), *question, read, review,* and *recite.* It was designed in the 1940s by Francis Robinson of Ohio State University, after he had examined the study habits of hundreds of successful and unsuccessful students. It consists of five simple steps:

S: *Survey* the entire chapter to get an idea of its scope and direction (its purpose). Instead of reading through any portion completely, look only for signals the writer has provided to focus your attention on especially important ideas and information. Pay particular attention to the title, the first paragraph or two, the subheadings, and a summary or review section if there is one.

[1] *The New Yorker,* January 16, 1978.

Q: Ask a *question* that you expect the first section of the chapter to answer (use the first subheading as the source for your question; that is, turn it into a question).

R: *Read* the first section, looking for an answer to your question.

R: *Recite* the various parts of the answer to the question. (Steps 2, 3, and 4 then are repeated on all sections of the chapter.)

R: *Review* the entire chapter, making certain that you understand how the various parts go together.

The method works especially well for textbooks that are set up as this one is. Notice that each chapter in this book is divided into major sections and subsections, that the headings for the major sections are listed in an outline at the beginning of the chapter, and that the last section is a summary of the entire chapter. That kind of organization makes both *surveying* or *skimming* and *studying by sections* easy to do.

LEARNING TO SKIM

If you are like most readers, you will have to learn to skim, and that will take some practice. You probably find it "natural" to read right through a work from the first word to the last, be it a business letter or a textbook chapter. And you may find it just as "natural" to let your mind drift away from the subject of the communication several times before you finish. The main purpose of the "skim-first" approach is to lessen the chances of that happening by pointing you in the direction the work is taking, that is, by giving you a sense of the writer's purpose.

Consider, for example, how a survey or skim-first approach can help you to stay on the track as you study Chapter One of this book. (If you have already read the chapter, go back to it again and try approaching it this new way. Remember, if you can, how you went about studying the chapter before and how much difficulty you had understanding it.)

First turn to the page that outlines Chapter One. Checking the chapter title and the objective statements, ask yourself, "What does this chapter emphasize? What theme or idea or purpose (sometimes one of these words will work better for you than another) do all these subsections appear to be developing?" Then read the first two paragraphs (in this case, the introduction to the chapter), looking particularly for generalizations about the chapter's scope and purpose. Finally, turn to the chapter summary and read just the first sentence of each paragraph (as you probably know, the first sentence of each paragraph is likely to be a topic sentence stating the main idea of the paragraph in a general way). Noting how often the words *message, analyzing, planning, constructing, writing,* and words with similar meaning occur, it won't take you long to conclude that the chapter emphasis is on writing planned and organized messages. And once you know this, you will be able to think along with the writer. For example, you won't be asking yourself, "Why isn't there anything here on job interviewing?" or "What does this material on achieving coherence have to do with business communication?" You will be able to sense how the topics covered relate to one another.

E SKIMMING IN READING BUSINESS COMMUNICATIONS

With much practice and continuing resistance to your urge to always "read right through," you will find that you can adapt the surveying or skimming-first approach (also sometimes called "previewing") to much of your college, work, or recreational reading. The approach works regardless of whether you are reading reports, essays, articles, or textbooks, for example.

In your previewing you will learn to recognize more subtle directional signals than subheadings. For example, words that are underlined or in boldface print and words that are repeated in key places, such as titles, introductions, and concluding statements, are directional signals. You will become very conscious of direct statements of the main ideas of pieces of writing. Also, you will learn to pick up implied main ideas where these are not directly stated. [One such clearly implied main idea is in the second paragraph of Chapter One: "How effective they (written business messages) are depends on how well the objectives are planned."]

As you develop the habit of at least briefly skimming or previewing everything you pick up to read, you will be developing a skill that will become very useful to you in business—the skill of making quick decisions about how each of the items in the pile of printed material on your desk fits *your purposes,* if it fits them at all. That is, you will learn how to spot quickly the writer's main idea or purpose and then to determine whether to read the work carefully yourself, to delegate responsibility for it to someone else, or to discard it altogether. As you probably know, the ability to make decisions of this kind efficiently is one that people in the business world value highly.

LEARNING THE Q AND THE R'S IN SQ3R

But there will be times in your business career when you will need to study material closely, noting details and remembering them. For that kind of reading, the study-by-sections part of SQ3R can be excellent preparation. It also can be adapted to the kind of reading you probably will do every day on the job, going through an article, memorandum, or letter quickly to find the main idea and the principal points that are made in developing that idea. First, though, it will be helpful to learn the method in its "pure" form (or nearly that) to apply to textbook study.

To get started, turn back to Chapter One and review briefly the subheadings that are listed on the outline page. Then take a few minutes to skim through the chapter again, section by section, framing a specific question for each major subheading as you note the ground that the section following that subheading appears to cover. This time in your skimming pay particular attention to opening and closing sentences of sections and to secondary subheadings. Sometimes these signals will provide clues that will help you find a more focused question than simply "What is _____?"—although sometimes that will be the obvious question to ask.

Then compare your questions with those listed at the end of this appendix. Those questions listed are not the only appropriate ones by any means, but they do illustrate specific, focused questioning.

When you have a set of appropriate questions for the chapter headings, you will be ready to go through the chapter a section at a time, applying the three "R" steps. (You may want to revise your original questions or use some of those at the end of this appendix.)

As you *read* through a section for the first time, you will be looking for a *general* answer to the question you have formed. You probably will find that you can concentrate better than you usually do because you will be reading purposefully. How many times in your study or other reading have you had the experience of suddenly realizing that you have been reading far too many paragraphs or pages without having any idea what the writer is saying? That is much less likely to happen when you are reading to answer a basic question.

When you move to step 4—*reciting*—you simply carry purposeful reading one step farther. At this point, you are concerned not only with the main idea of the chapter section but also with the way important details support any generalizations that are made—the kind of information you need to know for tests, for example. Robinson found that the easiest way to keep this kind of information in mind is to outline the material briefly in the margins of the pages. Outlining is particularly easy to do when you are studying a text such as this one because you can often use secondary headings or words in boldface print as major headings of your outline.

The point of *reviewing* is to demonstrate to yourself how much you remember of what you have studied and how much you understand about how the parts of the chapter fit together. In this last step of SQ3R, you will work through the chapter one last time, section by section, asking yourself the questions you raised in the first place and seeing how specifically and in how well organized a fashion you can answer those questions.

As you review Chapter One, if you find that you do understand the principles treated and you do recall much of the specific information covered, you should realize that you have discovered a useful study tool. If most of the material in Chapter One was new to you, then it was probably not an easy chapter to read. But by thoroughly applying SQ3R, that is by *purposeful studying,* the material becomes easier to master.

APPLYING SQ3R TO READING BUSINESS COMMUNICATIONS

In one important way, your purpose in reading professional materials will differ from your objective in studying a textbook. You will no longer be concerned with demonstrating to *someone else* how much you know about the subject you have been reading about. You will be *making your own use* of what you read. And since the study method you have been learning was designed primarily to help students do well on college tests, you should not expect to be able to apply it directly and literally to reading all of the items in that stack of papers on your desk. But what you can and will do in this reading is to apply the *questioning attitude* that you, as a reader, will have acquired by this time. Developing this questioning attitude is a by-product of working with SQ3R.

Even a very casual and general (and perhaps almost unconsciously asked) question can be useful as a way to begin to "think along" with the writer of a business message. Examples of such questions are "Why did Joe think he needed to write this memorandum, anyway?" or "Is Jones complaining about trivia again in this letter?"

Sometimes, however, particularly when you are reading formal reports or articles in professional magazines, you will question the writer's purpose in a more direct and specific way. (This happens also when the material you read is especially important to you.) Sometimes the title of a report or an article can be converted to a question that will lead you to the writer's main idea, the principal points that support this idea, and the details that back up these points—as they did in your textbook study.

And don't be surprised if you find yourself occasionally taking out a pencil and preparing a brief outline of sorts, much in the SQ3R fashion, to get a sense of the relationships of the parts of an article or report.

But whether your questioning and follow-up reading of professional materials is casual or systematic, if it follows years of consistent use of SQ3R for study purposes, it will always be inspired and directed by a sense of purpose. Such a sense is the result of a search for the writer's purpose and method of accomplishing it and a matching of the writer's purpose with your own.

Suggested Questions for Major Subheadings in Chapter One

1. How can the communicator plan and achieve writing objectives? (The steps for organizing a writing plan and the checklist will be helpful here.)

2. Why is reader analysis important? (An implied secondary question is, What is reader analysis? The list of points in the section will help here.)

3. How is coherence achieved in writing? (A subquestion is, What is coherence in writing? The minor subheadings will be useful clues for this section.)

4. Why is credibility important in writing? (Again, the minor subheadings will be helpful for this section.)

5. What are the kinds of emphasis techniques? (Subquestions are, What are emphasis techniques? and, What importance do these techniques have in writing? The list of ways to emphasize will help here.)

6. How can the communicator know whether messages are readable?

7. What is a good way to proofread messages?

8. How is copy prepared attractively? (Implied secondary questions are, Why prepare attractive copy? and, How can you know that prepared copy is attractive?)

Proofreading Marks

The following list shows standard proofreading marks for your use in proofreading copy. Illustrations of how to use these marks are included.

Instruction	Proofreading Marks	Marked Copy	Corrected Copy
align	//	// Make it work. Make it work.	Make it work. Make it work.
capitalize	≡	make it work.	Make it work.
close space	⌒	M ake it work.	Make it work.
delete	*ℓ*	Make its work.	Make it work.
double space	*ds*	*ds* (Make it work. Make it work.	Make it work. Make it work.
insert punctuation	○	Make it work⊙	Make it work.
insert word, phrase, clause, or more	∧	Make ∧ work. *it*	Make it work.
leave space	|	Make it work.	Make it work.
lower case	*lc or /*	Make it Work.	Make it work.

move left	[or ←	[Make it work.	Make it work.
move right	] or →	M]ake it work.	Make it work.
retain deleted material	*stet*	Make it work.	Make it work.
run in—do not paragraph	⌒	Make it work.⌐ ⌐Jo went.	Make it work. Jo went.
single space	*ss*	Make it work. Make it work.	Make it work. Make it work.
spell out	◯	Make ③ works.	Make three works.
start new paragraph	¶	Make it work.¶ Jo went.	Make it work. Jo went.
transpose	⌒	Make work it.	Make it work.
triple space	*ts*	Make it work. Make it work.	Make it work.
			Make it work.

Glossary

Abstract expression Word or phrase that refers to something intangible or nonmaterial. The word *value* is an example. The meaning will differ from instance to instance, and different people will understand the word differently.

Acceptance letter Researcher's reply to the authorization letter sent outside the company.

Acceptance memorandum Researcher's reply to the authorization memorandum sent within the company.

Active verb Verb that gives a person a precise and vivid image of the action in a thought. Note that this is not the same as active voice.

Adjustment correspondence Letter or memorandum that grants a claim or gives a receiver-centered reason why a claim cannot be granted.

A-I-D-A Mnemonic representing Attention, Interest, Desire, and Action, the four steps in an organizational plan for writing persuasive correspondence.

Analytical report Report that presents facts and also analyzes and interprets those facts.

Annotated bibliography A bibliography containing a brief summary of the contents of each information source.

Appendix Section that contains material that might interrupt the reader's thought flow if placed in the text, such as questionnaires and computer printouts.

Argumentum ad hominem Fallacy of reasoning that is associated with the personality or character of individuals rather than with the arguments presented.

Audience adaptation Shaping of information by a communicator to meet the needs, background, and predisposition of a particular audience.

Authorization letter Letter sent to the researcher from an outside authorizer giving permission to complete project.

Authorization memorandum Memorandum sent to the researcher from an authorizer from within the company giving permission to complete a project.

Authorization statement Statement telling who the authorizer is and perhaps also noting some of the requirements placed on the researcher.

Bar graph Graph prepared by using rectangular bars or boxes that have similar widths to show the relationship between data.

Begging the question Fallacy of reasoning where the proof offered is little more than a disguised repetition of the question or hypothesis.

Bibliography Section that provides the reader with the information sources consulted during the research.

Bona fide occupational qualifications (BFOQ) Pre-employment information gathered; must be limited to a job candidate's ability to perform a specific job satisfactorily.

Catalog system Alphabetical index of books, periodicals, and reference sources; index may be on cards or microform.

Central appeal Strongest argument in persuasive correspondence, the one most likely to persuade a receiver to take a desired action.

Chronological organizational plan Plan where the findings of a study are presented as they occurred over time.

Classifying data Procedure that involves identifying mutually exclusive intervals or groups of data that can be divided into manageable levels of related data.

Cliché Hackneyed or stereotyped expression that is worn out through overuse.

Coding data Procedure that involves assigning a number to each response classification.

Colloquialism Very informal expression used instead of standard English term.

Communication Use of written, oral, and nonverbal symbols to convey thoughts or ideas to others.

Complex claim correspondence Letter or memorandum in which a claim is placed about which the writer and reader may disagree.

Computer assisted retrieval (CAR) Process in which stored records can be retrieved rapidly by computer.

Computer graphics Means of producing visual aids automatically in both black and white and color and in different formats such as prints, transparencies, and slides.

Computer output microform (COM) Process to produce microform directly without first producing a paper copy.

Computerized literature search Computer process that can access various files or data bases for many subject areas and produce a related bibliography.

Conclusions Answers to the problem statement.

Concrete expression Word or phrase that refers to a tangible, material thing. The word *book* is an example. Different people will understand the word in much the same way.

Connective Word or phrase that smooths thought flow in communication by showing the progression of ideas and their relation to one another.

Copyright Publication rights given to owners of original written material by the office of the United States Register of Copyrights.

Cover letter Application letter in which job candidate explains why he or she is best qualified for a position.

Cross-tabulation Process where two or more questionnaire items are tabulated at one time.

Cumulative line graph Multiple line graphs, superimposed on one another, to show relationships between different trends over a time period.

Data analysis section Report section that presents the findings of the study.

Deductive organizational plan Plan that presents the results of a report from the general to the specific.

Deductive paragraph organization Direct presentation of ideas in which main thought or topic sentence is stated first followed by supporting details.

Deductive reasoning Type of logical reasoning where thought processes move from a general premise or proposition to a specific or particular conclusion.

Definitions Clarifications communicated using the following parts: term, class, and differentiation.

Dewey Decimal System Library classification

system using only numbers that classifies or catalogs books into 10 major categories and many subcategories.

Diagrams Visual aids that present a brief sketch of an item or show how a particular process works.

Dichotomous items Those questionnaire items that allow only two alternatives.

Dictation Message spoken by originator for transcription and later delivery to a receiver.

Dictation media equipment Equipment designed especially to record and replay dictation. The two types are *endless loop* (has continuous storage medium) and *discrete media* (has interchangeable storage medium—usually a cassette tape).

Direct-mail advertising Offering for sale goods and services in writing through the mails.

Direct refusal Explicit statement of refusal such as "no" or "We are unable to . . .".

Discrete media equipment Dictation equipment with interchangeable storage media. The three types are *centralized, portable,* and *desk-top units.*

Display work station Word/information processing system that uses a televisionlike screen (visual display unit) to display information entered into the system.

Documenting visual aids Acknowledging the source of a visual aid.

Dumb terminal Word/information processing work station in a shared system that will not operate if the computer is not operating because the terminal relies completely on the computer for logic and computing power, for storage, and for printing final copy.

Editing data Carefully checking data for any possible problems of understanding or interpretation.

Electronic mail Computer-augmented message distribution system in which messages are entered into a system at one location and are transmitted electronically to another location.

Electronic message distribution method Electronic method for storing and retrieving messages for distribution.

Endless loop dictation equipment Dictation equipment using magnetic tape that does not have to be replenished to store information.

Euphemism Term used for another term to convey an idea more tastefully and less offensively.

Experimental research method Primary research method that seeks to determine whether a change of one factor causes change in another factor.

External report Report that is routed outside the business where it is originated.

Facsimile (FAX) Electronic method for sending graphic information from one location to another.

Fair Labor Practices Code State and federal regulations designed to protect applicants from employer discrimination.

False analogy Fallacy of reasoning that occurs when two different statements or ideas are considered to be similar when they are not.

False dilemma Fallacy of reasoning that implies that there are only two sides to an issue when there can be others.

Favorable correspondence plan Direct (deductive) approach for organizing letters and memorandums to convey simple, positive messages.

Favorable message Message that a receiver will view positively.

Feasibility report Generally, an informal report that determines whether a particular project, equipment, or program procedure might help resolve a specific problem.

Feedback Reaction to a message, usually in the form of another message of some sort. Used to evaluate effectiveness of a communication process, feedback may be direct (immediate) or delayed.

"Floppy" disk Magnetic disk used for external

storage of information in a word/information processing system.

Flow chart   A visual aid that identifies significant areas in a process or precedure.

Fog Index   Formula used to compute the readability of written messages.

Follow-up interview   Callback or second screening interview in which the job applicant usually is introduced to the people with whom he or she will be working if hired.

Form documents   Written messages that are designed for repeated use but that will be sent to different people at different times.

Formal language level   Highest degree of formality in language use, appropriate for formal writing such as that in legal documents and treaties.

Formal report   Traditional, long report written in an impersonal writing style.

Formal table   Table that summarizes large amounts of quantitative and qualitative data that are to be separated from the report narrative.

Freedom of Information Act   Act allowing a person the right to review all records of federal agencies of the executive branch unless those records are exempted specifically by the act.

Frequency distribution   Distribution that shows how many responses were tabulated or tallied for each alternative for a particular questionnaire item.

Full-stroke keyboard   Keyboard with keys that actually move down when pressed and that are used to enter information into a word/information processing system.

Functional organization plan for reports   Plan where reports may be presented based on company divisions, departments, or other sections.

General expression   Word or phrase with a broad meaning. Opposite of "specific expression."

General purpose table   Formal table that contains complex or general reference data such as a computer printout and usually placed in the report appendix.

Geographical organizational plan   Plan that presents the results of a study based on relationships in area or space.

Glossary   Alphabetical list of technical or otherwise specialized terms that are defined for the reader.

Gobbledygook   Murky prose, sometimes called "double talk," used to distort meaning and perhaps to shirk responsibility.

Goodwill message   Message designed to create or maintain a favorable attitude in those with whom a person or firm does business.

Graphs or charts   Visual presentations of quantitative data.

Group interview   Interview session in which interviewer speaks to a number of interviewees (perhaps job applicants or employees) at the same time.

Grouped bar graph   Bar graph that compares two or more different values over a period of time or for a particular point in time.

Headings   Captions that show readers how the parts of a report or other message fit together.

Horizontal report   Report that is routed between individuals, departments, and divisions within the organization.

Hypothesis   Statement of proposed solution to a problem that will be tested during the research phase of the report process.

Identifying visual aids   Labeling, numbering, and titling of all visual aids used in a report.

Impact printer   Device used to print final form of a document with which characters are transferred by a typebar, a typing element, or a print wheel striking an inked or carbon ribbon against a paper.

Impersonal writing style   Formal style that uses third person throughout the report or other message.

Implied refusal   Implicit, indirectly stated refusal such as "The information you requested must be kept confidential."

Index Section that provides a cross-reference by name, subject, or both to the content of the report.

Inductive organizational plan Plan in which the physical presentation moves from the specific to the general or from the known to the unknown.

Inductive paragraph organization Indirect presentation of ideas in which supporting details are presented first followed by a main thought or topic sentence.

Inductive reasoning Type of logical reasoning where thought processes move from a specific premise or proposition to a general conclusion.

Informal language level Conversational, informal language use, appropriate for most business documents.

Informal report Usually a short report written in a personal writing style in either a letter or memorandum format.

Informal tables Tables used to emphasize or highlight several items by indenting them after a simple lead-in sentence; informal tables become a part of the regular narrative.

Informational report Report that presents facts in a comprehensive and organized manner and does not analyze or interpret facts.

Inkjet printer Type of nonimpact printer with which characters are formed by spraying a stream of ink on paper.

Input Information entered into a word/information processing system for processing.

Intelligent terminal Word/information processing work station in a shared system that has its own logic and computing power and therefore will operate regardless of whether a central computer to which it is connected is operating.

Interpersonal communication Direct exchange of information, on a face-to-face basis, between a limited number of individuals, usually two or three.

Interpreting visual aids Explanation of the significance of the data that appear in the visual.

Interviewer Person designated by a company to represent them in locating qualified applicants for specific jobs, usually only with authority to recommend—not hire. May be a company employee or one independently employed for this service.

Interviewing Specifically structured form of interpersonal meeting. Basic business applications include *problem solving, informative* (hiring, screening, and exit), *persuasive, counseling,* and *evaluation* interviewing.

Introducing visual aids Reference to the visual aid within the narrative or text of a report.

Introduction of the report Report part designed to acquaint reader with the report problem and establish the credibility and usefulness of the research.

Jargon Specialized language of a profession.

Job description Detailed explanation of job responsibilities and qualifications; normally includes salary and conditions of employment.

Judgment sampling Nonprobability sampling method that requires a selection of a representative sample based on an informal opinion that the sample would have some characteristics of the entire population.

Justification report Generally, an informal report that recommends taking an action and then explains and supports taking the action.

Language Organized construct of symbols agreed upon by users to communicate information. Assumed to be artificial, limited, abstract, arbitrary, and redundant.

Laser printer Type of nonimpact printer with which characters are formed by using a light beam to shape them on a light-sensitive paper surface.

Leadership Knowledgeable and sensitive application of natural and acquired skills to assist groups in accomplishing their goals.

Letter Written correspondence sent to a receiver who does not work for the same business as does the writer.

Letter report Short, informal report in letter format that communicates data to readers who are outside the writer's company.

Libel   Written defamation of another person's good reputation without good reason.

Library of Congress System   Library classification system that classifies or catalogs books by letters into 20 categories; a system of numbers after the letters further subdivides the categories.

Limitations   Outside constraints placed upon the researcher over which he or she has no control.

Line graphs   Graphs used to show trends or changes in data over a time period.

Mail questionnaires   Primary research survey technique that requires the researcher to prepare, print, and distribute survey questionnaires by mail to a group of people.

Managerial work station   Automated equipment designed for use by people (especially executives) who will produce and distribute messages without assistance from others. Some work stations can be used to read incoming electronic mail, file and retrieve stored documents electronically, and set up a reminder file of appointments and deadlines.

Maps   Visual aids that show a geographical representation of either qualitative or quantitative data.

Mean   Measure of central tendency that is computed by taking the sum of all the responses and dividing that sum by the number of responses.

Meaning   Intended or assigned significance of information agreed upon by users of the language. Divided for convenience into *denotation,* dictionary meaning, and *connotation,* individual interpretation based on experience.

Measures of central tendency   Summary statistics that measure or represent the center value of a distribution of data; these measures include the mean, median, and mode.

Measures of dispersion   Summary statistics that measure the variation or spreading out of the data in a distribution; these measures include the range, semi-interquartile range, and standard deviation.

Median   Measure of central tendency that is determined by locating the midpoint in a distribution of responses.

Meeting   Purposeful gathering of individuals. Basic business types include *organizational, informational, problem solving, brainstorming,* and *sensitivity.*

Membrane keyboard   Keyboard with flat surface without raised keys that is used to enter information into a word/information processing system.

Memorandum   Written correspondence sent to a receiver who works for the same business as does the writer.

Memorandum report   Short, informal report that communicates data within a company and uses a memorandum format.

Microforms   Photographic process that reduces the size of data and makes it easier to file; two common forms are microfilm and microfiche.

Micrographics filing system   Storage of records on microfilm or microfiche.

Mode   Measure of central tendency that is found by identifying the most frequently occurring response in a distribution of responses.

Mood   Verb form showing manner in which an action is expressed or a situation is described. Moods are indicative, imperative, or subjunctive.

Multiple choice items   Those questionnaire items that provide three or more alternatives that identify all the responses that are possible for each item.

Multiple line graph   Line graph that compares two or more values over a time period or for a particular point in time.

Networking   Use of basic patterns of channels that interlink communicators; valuable method for using "go-betweens" when seeking job leads and other primary information.

Nondisplay work station   Word/information processing system that uses paper to display information entered into the system.

Nonimpact printer   Device used to print final

form of a document with which characters are formed without direct impact. Two types of non-impact printers are inkjet and laser.

Nonstandard language level   Uneducated, ignorant language use, inappropriate for business communication.

Observational research method   Primary research method that involves either a human or mechanical viewing of the actions or results of some person or group of people.

Optical character recognition reader (OCR)   Electronic machine that can scan or read pages of a document automatically.

Organizational charts   Visual aids that identify the overall structure and directional line of authority for an organization.

Outline symbols   Pattern of Roman numeral, letter, number or decimal symbols that provides structure to an outline; one symbol corresponds to each main factor or subfactor in it.

Output   Final printing of a document produced on a word/information processing system.

Panel interview   Meeting in which a number of representatives of a company speak to the same job applicant.

Parallel construction   Construction in which ideas that are equal in thought are presented in the same grammatical form.

Percentages   Ratios that show a relationship between one or more data response classes to a base of 100.

Perception   Individual understanding, interpretation, or assignment of meaning to messages or stimuli.

Periodic report   Generally, an informal report written to tell managers what activities have taken place for a certain time period.

Personal computer   Automated equipment (microcomputer) designed to manipulate data electronically; can be used to perform language functions, given the appropriate program package.

Personal interviews   Primary research technique that acquires data through questions and answers in a face-to-face situation.

Personal writing style   Informal style that uses the first and second person throughout the report.

Persuasive correspondence plan   Indirect (inductive) approach for organizing letters and memorandums to convey complex, positive messages.

Persuasive message   An active attempt to alter someone else's attitudes, beliefs, or actions. The message often is complex and presented indirectly.

Phrase heading   Similar to a topic heading but subordinate to it. Phrase headings subdivide and clarify topic headings.

Physical message distribution method   Physical method for storing and retrieving messages for distribution; includes file and mail carrier systems.

Pictograms   Visual aids that use pictorial symbols to represent data.

Pie or circle graph   Graph that compares the parts of one value for a particular point in time.

Population   All the members of a group about which data are gathered; any useful sample of this population must be representative of the whole group.

Post hoc, ergo propter hoc   Fallacy of reasoning in which a before-after relationship between two events is represented as a cause-effect relationship

Preliminary report parts   Parts that prepare the audience for an understanding of the report body information.

Primacy effect   Special emphasis on the opening part of a message.

Primary data   Data or facts that come from an original source such as a questionnaire.

Private wire centralized dictation system   Discrete media dictation equipment system on which messages travel along a specially wired line between the dictating device and the recording unit.

Problem background   Section that provides the

reader with the framework within which the research problem is set.

Problem statement Statement that clearly and specifically identifies the problem to be researched.

Process or procedure description report Generally, an informal report that details the steps to be taken to complete some process or procedure such as operating a microcomputer.

Progress report Generally, an informal report written to let the reader know about the status of a particular project.

Proposal Generally, an informal report that is written to get projects, products, or services accepted either within or outside the business or to seek money by obtaining grants for research or special projects.

Questionnaire List of questions or statements designed for gathering raw data for later analysis to solve a research problem.

Quota sampling Nonprobability sampling method that involves selecting a representative sample based on certain characteristics of the population that are proportionate to the sample.

Range Measure of dispersion that is found by determining the difference between the value of the highest response and the value of the lowest response in a distribution.

Rating scales Type of multiple-choice items where the alternatives are based on some continuous scale.

Readability Ease with which a message can be read.

Reader's viewpoint Looking at a written communication situation from the reader's perspective.

Recency effect Special emphasis on the closing part of a message.

Recommendations Names, addresses, and telephone numbers of people who can be contacted by a potential employer to speak to an applicant's abilities, experience, and potential for success. Often takes the form of a letter of recommendation. *Also,* generalizations drawn di-

rectly from the conclusions such as what should be done to improve an auditing procedure.

Recourse A plan of action resorted to in order to aid or assist what was requested or desired originally.

Redundancy Unnecessary repetition of an idea.

Reliability Accuracy and reproduceability (consistency) of measurement.

Report Result of a process whose purpose is to transmit meaningful data to one or more people for either information or decision-making purposes.

Report authorizer Person granting permission to conduct a research study and/or to write the report.

Report body parts Divisions of a report; three major sections are introduction, data analysis or findings, and report ending.

Report ending section Last main section of the report body that generally is divided into the summary, conclusions, and recommendations.

Report factors Key items identified, after initial analysis, that provide the framework to begin data collection.

Report preview Transition statement, located between the introductory and data analysis sections of a report, which gives a brief overview of the report body.

Research plan Logical and organized pattern of material that gives the researcher guidance throughout the collecting, evaluating, and writing phases of a project.

Resignation Formal notification, usually in the form of a letter, to an employer of a person's intention to leave a position; considered a professional courtesy.

Résumé Objective description of a job applicant's qualifications prepared by (or for) the applicant.

Résumé package Written material gathered by a job applicant to support his or her application for employment. Usually includes a résumé, cover letter, and letters of recommendation.

Sampling Process of selecting from a large group or population a subgroup that is representative of the whole group.

Scope   Statement of the qualifying boundaries of the study.

Secondary data   Data or facts which come from an intermediate source such as material from books.

Segmented bar graph   Bar graph that shows the different parts that compose the whole amount of an item.

Semi-interquartile range   Measure of dispersion that is found by taking one-half the difference between the highest and lowest values of the middle 50 percent of all the values.

Sentence heading   Form of heading that states each report factor in a simple and complete sentence and that should not run over seven words in length.

Shared system   Word/information processing system that uses a central computer to process messages; several work stations or terminals may be connected to one central computer.

Simple bar graph   Bar graph that shows a comparison of two or more values and can be drawn either vertically or horizontally.

Simple claim correspondence   Letter or memorandum in which a claim is placed to which both writer and reader readily agree that the writer is entitled.

Simple random sampling   Probability sampling method that involves the selection of a sample where every member of the population has an equal chance of being selected.

Simulation session   Interview meeting in which an applicant is asked to act out or role play typical situations related to the job duties of the position under consideration.

Single line graph   Line graph that shows one series of value.

Sources and methods of data collection   Discussion that tells the reader how the researcher collected the data.

Special purpose tables   Formal tables that contain specific data that are related to a particular discussion in the text.

Specific expression   Word or phrase giving a definite, particular, precise meaning.

Speech styles   Manner in which oral messages are presented to audiences. Major variables include the nature of the information, the audience, and the occasion. Basic business applications are *impromptu* (informal and unrehearsed), *extemporaneous* (informal and planned), *manuscript* (formal and written), and *memorized* (formal, written, and delivered without aid of manuscript) speeches.

Stand-alone system   Word/information processing system consisting of a single work station not linked to any larger central processing unit.

Standard deviation   A measure of dispersion in a distribution that measures the relative distance of deviations from the mean.

Storage media   Media used in data processing to store information for later retrieval.

Stratified random sampling   Probability sampling method that consists of dividing the population into subgroups based on similar characteristics and then conducting a simple random selection within each subgroup.

Stress interview   Session structured by interviewer to put pressure on job applicant to evaluate how well an applicant performs under pressure.

Structured interview   Session controlled by interviewer in which the same procedures and questions are used for all job applicants, as contrasted to an *open* or nondirected meeting in which the applicant influences structure.

Structured or closed-ended response item   Questionnaire item that provides respondents with a set or list of possible responses to use in choosing appropriate responses.

Summary   Report section that draws together the main points of the data analysis section of a report.

Summary statistics   Statistical measures that reduce the data to a more manageable and meaningful level.

Superlative   Most extreme degree of an adjective or adverb, such as *loveliest* or *highest.*

Supplementary report parts   Sections that provide additional related material about the report for the reader; these parts consist of the bibliography, glossary, appendix, and index.

Supporting appeal Argument in persuasive correspondence designed to persuade a receiver to take a desired action. This appeal supports a central appeal.

Survey research method Primary research method that collects data from respondents by asking questions or posing statements to be responded to on questionnaires.

Syllogism Series of three statements that show how deductive reasoning works; these statements are a major premise, a minor premise, and a conclusion.

Synopsis Condensed version of the report body.

Systematic random sampling Probability sampling method that involves selecting a sample based on some predetermined interval. For example, a 10 percent sample would be selected by generating a random number between 1 and 10—say, 3—and then surveying the 3rd, 13th, 23rd, 33rd, and so on, members on the list of the population. (Note that this is one of many possible examples.)

Table of contents Listing that contains the headings or captions of all the major divisions and perhaps subdivisions of the report and the page number where each part begins.

Table of illustrations Listing that identifies the label, number, and title of the visual aids used in the report and the page number where each aid is located.

Table Systematic order of columns and rows that presents quantitative or qualitative data.

Tabulating data Procedure that involves counting the number of responses in each response classification for each statement or question.

Telecommunications Use of various media of technology to transmit messages over great distances.

Telephone interviews Primary research survey technique in which the interviewer can contact respondents by telephone more quickly and at a lower cost than by personal interviews.

Three P's Proofreading System Proofreading system based on preconditions, procedure, and postconditions; best used in proofreading long documents.

Time charts Visual aids that show a schedule of activities or events that are to be completed over a time period.

Title page Report part containing three sections: report title; name, title, and address of the individual for whom the report was prepared; and name, title, and address of the report writer and the date.

Topic heading Form of heading that consists of one, two, or three key words that show the specific factors that will be discussed in a report.

Transition statements Logical connections that provide a smooth continuity of thought between various parts of a written or spoken message.

Transmittal letter Letter written to deliver a report in writing to the report authorizer and used when report is sent outside the company where it originates.

Transmittal memorandum Memorandum written to deliver a report in writing to the report authorizer and used when report is sent to a reader or readers within the company where it originates.

Unbiased language Language use that reflects no sexual, racial, ethnic, or other type of unfounded discrimination.

Unfavorable correspondence plan Indirect (inductive) approach for organizing letters and memorandums that must convey negative messages.

Unfavorable message Message that a receiver will view as negative.

Unstructured or open-ended response item Questionnaire item in which the respondents are free to express any response to the item in their own words. Also applies to job interviewing questions.

Validity Characteristic of good measurement ensuring that the researcher actually has measured what he or she intended to measure.

Vertical report   Report that moves either up or down within the organizational structure of a company.

Video disk   Plastic disk used to store both visual and sound images.

Winchester disk   Hard disk packaged in a boxlike container and used for external storage of information in a word/information processing system.

Wordiness   Use of too many words to convey an idea.

Word/information   processing   equipment   Automated equipment used to compose, edit, and revise messages and to produce final copy for distribution to receivers.

Word processor   Automated equipment designed specifically (and only) to perform language functions such as preparing correspondence, reports, and graphics.

Work progress schedule   Planning aid that forces a researcher to think about the time needed to complete a report.

Writing style   Characteristic manner in which people express themselves in writing.

Writing tone   Manner in which people express a certain attitude in writing.

Index

Business and financial services, 430-
431
directory of, 173
Business Periodicals Index, 172
Business reference sources, 427-
428
abstracts, 428-429
bibliographies, 432-435
business and financial services,
430-431
computer-assisted information
services, 437-438
directories, 431-432
financial newspapers, 427-428
government documents and
statistics, 435-437
indexes, 428-429
periodicals, 427-428
subject dictionaries, 437
subject handbooks, 437

Campbell, William Giles, 245
Campus interviews, 337
Capitalization, 417-420
abbreviations, 417
first words, 417
miscellaneous, 420
proper nouns, 417-420
*Career Guide of Professional
Associations,* 349
Carruth, Gorton, 169
Catalog system, 169-171
Cathode ray tube (CRT), 301
Centralized dictation systems, 291,
293
Central tendency, measures of,
198-199
mean, 198
median, 199
mode, 199
Chalkboards, 392-393
Chronological organizational plan,
208
Churchill, Winston, 378-379
Circle graphs, 230-231
Civil Rights Act of 1964, 323
Claims against the company,
refused:
unfavorable letters, 105-107
unfavorable memorandums, 114-
115
Clarity, 34-39
abstract expressions, 35
concrete expressions, 35
foreign expressions, 37-38
general expressions, 35-36

jargon, 38-39
short, simple expressions, 36-37
specific expressions, 35-36
unfamiliar words, 37
Classified advertisements, 326
Classifying research data, 195
Clichés, figurative, 45
Closing statements for
correspondence, 70-72
action request, 71-72, 99, 126-
127
general, 71
Coding research data, 196
Coherent writing techniques, 7-13
active verbs, 8
connotative meanings, 8
denotative meanings, 8
descriptive adjectives and
adverbs, 8-9
effective sentences, 9-10
organized paragraphs, 11-12
parallel construction, 12-13
using appropriate words, 7-9
Collecting research data, *see*
Primary research data,
collecting; Secondary research
data, collecting
College Placement Annual, 350
Colloquialisms, 47
Colon, 414
Comma, 411-413
Commodore computers, 290
Communicate! (Verderber), 394,
396
Communication systems in
organizations, *see* Word/
information processing
Company literature, 327
Company publications as research
data, 169
Computer-assisted information
services, 437-438
Computer-assisted retrieval (CAR),
311, 312
Computer graphics as visual aids,
236
Computer output microfilm (COM),
310-311
Computerized literature search
services, 174
Computers, *see* Word/information
processing
Conciseness, 39-44
redundancies, 44
wordiness, 39-43
Concrete expressions, 35

Condolence messages, 78
Confidence, showing, 48-49
Confidentiality, safeguarding, 49
Congratulatory messages, 77-78
Conjunctions, 410
Connectives:
for paragraphs, 12
for sentences, 9-10
Connotative meanings, 8
Copy, attractive, 22-23
checkpoints for, 23
preparation of, 22-23
Copyright, 15
fair use of, 15-16
Cornucopia Softwear, 300
Correspondence, 59-74
closing statements, 70-72
favorable, *see* Favorable
correspondence
format and layout of, *see* Letters,
format and layout of;
Memorandums, format and
layout of
functions, 61
objectives, 61-62
opening statements, 68-70
organizational plans, 64-68
persuasive, *see* Persuasive
correspondence
psychology, 63-64
unfavorable, *see* Unfavorable
correspondence
Credibility, 13-16
complete information, 15
copyright and, 15-16
different viewpoints, 14-15
fairness, 14-15
libel and, 15
objectivity, 14
unrelated matters, 16
Credit information requests and
favorable responses, 72-74
Credit requests:
favorable responses, 74-76
unfavorable responses, 107-110
Cross-tabulation of research data,
196-197
Cumulative Book Index, 171
Cumulative line graphs, 230

Data processing, *see* Word/
information processing
Deductive organization, 11
Deductive organizational plan, 207-
208
Deductive reasoning, 203